Jeanie Shaw

Pen drawing by Kerr Eby,
after a photograph, 1854

RALPH WALDO EMERSON

*

AMERICAN WRITERS SERIES

*

HARRY HAYDEN CLARK

General Editor

*

✶ AMERICAN WRITERS SERIES ✶

Volumes of representative selections, prepared by American scholars under the general editorship of Harry Hayden Clark, University of Wisconsin. Volumes now ready are starred.

AMERICAN TRANSCENDENTALISTS, *Raymond Adams, University of North Carolina*

*WILLIAM CULLEN BRYANT, *Tremaine McDowell, University of Minnesota*

*JAMES FENIMORE COOPER, *Robert E. Spiller, Swarthmore College*

*JONATHAN EDWARDS, *Clarence H. Faust, University of Chicago, and Thomas H. Johnson, Lawrenceville School*

*RALPH WALDO EMERSON, *Frederic I. Carpenter, Harvard University*

*BENJAMIN FRANKLIN, *Frank Luther Mott, University of Iowa, and Chester E. Jorgenson, Wayne University*

*ALEXANDER HAMILTON AND THOMAS JEFFERSON, *Frederick C. Prescott, Cornell University*

BRET HARTE, *Joseph B. Harrison, University of Washington*

*NATHANIEL HAWTHORNE, *Austin Warren, Boston University*

OLIVER WENDELL HOLMES, *S. I. Hayakawa, University of Wisconsin, and Howard Mumford Jones, Harvard University*

*WASHINGTON IRVING, *Henry A. Pochmann, Mississippi State College*

HENRY JAMES, *Lyon Richardson, Western Reserve University*

*HENRY WADSWORTH LONGFELLOW, *Odell Shepard, Trinity College*

JAMES RUSSELL LOWELL, *Norman Foerster, University of Iowa, and Harry H. Clark, University of Wisconsin*

*HERMAN MELVILLE, *Willard Thorp, Princeton University*

*JOHN LOTHROP MOTLEY, *Chester P. Higby and B. T. Schantz, University of Wisconsin*

THOMAS PAINE, *Harry H. Clark, University of Wisconsin*

*FRANCIS PARKMAN, *Wilbur L. Schramm, University of Iowa*

*EDGAR ALLAN POE, *Margaret Alterton, University of Iowa, and Hardin Craig, Stanford University*

WILLIAM HICKLING PRESCOTT, *Michael Kraus, College of the City of New York, and William Charvat, New York University*

*SOUTHERN POETS, *Edd Winfield Parks, University of Georgia*

SOUTHERN PROSE, *Gregory Paine, University of North Carolina*

*HENRY DAVID THOREAU, *Bartholow Crawford, University of Iowa*

*MARK TWAIN, *Fred Lewis Pattee, Rollins College*

*WALT WHITMAN, *Floyd Stovall, University of Texas*

JOHN GREENLEAF WHITTIER, *Harry H. Clark, University of Wisconsin, and Bertha M. Stearns, Wellesley College*

Ralph Waldo Emerson

REPRESENTATIVE SELECTIONS, WITH INTRODUCTION, BIBLIOGRAPHY, AND NOTES

BY

FREDERIC I. CARPENTER

Instructor in English
Harvard University

AWS

AMERICAN BOOK COMPANY

New York · Cincinnati · Chicago
Boston · Atlanta

Carpenter's Emerson
W. P. 2.

Made in U. S. A.

PREFACE

The following selections from the writings of Ralph Waldo Emerson have been made, first, with a view to their intrinsic literary importance, and second, with a view to comprehensiveness. They illustrate, as far as possible, all the literary forms which he used, the whole period of his literary career, and the whole range of his thought. Too often he is studied only as the writer of formal, well-groomed essays. Often his later writing is shadowed by the brilliance of his earlier, more challenging pronouncements. Often his transcendental theories are emphasized at the expense of his shrewd, Yankee perceptions.

The Introduction follows the same general principles as the selections. More particularly it attempts to interpret Emerson in terms of the present day, and to test the value of his ideas for our own times. This involves a certain amount of personal opinion, and perhaps the editor should state that his sympathies are with the modernist, rather than with the classicist or humanist critics. Like any original and fertile writer, Emerson can be interpreted in many different ways, and the editor has attempted to follow Emerson's own principles, and treat him from a fresh, rather than from a strictly orthodox point of view. This will appear particularly in the sections on "Philosophy" and "Individualism and Socialism."

The Bibliography attempts to criticize the books and the more important articles which have been written about Emerson, and particularly to list those which have been published recently. The Notes supplement the Introduction with a more specific discussion of the text.

The text of Emerson's prose and verse included in the present volume is that of the Centenary Edition, which incorporates the author's final revisions. The selections from the *Journals* are used by permission of, and by arrangement with, Houghton Mifflin Company.

F. I. C.

CONTENTS

INTRODUCTION

I. AMERICA

Emerson's most famous address described his ideal of "The American Scholar"—"man thinking" in America. It also described the ideal by which he patterned his own life. That he wished to become an ideal scholar is clear, but that he wished to, and did become a representative American is less generally recognized. Judging him by his own standards, "Let us" (to use his own words) "see him in his school, and consider him in reference to the main influences he receives."

Upon Emerson, as upon the mind of his imaginary scholar, the first influence to be exerted was that of nature. "Every day, the sun; and, after sunset, Night and her stars. . . . Every day, men and women, conversing—beholding and beholden." The term "nature" includes not only the sun and the stars, or wild nature, but human nature—the whole environment of man.[1] Born as he was in the middle of the city of Boston, the human environment acted upon Emerson first. The America in which he lived exerted the most significant influence upon both his life and his writing.

To think of Emerson as one of the New England group of writers who flourished a century ago is to misrepresent him at the start. He was born to that group, but grew beyond it. By experience and by sympathy, he became a citizen of a larger America. Lowell declared that two men, Lincoln and Emerson, stood preëminent as products of American democracy.[2] Because modern Americans have been unwilling to couple Emerson

[1] For a discussion of "Nature," and natural law, see Introduction, IV and V.
[2] See Lowell's essay on "Democracy."

with Lincoln, they have too often overlooked the fact that Emerson was wholly a product of democracy. Mr. James Truslow Adams, who rather distrusts Emerson, yet recognizes that "in no other author can we get so close to the whole of the American spirit."[3]

To begin with, a long established myth must be destroyed. It has been repeated so often that Emerson was descended from seven generations of Puritan ministers that men have come to believe the statement literally. But only by a careful handpicking of the branches of his family tree can the assertion be justified, as Holmes, who originated it, cheerfully admitted. Emerson's mother was the daughter of a "cooper and distiller," and his maternal ancestors were largely innocent of ministerial proclivities.[4] In the direct line of his paternal descent a merchant and a baker intrude. The only generalization that can be made to include all his ancestors is that they were Americans for seven generations and that they shared between them almost all the experiences common to American pioneers. Thomas Emerson, the baker,[5] emigrated to New England in 1635, obtained a grant of land, and founded the family. His son, the Reverend Joseph Emerson, barely escaped with his life when the town of Mendon was destroyed by the Indians. His son, Edward Emerson, was a merchant. His grandson, Ralph Waldo's grandfather, William Emerson of Concord, died of camp fever while serving as chaplain in the patriot army of the Revolution. Lastly, the Reverend William Emerson of Boston, besides serving as chaplain of the Massachusetts Senate, delivered the official Fourth of July oration in Boston in 1802, the year before his son Ralph Waldo was born. In conversation with Bret Harte in 1872, Emerson could argue with justice that he "spoke also from Pilgrim experience." With the blood of

[3] *The Epic of America*, 198.

[4] See D. G. Haskins, *Emerson's Maternal Ancestors*.

[5] He is so described in the only surviving document; see *The Emersons of Ipswich*, by B. K. Emerson.

seven generations of American pioneers and patriots running in his veins, Emerson came naturally by the pioneer American philosophy of Self-Reliance.

The Boston into which Emerson was born was, perhaps, a Massachusetts town—in his youth, he used to lead the family cow to pasture on the common. But he lived to see Boston become a modern city, and a leader in the change from an agricultural to an industrial America. In his early years he saw it expand (very much as Chicago is doing today) by building new territory out of the sea, creating what is now called Back Bay. He saw the railroad bind together the outlying districts, and make possible a metropolitan center. He saw the influx of Irish immigrants challenge the supremacy of the old Yankee stock, and himself defended the rights of these immigrants against the one-hundred-per-centers of his day. It is false to project him against the conservatism of a modern Boston, and to imagine that he took his tone from that.

Emerson grew to maturity in a new America. The War of 1812 found him in school, with Boston in constant fear of British invasion. One day his class was asked to help throw up earthworks in Boston harbor for the defense of the city. Although the attack never came, it roused him and his generation to a consciousness of their common life, so that after the war a new patriotism had developed. After the war also, he saw the great wave of Western migration begin. At the age of nineteen he dedicated his Journal to "the spirit of America," using all the high-flown phrases of youth, but expressing the sincerity of a deeply felt conviction.[6]

This local patriotism soon expanded to include in its horizon not only Massachusetts, but also the new West that was then opening up. In 1823 he faced squarely the problem of a frontier,[7] with its opportunities and its dangers:

[6] See Selections following, p. 3.
[7] See Ernest Marchand, "Emerson and the Frontier."

The vast rapidity with which the desarts and forests of the interior of this country are peopled have led patriots to fear lest the nation grow *too fast* for its virtue and its peace. . . . Good men desire, and the great cause of human nature demands, that this abundant and overflowing richness wherewith God has blessed this country be not misapplied and made a curse of. . . . How to effect the check proposed is an object of momentous importance. And in view of an object of such magnitude, I know not who he is, that can complain that motive is lacking in this latter age, whereby men should become great.[8]

America was to supply the motive whereby Emerson became great.

Against the background of this enthusiasm for the new land, Emerson's "American Scholar" was projected. He devoted his life to the study of the "rapidity" of the American tempo. If, in youth, he often seemed to share the conservatives' desire for a "check" upon it, as soon as he began to think for himself, he realized that the best check for thoughtless expansion lay in the application of the intelligence of American scholars to it. Not by halting the car of progress would he save America, but by guiding it well. "Hitch your wagon to a star." All of his essays had as their main theme the application of the scholarship, or wisdom of man, to the problems of the present. He too turned to the present, writing in his Journal: "The dead sleep in their moonless night; my business is with the living."

At the time of the American Scholar address, two new factors were beginning to operate in America, and the nation was being forced to think seriously about the problems which her growth was creating. In 1828 the election of Jackson had focused attention on the problem of the West, while five years later the formation of the Anti-Slavery Society had emphasized the danger of slavery, and foreshadowed the conflict of the North with the South. In both these problems Emerson took a deep interest, but the excitement and the crusading spirit of reform which

[8] *Journals*, I, 247–8.

they engendered excited him even more. His relation to this spirit is vividly described by Lowell in his essay on "Thoreau," while Emerson's own attitude is expressed in his occasional essays, and in his Journals. Indeed, it may be said that Emerson was related to these momentous times both as cause and as effect; his addresses and essays were stimulating the young minds of Thoreau, Lowell, Holmes, and many lesser men, while at the same time the excitement of the times was urging him on to his best work. In his introductory essay to the *Dial*, he justified the new magazine as a vehicle of "a new spirit," and pointed out "the progress of a revolution" among the people of New England.[9]

Although Emerson's first knowledge of the West had come through books and travellers' reports, his intimate experience of the life of the nation was not limited to New England, or even to the East. In college he had roomed with a Southern student, and in early manhood made an extended trip to Florida for his health. Frequently thereafter he toured the Eastern states, delivering lectures in New York, Philadelphia, and Washington. Gradually he outgrew the natural provincialism of his youth. The years from the delivery of "The American Scholar" in 1837 to that of "The Young American" in 1844 were filled with new experiences and new thoughts. In the latter address he emphasized the importance of the newly constructed railroads, by means of which "the nervous, rocky West is intruding a new and continental element into the national mind, and we shall yet have an American genius." Beginning in the 1840's, as the railroads pushed their way over the mountains, Emerson followed them farther and farther West, delivering his lectures, first in Pittsburgh and Cincinnati (where his earliest poems had already been published in James Freeman Clarke's *Western Messenger*), then in Chicago and Milwaukee, and finally across the Mississippi in Iowa. On December 31, 1855, he noted in his

[9] *Uncollected Writings*, 31–2.

Journal: "I have crossed the Mississippi on foot three times." And in 1871, at the age of sixty-eight, he travelled to California, delivering several lectures there.

Emerson's life was lived in the days of Westward expansion. It included the War of 1812, the Annexation of Texas, the Gold Rush, the Civil War, and the completion of the Union Pacific Railroad. He was intensely aware of all these events. Only in the light of them can the significance of his writings be appreciated, for before being a scholar, he was first of all an American.

II. BOOKS

This emphasis is as Emerson would have had it, for he declared that books, or "the mind of the past" should be of secondary importance in the training of the American Scholar. "Books," he said, "are for the scholar's idle times." But presumably the scholar must have a great many idle times—certainly Emerson himself did. Although he never forced himself to read when he did not feel inclined, he managed to become intimate with a large group of authors. Those whom he considered most important, he listed in his Journal for October, 1842, with characteristic emphasis:

> Thou shalt read Homer, Æschylus, Sophocles, Euripides, Aristophanes, Plato, Proclus, Plotinus, Jamblichus, Porphyry, Aristotle, Virgil, Plutarch, Apuleius, Chaucer, Dante, Rabelais, Montaigne, Cervantes, Shakspeare, Jonson, Ford, Chapman, Beaumont and Fletcher, Bacon, Marvell, More, Milton, Molière, Swedenborg, Goethe.

It would be rash to deny the title of scholar to one who had read, and pondered over, all of these.[10]

This list of authors includes most of Emerson's favorites, but there are some striking omissions. Since there are revealing

[10] Emerson's debt to these, and other authors, has been studied extensively. See the Bibliography, III, for special references.

But for Emerson they performed an important function. They helped him to fuse the intellectual philosophy of Plato with the religious thought of the Bible and of the ancient East.[16] For better or for worse Emerson was part mystic, and these books became part of him. They, much more than the German idealistic philosophers, influenced his transcendental thought.[17] But perhaps their chief function was to furnish him with that length of perspective which most distinguishes him from his contemporaries.

There remain the moderns, whom Emerson always read, although often out of school. In his day in college it was impossible to study English Literature as such, and as a result he often neglected his official tasks in favor of reading the modern dramatists and poets. He loved especially the Elizabethans, and mentions Shakespeare more often than any other author. Indeed, Shakespeare may be compared with Plato as furnishing the substance, as opposed to the form, of Emerson's literary thinking. For him Shakespeare expressed the beauty and the color of the world in so far as these could be expressed in words. Shakespeare became "the poet."

Finally among the moderns was Montaigne, "the grand old sloven," to whom Emerson seems to have been attracted by the law of opposites. In any grouping of his favorite authors, the Frenchman should occupy the prominent position on the extreme left. For Emerson's mind took in the whole range of literature, and if he adopted many conventional favorites such as Plato and Shakespeare, he also went further afield to include extreme mystics such as Plotinus, and extreme skeptics, such as Montaigne. All his life a lover of the earth and the raciness of common men, Montaigne furnished him in literary form with this element that he most needed. With Montaigne Emerson's intellectual equipment became rounded and complete.

[16] See F. I. Carpenter, *Emerson and Asia.*

[17] See *Emerson and Asia*, 94–100; and J. S. Harrison, *The Teachers of Emerson.*

reasons for these, and since they exerted a greater influence upon him than any of his listed favorites, we may consider them first. One is the Bible, and second is the body of contemporary poetry and essays and fiction in the midst of which he grew up. These two types of literature had become so familiar to him that in later life he forgot their importance.

Just as the American background of Emerson's life has often been neglected, because it was so obvious, so his lifelong acquaintance with the Bible can easily be overlooked in favor of his more unusual enthusiasms for Plotinus or Montaigne. If the greatest practical influence on his life was the growth of a new America, the greatest spiritual influence was undoubtedly the old Bible. For that matter, pioneer Americans had read the Bible as universally as he. But like so many things we grow up with, Emerson reacted against the Bible when he came of age. In his radical "Divinity School Address," emphasizing the first-hand quality of religious inspiration, he opposed the fundamentalist interpretation of sacred literature, and seemed to oppose the Bible itself. Many orthodox ministers of the time accused him of ignorance of it, but the accusation was baseless. He was in the fortunate position of one who knew it so well that he did not need to quote it. Actually he was describing his own experience when he spoke (in the same address) of "the unique impression of Jesus upon mankind, whose name is not so much written as ploughed into the history of the world."

In reaction from such "required reading" as the Bible, Emerson turned to many contemporary books and magazines. This unconscious bent toward the natural reading of youth was his defense against the ministerial side of his inheritance, and fitted him to become the spokesman of his generation. Moreover, he fully recognized its importance. "The regular course of studies," he wrote, "the years of academical and professional education have not yielded me better facts than some idle books under the bench at Latin School. What we do not call education is more precious than that which we call so."[11] Just as he distrusted books in general, and turned to the life around him for much of his education, so he distrusted many of the required books, and turned to the "idle books" which his contemporaries were writing.

Chief of these in youth were the novels of Scott, the poetry of Scott, Byron, and Wordsworth, and, later, the essays of Carlyle and Coleridge.[12] The novels served to enlarge the boy's horizon beyond the narrowness of his early life, the essays suggested new ideas, but the poems performed an even more important service in turning his mind to the actual creation of poetry. Before he reached his 'teens, he had been inspired to celebrate in verse the naval victories of the War of 1812; and at an early age had composed a narrative poem entitled "Fortus." He wrote many of his early letters in verse, and, what is more, seems to have pleased his friends with his rhymes. On leaving school at Concord, he was raised to the top of a barrel and made to declaim an ode of farewell, beginning:

> I rise to bid adieu
> To you, my schoolmates, and, kind sir, to you.

Out of these unforced beginnings grew his tastes for poetic creation. He regarded this creation not as a duty, but as a sort of happy recreation.

So, when Emerson came to list the books which "thou shalt read," he omitted the Bible because, as he said, it "wore black cloth," and he omitted Scott and Carlyle and Wordsworth because their significance was chiefly personal, or contemporary. But the authors that he did choose were sufficiently unusual. Half of his list were ancient, many of them almost unknown.

[11] *Works*, II, 133; "Spiritual Laws."

[12] The influence of these writers on his thinking was great. For a detailed discussion of the influence on Emerson of Carlyle, Coleridge, and Wordsworth, see articles by F. T. Thompson, as listed in the Bibliography.

"Proclus, Plotinus, Jamblichus, Porphyry . . . Apuleius" ar certainly not on usual reading lists. And the modern half of th list includes authors which conservative people have often bee compelled to omit. Emerson's reading was both unusual an varied.

First in time, as well as in importance in his formal educatio were the Greek Classics. From his early days in the Bosto Latin School he had been made to read these, and although l constantly rebelled against the way they were taught, he gr to love them as literature. In later life he became one of t first opponents of compulsory Greek and Latin, and ridicul "our scholastic devotion to the dead languages. . . . In a hu dred high schools and colleges this warfare against comm sense still goes on."[13] President Eliot of Harvard traced b many of the reforms of his own administration to Emerso But neither Eliot nor Emerson would have had students fo the value of the Greek Classics, and Emerson read them v enthusiasm throughout his life.

Foremost among the Classics, and probably the gre single influence on Emerson's intellectual life was Plato— Bible of the learned for twenty-two hundred years." He the philosopher from an early age, and there can be no d that Plato dictated the form which his thinking was to The preëxistent Platonic ideas held the same fascination him that they have for almost every great thinker, and he brated the Greek as the first and greatest of his "Represent Men."[15]

Next in Emerson's list of favorites were included the es Neo-Platonists, headed by Proclus and Plotinus. These w probably represent all that the average man would set do "transcendental," and to most they make heavy enough rea

[13] *Works*, III, 258–9.

[14] See C. W. Eliot, *Four American Leaders* (Boston, 1906).

[15] For a further discussion of Emerson's Platonism, see Introducti "Philosophy," and J. S. Harrison, *The Teachers of Emerson*.

reasons for these, and since they exerted a greater influence upon him than any of his listed favorites, we may consider them first. One is the Bible, and second is the body of contemporary poetry and essays and fiction in the midst of which he grew up. These two types of literature had become so familiar to him that in later life he forgot their importance.

Just as the American background of Emerson's life has often been neglected, because it was so obvious, so his lifelong acquaintance with the Bible can easily be overlooked in favor of his more unusual enthusiasms for Plotinus or Montaigne. If the greatest practical influence on his life was the growth of a new America, the greatest spiritual influence was undoubtedly the old Bible. For that matter, pioneer Americans had read the Bible as universally as he. But like so many things we grow up with, Emerson reacted against the Bible when he came of age. In his radical "Divinity School Address," emphasizing the first-hand quality of religious inspiration, he opposed the fundamentalist interpretation of sacred literature, and seemed to oppose the Bible itself. Many orthodox ministers of the time accused him of ignorance of it, but the accusation was baseless. He was in the fortunate position of one who knew it so well that he did not need to quote it. Actually he was describing his own experience when he spoke (in the same address) of "the unique impression of Jesus upon mankind, whose name is not so much written as ploughed into the history of the world."

In reaction from such "required reading" as the Bible, Emerson turned to many contemporary books and magazines. This unconscious bent toward the natural reading of youth was his defense against the ministerial side of his inheritance, and fitted him to become the spokesman of his generation. Moreover, he fully recognized its importance. "The regular course of studies," he wrote, "the years of academical and professional education have not yielded me better facts than some idle books under the bench at Latin School. What we do not call education is more precious than that which we call so."[11] Just as he distrusted books in general, and turned to the life around him for much of his education, so he distrusted many of the required books, and turned to the "idle books" which his contemporaries were writing.

Chief of these in youth were the novels of Scott, the poetry of Scott, Byron, and Wordsworth, and, later, the essays of Carlyle and Coleridge.[12] The novels served to enlarge the boy's horizon beyond the narrowness of his early life, the essays suggested new ideas, but the poems performed an even more important service in turning his mind to the actual creation of poetry. Before he reached his 'teens, he had been inspired to celebrate in verse the naval victories of the War of 1812; and at an early age had composed a narrative poem entitled "Fortus." He wrote many of his early letters in verse, and, what is more, seems to have pleased his friends with his rhymes. On leaving school at Concord, he was raised to the top of a barrel and made to declaim an ode of farewell, beginning:

> I rise to bid adieu
> To you, my schoolmates, and, kind sir, to you.

Out of these unforced beginnings grew his tastes for poetic creation. He regarded this creation not as a duty, but as a sort of happy recreation.

So, when Emerson came to list the books which "thou shalt read," he omitted the Bible because, as he said, it "wore black cloth," and he omitted Scott and Carlyle and Wordsworth because their significance was chiefly personal, or contemporary. But the authors that he did choose were sufficiently unusual. Half of his list were ancient, many of them almost unknown.

[11] *Works*, II, 133; "Spiritual Laws."

[12] The influence of these writers on his thinking was great. For a detailed discussion of the influence on Emerson of Carlyle, Coleridge, and Wordsworth, see articles by F. T. Thompson, as listed in the Bibliography.

"Proclus, Plotinus, Jamblichus, Porphyry . . . Apuleius" are certainly not on usual reading lists. And the modern half of the list includes authors which conservative people have often been compelled to omit. Emerson's reading was both unusual and varied.

First in time, as well as in importance in his formal education, were the Greek Classics. From his early days in the Boston Latin School he had been made to read these, and although he constantly rebelled against the way they were taught, he grew to love them as literature. In later life he became one of the first opponents of compulsory Greek and Latin, and ridiculed "our scholastic devotion to the dead languages. . . . In a hundred high schools and colleges this warfare against common-sense still goes on."[13] President Eliot of Harvard traced back many of the reforms of his own administration to Emerson.[14] But neither Eliot nor Emerson would have had students forget the value of the Greek Classics, and Emerson read them with enthusiasm throughout his life.

Foremost among the Classics, and probably the greatest single influence on Emerson's intellectual life was Plato—"the Bible of the learned for twenty-two hundred years." He read the philosopher from an early age, and there can be no doubt that Plato dictated the form which his thinking was to take. The preëxistent Platonic ideas held the same fascination for him that they have for almost every great thinker, and he celebrated the Greek as the first and greatest of his "Representative Men."[15]

Next in Emerson's list of favorites were included the esoteric Neo-Platonists, headed by Proclus and Plotinus. These writers probably represent all that the average man would set down as "transcendental," and to most they make heavy enough reading.

[13] *Works*, III, 258–9.
[14] See C. W. Eliot, *Four American Leaders* (Boston, 1906).
[15] For a further discussion of Emerson's Platonism, see Introduction, V, "Philosophy," and J. S. Harrison, *The Teachers of Emerson.*

But for Emerson they performed an important function. They helped him to fuse the intellectual philosophy of Plato with the religious thought of the Bible and of the ancient East.[16] For better or for worse Emerson was part mystic, and these books became part of him. They, much more than the German idealistic philosophers, influenced his transcendental thought.[17] But perhaps their chief function was to furnish him with that length of perspective which most distinguishes him from his contemporaries.

There remain the moderns, whom Emerson always read, although often out of school. In his day in college it was impossible to study English Literature as such, and as a result he often neglected his official tasks in favor of reading the modern dramatists and poets. He loved especially the Elizabethans, and mentions Shakespeare more often than any other author. Indeed, Shakespeare may be compared with Plato as furnishing the substance, as opposed to the form, of Emerson's literary thinking. For him Shakespeare expressed the beauty and the color of the world in so far as these could be expressed in words. Shakespeare became "the poet."

Finally among the moderns was Montaigne, "the grand old sloven," to whom Emerson seems to have been attracted by the law of opposites. In any grouping of his favorite authors, the Frenchman should occupy the prominent position on the extreme left. For Emerson's mind took in the whole range of literature, and if he adopted many conventional favorites such as Plato and Shakespeare, he also went further afield to include extreme mystics such as Plotinus, and extreme skeptics, such as Montaigne. All his life a lover of the earth and the raciness of common men, Montaigne furnished him in literary form with this element that he most needed. With Montaigne Emerson's intellectual equipment became rounded and complete.

16 See F. I. Carpenter, *Emerson and Asia.*

17 See *Emerson and Asia*, 94–100; and J. S. Harrison, *The Teachers of Emerson.*

III. DOMESTIC LIFE

We have considered two important influences acting upon Emerson to form him into his ideal of the American Scholar—namely, the American scene, and the literature of the past—but a third acted more powerfully and constantly than either of these, and contributed the element of strength to his character which most distinguishes it. As Emerson wrote, "Action is with the scholar subordinate, but it is essential. . . . Only so much do I know, as I have lived." Since he acted very little in the sphere of public life,[18] but very fully in private, or domestic life, we may consider this as the third influence upon his character and philosophy.

In a famous passage of his essay on "Domestic Life," Emerson drew upon his own experience to describe its formative effect upon character. Speaking of himself and his brothers, he asked: "What is the hoop that holds them staunch? It is the iron band of poverty, of necessity, of austerity. . . . The angels that dwell with them and are weaving the laurels of life for their youthful brows, are Toil and Want, Truth and Mutual Faith."[19] These words are important, as they suggest both the usual and the unusual aspects of Emerson's life. "Toil and Want" were always present, so that poverty was one of the driving forces of his life, as it has been in the lives of many young Americans. But "Truth and Mutual Faith" were also present in an unusual degree, and gave his character the simplicity and sincerity which distinguishes it.

Emerson was a poor boy. Unlike Longfellow and Lowell and Holmes, he was never one of the true "Brahmins" of Boston. In 1854 he exclaimed to his Journal: "If Socrates were here, we could go and talk with him; but Longfellow, we cannot talk with; there is a palace, and servants, and a row of bottles of different coloured wines, and wine glasses, and fine coats."

[18] See section VII, "Public Affairs." [19] *Works*, VII, 121.

Emerson's family had always been poor, and, in spite of success in later life, he always avoided luxury. In his essay on "Napoleon," he criticized the "man of the world" as one who, when he had made all the money he needed, did not know what to do with it, and could find satisfaction only in making more money. Emerson knew the value of poverty as a driving force, spurring the individual to his best efforts, and disciplining him in the school of "necessity and austerity." And he also knew the value of money, which makes social independence possible. So he was able to enjoy the advantages of both, keeping the balance between them. Throughout his life he practiced a self-reliant poverty. He concluded his essay on "Self-Reliance": "So use all that is called Fortune. Most men gamble with her, and gain all, and lose all, as her wheel rolls. But do thou leave as unlawful these winnings, and deal with Cause and Effect, the chancellors of God."

Together with poverty, his domestic life trained him in the virtues of "Truth and Mutual Faith." Here the many generations of puritan ancestry exerted themselves to inculcate the personal integrity which had always been their highest ideal. Anyone reading his Journals must be impressed with his remarkable honesty, both with himself and with other men. He always faced the facts of his life squarely, without evasion. Indeed, in his efforts not to deceive himself, or others, he often criticized himself too severely. At the early age of ten years, he wrote to his Aunt Mary,[20] describing his daily routine of life, and confessing to the faults of occasional anger at his brothers, and a desire to play during the time that should have been devoted to reading. In his later life, he criticized himself not so much for his lack of the puritan virtues, as for his possession of the puritan faults. The famous passage beginning "I was born cold" has been quoted too often. At the start of his essay on

[20] The complete letter is of great interest. See J. E. Cabot, *A Memoir*, I, 34–36.

"Experience," he criticized himself, in this case unduly, for his inability to feel grief at the death of his eldest son. His absolute honesty with himself and with the world is one of his outstanding characteristics. It is interesting to speculate whether his knowledge of his own faults did not overbalance those faults. A man may perhaps see the world steadily and whole, even with a defect of vision, if he recognizes his defect sufficiently to make exact allowances for it.

Emerson's training in a self-reliant poverty, and his training in truthfulness and sincerity, are two of the keys to his personality and philosophy. They help to explain his optimism, and his wisdom. Considered together they may be taken to illustrate one of the central principles of religious truth—"Blessed are the poor in spirit, for theirs is the kingdom of heaven." Trained in poverty, Emerson knew that unlimited "prosperity" was not only not possible, but not advisable. Trained in truthfulness and self-knowledge, he knew the faults of men too well to be proud.

But one does not usually think of the philosopher of self-reliance as "poor in spirit." He did not try, like Franklin, to "imitate Jesus," and cultivate humility. Rather, he "took himself for better or for worse as his portion in life," cheerfully. But he remained poor in spirit because he did not ask too much of life. He accepted thankfully whatever good was offered him as pure gain. In the language of materialism, he did not list his stock at a par of one hundred, and then despair when its value depreciated; rather he listed it at zero, and rejoiced if his efforts made it climb above that point. His own words, in his essay on "Experience," explain this attitude most clearly, and also explain why his optimism was so at variance with the pessimism of "the modern temper," both in our time and in his own:

> The fine young people despise life [he wrote] but . . . I am thankful for small mercies. I compared notes with one of my

friends who expects everything of the universe, and is disappointed when anything is less than the best, and I found that I begin at the other extreme, expecting nothing, and am always full of thanks for moderate good.

"Expecting nothing from the universe," Emerson was always optimistic. Trained to live simply, he was easily contented. Knowing his faults, and those of other men, he did not wish for too much. "Ask nothing of men, and, in the endless mutation, thou only firm column must presently appear the upholder of all that surrounds thee."[21] Thus it happened that Emerson himself became one of the "firm columns" of the pantheon of American literature.

IV. RELIGION

Emerson's life was closely connected with his writing, so that the transition from one to the other is natural and inevitable—especially in the field of religion, where Emerson lived most completely the theories which he preached. Like Tolstoi he held that "Religion . . . is a life," and indeed the master purpose of his writing is, perhaps, the application and illustration of religious truths in practical affairs. But even if his religion was personal, he used the forms of his time in which to express his ideas, and hence these forms take on a certain importance. The words "Calvinism," "Unitarianism," and "Transcendentalism" are vague, and need description.

Contrary to common belief, the progression from Calvinism to Transcendentalism represents a steady development from the theological to the practical—from exclusive religion to the religious practice of common life. The various stages of this development may be described briefly with reference to their changing conceptions of God. Calvinism, which dominated New England until late in the eighteenth century, worshiped "God in three persons," conceiving of God somewhat anthro-

[21] *Works*, II, 89; "Self-Reliance."

pomorphically, and of Jesus as divine. Unitarianism, according to whose tenets Emerson was brought up, broke away from this conception of God, contending that there could be but one God, and that Jesus had not been divine, but rather the perfect "Son of Man." Transcendentalism carried the process to its logical conclusion, and denied the "personality" of God altogether, speaking of God as an impersonal force, which operated by means of "the moral law." In abandoning the personal conception of God, it accepted the findings of contemporary science and idealistic philosophy, basing its belief in God on the fact that the world was governed by law. But there were two laws, as Emerson wrote: "law for man, and law for thing"—"moral law," and "natural law." Transcendentalism derived its peculiar quality (which differentiated it from the mechanical Deism of the eighteenth century) from its emphasis on the moral law, or the place of man in the universe. Of course it sought to discover moral law through the preliminary observation of natural law—hence the term "Transcendentalism,"[22] indicating that beyond or "transcending" the natural law a human or spiritual truth might be discerned. The laws of the soul were its chief interest, and it differed from modern psychology in its method, but not in its subject matter. Emerson's "Over-Soul" affirms general truths where William James's *Varieties of Religious Experience* collects specific observations to illustrate the same principles. In opposition to the earlier theologians, both Emerson and James wrote impersonally of the laws of human nature as revealed in experience, rather than as revealed *a priori* in the Biblical revelations of a personal God.

For the first twenty-nine years of his life Emerson remained a Unitarian.[23] He studied in a Unitarian divinity school, and for

[22] For a detailed study of Transcendentalism, see H. C. Goddard, *Studies in New England Transcendentalism* (New York, 1908). Emerson's essay on "The Transcendentalist" is also important.

[23] Often Transcendentalism and Unitarianism are combined. Thus the article on "Unitarianism" in the *Encyclopædia Britannica* (14th ed.) calls Emerson one of the leaders of the "second stage" of Unitarianism.

three years preached successfully to one of the most important Unitarian congregations of Boston. Like his father he was chaplain of the State Senate. His sermons were universally accepted and admired, and as a visiting preacher he was much in demand. He did not leave the Unitarian ministry because of any failure on his own part to measure up to the conventional religious standards of his congregation, or because of any misunderstanding. He resigned from it because, as he began to think things out for himself, he saw that he could not continue to believe in its tenets. A remark which he made to a friend soon after his resignation puts the matter more forcefully than anything he ever actually wrote: "Whoever would preach Christ in these times must say nothing about him."[24] Put bluntly, he believed that the influence of the Church as a religious force was narrow. In the Church, one preached theology; outside it, one could proclaim the laws of human life. In the Church, people listened on Sunday; outside, on all the days of the week. Emerson sought to break down the distinction between the religious and the secular, and therefore abandoned the Church.

The only important evidence so far published of his early ideas as a Unitarian minister is his extraordinary farewell sermon on "The Lord's Supper."[25] This sermon shows him in the moment of transition from the old religion to the new, when he was still conforming to the rules of the old. Specifically, he had based his resignation on his objection to administering the bread and wine of the sacrament, and in this sermon he argued, from theological grounds, that the Lord's Supper had no justification in scripture or in practice. For the only time in his career as a writer, he played the game according to the rules of his opponents, arguing from text to text, and from precedent to historical precedent. He displayed the greatest shrewdness and

[24] Elizabeth P. Peabody, "Emerson as Preacher," in *The Genius and Character of Emerson*, 161.

[25] See *Works*, XI, 1–25. It is not included in the Selections because of the limited scope of its subject matter.

logical precision in this. He declared that the Lord's Supper was not originally meant to be part of a Christian service. First he cited scriptural text, then Jewish custom, then historical usage, and then the question of modern expediency. Only finally did he come to the ground from which he wrote during all the rest of his life—that of intuition, or personal conviction. Meanwhile he had composed the most convincing proof possible of the fact that he did not abandon theology and logical exposition because he was incapable of them. For twenty-nine years he had conformed, had become proficient, and had gained success. For the rest of his life he was to follow his own path and describe religious truth at first-hand, as he observed and experienced it.

This break from the religion of the past was largely caused by an increasing preoccupation with the events and ideas of the present—especially the ideas of modern science. He felt that the truths of the old religion must be fused with those of science, and that this was possible only if the forms of the old religion were modified. The year before he resigned his ministry he read widely in science, especially in the astronomy of the time.[26] Shortly before making his decision to resign he wrote significantly in his Journal: "The Religion that is afraid of science dishonours God and commits suicide." He himself opened his arms to science, and on his trip to Europe visited many scientific museums and lectures with increasing interest, until, standing in the Jardin des Plantes in Paris, he thought to himself: "I am moved by strange sympathies; I say continually, 'I will be a naturalist.'"[27] Of course he never carried out this resolve to the letter, but throughout his life he read continually of the new theories and discoveries of science, constantly coloring his own thought with them.

Between his farewell sermon in 1832 and his famous address to the Divinity School at Harvard in 1838 he had advanced far,

[26] See H. H. Clark, "Emerson and Science," 234. [27] *Journals*, III, 163.

in confidence, in method, and in ideas. In his farewell sermon he had attacked the relatively minor institution of the Lord's Supper; in the Divinity School Address he attacked the whole structure of formalized Christianity. In the sermon, he had argued from verse and text, accepting, for the purposes of argument, the literal authority of the Scriptures; in the address, he abandoned historical argument and wrote from the broader ground of intuition and experience. In the sermon, he had offered no substitute for the formal religious observance he was attacking; in the address, he attempted to describe the true "religious sentiment," before criticizing the formalism which, as he believed, obscured it. The Divinity School Address was primarily a challenge to the old religion, and was so understood by those who heard it and read it. Immediately on its delivery a storm of protest and acclaim arose, making its author so notorious that for more than a generation he was denied the halls of the University where he had spoken.

The Divinity School Address is one of his most powerful attacks on the old order, and since he attacked it on its most sensitive point—religion—the radicalism of his ideas here became immediately apparent. In its larger implications, this address merely restated the ideas which he had already set forward in *Nature* and "The American Scholar," but these seemed most striking and dangerous when applied to the religious life of man. Generally speaking, he now flatly denied the validity of preaching from tradition, or from Scriptural text. "It is the office of the true teacher to show us that God is, not was; that He speaketh, not spake." He opposed historical Christianity because it was historical—because it spoke "as if God were dead." Instead, he would have men live wholly in the present, and seek God in their daily life about them. "One mind is everywhere active, in each ray of the star, in each wavelet of the pool. . . . The old is for slaves. Wherever a man comes, there comes revolution."

That this preaching was dangerous, Emerson knew. Essentially it was an early statement of the experimental way of life, which has always been recognized as radical. If tradition is to be abandoned and the present accepted as the only test of truth, men must find truth for themselves by living experiments with it. Here Emerson came very close to the spirit of science, as that can be applied to the realm of the "moral law." In his Journal he put the idea most clearly: "All life is an experiment. The more experiments you make the better. . . . What if you do fail, and get fairly rolled in the dirt once or twice? Up again, you shall never be so afraid of a tumble."[28] Partly by reaction from the old religion, he developed the new, or scientific way of life, which was to lead him to the formulation of "Self-Reliance," his greatest essay.

It was apparent that this radicalism needed qualification, and therefore he attempted a better rounded scheme of religion in his essay on "The Over-Soul." Although this lacks the bite of the Divinity School Address, it has been accepted as the classical statement of his religious ideas. It uses a rather mystical terminology, but, because of its individual quality, has survived the years. But Emerson himself clearly saw the difficulty of trying to describe an infinite God in finite words, and in all his later writings abandoned the attempt—the "Over-Soul" remaining his last purely religious essay.

Technically, the idea of the Over-Soul derives largely from the "emanation theory" of the Neo-Platonists, especially of Plotinus, colored by the mysticism of later writers, and by the "inner light" of the Quakers. God is thought of as a sort of reservoir of spiritual energy—sometimes the metaphor of "the divine water" is used, sometimes that of an "ocean of light," sometimes that of a more subtle, radiant energy. Religion is conceived as the emanation of this energy from its divine source, and its influx into the individual life, which is thereby

[28] *Journals*, VI, 302.

enriched and illuminated. The idea is as old as the hills, and as vague, and is so recognized by Emerson. Therefore he asks how it can be applied, specifically. "The only answer to these questions of the senses is to forego all low curiosity, and, accepting the tide of being which floats us into the secret of nature, work and live, work and live, and all unawares the advancing soul has built and forged for itself a new condition, and the question and the answer are one." This advice sounds not unlike modern Pragmatism, although it is clothed in the emotion of mysticism.

The particular value of Emerson's religion of the Over-Soul lies in its emphasis on the spirit as opposed to the letter of the religious law; in its emphasis upon personal experience rather than formal tradition as a means of discovering this law; and in its emphasis on education rather than prohibition as the means of administering it. For educated and civilized men and women, this radical religion offers a challenge and an opportunity. Fortunately, uneducated and uncivilized men and women will probably never read it.

V. PHILOSOPHY

Emerson's philosophy grew out of his religion, both in practice and in theory. He had always read widely in philosophy, and after resigning from the ministry in 1832, he devoted himself more than ever before to it. In his first book on *Nature*, he attempted an ordered presentation of his own ideas. But just as the individualism of his temperament had led him to deny allegiance to any creed or system of theology, so it kept him from formulating any philosophic system. Although in his lifetime men thought of him as a philosopher, and after his death Harvard named its new philosophy building in his honor, modern writers have sometimes denied his right to the title of philosopher, at all.

Emerson, with his usual self-knowledge, did not claim to be a philosopher. And he offered several significant reasons for not becoming one. "I can very confidently announce one or another law," he wrote, "which throws itself into relief and form, but I am too young yet by some ages to compile a code."[29] Knowing well that he was living in an age of transition, "between two worlds," he did not attempt to formulate a fixed and final system. Later he wrote: "I cannot myself use that systematic form which is reckoned essential in treating the science of the mind. But if one can say so without arrogance, I might suggest that he who contents himself with dotting a fragmentary curve, recording only what facts he has observed, without attempting to arrange them within one outline, follows a system also."[30] Recording "only what facts he has observed," Emerson imported the rules of science into the practice of philosophy. Lastly he declared: "My metaphysics are to the end of use. I wish to know the laws of this wonderful power, that I may domesticate it."[31] Wishing to make his idealism practical, and apply it to the life of his America, he avoided any self-sufficient, metaphysical system. Emerson's sentences will suggest much to the student of modern philosophy, but before trying to follow out their implications, his thought should be related briefly to the philosophical systems of the past.

Given the religious training of his youth, and his lifelong devotion to Plato, it was almost inevitable that Emerson should become an idealist. But "idealism" is a much-abused word, which means little to the modern world unless it is defined. Emerson believed that mind is more important than matter, and that the observer gives color to the thing observed. But he was not an "idealist" who denied the existence or the reality of matter. Nothing could be further from him than the doctrines

[29] *Works*, III, 83; "Experience."
[30] *Works*, XII, 11; "Natural History of Intellect."
[31] *Works*, XII, 13–14.

of Christian Science, which have been compared to his own. "Does the fact look crass and material, threatening to degrade thy theory of spirit? Resist it not; it goes to refine and raise thy theory of matter just as much."[32] He was not an absolutist.

Recognizing the limitations of Emerson's idealism, many philosophical critics[33] have been driven to calling him a "dualist"—one who believed in the parallel existence of mind and matter. Certainly there is much in his writings to justify this view. "Dualism" gave form to his philosophy, and lies behind the general theory of Transcendentalism, which implies that there are two planes of existence—the natural and the human—and that the second transcends, or develops out of the first. He described the dual aspect of life most completely in his essay on "Plato," where he contrasts: "Unity and Variety," "the One and the Many," "East and West." "The unity of Asia and the detail of Europe . . . Plato came to join, and by contact to enhance the energy of each." Indeed, whenever Emerson described one of these aspects of life, he always related it to its opposite. "Self-reliance" he qualified by reliance upon the unity of the "Over-Soul." "Nature" implied an observer to see and to understand her. "Fate," or "form," cannot be understood without reference to the "Power" which directs the currents of life through its preordained channels. The "Illusions," or moods, which seem to be "the lords of life," fall into perspective when seen as a whole by the mature mind of man. The "Experience" of the senses must be complemented by the religious experience.

> There are two laws discrete,
> Not reconciled,—
> Law for man, and law for thing;

[32] *Works*, II, 285; "Circles."

[33] Especially the classical and humanistic critics, such as W. C. Brownell, P. E. More, Norman Foerster, and H. H. Clark. For the best expression of a contrary view, see H. D. Gray, *Emerson*, 25–70.

The last builds town and fleet,
But it runs wild,
And doth the man unking.[34]

But always parallel with this dualism, Emerson expressed his mystical belief in "the eternal ONE." By religion, rather than by philosophy, he was a monist, as "The Over-Soul" and "Brahma" bear witness.

Emerson never fully formulated any explanation of the unity which he felt to underlie the dualism of life; but two theories which he adapted to his own usage show how he might have done so, and one concept which he developed for himself, prepared the way for later thinkers to do so. The first of the two theories is that of emanation, which he found originally in Plotinus, and whose import was primarily religious. The second is the theory of evolution, which had been in the air for fifty years before Darwin gave it scientific formulation.[35] Emanation may be described as an idealistic monism; evolution as a materialistic monism. The first readily adapted itself to the theory (then merely a suggestion, but now well established), of the identity of energy and matter—energy continually "emanating" from God, and condensing itself, as it were, in the forms of the material world. The second, describing the gradual evolution of life from inanimate to animate matter, and from lower to higher forms until it issues at last in the intelligence of man, also seemed to furnish such a satisfactory monistic theory, and recommended itself especially to Emerson as confirming his idea of progress, or melioration. In the poetic motto of *Nature*, he wrote:

[34] "Ode Inscribed to W. H. Channing." Evidence regarding Emerson's interpretation of the classical-Christian dualism between good and evil has been collected by C. E. Jorgenson; see Bibliography.

[35] See H. D. Gray, *Emerson*, 40–46. For the sources of Emerson's ideas on evolution, see H. H. Clark, "Emerson and Science," 247 ff. Professor Clark argues that Emerson reconciled the doctrine of evolution to his Platonic dualism.

And, striving to be man, the worm
Mounts through all the spires of form.

Indeed, the whole organization of his book on *Nature*, starting from its most materialistic aspect as "Commodity," and progressing to its most idealistic aspect as "Spirit," suggested this evolutionary approach. But Emerson never formulated either of these theories specifically.

The original concept by which Emerson suggested the solution of the problem of dualism, is that of experience, considered in its most general sense. This concept is fundamental to his philosophy, as his serious critics agree.[36] But he conceived of experience inclusively. He described two types of experience: the mystical and the sensuous. There were "spiritual facts" and "physical facts," but both were "facts." Like William James, he based his belief in theism on the evidence of what he called "God the phenomenon."[37] And in his essay on "Experience," he described life as "sensations *and* states of mind," unified by the consciousness of man. By considering experience both in its objective and subjective aspects, he avoided both "absolutism," which denied the validity of the test of experience, and "empiricism," which denied the reality of human consciousness. In all of this he foreshadowed the Pragmatism of later American thinkers.[38]

Experience, thus defined, is what William James called a "double-barreled" fact. In itself it includes both the subjective and the objective: the mystical experience merely emphasizes the one, the sensuous experience the other. But always, unless there is a subject to perceive, there can be no experience; unless there is an objective world to suggest the impression, there can

[36] O. W. Firkins writes: "The secret of Emerson may be conveyed in one word, the superlative, even the superhuman, value which he found in the unit of experience." (*Emerson*, 297.) See also G. E. Woodberry, *Emerson*, 109; and R. M. Gay, *Emerson*, 8–9.

[37] *Works*, I, 60; "Nature."

[38] See W. James, *Varieties of Religious Experience*, and J. Dewey, *Experience and Nature*, chap. I.

be none. Experience is a bridge between subject and object. Neither the soul, nor nature, can possess any reality, separately. Only by the interaction of the two can the true meaning of life be discovered. "Power ceases in the instant of repose; it resides in the moment of transition from a past to a new state, in the shooting of the gulf, in the darting to an aim."[39] Reality lies in the fact of experience.

The chief obscurity of Emerson's writing results from his custom of never using the same word twice in the same context, but of always varying his terminology. Thus he did not often speak of "experience" as such, and his ideas concerning it are not always self-evident. To show how the concept dominated his thought, even when he did not use the word, we may analyze briefly his first book on *Nature*. Besides being his first, *Nature* has the advantage of being his most carefully organized book, and of announcing all of his ideas, at least in embryo. In it, Emerson described his theory of experience, under the title of "Discipline." After an introductory and general discussion, he wrote successively of three common uses, or aspects, of Nature. His discussion of "Commodity" is simple and clear. That of "Beauty" is hardly less so—it describes the artistic or esthetic aspect of nature. "Language" carries the reader to the realm of the transcendental, but on analysis it is a restatement of the old idea of symbolism, strongly colored by the more modern theory of "correspondence."[40] The material for these earlier chapters Emerson borrowed, and reshaped to his own usage. But with "Discipline," he introduced a radically new idea. What is more, he immediately advertised it as such, stating: "In view of the significance of nature, we arrive at once at a new fact, that nature is a discipline. This use of the world includes the preceding uses [Commodity, Beauty, and Language], as parts

[39] *Works*, II, 69; "Self-Reliance."

[40] See C. P. Hotson, "Emerson and the Doctrine of Correspondence," *New-Church Review*, XXXVI, 47–59; 173–186; 304–316; 435–448 (1929).

of itself." The theory of discipline is "new," and its significance is inclusive. It means not only merely "discipline," but more broadly "education through experience," and it points the way to *The Education of Henry Adams*, as well as to Dewey's *Experience and Nature*. Also, it leads the way to Emerson's Transcendentalism, as expressed in the last three chapters of his little book. It bridges the chasm between external nature and the soul. He reaches his chapter on "Idealism" by means of this bridge:

> To this one end of Discipline, all parts of nature conspire.
> A noble doubt perpetually suggests itself,—whether this end be not the Final Cause of the Universe; and whether nature outwardly exists.

Since "discipline," or experience, suggests to man his only ideas of the Universe, is not this "suggestion" the ultimate reality?

But exactly how does "experience" comport with "idealism"? The answer is to be found in Emerson's essays on "Experience" and "Illusions," as well as in James's book on *The Will to Believe*. Both Emerson and James put the mystical experience first, as, indeed, it seems to come first in the consciousness of man. For by the mystical experience Emerson did not mean merely the supersensitive, visionary experience of religious enthusiasts; but rather that simple, universal experience of every common man with nature, which, unconsciously and irrationally, forces upon him the belief that "life is worth living." Emerson had written that "*the universal impulse to believe* . . . is the principal factor in the history of the globe."[41] James described this same experience at greater length as the "will" to believe, and gave it also a central place in his philosophy.

From this simple, mystical experience, all others derive their meaning. It is the first and the last thing, and Emerson described the others, in the language of the ancient East, as "illu-

[41] *Works*, III, 74; "Experience."

sions," or partial experiences. By illusion, nature educates man, and gives content and specific meaning to the vague or mystical experience of "Pure Being." By the process of everyday experience, the mystical experience takes on the form, and becomes "the sense of being something." So life becomes complex, and the young mortal feels as though he had lost his way in the world, and becomes confused. But at length the fundamental, mystical experience reasserts itself, and he once again sees "the gods sitting around him on their thrones,—they alone with him alone."[42]

Emerson's philosophy may perhaps be described as a Pragmatic Mysticism.[43] It is idealistic in that it puts the mystical experience first. It is dualistic in that it looks both ways from its position on the bridge between the soul and nature. It is monistic in that it maintains that this bridge is the only reality. But it is pragmatic in that it tests all truths (including the mystical belief in the value of life) by experience.

It remains to suggest that this pragmatic mysticism is essentially *the* American philosophy, or, as it has been called, "the American Dream." America was founded by men who held an irrational and fundamentally mystical belief in the potentialities of life in the New World. The Declaration of Independence was written by an idealist, and its principles were based on an act of faith. Liberty and equality were originally transcendental ideas.[44] These ideas have been experimentally tested by succeeding generations of Americans, and are still being so tested. But fundamentally they are mystical. As Mr. Adams writes: "The American Dream was not a logical concept of thought. Like every great thought that has stirred and advanced humanity, it was a religious emotion, a great act of faith, a courageous

[42] See end of "Illusions." *Works*, VI, 325.

[43] See H. D. Gray, *Emerson*, 14.

[44] "Transcendental," in the sense of mystical, and not yet tested by sensuous experience. See H. S. Commager, "Theodore Parker," *New England Quarterly*, VI, 275–6 (June, 1933).

leap into the dark unknown. As long as that dream persists to strengthen the heart of man, Emerson will remain one of its prophets."[45]

VI. POETRY

In the theory and practice of poetry, as in philosophy, Emerson derived many ideas from the literature of the past, but recreated them into an original and modern esthetic. His essay on "The Poet" sounded a call for an authentically American poet, which was answered by Whitman—and he even prophesied the exact paths which that poet must follow. Emerson's theory of literature as expression has been repeated and elaborated by many writers: In 1860 John Burroughs published an anonymous essay on "Expression" in the *Atlantic Monthly*, which was long attributed to Emerson. Recently Benedetto Croce, the Italian pragmatist, has repeated Emerson's theory of the inseparability of the artistic ideal and the expression of it. In 1932, Mr. Ludwig Lewisohn made Emerson's words a starting-point for his study *Expression in America*. In his essay on "Beauty" Emerson foreshadowed the whole modern theory of art and architecture, declaring flatly that "outside embellishment is deformity. . . . Our taste in building . . . refuses pilasters and columns that support nothing, and allows the real supporters of the house honestly to show themselves." By the same token he preceded John Dewey's protest against the separation of the "fine arts" from the "useful arts": "Nothing merely ornamental can be beautiful."[46] In almost every phase of his esthetic theory, he cleared the path that has been followed by later men.

As always, Emerson's ideas concerning poetry are bound up with his whole philosophy of life. They are a part of his revolt from the past. In "The American Scholar" he had announced this revolt in ringing words, and applied it particularly to the

[45] J. T. Adams, *The Epic of America*, 198. [46] *Journals*, IV, 88.

realm of philosophy and intellect. In his essay on "The Poet" he applied it to the field of creative writing. Here he divided human endeavor into three representative fields: knowledge, action, and expression; represented by the philosopher, the man of action, and the poet. Having already specified his ideal for the American scholar, or philosopher, he now went on to describe his ideal for the American poet. Both his American Scholar and Poet were to express the thoughts and emotions common to humanity in all ages; but they were to describe these as they appeared in the native life about them, and were to use new forms, appropriate to this new life.

It is illuminating to read "The Poet" with Whitman's later practice of poetry in mind. Emerson first attacked "our poets" (much as Mr. Van Wyck Brooks has attacked them) for putting poetical finish before genuine inspiration, declaring "it is not metres, but a metre-making argument that makes a poem." Then, having bewailed the absence of the genuinely inspired poet in America, he went on to describe this poet's characteristics: "The vocabulary . . . would embrace words and images excluded from polite conversation. What would be base, or even obscene, to the obscene, becomes illustrious spoken in a new connection of thought." Even "bare lists of words are found suggestive to an imaginative and excited mind." He went on to celebrate "the factory village and the railway" as proper subjects for the American poet. Then, after a more general discussion of the theory of poetry, he came to his conclusion: "Yet America is a poem in our eyes . . . and it will not wait long for metres." "Doubt not, O poet, but persist. Say 'It is in me, and shall out.'" Following these exhortations, Whitman wrote in his "Song of Myself": "Walt you contain enough, why don't you let it out then?" He followed Emerson's suggestions in almost every particular. So Emerson welcomed him at the beginning of his career, not at random, but as a true disciple.

In the phrase "It is in me, and shall out" lies the germ of

Emerson's esthetic theory. All great art is organic and necessary: it is a functional part of human life, and if it is denied to man, his soul dies. In the extreme form of the doctrine, expression is man's only spiritual necessity: "Expression is all we need, not knowledge, but vent." Indeed Santayana sees it as the key to Emerson's thought: "Imagination is his single theme . . . Emerson traces in every sphere the same spiritual laws of experience—compensation, continuity, the self-expression of the Soul in the forms of Nature and of society."[47] But in the very centrality of the idea of self-expression lies the guarantee of its sanity. Expression cannot be arbitrary or superficial, because it springs from the center of human life. The merely ornamental is essentially false, because it is untrue to man's nature. Great art must be necessary, and unconscious. At the opposite pole from Poe, Emerson's philosophy of composition demanded that the artist forget his means in the pursuit of his end. Poe was "the jingle man," because he lost sight of the functional necessity of beauty, in his preoccupation with the means of composition. Whitman was the true poet, because he subordinated the means of expression to the imaginative truth to be expressed.[48]

Emerson's theory of the organic nature of art was essentially modern, but his practice of it was not always successful. His own poetry could not wholly free itself from the conventions of the past—Whitman practiced his ideal better than he did. Although Emerson disparaged metres, he never abandoned them. His vocabulary did not embrace words or images excluded from polite conversation. He seldom described "the factory village and the railway" in his poems. And he did not celebrate an America set free in his poetry, as he had done in his prose.

[47] *Interpretations of Poetry and Religion*, 221.

[48] For the philosophic background of Emerson's theory, see Norman Foerster, *American Criticism*, 52–110; F. I. Carpenter, *Emerson and Asia*, 86–94; and E. G. Sutcliffe, *Emerson's Theories of Literary Expression.*

Emerson's poetry always threatens to escape from metre and from rhyme, but never quite does so. The reader of his verses at first is led to expect the regularity which the use of metre and rhyme seems to guarantee, but soon is startled and confused by sudden variations of metre, and abandonments of rhyme. While this shock heightens the reader's awareness to the meaning, it is as if the poet had taken an unfair advantage of him. If Emerson cared no more than this for metre and rhyme, he should have abandoned them altogether. One instinctively objects to so much freedom in verse which is not free verse.

Nevertheless this freedom is an integral part of Emerson's poetry, and often imparts to it its greatest power. Many of his best poems partially or wholly abandon rhyme. "Days," although brief and essentially lyrical, does not employ it. "The Snow-Storm" and "Seashore" also succeed in this most difficult form—the blank verse lyric. Moreover, when rhyme is not abandoned, it often is distorted. Imperfect rhymes and assonances appear, which, because exceptional, seem clumsy. Critics object to the pairing of "arms" and "psalms," "hurry" and "busy," although these were obviously not intended as true rhymes. Here Emerson appears as the unconscious forerunner of Emily Dickinson and of the modern experimentalists. Finally such poems as "Bacchus" and "Give All to Love" use rhyme so at random as practically to destroy the effect of it.

Emerson uses metre no less freely. A single poem, "Hamatreya," includes many of the variations which he uses. Its first line,

> "Bulkeley, Hunt, Willard, Hosmer, Meriam, Flint,"

although technically regular, strikes a new note, anticipating Robert Frost. The rest of the blank verse introduction contains two unfinished lines, used for emphasis. Then the "Earth-Song" skips about, making utterly free with both metre and rhyme, until finally the last quatrain closes without ceremony, in two different metres:

When I heard the Earth-song,
I was no longer brave;
My avarice cooled
Like lust in the chill of the grave.

Many other poems, such as "Threnody," "The Sphinx," "Merlin," "Bacchus," and "Terminus," use the same irregularity of metre.

The trouble is that Emerson's poetry is not even regularly irregular. The famous "Brahma," "The Concord Hymn," and "The Rhodora" are as regular as clockwork, yet no less typical of Emerson, and no less successful. If Emerson had developed exclusively the technique of free verse, American literature would have lost some of its most perfect poems. As a poet Emerson followed his own law, ascended sometimes to the heights, and—like all who practice the experimental life—got rolled in the dust frequently. But with all its imperfections his poetry has endured exceptionally well, as the critics and anthologists of the twentieth century bear witness. Bryant, Holmes, Whittier, Longfellow, Lowell, with their metrically regular poetry, often sound flat to the modern ear. Poe survives for other reasons. But only Whitman, who practiced most completely what Emerson preached, clearly surpassed his master in poetic stature.

VII. POLITICS AND PUBLIC AFFAIRS

Emerson succeeded to a high degree as "philosopher," and "poet," but he was not a "man of the world." According to his own ideal, and according to most popular ideals, he should have been. Undoubtedly, his aloofness from public life was his greatest weakness. But in two instances, at the two extremes of local politics, and of national politics, he did act. As a citizen of Concord, and as a spokesman for the cause of anti-slavery, he entered into public affairs as a leader.

Emerson's first published address was delivered at the second centenary of the town of Concord, in 1835, and consisted of a faithful history of the town and of its method of government. Throughout his life he identified himself with the town so as to become its leading citizen. His famous "Concord Hymn" and Concord "Ode" were devoted to its celebration, as were numerous addresses on other public occasions.[49] More practically he was president of the Lyceum Board, attended and debated at the town meetings, and acted on numerous committees of the town. As individual citizen he performed every duty, with ability.

At the other extreme, in his rôle of national idealist, he identified himself with the anti-slavery movement from its early days. In 1831 he opened his pulpit to the unpopular agitators of the time, defending their rights to free speech. In 1835, he wrote: "I confess that I do not want to live in a nation where slavery exists."[50] From 1844 on he delivered increasingly frequent and effective public addresses on the subject, centering his attacks on the Fugitive Slave Law, and on the case of John Brown. Brown had early visited in his house at Concord, so that his trial and execution moved Emerson more deeply than the mere principles involved. Likewise Charles Sumner was a personal friend and admirer of Emerson, and the assault upon him roused Emerson to a high pitch. By frequent speeches during the Civil War, he succeeded in communicating this depth of feeling to the public.

But between the local and the national extremes, Emerson took little interest in practical politics. By temperament he was opposed to all fixed institutions. He began his essay on "Politics" in a negative vein, and went on to cite the derogatory connotation of the word "politic" as "cunning." So it is not surprising to find him showing less original thought in his active relations to the politics of the time than he did in any other

[49] See *Works*, XI. [50] *Journals*, III, 446.

field of contemporary endeavor. Thus his early political sympathies were blindly with the Whig, or conservative party, so that for many years he opposed Jacksonianism as the greatest of political evils.[51] He had reached a more intelligent and disinterested viewpoint before writing his essay on "Politics" in 1844, but only with the rise of the slavery issue, and the apostasy of Daniel Webster, did he abandon his practical conservatism. This issue forced him to apply his idealistic theories to politics, so that from 1850 on he supported the liberal parties. A letter of Webster's suggests the political associations of Emerson's ideas at this time. To a Concord friend, Webster wrote: "Many of those whom I so highly esteemed, in your beautiful and quiet village, have become a good deal estranged, to my great grief, by abolitionism, free-soilism, transcendentalism, and other notions which I cannot [but] regard as so many vagaries of the imagination."[52]

Emerson's failure to join actively in the various reform movements of his time (other than anti-slavery) has been criticized. He did not enroll in the Brook Farm community, nor in Alcott's Fruitlands; he refused to become excited by Margaret Fuller's crusade for woman's rights; he paid his taxes regularly (unlike Thoreau); and he regarded the whole group of radical reformers with the amused tolerance shown by his essay on "The Chardon St. Convention." It is true that he gave all these his blessing—attending the conventions, and delivering a speech in favor of woman's rights; but his heart was not with them. In the essay on "New England Reformers," he explains why: "But many a reformer perishes in his removal of rubbish; and that makes the offensiveness of the class. They are partial; they are not equal to the work they pretend. They lose their way; in the assault on the kingdom of darkness they expend all their energy on some accidental evil." The trouble with these reformers was

[51] See R. McQuiston, *The Relation of Emerson to Public Affairs*, 18–19.
[52] F. B. Sanborn, *Henry D. Thoreau* (Boston, 1882), 94.

that they were not radical enough, but only attacked partial abuses. When a truly fundamental reform like anti-slavery appeared, Emerson supported it actively. For the rest, he preferred to reform the human race from within, by educating the individual, rather than from without, by political and legal means.

VIII. INDIVIDUALISM AND SOCIALISM

Emerson's individualistic idealism probably reached its height in a conversation with Carlyle and others, described in *English Traits:*

> My friends asked, whether there were any Americans?—any with an American idea,—any theory of the right future of that country? Thus challenged I bethought myself neither of caucuses nor congress, neither of presidents nor of cabinet-ministers, nor of such as would make of America another Europe. . . . I said, "Certainly yes;—but those who hold it are fanatics of a dream which I should hardly care to relate to your English ears, to which it might be only ridiculous,—and yet it is the only true."[53]

But when asked what was this American dream of government, Emerson explained somewhat lamely: "So I opened the dogma of no-government and non-resistance." This dogma, of course, was the logical outcome of his individualistic philosophy of self-reliance. When the individual shall have become sufficiently educated and perfected to rely wholly upon himself, he will need no external government to reform him. Emerson's thought was consistent. But none the less, this sort of American dream, in its extreme form, sounds remote to modern ears. Without Emerson's eloquence, it would be ridiculous—so far is it from realization. Indeed, modern writers have described the failure of the dream so as to make it seem a nightmare. Was Emerson's optimism shallow, and his dream fantastic? What of the facts—

[53] *Works,* V, 286–7.

the "stubborn, irreducible facts"? And what of the means by which these facts were to be improved? Did Emerson forget all these things, in dreaming fanatically of his ideal America?

The answer is that Emerson did not forget, but that his eloquence sounded so persuasive when he was describing the ideal to be striven for, that the actual facts, and the means of striving to better them, sounded flat. Men remember "Self-Reliance," but they do not so readily remember "The Young American." They remember the challenging, individualistic ideal; but they conveniently forget the criticism of present American conditions lying behind it, and even more they forget the prophecy of the social compulsions by means of which this ideal may be realized by the mass of the American people. Emerson's self-reliance was an ideal for the educated, creative individual; while a better governmental organization, tending perhaps toward socialism, was his temporary solution for American society as a whole. In the famous essay on "Civil Disobedience," Thoreau wrote: "To speak practically . . . I ask for, not at once no government, but *at once* a better government." No less than his radical disciple, Emerson asked for a "new deal" in government, even though this might not seem to tend toward the realization of his ultimate individualistic ideal.

First, he criticized American government as it existed. In "Politics" he exclaimed: "We think our civilization near its meridian, but we are yet only at the cock-crowing and the morning star. In our barbarous society the influence of character is in its infancy. . . . We live in a very low state of the world. . . . A man has a right to be employed, to be trusted, to be loved, to be revered." And in "The Young American" he criticized American government more specifically: "Feudalism is not ended yet. Our governments still partake largely of that element. . . . In consequence of the revolution in the state of society wrought by trade, Government in our times is beginning to wear a clumsy and cumbrous appearance." He believed that the communal experiments such as Brook Farm proceeded "in great part from a feeling that the true offices of the State, the State had let fall to the ground; that in the scramble of parties for the public purse, the main duties of government were omitted,—the duty to instruct the ignorant, to supply the poor with work and with good guidance, . . . and the . . . mediation between want and supply."[54]

Many critics, reading only the essay on "Politics," in which Emerson's thought moves swiftly from a criticism of American government to an absolute ideal, interpret his political philosophy as "rugged individualism," and oppose it to modern socialism. A socialistic critic, for instance, declares: "While it is doubtful whether Emerson knew anything of the works of Marx or of the Marxian socialists, there can be no question that if he had, the whole direction of his philosophy would have made him their instant opponent."[55] But the question is doubtful. Emerson would have opposed the artificial restraints and levelings of Marxian socialism, as contrary to the trend of American freedom and independence. But Emerson would have accepted the positive qualities of the modern social philosophy—especially when they applied to government and public life. Emerson's self-reliant individualism was a private and essentially religious, or ethical philosophy. In the material world he recognized the necessity of regulation, and opposed the government of his time exactly because it did not properly "mediate between want and supply."

Let us conclude by piecing together some passages from his writings which illustrate this social thought: "Destiny is . . . a terrible communist, reserving all profits to the community, without dividend to individuals. Its law is, you shall have everything as a member, nothing to yourself. . . . This is the value of the Communities, not what they have done, but the

[54] *Works*, I, 363–395.
[55] V. F. Calverton, *The Liberation of American Literature*, 248.

revolution which they indicate as on the way. . . . The [aristocratic social] system is an invasion of the sentiment of justice and the native rights of men. . . . If only the men are employed in conspiring with the designs of the Spirit who led us hither and is leading us still, we shall quickly enough advance . . . into a new and more excellent *social state* than history has recorded."[56] "The evolution of a highly destined society must be moral. . . . What is *moral?* It is the respecting in action catholic or universal ends. . . . And the highest proof of civility is that the whole public action of the State is directed on securing the greatest good of the greatest number."[57]

If Emerson dreamed the American dream, he knew that it involved a revolution in the political and economic life of America. In its present "barbarous" state, "Good men must not obey the laws too well." Self-reliance requires a revolution privately conducted, until, through the proper governmental regulation of commerce, and governmental education of the poor, men can conduct their social affairs without the aid of government, at all. Self-reliance is for the educated individual, who understands the purposes of the Over-Soul, and to him Emerson addressed his writing. But he did not forget, and certainly he did not oppose, the gradual improvement of society, by the evolution of a better form of government, for the sake of the greatest number. In this, as in many other things, his ideas foreshadowed the liberal thought of modern America.

[56] From "The Young American." See Selections following, pp. 157, 164, 169. Italics added.
[57] From "Civilization." See Selections following, pp. 359, 363.

SELECTED BIBLIOGRAPHY

The following bibliography is critical as well as selective.

I. TEXT

The Complete Works of Ralph Waldo Emerson. Boston: 1903–4. Centenary Edition. 12 vols. (This is the standard edition of Emerson's Works. A biographical introduction and detailed notes by Emerson's son, Edward Waldo Emerson, and an index, add to the value of this authoritative collection.)

The Journals of Ralph Waldo Emerson. Ed. by Edward Waldo Emerson and Waldo Emerson Forbes. Boston: 1909–14. 10 vols. (This is the standard edition of the Journals.)

The Heart of Emerson's Journals. Ed. by Bliss Perry. Boston: 1926. (Offers an excellent one-volume selection from the above.)

The Uncollected Writings. Essays, Addresses, Poems, Reviews and Letters by Ralph Waldo Emerson. Ed. by Charles C. Bigelow. New York: 1912. (Contains supplementary material of importance.)

Uncollected Lectures by Ralph Waldo Emerson. Ed. by Clarence Gohdes. New York: 1932.

The unpublished letters of Ralph Waldo Emerson are now being prepared by Professor R. L. Rusk for publication by the Columbia University Press in four or five volumes. This authorized collection will include a check-list of all the Emerson letters now published. Of these, the most important collections are:

The Correspondence of Thomas Carlyle and Ralph Waldo Emerson, 1834–1872. Edited by C. E. Norton. Revised edition, Boston: 1888. 2 vols.

"The Emerson-Thoreau Correspondence," ed. by F. B. Sanborn, *Atlantic Monthly*, LXIX, 577–596 and 736–753 (May and June, 1892).

A Correspondence between John Sterling and Ralph Waldo Emerson. Ed. by E. W. Emerson. Boston: 1897.

Letters from Ralph Waldo Emerson to a Friend [Samuel Gray Ward]. Ed. by C. E. Norton. Boston: 1899.

Correspondence between Ralph Waldo Emerson and Herman Grimm. Ed. by F. W. Holls, *Atlantic Monthly*, XCI, 467–479 (April, 1903).

Records of a Lifelong Friendship, 1807–1882. Ralph Waldo Emerson and William Henry Furness. Ed. by H[enry] H[oward] F[urness]. Boston: 1910. (This volume also prints Emerson's juvenile poem, "Fortus.")

II. BIOGRAPHY

The definitive biography of Emerson is yet to be written. Probably the best approach to Emerson's life is through his own *Journals*, and especially through *The Heart of Emerson's Journals*, edited by Bliss Perry. Those biographies which seem most important to the editor are starred:

Alcott, Amos B. *Ralph Waldo Emerson: Philosopher and Seer.* Boston: 1882. (Mostly Alcott, and very little of that.)

Brooks, Van Wyck. *The Life of Emerson.* New York: 1932. (By one of our most distinguished critics. Using mostly the words of Emerson's *Journals*, this *Life* competes rather unsuccessfully with *The Heart of Emerson's Journals*, and gives the [false] impression of a secondhand presentation.)

*Cabot, James E. *A Memoir of Ralph Waldo Emerson.* Boston: 1887. 2 vols. (The standard biography, by Emerson's literary executor, and the most complete yet published. Contains many quotations from the *Journals* and Letters that have since been reprinted. Omits criticism and interpretation.)

Cary, Elizabeth L. *Emerson, Poet and Thinker.* New York: 1904. (Thoughtful. A final chapter on "The French Estimate" is especially valuable.)

Conway, Moncure D. *Emerson at Home and Abroad.* Boston: 1882. (A discursive study by a disciple, containing, however, much original material.)

Cooke, George W. *Ralph Waldo Emerson: His Life, Writings, and Philosophy*. Boston: 1881. (An able, but uninspired interpretation, stressing the writings.)

Dugard, Marie. *Ralph Waldo Emerson, sa Vie et son Œuvre*. Paris: 1907. (Enthusiastic, and sometimes illuminating. The best biography by a European.)

Emerson, Edward W. *Emerson in Concord: A Memoir*. Boston: 1889. (A biography by Emerson's son, composed mostly of excerpts from the *Journals*, which have since been published.)

*Firkins, Oscar W. *Ralph Waldo Emerson*. Boston: 1915. (A brilliant but uneven biographical and critical study.)

Garnett, Richard. *Life of Ralph Waldo Emerson*. London: 1888. (Unsympathetic, and often external, although by a distinguished man of letters.)

Gay, Robert M. *Emerson: A Study of the Poet as Seer*. Murray Hill Biographies. New York: 1928. (A thoughtful study.)

Guernsey, Alfred H. *Ralph Waldo Emerson: Philosopher and Poet*. New York: 1881. (Minor.)

*Holmes, Oliver W. *Ralph Waldo Emerson*. American Men of Letters series. Boston: 1884. (A readable and suggestive biography by a lifelong friend and admirer, who never understood Emerson. Better as biography than as criticism.)

Ireland, Alexander. *Ralph Waldo Emerson: His Life, Genius and Writings*. London: 1882. (By an English journalist and friend, containing some personal reminiscences.)

Michaud, Régis. *Emerson: The Enraptured Yankee*. Tr. by George Boas. New York: 1930. (An attempt at popular interpretation by a French scholar of note. The style is exclamatory and rhapsodic.)

Russell, Phillips. *Emerson: The Wisest American*. New York: 1929. (A popular biography, omitting all serious discussion of ideas. A vivid picture of the man emerges, however.)

Sanborn, F. B. *Ralph Waldo Emerson*. Beacon Biographies. Boston: 1901. (Very brief.)

Searle, January [George Searle Phillips]. *Emerson: His Life and Writings*. London: 1855. (The first volume upon Emerson. Brief.)

Snider, Denton J. *The Life of Emerson.* St. Louis: 1921. (Minor.)

*Woodberry, George E. *Ralph Waldo Emerson.* English Men of Letters series. New York: 1907. (A brilliant criticism and interpretation by one who nevertheless admits to "little intellectual sympathy with [Emerson]." Probably the best short biography.)

III. CRITICISM

This section of the bibliography lists not only critical and scholarly studies, but also a few brief critical estimates and interpretations included in books not confined to treatment of Emerson alone.

Albee, John. *Remembrances of Emerson.* New York: 1901 and 1903. ("A narrative of Emerson's influence upon the thoughtful young men of his time.")

Andler, C. "Emerson," in *Nietzsche, sa Vie et sa Pensée.* Paris: 1920. Vol. I, 340–371. (Contains a full account of Nietzsche's enthusiasm for Emerson.)

Arnold, Matthew. "Emerson," in *Discourses in America.* London: 1885, pp. 138–207.

Barton, Joel E. *Emerson as a Poet.* New York: 1883. (Over-enthusiastic, but occasionally critical and interesting.)

Boynton, Percy H. "Emerson in His Period," *International Journal of Ethics*, XXXIX, 177–189 (January, 1929).

Brooks, Van Wyck. *Emerson and Others.* New York: 1927. (Contains "six episodes" of Emerson's life in Concord. See also Mr. Brooks's *Life.*)

Brownell, William C. "Emerson," in *American Prose Masters.* New York: 1909, pp. 131–204.

Bruel, André. *Emerson et Thoreau.* Paris: 1929. (A detailed story of the relations of the two men, told chronologically, in a readable style.)

Canby, H. S. "Emerson," in *Classic Americans.* New York: 1931, pp. 143–183.

Carpenter, F. I. *Emerson and Asia.* Cambridge, Mass.: 1930. (A study of Emerson's Orientalism, and of his Neo-Platonism.)

Carpenter, F. I. "Points of Comparison Between Emerson and William James," *New England Quarterly*, II, 458–474 (July, 1929).

The Centenary of the Birth of Ralph Waldo Emerson. Concord, Mass.: 1903. (Fifteen addresses, by various speakers, including LeB. R. Briggs, Charles E. Norton, T. W. Higginson, William James, and Hugo Münsterberg.)

Chapman, John J. "Emerson, Sixty Years After," in *Emerson and Other Essays*. New York: 1898, pp. 3–108.

Christy, A. E. *The Orient in American Transcendentalism.* New York: 1932. (The chapter on Emerson occupies pp. 61–185. A scholarly study.)

Clark, H. H. "Emerson and Science," *Philological Quarterly*, X, 225–260 (July, 1931). (A scholarly and illuminating study of the subject.)

Crothers, S. McC. *Ralph Waldo Emerson: How to Know Him.* Indianapolis: 1921. (An original and well-written interpretation of Emerson and his thought, for modern readers. Not biographical.)

Dewey, John. "Emerson," in *Character and Events*. New York: 1929. Vol. I, 69–77.

Emerson, B. K. *The Ipswich Emersons.* Boston: 1900. (Genealogical.)

Firkins, Oscar W. "Has Emerson a Future?" in *Selected Essays*. Minneapolis, Minn.: 1933, pp. 79–93.

Foerster, Norman. *Nature in American Literature.* Boston: 1923. (Includes a long chapter on Emerson's view of nature.)

Foerster, Norman. *American Criticism.* Boston: 1928. (The chapter on Emerson's criticism occupies pp. 52–111, and is probably the best brief study of the subject.)

The Genius and Character of Emerson. Ed. by F. B. Sanborn. Boston: 1885. (Sixteen essays by various writers, including A. B. Alcott, Julian Hawthorne, Elizabeth P. Peabody, Julia

Ward Howe, and W. T. Harris. Much valuable reminiscence, and some good criticism.)

Gray, Henry D. *Emerson: A Statement of New England Transcendentalism as Expressed in the Philosophy of its Chief Exponent*. Stanford, Calif.: 1917. (The best discussion of Emerson's philosophy.)

Harrison, John S. *The Teachers of Emerson*. New York: 1910. (A valuable, but one-sided scholarly study. "The" teachers of Emerson are Plato and the Neo-Platonists.)

Haskins, David G. *Emerson's Maternal Ancestors*. Boston: 1887. (Of minor importance.)

Hill, J. A. *Emerson and his Philosophy*. London: 1919. (Minor.)

Hotson, C. P. *Emerson and Swedenborg*. 1929. Published in part in magazines. See *American Literature*, IV, 427–8 (January, 1933). (A scholarly study, with a strong Swedenborgian bias.)

Hubbell, G. S. *A Concordance to the Poems of Ralph Waldo Emerson*. New York: 1932. (A similar concordance to Emerson's prose is much needed.)

James, Henry, Jr. "Emerson," in *Partial Portraits*. London: 1888, pp. 1–33.

Jorgenson, C. E. "Emerson's Paradise under the Shadow of Swords," *Philological Quarterly*, XI, 274–292 (July, 1932). (A detailed discussion of Emerson's view of evil.)

Keller, Hans. *Emerson in Frankreich*. Giessen: 1932. (A doctoral dissertation.)

Kreymborg, Alfred. "The Intoxicated Emerson," in *Our Singing Strength*. New York: 1929, pp. 67–83. (An excellent criticism of Emerson as a poet.)

Lowell, James Russell. "Emerson, the Lecturer," in *My Study Windows*. Boston: 1871, pp. 375–384.

Marchand, Ernest. "Emerson and the Frontier," *American Literature*, III, 149–174 (May, 1931). (An excellent study, which might well be expanded.)

Maulsby, D. L. *The Contribution of Emerson to Literature*. Tufts College, Mass.: 1911. (A minor study of sources.)

McQuiston, R. *The Relation of Ralph Waldo Emerson to Public Affairs*. Lawrence, Kansas: 1923. Humanistic Studies, Vol. III, No. 1. (An able but not exhaustive study of the subject.)

Michaud, Régis. *Autour d'Emerson*. Paris: 1924. (Contains four essays on Emerson, and on his relation to Nietzsche, Achille Murat and Swedenborg.)

Michaud, Régis. *L'Esthétique d'Emerson*. Paris: 1927. (A detailed and scholarly study of Emerson's philosophy, under the three topics of "genius," "art," and "history.")

More, Paul Elmer. "Emerson," in *Cambridge History of American Literature*. New York: 1917. Vol. I, 349–362.

Parrington, Vernon L. "Emerson," in *Main Currents of American Thought*. New York: 1927. Vol. II, 386–399.

Perry, Bliss. *The Praise of Folly and Other Papers*. Boston: 1923. (Contains a vivid reconstruction of the circumstances of Emerson's "American Scholar" speech, and an essay on his *Journals*.)

Perry, Bliss. *Emerson Today*. Princeton, New Jersey: 1931. (A vivid interpretation of Emerson as a human being, for the modern world.)

Sakmann, Paul. *Emerson's Geisteswelt*. Stuttgart: 1927. (A comprehensive and well-considered study of Emerson's philosophy.)

Sanborn, F. B. *The Personality of Emerson*. Boston: 1903. (Personal reminiscences of Emerson, from 1853 on. Includes some original letters, and table-talk.)

Santayana, George. "Emerson," in *Interpretations of Poetry and Religion*. New York: 1900, pp. 217–233.

Sherman, Stuart P. "The Emersonian Liberation," in *Americans*. New York: 1922, pp. 62–121.

Sutcliffe, E. G. *Emerson's Theories of Literary Expression*. University of Illinois: 1923. (A thoroughly scholarly discussion.)

Thayer, James B. *A Western Journey with Emerson*. Boston: 1884. (An account of Emerson's trip to California in 1871.)

Thompson, F. T. "Emerson's Indebtedness to Coleridge," *Studies in Philology*, XXIII, 55–76 (Jan., 1926).

Thompson, F. T. "Emerson and Carlyle," *Studies in Philology*, XXIV, 438–453 (July, 1927).

Thompson, F. T. "Emerson's Theory and Practice of Poetry," *Pub. Mod. Lang. Assn.*, XLIII, 1170–1184 (Dec., 1928). (Deals with Emerson's debt to Coleridge and, especially, to Wordsworth.)

Wahr, F. W. *Emerson and Goethe.* Ann Arbor, Mich.: 1915. (A detailed, scholarly study.)

Woodbury, C. J. *Talks with Emerson.* London: 1890. (Extended reminiscences and notes by a student at Williams College who "Boswellized" Emerson. First-hand, and often uniquely interesting.)

IV. BIBLIOGRAPHY

Cooke, George W. *Bibliography of Ralph Waldo Emerson.* Boston: 1908.

The Cambridge History of American Literature. New York: 1917. Vol. I, 551–556. (For material up to 1917.)

Since 1923, the most important Emerson items have been listed in the annual "American Bibliography" of the *Publications of the Modern Language Association.* The present bibliography has emphasized material since 1917.

CHRONOLOGICAL TABLE

1803. May 25. Emerson born in Boston.
1811. His father, William Emerson, died.
1813–17. At the Boston Latin School.
1817–21. At Harvard College. February, 1820, first entry in Journal.
1821–28. School-teaching, and studying at the Harvard Divinity School. 1826–27, visit to Florida.
1829. March 11. Pastor of Second Church of Boston. September, married to Ellen Louisa Tucker.
1831. February 8. Ellen Tucker Emerson died.
1832. September 9. Resigned pastorate, and preached farewell sermon. December 25, sailed for Europe.
1833. August 25. First visit to Carlyle.
1835. September. Married Lydia Jackson. Moved to Concord.
1836. September. *Nature* published. October 30, his son, Waldo, born.
1837. August 31. "The American Scholar" Address.
1838. July 15. The Divinity School Address.
1841. March. *Essays, First Series.*
1842. January 27. Waldo died. Edited the *Dial* (till 1844).
1844. *Essays, Second Series.*
1847. *Poems.* Second visit to Europe.
1849. *Nature, Addresses and Lectures* collected.
1850. *Representative Men.*
1856. *English Traits.*
1860. *Conduct of Life.*
1867. *May Day* (second volume of poems).
1870. *Society and Solitude.*
1872. House burned. Third visit to Europe.
1875. *Letters and Social Aims.*
1876. Last entry in Journal.
1882. April 27. Died in Concord.

CHRONOLOGICAL TABLE

1803. May 25. Emerson born in Boston.
1811. His father, William Emerson, died.
1812–17. At the Boston Latin School.
1817–21. At Harvard College. (February, 1820, first entry in Journal.)
1821–28. School-teaching, and studying at the Harvard Divinity School. 1826–27, visit to Florida.
1829. March 11. Pastor of Second Church of Boston. September, married to Ellen Louisa Tucker.
1831. February 8. Ellen Tucker Emerson died.
1832. September 9. Resigned pastorate, and preached farewell sermon. December 25, sailed for Europe.
1833. August 25. First visit to Carlyle.
1835. September. Married Lydia Jackson. Moved to Concord.
1836. September. *Nature* published. October 30, his son Waldo born.
1837. August 31. "The American Scholar" Address.
1838. July 15. The Divinity School Address.
1841. March. *Essays, First Series.*
1842. January 27. Waldo died. Edited the *Dial* (till 1844).
1844. *Essays, Second Series.*
1847. *Poems.* Second visit to Europe.
1849. *Nature, Addresses and Lectures* collected.
1850. *Representative Men.*
1856. *English Traits.*
1860. *Conduct of Life.*
1867. *May Day* (second volume of poems).
1870. *Society and Solitude.*
1872. House burned. Third visit to Europe.
1875. *Letters and Social Aims.*
1875. Last entry in Journal.
1882. April 27. Died at Concord.

*

Selections from

RALPH WALDO EMERSON

*

PROSE SELECTIONS

From EMERSON'S JOURNALS[1]

Boston, July 11, 1822.

I dedicate my book to the Spirit of America. I dedicate it to that living soul, which doth exist somewhere beyond the Fancy, to whom the Divinity hath assigned the care of this bright corner of the Universe. I bring my little offering, in this month, which covers the continent with matchless beauty, to the shrine, which distant generations shall load with sacrifice, and distant ages shall admire afar off. With a spark of prophetic devotion, I hasten to hail the Genius, who yet counts the tardy years of childhood, but who is increasing unawares in the twilight, and swelling into strength, until the hour when he shall break the cloud, to shew his colossal youth, and cover the firmament with the shadow of his wings.

Canterbury, undated [1825].

It is my own humor to despise pedigree. I was educated to prize it. The kind Aunt whose cares instructed my youth (and whom may God reward) told me oft the virtues of her and mine ancestors. They have been clergymen for many generations, and the piety of all and the eloquence of many is yet praised in the Churches. But the dead sleep in their moonless night; my business is with the living.

[1] The selections from the *Journals* of Ralph Waldo Emerson are used by permission of, and by arrangement with, Houghton Mifflin Company.

EMERSON'S FIRST LETTER TO CARLYLE

Boston, Massachusetts, 14 May, 1834.

My Dear Sir,—There are some purposes which we delay long to execute simply because we have them more at heart than others, and such an one has been for many weeks, I may say months, my design of writing you an epistle.

Some chance wind of Fame blew your name to me, perhaps two years ago, as the author of papers which I had already distinguished (as indeed it was very easy to do) from the mass of English periodical criticism as by far the most original and profound essays of the day,—the works of a man of Faith as well as Intellect, sportive as well as learned, and who, belonging to the despairing and deriding class of philosophers, was not ashamed to hope and to speak sincerely. Like somebody in *Wilhelm Meister*, I said: This person has come under obligations to me and to all whom he has enlightened. He knows not how deeply I should grieve at his fall, if, in that exposed England where genius always hears the Devil's whisper, "All these kingdoms will I give thee," his virtue also should be an initial growth put off with age. When therefore I found myself in Europe, I went to your house only to say, "Faint not,—the word you utter is heard, though in the ends of the earth and by humblest men; it works, prevails." Drawn by strong regard to one of my teachers I went to see his person, and as he might say his environment at Craigenputtock. Yet it was to fulfil my duty, finish my mission, not with much hope of gratifying him,—in the spirit of "If I love you, what is that to you?" Well, it happened to me that I was delighted with my visit, justified to myself in my respect, and many a time upon the sea in my homeward voyage I remembered with joy the favored condition of my lonely philosopher, his happiest wedlock, his steadfast simplicity, his all means of happiness;—not that I had the remotest hope that he should so far depart from his theories as to expect happiness. On my arrival at home I rehearsed to several attentive ears what I had seen and heard, and they with joy received it.

In Liverpool I wrote to Mr. Fraser to send me his Magazine,

and I have now received four numbers of the *Sartor Resartus*, for whose light thanks evermore. I am glad that one living scholar is self-centred, and will be true to himself though none ever were before; who, as Montaigne says, "puts his ear close by himself, and holds his breath and listens." And none can be offended with the self-subsistency of one so catholic and jocund. And 'tis good to have a new eye inspect our mouldy social forms, our politics, and schools, and religion. I say *our*, for it cannot have escaped you that a lecture upon these topics written for England may be read in America. Evermore thanks for the brave stand you have made for Spiritualism in these writings. But has literature any parallel to the oddity of the vehicle you have chosen to convey this treasure? I delight in the contents; the form, which my defective apprehension for a joke makes me not appreciate, I leave to your merry discretion. And yet did ever wise and philanthropic author use so defying a diction? As if society were not sufficiently shy of truth without providing it beforehand with an objection to the form. Can it be that this humor proceeds from a despair of finding a contemporary audience, and so the Prophet feels at liberty to utter his message in droll sounds. Did you not tell me, Mr. Thomas Carlyle, sitting upon one of your broad hills, that it was Jesus Christ built Dunscore Kirk yonder? If you love such sequences, then admit, as you will, that no poet is sent into the world before his time; that all the departed thinkers and actors have paved your way; that (at least when you surrender yourself) nations and ages do guide your pen, yes, and common goose-quills as well as your diamond graver. Believe then that harp and ear are formed by one revolution of the wheel; that men are waiting to hear your epical song; and so be pleased to skip those excursive involved glees, and give us the simple air, without the volley of variations. At least in some of your prefaces you should give us the theory of your rhetoric. I comprehend not why you should lavish in that spendthrift style of yours celestial truths. Bacon and Plato have something too solid to say than that they can afford to be humorists. You are dispensing that which is rarest, namely, the simplest truths,—truths which lie next to consciousness, and which only the Platos and Goethes perceive. I look for the hour with impatience when the vehicle will be worthy of the spirit,—when the word will be as simple, and so as resistless, as the thought,—and, in short, when your words will be one with things. I have no hope that you will find suddenly a large audience. Says not the sarcasm, "Truth hath the plague in his house?" Yet all men are *potentially* (as Mr. Coleridge would say) your audience, and if you will not in very Mephistophelism repel and defy them, shall be actually; and whatever the great or the small may say about the charm of diabolism, a true and majestic genius can afford to despise it.

I venture to amuse you with this homiletic criticism because it is the sense of uncritical truth-seekers, to whom you are no more than Hecuba, whose instincts assure them that there is Wisdom in this grotesque Teutonic apocalyptic strain of yours, but that 'tis hence hindered in its effect. And though with all my heart I would stand well with my Poet, yet if I offend I shall quietly retreat into my universal relations, wherefrom I affectionately espy you as a man, myself as another.

And yet before I come to the end of my letter I may repent of my temerity and unsay my charge. For are not all our circlets of will as so many little eddies rounded in by the great Circle of Necessity, and *could* the Truth-speaker, perhaps now the best Thinker of the Saxon race, have written otherwise? And must not we say that Drunkenness is a virtue rather than that Cato has erred?

I wish I could gratify you with any pleasing news of the regeneration, education, prospects, of man on this continent. But your philanthropy is so patient, so far-sighted, that present evils give you less solicitude. In the last six years government in the United States has been fast becoming a job, like great charities. A most unfit person in the Presidency has been doing the worst things; the worse he grew, the more popular. Now things seem to mend. Webster, a good man and as strong as if he were a sinner, begins to find himself the centre of a great and enlarging party and his eloquence incarnated and enacted by them; yet men dare not hope that the majority shall be suddenly unseated.

I send herewith a volume of Webster's that you may see his speech on Foot's Resolution, a speech which Americans have never done praising. I have great doubts whether the book reaches you, as I know not my agents. I shall put with it the little book of my Swedenborgian druggist, of whom I told you. And if, which is hardly to be hoped, any good book should be thrown out of our vortex of trade and politics, I shall not fail to give it the same direction.

I need not tell you, my dear sir, what pleasure a letter from you would give me when you have a few moments to spare to so remote a friend. If any word in my letter should provoke you to a reply, I shall rejoice in my sauciness. I am spending the summer in the country, but my address is Boston, care of Barnard, Adams & Co. Care of O. Rich, London. Please to make my affectionate respects to Mrs. Carlyle, whose kindness I shall always gratefully remember. I depend upon her intercession to assure your writing to me. May God grant you both his best blessing.

Your friend,

R. WALDO EMERSON.

TO THE REVEREND HENRY WARE, JR.

Concord, October 8, 1838.

My dear Sir,—I ought sooner to have acknowledged your kind letter of last week, and the Sermon it accompanied. The letter was right manly and noble. The Sermon, too, I have read with attention. If it assails any doctrines of mine, perhaps I am not so quick to see it as writers generally—certainly I did not feel any disposition to depart from my habitual contentment that you should say your thought, whilst I say mine.

I believe I must tell you what I think of my new position. It strikes me very oddly that good and wise men at Cambridge and Boston should think of raising me into an object of criticism. I have always been, from my very incapacity of methodical writing, "a chartered libertine," free to worship and free to rail; lucky when I could make myself understood, but never esteemed near enough to the institutions and mind of society to deserve the notice of the masters of literature and religion. I have appreciated fully the advantage of my position; for I well know that there is no scholar less willing or less able to be a polemic. I could not give account of myself, if challenged. I could not possibly give you one of the "arguments" you cruelly hint at, on which any doctrine of mine stands. For I do not know what arguments mean in reference to any expression of a thought. I delight in telling what I think, but if you ask how I dare say so, or why it is so, I am the most helpless of mortal men. I do not even see that either of these questions admits of an answer. So that, in the present droll posture of my affairs, when I see myself suddenly raised into the importance of a heretic, I am very uneasy when I advert to the supposed duties of such a personage, who is expected to make good his thesis against all comers.

I certainly shall do no such thing. I shall read what you and other good men write, as I have always done,—glad when you speak my thought, and skipping the page that has nothing for me. I shall go on, just as before, seeing whatever I can, and telling what I see; and, I suppose, with the same fortune that has hitherto attended me,—the joy of finding that my abler and better brothers, who work with the sympathy of society, loving and beloved, do now and then unexpectedly confirm my perceptions, and find my nonsense is only their own thought in motley. And so I am

Your affectionate servant,

R. W. Emerson.

NATURE

A subtle chain of countless rings
The next unto the farthest brings;
The eye reads omens where it goes,
And speaks all languages the rose;
And, striving to be man, the worm
Mounts through all the spires of form.

Introduction

Our age is retrospective. It builds the sepulchres of the fathers. It writes biographies, histories, and criticism. The foregoing generations beheld God and nature face to face; we, through their eyes. Why should not we also enjoy an original relation to the universe? Why should not we have a poetry and philosophy of insight and not of tradition, and a religion by revelation to us, and not the history of theirs? Embosomed for a season in nature, whose floods of life stream around and through us, and invite us, by the powers they supply, to action proportioned to nature, why should we grope among the dry bones of the past, or put the living generation into masquerade out of its faded wardrobe? The sun shines to-day also. There is more wool and flax in the fields. There are new lands, new men, new thoughts. Let us demand our own works and laws and worship.

Undoubtedly we have no questions to ask which are unanswerable. We must trust the perfection of the creation so far as to believe that whatever curiosity the order of things has awakened in our minds, the order of things can satisfy. Every man's condition is a solution in hieroglyphic to those inquiries he would put. He acts it as life, before he apprehends it as truth. In like manner, nature is already, in its forms and tendencies, describing its own design. Let us interrogate the great apparition that shines so peacefully around us. Let us inquire, to what end is nature?

All science has one aim, namely, to find a theory of nature.

We have theories of races and of functions, but scarcely yet a remote approach to an idea of creation. We are now so far from the road to truth, that religious teachers dispute and hate each other, and speculative men are esteemed unsound and frivolous. But to a sound judgment, the most abstract truth is the most practical. Whenever a true theory appears, it will be its own evidence. Its test is, that it will explain all phenomena. Now many are thought not only unexplained but inexplicable; as language, sleep, madness, dreams, beasts, sex.

Philosophically considered, the universe is composed of Nature and the Soul. Strictly speaking, therefore, all that is separate from us, all which Philosophy distinguishes as the NOT ME, that is, both nature and art, all other men and my own body, must be ranked under this name, NATURE. In enumerating the values of nature and casting up their sum, I shall use the word in both senses;—in its common and in its philosophical import. In inquiries so general as our present one, the inaccuracy is not material; no confusion of thought will occur. *Nature*, in the common sense, refers to essences unchanged by man; space, the air, the river, the leaf. *Art* is applied to the mixture of his will with the same things, as in a house, a canal, a statue, a picture. But his operations taken together are so insignificant, a little chipping, baking, patching, and washing, that in an impression so grand as that of the world on the human mind, they do not vary the result.

I. NATURE

To go into solitude, a man needs to retire as much from his chamber as from society. I am not solitary whilst I read and write, though nobody is with me. But if a man would be alone, let him look at the stars. The rays that come from those heavenly worlds will separate between him and what he touches. One might think the atmosphere was made transparent with this design, to give man, in the heavenly bodies, the perpetual presence of the sublime. Seen in the streets of cities, how great they are! If the stars should appear one night in a thousand years, how would men believe and adore; and preserve for many generations the remembrance of the city of God which had been shown! But every night come out these envoys of beauty, and light the universe with their admonishing smile.

The stars awaken a certain reverence, because though always present, they are inaccessible; but all natural objects make a kindred impression, when the mind is open to their influence. Nature never wears a mean appearance. Neither does the wisest man extort her secret, and lose his curiosity by finding out all her perfection. Nature never became a toy to a wise spirit. The flowers, the animals, the mountains, reflected the wisdom of his best hour, as much as they had delighted the simplicity of his childhood.

When we speak of nature in this manner, we have a distinct but most poetical sense in the mind. We mean the integrity of impression made by manifold natural objects. It is this which distinguishes the stick of timber of the wood-cutter from the tree of the poet. The charming landscape which I saw this morning is indubitably made up of some twenty or thirty farms. Miller owns this field, Locke that, and Manning the woodland beyond. But none of them owns the landscape. There is a property in the horizon which no man has but he whose eye can integrate all the parts, that is, the poet. This is the best part of these men's farms, yet to this their warranty-deeds give no title.

To speak truly, few adult persons can see nature. Most persons do not see the sun. At least they have a very superficial seeing. The sun illuminates only the eye of the man, but shines into the eye and the heart of the child. The lover of nature is he whose inward and outward senses are still truly adjusted to each other; who has retained the spirit of infancy even into the era of manhood. His intercourse with heaven and earth becomes part of his daily food. In the presence of nature a wild delight runs through the man, in spite of real sorrows. Nature says,—he is my creature, and maugre all his impertinent griefs, he shall be glad with me. Not the sun or the summer alone, but every hour and season yields its tribute of delight; for every hour and change corresponds to and authorizes a different state of the mind, from breathless noon to grimmest midnight. Nature is a setting that fits equally well a comic or a mourning piece. In good health, the air is a cordial of incredible virtue. Crossing a bare common, in snow puddles, at twilight, under a clouded sky, without having in my thoughts any occurrence of special good fortune, I have enjoyed a perfect exhilaration. I am glad to the brink of fear. In the woods, too, a man casts off his years, as the snake his slough, and at what period soever of life, is always a child. In the woods is perpetual youth. Within these plantations of God, a decorum and sanctity reign, a perennial festival is dressed, and the guest sees not how he should tire of them in a thousand years. In the woods, we return to reason and faith. There I feel that nothing can befall me in life,—no disgrace, no calamity (leaving me my eyes), which nature cannot repair. Standing on the bare ground,—my head bathed by the blithe air, and uplifted into infinite space,—all mean egotism vanishes. I become a transparent eyeball; I am nothing; I see all; the currents of the Universal Being circulate through me; I am part or parcel of God. The name of the nearest friend sounds then foreign and accidental: to be brothers, to be acquaintances,—master or servant, is then a trifle and a disturbance. I am the lover of uncontained and immortal beauty. In the wilderness, I find something more dear and connate than in streets or villages. In the tranquil landscape, and especially in the distant line of the horizon, man beholds somewhat as beautiful as his own nature.

The greatest delight which the fields and woods minister is the suggestion of an occult relation between man and the vegetable. I am not alone and unacknowledged. They nod to me, and I to them. The waving of the boughs in the storm is new to me and old. It takes me by surprise, and yet is not unknown. Its effect is like that of a higher thought or a better emotion coming over me, when I deemed I was thinking justly or doing right.

Yet it is certain that the power to produce this delight does not reside in nature, but in man, or in a harmony of both. It is necessary to use these pleasures with great temperance. For nature is not always tricked in holiday attire, but the same scene which yesterday breathed perfume and glittered as for the frolic of the nymphs, is overspread with melancholy to-day. Nature always wears the colors of the spirit. To a man laboring under calamity, the heat of his own fire hath sadness in it. Then there is a kind of contempt of the landscape felt by him who has just lost by death a dear friend. The sky is less grand as it shuts down over less worth in the population.

II. Commodity

Whoever considers the final cause of the world will discern a multitude of uses that enter as parts into that result. They all admit of being thrown into one of the following classes: Commodity; Beauty; Language; and Discipline.

Under the general name of commodity, I rank all those advantages which our senses owe to nature. This, of course, is a benefit which is temporary and mediate, not ultimate, like its service to the soul. Yet although low, it is perfect in its kind, and is the only use of nature which all men apprehend. The misery of man appears like childish petulance, when we explore the steady and prodigal provision that has been made for his support and delight on this green ball which floats him through the heavens. What angels invented these splendid ornaments, these rich conveniences, this ocean of air above, this ocean of water beneath, this firmament of earth between? this zodiac of lights, this tent of dropping clouds, this striped coat of climates, this fourfold year? Beasts, fire, water, stones, and corn serve him. The field is at once his floor, his work-yard, his play-ground, his garden, and his bed.

> "More servants wait on man
> Than he'll take notice of."

Nature, in its ministry to man, is not only the material, but is also the process and the result. All the parts incessantly work into each other's hands for the profit of man. The wind sows the seed; the sun evaporates the sea; the wind blows the vapor to the field; the ice, on the other side of the planet, condenses rain on this; the rain feeds the plant; the plant feeds the animal; and thus the endless circulations of the divine charity nourish man.

The useful arts are reproductions or new combinations by the wit of man, of the same natural benefactors. He no longer waits for favoring gales, but by means of steam, he realizes the fable of Æolus's bag, and carries the two and thirty winds in the boiler of his boat. To diminish friction, he paves the road with iron bars, and, mounting a coach with a ship-load of men, animals, and merchandise behind him, he darts through the country, from town to town, like an eagle or a swallow through the air. By the aggregate of these aids, how is the face of the world changed, from the era of Noah to that of Napoleon! The private poor man hath cities, ships, canals, bridges, built for him. He goes to the post-office, and the human race run on his errands; to the book-shop, and the human race read and write of all that happens, for him; to the court-house, and nations repair his wrongs. He sets his house upon the road, and the human race go forth every morning, and shovel out the snow, and cut a path for him.

But there is no need of specifying particulars in this class of uses. The catalogue is endless, and the examples so obvious, that I shall leave them to the reader's reflection, with the general remark, that this mercenary benefit is one which has respect to a farther good. A man is fed, not that he may be fed, but that he may work.

III. Beauty

A nobler want of man is served by nature, namely, the love of Beauty.

The ancient Greeks called the world *κόσμος*, beauty. Such is the constitution of all things, or such the plastic power of the human eye, that the primary forms, as the sky, the mountain, the tree, the animal, give us a delight *in and for themselves;* a pleasure arising from outline, color, motion, and grouping. This seems partly owing to the eye itself. The eye is the best of artists. By the mutual action of its structure and of the laws of light, perspective is produced, which integrates every mass of objects, of what character soever, into a well colored and shaded globe, so that where the particular objects are mean and unaffecting, the landscape which they compose is round and symmetrical. And as the eye is the best composer, so light is the first of painters. There is no object so foul that intense light will not make beautiful. And the stimulus it affords to the sense, and a sort of infinitude which it hath, like space and time, make all matter gay. Even the corpse has its own beauty. But besides this general grace diffused over nature, almost all the individual forms are agreeable to the eye, as is proved by our endless imitations of some of them, as the acorn, the grape, the pine-cone, the wheat-ear, the egg, the wings and forms of most birds, the lion's claw, the serpent, the butterfly, sea-shells, flames, clouds, buds, leaves, and the forms of many trees, as the palm.

For better consideration, we may distribute the aspects of Beauty in a threefold manner.

1. First, the simple perception of natural forms is a delight. The influence of the forms and actions in nature is so needful to man, that, in its lowest functions, it seems to lie on the confines of commodity and beauty. To the body and mind which have been cramped by noxious work or company, nature is medicinal and restores their tone. The tradesman, the attorney comes out of the din and craft of the street and sees the sky and the woods, and is a man again. In their eternal calm, he finds himself. The health of the eye seems to demand a horizon. We are never tired, so long as we can see far enough.

But in other hours, Nature satisfies by its loveliness, and without any mixture of corporeal benefit. I see the spectacle of morning from the hilltop over against my house, from daybreak to sunrise, with emotions which an angel might share. The long slender bars of cloud float like fishes in the sea of crimson light. From the earth, as a shore, I look out into that silent sea. I seem to partake its rapid transformations; the active enchantment reaches my dust, and I dilate and conspire with the morning wind. How does Nature deify us with a few and cheap elements! Give me health and a day, and I will make the pomp of emperors ridiculous. The dawn is my Assyria; the sunset and moonrise my Paphos, and unimaginable realms of faerie; broad noon shall be my England of the senses and the understanding; the night shall be my Germany of mystic philosophy and dreams.

Not less excellent, except for our less susceptibility in the afternoon, was the charm, last evening, of a January sunset. The western clouds divided and subdivided themselves into pink flakes modulated with tints of unspeakable softness, and the air had so much life and sweetness that it was a pain to come within doors. What was it that nature would say? Was there no meaning in the live repose of the valley behind the mill, and which Homer or Shakespeare could not re-form for me in words? The leafless trees become spires of flame in the sunset, with the blue east for their background, and the stars of the dead calices of flowers, and every withered stem and stubble rimed with frost, contribute something to the mute music.

The inhabitants of cities suppose that the country landscape is pleasant only half the year. I please myself with the graces of the winter scenery, and believe that we are as much touched by it as by the genial influences of summer. To the attentive eye, each moment of the year has its own beauty, and in the same field, it beholds, every hour, a picture which was never seen before, and which shall never be seen again. The heavens change every moment, and reflect their glory or gloom on the plains beneath. The state of the crop in the surrounding farms alters the expression of the earth from week to week. The succession of native plants in the pastures and roadsides, which makes the silent clock by which time tells the summer hours, will make even the divisions of the day sensible to a keen observer. The tribes of birds and insects, like the plants punctual to their time, follow each other, and the year has room for all. By water-courses, the variety is greater. In July, the blue pontederia or pickerel-weed blooms in large beds in the shallow parts of our pleasant river, and swarms with yellow butterflies in continual motion. Art cannot rival this pomp of purple and gold. Indeed the river is a perpetual gala, and boasts each month a new ornament.

But this beauty of Nature which is seen and felt as beauty, is the least part. The shows of day, the dewy morning, the rainbow, mountains, orchards in blossom, stars, moonlight, shadows in still water, and the like, if too eagerly hunted, become shows merely, and mock us with their unreality. Go out of the house to see the moon, and 'tis mere tinsel; it will not please as when its light shines upon your necessary journey. The beauty that shimmers in the yellow afternoons of October, who ever could clutch it? Go forth to find it, and it is gone; 'tis only a mirage as you look from the windows of diligence.

2. The presence of a higher, namely, of the spiritual element is essential to its perfection. The high and divine beauty which can be loved without effeminacy, is that which is found in combination with the human will. Beauty is the mark God sets upon virtue. Every natural action is graceful. Every heroic act is also decent, and causes the place and the bystanders to shine. We are taught by great actions that the universe is the property of every individual in it. Every rational creature has all nature for his dowry and estate. It is his, if he will. He may divest himself of it; he may creep into a corner, and abdicate his kingdom, as most men do, but he is entitled to the world by his constitution. In proportion to the energy of his thought and will, he takes up the world into himself. "All those things for which men plough, build, or sail, obey virtue;" said Sallust. "The winds and waves," said Gibbon, "are always on the side of the ablest navigators." So are the sun and moon and all the stars of heaven. When a noble act is done,—perchance in a scene of great natural beauty; when Leonidas and his three hundred martyrs consume one day in dying, and the sun and moon come each and look at them once in the steep defile of Thermopylæ; when Arnold Winkelried, in the high Alps, under the shadow of the avalanche, gathers in his side a sheaf of Austrian spears to break the line for his comrades; are not these heroes entitled to add the beauty of the scene to the beauty of the deed? When the bark of Columbus nears the shore of America;—before it, the beach lined with savages, fleeing out of all their huts of cane; the sea behind; and the purple moun-

tains of the Indian Archipelago around, can we separate the man from the living picture? Does not the New World clothe his form with her palm-groves and savannahs as fit drapery? Ever does natural beauty steal in like air, and envelope great actions. When Sir Harry Vane was dragged up the Tower-hill, sitting on a sled, to suffer death as the champion of the English laws, one of the multitude cried out to him, "You never sate on so glorious a seat!" Charles II., to intimidate the citizens of London, caused the patriot Lord Russell to be drawn in an open coach through the principal streets of the city on his way to the scaffold. "But," his biographer says, "the multitude imagined they saw liberty and virtue sitting by his side." In private places, among sordid objects, an act of truth or heroism seems at once to draw to itself the sky as its temple, the sun as its candle. Nature stretches out her arms to embrace man, only let his thoughts be of equal greatness. Willingly does she follow his steps with the rose and the violet, and bend her lines of grandeur and grace to the decoration of her darling child. Only let his thoughts be of equal scope, and the frame will suit the picture. A virtuous man is in unison with her works, and makes the central figure of the visible sphere. Homer, Pindar, Socrates, Phocion, associate themselves fitly in our memory with the geography and climate of Greece. The visible heavens and earth sympathize with Jesus. And in common life whosoever has seen a person of powerful character and happy genius, will have remarked how easily he took all things along with him,—the persons, the opinions, and the day, and nature became ancillary to a man.

3. There is still another aspect under which the beauty of the world may be viewed, namely, as it becomes an object of the intellect. Beside the relation of things to virtue, they have a relation to thought. The intellect searches out the absolute order of things as they stand in the mind of God, and without the colors of affection. The intellectual and the active powers seem to succeed each other, and the exclusive activity of the one generates the exclusive activity of the other. There is something unfriendly in each to the other, but they are like the alternate periods of feeding and working in animals; each prepares

and will be followed by the other. Therefore does beauty, which, in relation to actions, as we have seen, comes unsought, and comes because it is unsought, remain for the apprehension and pursuit of the intellect; and then again, in its turn, of the active power. Nothing divine dies. All good is eternally reproductive. The beauty of nature re-forms itself in the mind, and not for barren contemplation, but for new creation.

All men are in some degree impressed by the face of the world; some men even to delight. This love of beauty is Taste. Others have the same love in such excess, that, not content with admiring, they seek to embody it in new forms. The creation of beauty is Art.

The production of a work of art throws a light upon the mystery of humanity. A work of art is an abstract or epitome of the world. It is the result or expression of nature, in miniature. For although the works of nature are innumerable and all different, the result or the expression of them all is similar and single. Nature is a sea of forms radically alike and even unique. A leaf, a sunbeam, a landscape, the ocean, make an analogous impression on the mind. What is common to them all,—that perfectness and harmony, is beauty. The standard of beauty is the entire circuit of natural forms,—the totality of nature; which the Italians expressed by defining beauty "il più nell' uno." Nothing is quite beautiful alone; nothing but is beautiful in the whole. A single object is only so far beautiful as it suggests this universal grace. The poet, the painter, the sculptor, the musician, the architect, seek each to concentrate this radiance of the world on one point, and each in his several work to satisfy the love of beauty which stimulates him to produce. Thus is Art a nature passed through the alembic of man. Thus in art does Nature work through the will of a man filled with the beauty of her first works.

The world thus exists to the soul to satisfy the desire of beauty. This element I call an ultimate end. No reason can be asked or given why the soul seeks beauty. Beauty, in its largest and profoundest sense, is one expression for the universe. God is the all-fair. Truth, and goodness, and beauty, are but different faces of the same All. But beauty in nature is not ultimate. It is the herald of inward and eternal beauty, and is not alone a solid and satisfactory good. It must stand as a part, and not as yet the last or highest expression of the final cause of Nature.

IV. Language

Language is a third use which Nature subserves to man. Nature is the vehicle of thought, and in a simple, double, and three-fold degree.

1. Words are signs of natural facts.

2. Particular natural facts are symbols of particular spiritual facts.

3. Nature is the symbol of spirit.

1. Words are signs of natural facts. The use of natural history is to give us aid in supernatural history; the use of the outer creation, to give us language for the beings and changes of the inward creation. Every word which is used to express a moral or intellectual fact, if traced to its root, is found to be borrowed from some material appearance. *Right* means *straight; wrong* means *twisted. Spirit* primarily means *wind; transgression*, the crossing of a *line; supercilious*, the *raising of the eyebrow*. We say the *heart* to express emotion, the *head* to denote thought; and *thought* and *emotion* are words borrowed from sensible things, and now appropriated to spiritual nature. Most of the process by which this transformation is made, is hidden from us in the remote time when language was framed; but the same tendency may be daily observed in children. Children and savages use only nouns or names of things, which they convert into verbs, and apply to analogous mental acts.

2. But this origin of all words that convey a spiritual import,—so conspicuous a fact in the history of language,—is our least debt to nature. It is not words only that are emblematic; it is things which are emblematic. Every natural fact is a symbol of some spiritual fact. Every appearance in nature corresponds to some state of the mind, and that state of the mind can only be described by presenting that natural appearance as its picture. An enraged man is a lion, a cunning man is a fox, a firm man is

a rock, a learned man is a torch. A lamb is innocence; a snake is subtle spite; flowers express to us the delicate affections. Light and darkness are our familiar expression for knowledge and ignorance; and heat for love. Visible distance behind and before us, is respectively our image of memory and hope.

Who looks upon a river in a meditative hour and is not reminded of the flux of all things? Throw a stone into the stream, and the circles that propagate themselves are the beautiful type of all influence. Man is conscious of a universal soul within or behind his individual life, wherein, as in a firmament, the natures of Justice, Truth, Love, Freedom, arise and shine. This universal soul he calls Reason: it is not mine, or thine, or his, but we are its; we are its property and men. And the blue sky in which the private earth is buried, the sky with its eternal calm, and full of everlasting orbs, is the type of Reason. That which intellectually considered we call Reason, considered in relation to nature, we call Spirit. Spirit is the Creator. Spirit hath life in itself. And man in all ages and countries embodies it in his language as the FATHER.

It is easily seen that there is nothing lucky or capricious in these analogies, but that they are constant, and pervade nature. These are not the dreams of a few poets, here and there, but man is an analogist, and studies relations in all objects. He is placed in the centre of beings, and a ray of relation passes from every other being to him. And neither can man be understood without these objects, nor these objects without man. All the facts in natural history taken by themselves, have no value, but are barren, like a single sex. But marry it to human history, and it is full of life. Whole floras, all Linnæus' and Buffon's volumes, are dry catalogues of facts; but the most trivial of these facts, the habit of a plant, the organs, or work, or noise of an insect, applied to the illustration of a fact in intellectual philosophy, or in any way associated to human nature, affects us in the most lively and agreeable manner. The seed of a plant,—to what affecting analogies in the nature of man is that little fruit made use of, in all discourse, up to the voice of Paul, who calls the human corpse a seed,—"It is sown a natural body; it is raised a spiritual body." The motion of the earth round its axis and round the sun, makes the day and the year. These are certain amounts of brute light and heat. But is there no intent of an analogy between man's life and the seasons? And do the seasons gain no grandeur or pathos from that analogy? The instincts of the ant are very unimportant considered as the ant's; but the moment a ray of relation is seen to extend from it to man, and the little drudge is seen to be a monitor, a little body with a mighty heart, then all its habits, even that said to be recently observed, that it never sleeps, become sublime.

Because of this radical correspondence between visible things and human thoughts, savages, who have only what is necessary, converse in figures. As we go back in history, language becomes more picturesque, until its infancy, when it is all poetry; or all spiritual facts are represented by natural symbols. The same symbols are found to make the original elements of all languages. It has moreover been observed, that the idioms of all languages approach each other in passages of the greatest eloquence and power. And as this is the first language, so is it the last. This immediate dependence of language upon nature, this conversion of an outward phenomenon into a type of somewhat in human life, never loses its power to affect us. It is this which gives that piquancy to the conversation of a strong-natured farmer or backwoodsman, which all men relish.

A man's power to connect his thought with its proper symbol, and so to utter it, depends on the simplicity of his character, that is, upon his love of truth and his desire to communicate it without loss. The corruption of man is followed by the corruption of language. When simplicity of character and the sovereignty of ideas is broken up by the prevalence of secondary desires,—the desire of riches, of pleasure, of power, and of praise,—and duplicity and falsehood take place of simplicity and truth, the power over nature as an interpreter of the will is in a degree lost; new imagery ceases to be created, and old words are perverted to stand for things which are not; a paper currency is employed, when there is no bullion in the vaults. In due time the fraud is manifest, and words lose all power to stimulate the understanding or the affections. Hundreds of writers may be found in every long-civilized nation who for a short time believe and make others believe that they see and utter truths, who do not of themselves clothe one thought in its natural garment, but who feed unconsciously on the language created by the primary writers of the country, those, namely, who hold primarily on nature.

But wise men pierce this rotten diction and fasten words again to visible things; so that picturesque language is at once a commanding certificate that he who employs it is a man in alliance with truth and God. The moment our discourse rises above the ground line of familiar facts and is inflamed with passion or exalted by thought, it clothes itself in images. A man conversing in earnest, if he watch his intellectual processes, will find that a material image more or less luminous arises in his mind, contemporaneous with every thought, which furnishes the vestment of the thought. Hence, good writing and brilliant discourse are perpetual allegories. This imagery is spontaneous. It is the blending of experience with the present action of the mind. It is proper creation. It is the working of the Original Cause through the instruments he has already made.

These facts may suggest the advantage which the country-life possesses, for a powerful mind, over the artificial and curtailed life of cities. We know more from nature than we can at will communicate. Its light flows into the mind evermore, and we forget its presence. The poet, the orator, bred in the woods, whose senses have been nourished by their fair and appeasing changes, year after year, without design and without heed,—shall not lose their lesson altogether, in the roar of cities or the broil of politics. Long hereafter, amidst agitation and terror in national councils,—in the hour of revolution,—these solemn images shall reappear in their morning lustre, as fit symbols and words of the thoughts which the passing events shall awaken. At the call of a noble sentiment, again the woods wave, the pines murmur, the river rolls and shines, and the cattle low upon the mountains, as he saw and heard them in his infancy. And with these forms, the spells of persuasion, the keys of power are put into his hands.

3. We are thus assisted by natural objects in the expression of particular meanings. But how great a language to convey such pepper-corn informations! Did it need such noble races of creatures, this profusion of forms, this host of orbs in heaven, to furnish man with the dictionary and grammar of his municipal speech? Whilst we use this grand cipher to expedite the affairs of our pot and kettle, we feel that we have not yet put it to its use, neither are able. We are like travellers using the cinders of a volcano to roast their eggs. Whilst we see that it always stands ready to clothe what we would say, we cannot avoid the question whether the characters are not significant of themselves. Have mountains, and waves, and skies, no significance but what we consciously give them when we employ them as emblems of our thoughts? The world is emblematic. Parts of speech are metaphors, because the whole of nature is a metaphor of the human mind. The laws of moral nature answer to those of matter as face to face in a glass. "The visible world and the relation of its parts, is the dial plate of the invisible." The axioms of physics translate the laws of ethics. Thus, "the whole is greater than its part;" "reaction is equal to action;" "the smallest weight may be made to lift the greatest, the difference of weight being compensated by time;" and many the like propositions, which have an ethical as well as physical sense. These propositions have a much more extensive and universal sense when applied to human life, than when confined to technical use.

In like manner, the memorable words of history and the proverbs of nations consist usually of a natural fact, selected as a picture or parable of a moral truth. Thus; A rolling stone gathers no moss; A bird in the hand is worth two in the bush; A cripple in the right way will beat a racer in the wrong; Make hay while the sun shines; 'T is hard to carry a full cup even; Vinegar is the son of wine; The last ounce broke the camel's back; Long-lived trees make roots first;—and the like. In their primary sense these are trivial facts, but we repeat them for the value of their analogical import. What is true of proverbs, is true of all fables, parables, and allegories.

This relation between the mind and matter is not fancied by

some poet, but stands in the will of God, and so is free to be known by all men. It appears to men, or it does not appear. When in fortunate hours we ponder this miracle, the wise man doubts if at all other times he is not blind and deaf;

> "Can such things be,
> And overcome us like a summer's cloud,
> Without our special wonder?"

for the universe becomes transparent, and the light of higher laws than its own shines through it. It is the standing problem which has exercised the wonder and the study of every fine genius since the world began; from the era of the Egyptians and the Brahmins to that of Pythagoras, of Plato, of Bacon, of Leibnitz, of Swedenborg. There sits the Sphinx at the road-side, and from age to age, as each prophet comes by, he tries his fortune at reading her riddle. There seems to be a necessity in spirit to manifest itself in material forms; and day and night, river and storm, beast and bird, acid and alkali, preëxist in necessary Ideas in the mind of God, and are what they are by virtue of preceding affections in the world of spirit. A Fact is the end or last issue of spirit. The visible creation is the terminus or the circumference of the invisible world. "Material objects," said a French philosopher, "are necessarily kinds of *scoriæ* of the substantial thoughts of the Creator, which must always preserve an exact relation to their first origin; in other words, visible nature must have a spiritual and moral side."

This doctrine is abstruse, and though the images of "garment," "scoriæ," "mirror," etc., may stimulate the fancy, we must summon the aid of subtler and more vital expositors to make it plain. "Every scripture is to be interpreted by the same spirit which gave it forth,"—is the fundamental law of criticism. A life in harmony with Nature, the love of truth and of virtue, will purge the eyes to understand her text. By degrees we may come to know the primitive sense of the permanent objects of nature, so that the world shall be to us an open book, and every form significant of its hidden life and final cause.

A new interest surprises us, whilst, under the view now suggested, we contemplate the fearful extent and multitude of objects; since "every object rightly seen, unlocks a new faculty of the soul." That which was unconscious truth, becomes, when interpreted and defined in an object, a part of the domain of knowledge,—a new weapon in the magazine of power.

V. Discipline

In view of the significance of nature, we arrive at once at a new fact, that nature is a discipline. This use of the world includes the preceding uses, as parts of itself.

Space, time, society, labor, climate, food, locomotion, the animals, the mechanical forces, give us sincerest lessons, day by day, whose meaning is unlimited. They educate both the Understanding and the Reason. Every property of matter is a school for the understanding,—its solidity or resistance, its inertia, its extension, its figure, its divisibility. The understanding adds, divides, combines, measures, and finds nutriment and room for its activity in this worthy scene. Meantime, Reason transfers all these lessons into its own world of thought, by perceiving the analogy that marries Matter and Mind.

1. Nature is a discipline of the understanding in intellectual truths. Our dealing with sensible objects is a constant exercise in the necessary lessons of difference, of likeness, of order, of being and seeming, of progressive arrangement; of ascent from particular to general; of combination to one end of manifold forces. Proportioned to the importance of the organ to be formed, is the extreme care with which its tuition is provided, —a care pretermitted in no single case. What tedious training, day after day, year after year, never ending, to form the common sense; what continual reproduction of annoyances, inconveniences, dilemmas; what rejoicing over us of little men; what disputing of prices, what reckonings of interest,—and all to form the Hand of the mind;—to instruct us that "good thoughts are no better than good dreams, unless they be executed!"

The same good office is performed by Property and its filial systems of debt and credit. Debt, grinding debt, whose iron face the widow, the orphan, and the sons of genius fear and hate; —debt, which consumes so much time, which so cripples and disheartens a great spirit with cares that seem so base, is a preceptor whose lessons cannot be foregone, and is needed most by those who suffer from it most. Moreover, property, which has been well compared to snow,—"if it fall level to-day, it will be blown into drifts to-morrow,"—is the surface action of internal machinery, like the index on the face of a clock. Whilst now it is the gymnastics of the understanding, it is hiving, in the foresight of the spirit, experience in profounder laws.

The whole character and fortune of the individual are affected by the least inequalities in the culture of the understanding; for example, in the perception of differences. Therefore is Space, and therefore Time, that man may know that things are not huddled and lumped, but sundered and individual. A bell and a plough have each their use, and neither can do the office of the other. Water is good to drink, coal to burn, wool to wear; but wool cannot be drunk, nor water spun, nor coal eaten. The wise man shows his wisdom in separation, in gradation, and his scale of creatures and of merits is as wide as nature. The foolish have no range in their scale, but suppose every man is as every other man. What is not good they call the worst, and what is not hateful, they call the best.

In like manner, what good heed Nature forms in us! She pardons no mistakes. Her yea is yea, and her nay, nay.

The first steps in Agriculture, Astronomy, Zoölogy (those first steps which the farmer, the hunter, and the sailor take), teach that Nature's dice are always loaded; that in her heaps and rubbish are concealed sure and useful results.

How calmly and genially the mind apprehends one after another the laws of physics! What noble emotions dilate the mortal as he enters into the councils of the creation, and feels by knowledge the privilege to Be! His insight refines him. The beauty of nature shines in his own breast. Man is greater that he can see this, and the universe less, because Time and Space relations vanish as laws are known.

Here again we are impressed and even daunted by the

immense Universe to be explored. "What we know is a point to what we do not know." Open any recent journal of science, and weigh the problems suggested concerning Light, Heat, Electricity, Magnetism, Physiology, Geology, and judge whether the interest of natural science is likely to be soon exhausted.

Passing by many particulars of the discipline of nature, we must not omit to specify two.

The exercise of the Will, or the lesson of power, is taught in every event. From the child's successive possession of his several senses up to the hour when he saith, "Thy will be done!" he is learning the secret that he can reduce under his will not only particular events but great classes, nay, the whole series of events, and so conform all facts to his character. Nature is thoroughly mediate. It is made to serve. It receives the dominion of man as meekly as the ass on which the Saviour rode. It offers all its kingdoms to man as the raw material which he may mould into what is useful. Man is never weary of working it up. He forges the subtile and delicate air into wise and melodious words, and gives them wing as angels of persuasion and command. One after another his victorious thought comes up with and reduces all things, until the world becomes at last only a realized will,—the double of the man.

2. Sensible objects conform to the premonitions of Reason and reflect the conscience. All things are moral; and in their boundless changes have an unceasing reference to spiritual nature. Therefore is nature glorious with form, color, and motion; that every globe in the remotest heaven, every chemical change from the rudest crystal up to the laws of life, every change of vegetation from the first principle of growth in the eye of a leaf, to the tropical forest and antediluvian coal-mine, every animal function from the sponge up to Hercules, shall hint or thunder to man the laws of right and wrong, and echo the Ten Commandments. Therefore is Nature ever the ally of Religion: lends all her pomp and riches to the religious sentiment. Prophet and priest, David, Isaiah, Jesus, have drawn deeply from this source. This ethical character so penetrates

the bone and marrow of nature, as to seem the end for which it was made. Whatever private purpose is answered by any member or part, this is its public and universal function, and is never omitted. Nothing in nature is exhausted in its first use. When a thing has served an end to the uttermost, it is wholly new for an ulterior service. In God, every end is converted into a new means. Thus the use of commodity, regarded by itself, is mean and squalid. But it is to the mind an education in the doctrine of Use, namely, that a thing is good only so far as it serves; that a conspiring of parts and efforts to the production of an end is essential to any being. The first and gross manifestation of this truth is our inevitable and hated training in values and wants, in corn and meat.

It has already been illustrated, that every natural process is a version of a moral sentence. The moral law lies at the centre of nature and radiates to the circumference. It is the pith and marrow of every substance, every relation, and every process. All things with which we deal, preach to us. What is a farm but a mute gospel? The chaff and the wheat, weeds and plants, blight, rain, insects, sun,—it is a sacred emblem from the first furrow of spring to the last stack which the snow of winter overtakes in the fields. But the sailor, the shepherd, the miner, the merchant, in their several resorts, have each an experience precisely parallel, and leading to the same conclusion: because all organizations are radically alike. Nor can it be doubted that this moral sentiment which thus scents the air, grows in the grain, and impregnates the waters of the world, is caught by man and sinks into his soul. The moral influence of nature upon every individual is that amount of truth which it illustrates to him. Who can estimate this? Who can guess how much firmness the sea-beaten rock has taught the fisherman? how much tranquillity has been reflected to man from the azure sky, over whose unspotted deeps the winds forevermore drive flocks of stormy clouds, and leave no wrinkle or stain? how much industry and providence and affection we have caught from the pantomime of brutes? What a searching preacher of self-command is the varying phenomenon of Health!

Herein is especially apprehended the unity of Nature,—the unity in variety,—which meets us everywhere. All the endless variety of things make an identical impression. Xenophanes complained in his old age, that, look where he would, all things hastened back to Unity. He was weary of seeing the same entity in the tedious variety of forms. The fable of Proteus has a cordial truth. A leaf, a drop, a crystal, a moment of time, is related to the whole, and partakes of the perfection of the whole. Each particle is a microcosm, and faithfully renders the likeness of the world.

Not only resemblances exist in things whose analogy is obvious, as when we detect the type of the human hand in the flipper of the fossil saurus, but also in objects wherein there is great superficial unlikeness. Thus architecture is called "frozen music," by De Staël and Goethe. Vitruvius thought an architect should be a musician. "A Gothic church," said Coleridge, "is a petrified religion." Michael Angelo maintained, that, to an architect, a knowledge of anatomy is essential. In Haydn's oratorios, the notes present to the imagination not only motions, as of the snake, the stag, and the elephant, but colors also; as the green grass. The law of harmonic sound reappears in the harmonic colors. The granite is differenced in its laws only by the more or less of heat from the river that wears it away. The river, as it flows, resembles the air that flows over it; the air resembles the light which traverses it with more subtile currents; the light resembles the heat which rides with it through Space. Each creature is only a modification of the other; the likeness in them is more than the difference, and their radical law is one and the same. A rule of one art, or a law of one organization, holds true throughout nature. So intimate is this Unity, that, it is easily seen, it lies under the undermost garment of Nature, and betrays its source in Universal Spirit. For it pervades Thought also. Every universal truth which we express in words, implies or supposes every other truth. *Omne verum vero consonat*. It is like a great circle on a sphere, comprising all possible circles; which, however, may be drawn and comprise it in like manner. Every such truth is the absolute Ens seen from one side. But it has innumerable sides.

The central Unity is still more conspicuous in actions. Words are finite organs of the infinite mind. They cannot cover the dimensions of what is in truth. They break, chop, and impoverish it. An action is the perfection and publication of thought. A right action seems to fill the eye, and to be related to all nature. "The wise man, in doing one thing, does all; or, in the one thing he does rightly, he sees the likeness of all which is done rightly."

Words and actions are not the attributes of brute nature. They introduce us to the human form, of which all other organizations appear to be degradations. When this appears among so many that surround it, the spirit prefers it to all others. It says, "From such as this have I drawn joy and knowledge; in such as this have I found and beheld myself; I will speak to it; it can speak again; it can yield me thought already formed and alive." In fact, the eye,—the mind,—is always accompanied by these forms, male and female; and these are incomparably the richest informations of the power and order that lie at the heart of things. Unfortunately every one of them bears the marks as of some injury; is marred and superficially defective. Nevertheless, far different from the deaf and dumb nature around them, these all rest like fountain-pipes on the unfathomed sea of thought and virtue whereto they alone, of all organizations, are the entrances.

It were a pleasant inquiry to follow into detail their ministry to our education, but where would it stop? We are associated in adolescent and adult life with some friends, who, like skies and waters, are coextensive with our idea; who, answering each to a certain affection of the soul, satisfy our desire on that side; whom we lack power to put at such focal distance from us, that we can mend or even analyze them. We cannot choose but love them. When much intercourse with a friend has supplied us with a standard of excellence, and has increased our respect for the resources of God who thus sends a real person to outgo our ideal; when he has, moreover, become an object of thought, and, whilst his character retains all its unconscious effect, is converted in the mind into solid and sweet wisdom,—it is a sign to us that his office is closing, and he is commonly withdrawn from our sight in a short time.

VI. Idealism

Thus is the unspeakable but intelligible and practicable meaning of the world conveyed to man, the immortal pupil, in every object of sense. To this one end of Discipline, all parts of nature conspire.

A noble doubt perpetually suggests itself,—whether this end be not the Final Cause of the Universe; and whether nature outwardly exists. It is a sufficient account of that Appearance we call the World, that God will teach a human mind, and so makes it the receiver of a certain number of congruent sensations, which we call sun and moon, man and woman, house and trade. In my utter impotence to test the authenticity of the report of my senses, to know whether the impressions they make on me correspond with outlying objects, what difference does it make, whether Orion is up there in heaven, or some god paints the image in the firmament of the soul? The relations of parts and the end of the whole remaining the same, what is the difference, whether land and sea interact, and worlds revolve and intermingle without number or end,—deep yawning under deep, and galaxy balancing galaxy, throughout absolute space,—or whether, without relations of time and space, the same appearances are inscribed in the constant faith of man? Whether nature enjoy a substantial existence without, or is only in the apocalypse of the mind, it is alike useful and alike venerable to me. Be it what it may, it is ideal to me so long as I cannot try the accuracy of my senses.

The frivolous make themselves merry with the Ideal theory, as if its consequences were burlesque; as if it affected the stability of nature. It surely does not. God never jests with us, and will not compromise the end of nature by permitting any inconsequence in its procession. Any distrust of the permanence of laws would paralyze the faculties of man. Their permanence is sacredly respected, and his faith therein is perfect. The wheels and springs of man are all set to the hypothesis of the permanence of nature. We are not built like a ship to be tossed, but like a house to stand. It is a natural consequence of this structure, that so long as the active powers predominate over the reflective, we resist with indignation any hint that nature is more short-lived or mutable than spirit. The broker, the wheelwright, the carpenter, the tollman, are much displeased at the intimation.

But whilst we acquiesce entirely in the permanence of natural laws, the question of the absolute existence of nature still remains open. It is the uniform effect of culture on the human mind, not to shake our faith in the stability of particular phenomena, as of heat, water, azote; but to lead us to regard nature as phenomenon, not a substance; to attribute necessary existence to spirit; to esteem nature as an accident and an effect.

To the senses and the unrenewed understanding, belongs a sort of instinctive belief in the absolute existence of nature. In their view man and nature are indissolubly joined. Things are ultimates, and they never look beyond their sphere. The presence of Reason mars this faith. The first effort of thought tends to relax this despotism of the senses which binds us to nature as if we were a part of it, and shows us nature aloof, and, as it were, afloat. Until this higher agency intervened, the animal eye sees, with wonderful accuracy, sharp outlines and colored surfaces. When the eye of Reason opens, to outline and surface are at once added grace and expression. These proceed from imagination and affection, and abate somewhat of the angular distinctness of objects. If the Reason be stimulated to more earnest vision, outlines and surfaces become transparent, and are no longer seen; causes and spirits are seen through them. The best moments of life are these delicious awakenings of the higher powers, and the reverential withdrawing of nature before its God.

Let us proceed to indicate the effects of culture.

1. Our first institution in the Ideal philosophy is a hint from Nature herself.

Nature is made to conspire with spirit to emancipate us. Certain mechanical changes, a small alteration in our local position, apprises us of a dualism. We are strangely affected by seeing the shore from a moving ship, from a balloon, or through the tints of an unusual sky. The least change in our point of view gives the whole world a pictorial air. A man who seldom rides, needs only to get into a coach and traverse his own town, to turn the street into a puppet-show. The men, the women,—talking, running, bartering, fighting,—the earnest mechanic, the lounger, the beggar, the boys, the dogs, are unrealized at once, or, at least, wholly detached from all relation to the observer, and seen as apparent, not substantial beings. What new thoughts are suggested by seeing a face of country quite familiar, in the rapid movement of the railroad car! Nay, the most wonted objects, (make a very slight change in the point of vision,) please us most. In a camera obscura, the butcher's cart, and the figure of one of our own family amuse us. So a portrait of a well-known face gratifies us. Turn the eyes upside down, by looking at the landscape through your legs, and how agreeable is the picture, though you have seen it any time these twenty years!

In these cases, by mechanical means, is suggested the difference between the observer and the spectacle—between man and nature. Hence arises a pleasure mixed with awe; I may say, a low degree of the sublime is felt, from the fact, probably, that man is hereby apprised that whilst the world is a spectacle, something in himself is stable.

2. In a higher manner the poet communicates the same pleasure. By a few strokes he delineates, as on air, the sun, the mountain, the camp, the city, the hero, the maiden, not different from what we know them, but only lifted from the ground and afloat before the eye. He unfixes the land and the sea, makes them revolve around the axis of his primary thought, and disposes them anew. Possessed himself by a heroic passion, he uses matter as symbols of it. The sensual man conforms thoughts to things; the poet conforms things to his thoughts. The one esteems nature as rooted and fast; the other, as fluid, and impresses his being thereon. To him, the refractory world is ductile and flexible; he invests dust and stones with humanity, and makes them the words of the Reason. The Imagination

may be defined to be the use which the Reason makes of the material world. Shakspeare possesses the power of subordinating nature for the purposes of expression, beyond all poets. His imperial muse tosses the creation like a bauble from hand to hand, and uses it to embody any caprice of thought that is uppermost in his mind. The remotest spaces of nature are visited, and the farthest sundered things are brought together, by a subtile spiritual connection. We are made aware that magnitude of material things is relative, and all objects shrink and expand to serve the passion of the poet. Thus in his sonnets, the lays of birds, the scents and dyes of flowers he finds to be the *shadow* of his beloved; time, which keeps her from him, is his *chest;* the suspicion she has awakened, is her *ornament;*

> The ornament of beauty is Suspect,
> A crow which flies in heaven's sweetest air.

His passion is not the fruit of chance; it swells, as he speaks, to a city, or a state.

> No, it was builded far from accident;
> It suffers not in smiling pomp, nor falls
> Under the brow of thralling discontent;
> It fears not policy, that heretic,
> That works on leases of short numbered hours,
> But all alone stands hugely politic.

In the strength of his constancy, the Pyramids seem to him recent and transitory. The freshness of youth and love dazzles him with its resemblance to morning;

> Take those lips away
> Which so sweetly were forsworn;
> And those eyes,—the break of day,
> Lights that do mislead the morn.

The wild beauty of this hyperbole, I may say in passing, it would not be easy to match in literature.

This transfiguration which all material objects undergo through the passion of the poet,—this power which he exerts to dwarf the great, to magnify the small,—might be illustrated by a thousand examples from his Plays. I have before me the Tempest, and will cite only these few lines.

> Ariel. The strong based promontory
> Have I made shake, and by the spurs plucked up
> The pine and cedar.

Prospero calls for music to soothe the frantic Alonzo, and his companions;

> A solemn air, and the best comforter
> To an unsettled fancy, cure my brains
> Now useless, boiled within thy skull.

Again;

> The charm dissolves apace,
> And, as the morning steals upon the night,
> Melting the darkness, so their rising senses
> Begin to chase the ignorant fumes that mantle
> Their clearer reason.
> Their understanding
> Begins to swell: and the approaching tide
> Will shortly fill the reasonable shores
> That now lie foul and muddy.

The perception of real affinities between events (that is to say, of *ideal* affinities, for those only are real), enables the poet thus to make free with the most imposing forms and phenomena of the world, and to assert the predominance of the soul.

3. Whilst thus the poet animates nature with his own thoughts, he differs from the philosopher only herein, that the one proposes Beauty as his main end; the other Truth. But the philosopher, not less than the poet, postpones the apparent order and relations of things to the empire of thought. "The problem of philosophy," according to Plato, "is, for all that exists conditionally, to find a ground unconditioned and absolute." It proceeds on the faith that a law determines all phenomena, which being known, the phenomena can be predicted. That law,

when in the mind, is an idea. Its beauty is infinite. The true philosopher and the true poet are one, and a beauty, which is truth, and a truth, which is beauty, is the aim of both. Is not the charm of one of Plato's or Aristotle's definitions strictly like that of the Antigone of Sophocles? It is, in both cases, that a spiritual life has been imparted to nature; that the solid seeming block of matter has been pervaded and dissolved by a thought; that this feeble human being has penetrated the vast masses of nature with an informing soul, and recognized itself in their harmony, that is, seized their law. In physics, when this is attained, the memory disburthens itself of its cumbrous catalogues of particulars, and carries centuries of observation in a single formula.

Thus even in physics, the material is degraded before the spiritual. The astronomer, the geometer, rely on their irrefragable analysis, and disdain the results of observation. The sublime remark of Euler on his law of arches, "This will be found contrary to all experience, yet is true;" had already transferred nature into the mind, and left matter like an outcast corpse.

4. Intellectual science has been observed to beget invariably a doubt of the existence of matter. Turgot said, "He that has never doubted the existence of matter, may be assured he has no aptitude for metaphysical inquiries." It fastens the attention upon immortal necessary uncreated natures, that is, upon Ideas; and in their presence we feel that the outward circumstance is a dream and a shade. Whilst we wait in this Olympus of gods, we think of nature as an appendix to the soul. We ascend into their region, and know that these are the thoughts of the Supreme Being. "These are they who were set up from everlasting, from the beginning, or ever the earth was. When he prepared the heavens, they were there; when he established the clouds above, when he strengthened the fountains of the deep. Then they were by him, as one brought up with him. Of them took he counsel."

Their influence is proportionate. As objects of science they are accessible to few men. Yet all men are capable of being raised by piety or by passion, into their region. And no man touches these divine natures, without becoming, in some degree, himself divine. Like a new soul, they renew the body. We become physically nimble and lightsome; we tread on air; life is no longer irksome, and we think it will never be so. No man fears age or misfortune or death in their serene company, for he is transported out of the district of change. Whilst we behold unveiled the nature of Justice and Truth, we learn the difference between the absolute and the conditional or relative. We apprehend the absolute. As it were, for the first time, *we exist.* We become immortal, for we learn that time and space are relations of matter; that with a perception of truth or a virtuous will they have no affinity.

5. Finally, religion and ethics, which may be fitly called the practice of ideas, or the introduction of ideas into life, have an analogous effect with all lower culture, in degrading nature and suggesting its dependence on spirit. Ethics and religion differ herein; that the one is the system of human duties commencing from man; the other, from God. Religion includes the personality of God; Ethics does not. They are one to our present design. They both put nature under foot. The first and last lesson of religion is, "The things that are seen, are temporal; the things that are unseen, are eternal." It puts an affront upon nature. It does that for the unschooled, which philosophy does for Berkeley and Viasa. The uniform language that may be heard in the churches of the most ignorant sects is,—"Contemn the unsubstantial shows of the world; they are vanities, dreams, shadows, unrealities; seek the realities of religion." The devotee flouts nature. Some theosophists have arrived at a certain hostility and indignation towards matter, as the Manichean and Plotinus. They distrusted in themselves any looking back to these flesh-pots of Egypt. Plotinus was ashamed of his body. In short, they might all say of matter, what Michael Angelo said of external beauty, "It is the frail and weary weed, in which God dresses the soul which he has called into time."

It appears that motion, poetry, physical and intellectual science, and religion, all tend to affect our convictions of the reality of the external world. But I own there is something ungrateful in expanding too curiously the particulars of the general proposition, that all culture tends to imbue us with idealism. I have no hostility to nature, but a child's love to it. I expand and live in the warm day like corn and melons. Let us speak her fair. I do not wish to fling stones at my beautiful mother, nor soil my gentle nest. I only wish to indicate the true position of nature in regard to man, wherein to establish man all right education tends; as the ground which to attain is the object of human life, that is, of man's connection with nature. Culture inverts the vulgar views of nature, and brings the mind to call that apparent which it uses to call real, and that real which it uses to call visionary. Children, it is true, believe in the external world. The belief that it appears only, is an afterthought, but with culture this faith will as surely arise on the mind as did the first.

The advantage of the ideal theory over the popular faith is this, that it presents the world in precisely that view which is most desirable to the mind. It is, in fact, the view which Reason, both speculative and practical, that is, philosophy and virtue, take. For seen in the light of thought, the world always is phenomenal; and virtue subordinates it to the mind. Idealism sees the world in God. It beholds the whole circle of persons and things, of actions and events, of country and religion, not as painfully accumulated, atom after atom, act after act, in an aged creeping Past, but as one vast picture which God paints on the instant eternity for the contemplation of the soul. Therefore the soul holds itself off from a too trivial and microscopic study of the universal tablet. It respects the end too much to immerse itself in the means. It sees something more important in Christianity than the scandals of ecclesiastical history or the niceties of criticism; and, very incurious concerning persons or miracles, and not at all disturbed by chasms of historical evidence, it accepts from God the phenomenon, as it finds it, as the pure and awful form of religion in the world. It is not hot and passionate at the appearance of what it calls its own good or bad fortune, at the union or opposition of other persons. No man is its enemy. It accepts whatsoever befalls, as part of its lesson. It is a watcher more than a doer, and it is a doer, only that it may the better watch.

VII. Spirit

It is essential to a true theory of nature and of man, that it should contain somewhat progressive. Uses that are exhausted or that may be, and facts that end in the statement, cannot be all that is true of this brave lodging wherein man is harbored, and wherein all his faculties find appropriate and endless exercise. And all the uses of nature admit of being summed in one, which yields the activity of man an infinite scope. Through all its kingdoms, to the suburbs and outskirts of things, it is faithful to the cause whence it had its origin. It always speaks of Spirit. It suggests the absolute. It is a perpetual effect. It is a great shadow pointing always to the sun behind us.

The aspect of Nature is devout. Like the figure of Jesus, she stands with bended head, and hands folded upon the breast. The happiest man is he who learns from nature the lesson of worship.

Of that ineffable essence which we call Spirit, he that thinks most, will say least. We can foresee God in the coarse, and, as it were, distant phenomena of matter; but when we try to define and describe himself, both language and thought desert us, and we are as helpless as fools and savages. That essence refuses to be recorded in propositions, but when man has worshipped him intellectually, the noblest ministry of nature is to stand as the apparition of God. It is the organ through which the universal spirit speaks to the individual, and strives to lead back the individual to it.

When we consider Spirit, we see that the views already presented do not include the whole circumference of man. We must add some related thoughts.

Three problems are put by nature to the mind: What is matter? Whence is it? and Whereto? The first of these questions only, the ideal theory answers. Idealism saith: matter is a phenomenon, not a substance. Idealism acquaints us with the total disparity between the evidence of our own being and the evidence of the world's being. The one is perfect; the other, incapable of any assurance; the mind is a part of the nature of things; the world is a divine dream, from which we may presently awake to the glories and certainties of day. Idealism is a hypothesis to account for nature by other principles than those of carpentry and chemistry. Yet, if it only deny the existence of matter, it does not satisfy the demands of the spirit. It leaves God out of me. It leaves me in the splendid labyrinth of my perceptions, to wander without end. Then the heart resists it, because it balks the affections in denying substantive being to men and women. Nature is so pervaded with human life that there is something of humanity in all and in every particular. But this theory makes nature foreign to me, and does not account for that consanguinity which we acknowledge to it.

Let it stand then, in the present state of our knowledge, merely as a useful introductory hypothesis, serving to apprise us of the eternal distinction between the soul and the world.

But when, following the invisible steps of thought, we come to inquire, Whence is matter? and Whereto? many truths arise to us out of the recesses of consciousness. We learn that the highest is present to the soul of man; that the dread universal essence, which is not wisdom, or love, or beauty, or power, but all in one, and each entirely, is that for which all things exist, and that by which they are; that spirit creates; that behind nature, throughout nature, spirit is present; one and not compound it does not act upon us from without, that is, in space and time, but spiritually, or through ourselves: therefore, that spirit, that is, the Supreme Being, does not build up nature around us, but puts it forth through us, as the life of the tree puts forth new branches and leaves through the pores of the old. As a plant upon the earth, so a man rests upon the bosom of God; he is nourished by unfailing fountains, and draws at his need inexhaustible power. Who can set bounds to the possibilities of man? Once inhale the upper air, being admitted to behold the absolute natures of justice and truth, and we learn that man has access to the entire mind of the Creator, is himself the creator in the finite. This view, which admonishes me where the sources of wisdom and power lie, and points to virtue as to

> "The golden key
> Which opes the palace of eternity,"

carries upon its face the highest certificate of truth, because it animates me to create my own world through the purification of my soul.

The world proceeds from the same spirit as the body of man. It is a remoter and inferior incarnation of God, a projection of God in the unconscious. But it differs from the body in one important respect. It is not, like that, now subjected to the human will. Its serene order is inviolable by us. It is, therefore, to us, the present expositor of the divine mind. It is a fixed point whereby we may measure our departure. As we degenerate, the contrast between us and our house is more evident. We are as much strangers in nature as we are aliens from God. We do not understand the notes of birds. The fox and the deer run away from us; the bear and tiger rend us. We do not know the uses of more than a few plants, as corn and the apple, the potato and the vine. Is not the landscape, every glimpse of which hath a grandeur, a face of him? Yet this may show us what discord is between man and nature, for you cannot freely admire a noble landscape if laborers are digging in the field hard by. The poet finds something ridiculous in his delight until he is out of the sight of men.

VIII. Prospects

In inquiries respecting the laws of the world and the frame of things, the highest reason is always the truest. That which seems faintly possible, it is so refined, is often faint and dim because it is deepest seated in the mind among the eternal verities. Empirical science is apt to cloud the sight, and by the very knowledge of functions and processes to bereave the student of the manly contemplation of the whole. The savant becomes unpoetic. But the best read naturalist who lends an entire and devout attention to truth, will see that there remains much to learn of his relation to the world, and that it is not to be learned by any addition or subtraction or other comparison of known quantities, but is arrived at by untaught sallies of the spirit, by a continual self-recovery, and by entire humility. He will perceive that there are far more excellent qualities in the student than preciseness and infallibility; that a guess is often more fruitful than an indisputable affirmation, and that a dream may let us deeper into the secret of nature than a hundred concerted experiments.

For the problems to be solved are precisely those which the physiologist and the naturalist omit to state. It is not so pertinent to man to know all the individuals of the animal kingdom, as it is to know whence and whereto is this tyrannizing unity in his constitution, which evermore separates and classifies things, endeavoring to reduce the most diverse to one form. When I behold a rich landscape, it is less to my purpose to recite correctly the order and superposition of the strata, than to know why all thought of multitude is lost in a tranquil sense of unity. I cannot greatly honor minuteness in details, so long as there is no hint to explain the relation between things and thoughts; no ray upon the *metaphysics* of conchology, of botany, of the arts, to show the relation of the forms of flowers, shells, animals, architecture, to the mind, and build science upon ideas. In a cabinet of natural history, we become sensible of a certain occult recognition and sympathy in regard to the most unwieldy and eccentric forms of beast, fish, and insect. The American who has been confined, in his own country, to the sight of buildings designed after foreign models, is surprised on entering York Minster or St. Peter's at Rome, by the feeling that these structures are imitations also,—faint copies of an invisible archetype. Nor has science sufficient humanity, so long as the naturalist overlooks that wonderful congruity which subsists between man and the world; of which he is lord, not because he is the most subtile inhabitant, but because he is its head and heart, and finds something of himself in every great and small thing, in every mountain stratum, in every new law of color, fact of astronomy, or atmospheric influence which observation or analysis lays open. A perception of this mystery inspires the muse of George Herbert, the beautiful psalmist of the seventeenth century. The following lines are part of his little poem on Man.

> Man is all symmetry,
> Full of proportions, one limb to another,
> And all to all the world besides.
> Each part may call the farthest, brother;
> For head with foot hath private amity,
> And both with moons and tides.
>
> Nothing hath got so far
> But man hath caught and kept it as his prey;
> His eyes dismount the highest star:
> He is in little all the sphere.
> Herbs gladly cure our flesh, because that they
> Find their acquaintance there.
>
> For us, the winds do blow,
> The earth doth rest, heaven move, and fountains flow;
> Nothing we see, but means our good,
> As our delight, or as our treasure;
> The whole is either our cupboard of food,
> Or cabinet of pleasure.
>
> The stars have us to bed:
> Night draws the curtain; which the sun withdraws.
> Music and light attend our head.
> All things unto our flesh are kind,
> In their descent and being; to our mind,
> In their ascent and cause.
>
> More servants wait on man
> Than he'll take notice of. In every path,
> He treads down that which doth befriend him
> When sickness makes him pale and wan.
> Oh mighty love! Man is one world, and hath
> Another to attend him.

The perception of this class of truths makes the attraction which draws men to science, but the end is lost sight of in attention to the means. In view of this half-sight of science, we accept the sentence of Plato, that "poetry comes nearer to vital truth than history." Every surmise and vaticination of the mind is entitled to a certain respect, and we learn to prefer imperfect theories, and sentences which contain glimpses of truth, to digested systems which have no one valuable suggestion. A wise writer will feel that the ends of study and composition are best answered by announcing undiscovered regions of thought, and so communicating, through hope, new activity to the torpid spirit.

I shall therefore conclude this essay with some traditions of man and nature, which a certain poet sang to me; and which, as they have always been in the world, and perhaps reappear to every bard, may be both history and prophecy.

"The foundations of man are not in matter, but in spirit. But the element of spirit is eternity. To it, therefore, the longest series of events, the oldest chronologies are young and recent. In the cycle of the universal man, from whom the known individuals proceed, centuries are points, and all history is but the epoch of one degradation.

"We distrust and deny inwardly our sympathy with nature. We own and disown our relation to it, by turns. We are like Nebuchadnezzar, dethroned, bereft of reason, and eating grass like an ox. But who can set limits to the remedial force of spirit?

"A man is a god in ruins. When men are innocent, life shall be longer, and shall pass into the immortal as gently as we awake from dreams. Now, the world would be insane and rabid, if these disorganizations should last for hundreds of years. It is kept in check by death and infancy. Infancy is the perpetual Messiah, which comes into the arms of fallen men, and pleads with them to return to paradise.

"Man is the dwarf of himself. Once he was permeated and dissolved by spirit. He filled nature with his overflowing currents. Out from him sprang the sun and moon; from man the sun, from woman the moon. The laws of his mind, the periods of his actions externized themselves into day and night, into the year and the seasons. But, having made for himself this huge shell, his waters retired; he no longer fills the veins and veinlets; he is shrunk to a drop. He sees that the structure still fits him, but fits him colossally. Say, rather, once it fitted him, now it corresponds to him from far and on high. He adores timidly his own work. Now is man the follower of the sun, and woman the follower of the moon. Yet sometimes he starts in his slumber, and wonders at himself and his house, and muses strangely at the resemblance betwixt him and it. He perceives that if his law is still paramount, if still he have elemental power, if his word is sterling yet in nature, it is not conscious power, it is not inferior but superior to his will. It is instinct." Thus my Orphic poet sang.

At present, man applies to nature but half his force. He works on the world with his understanding alone. He lives in it and masters it by a penny-wisdom; and he that works most in it is but a half-man, and whilst his arms are strong and his digestion good, his mind is imbruted, and he is a selfish savage. His relation to nature, his power over it, is through the understanding, as by manure; the economic use of fire, wind, water, and the mariner's needle; steam, coal, chemical agriculture; the repairs of the human body by the dentist and the surgeon. This is such a resumption of power as if a banished king should buy his territories inch by inch, instead of vaulting at once into his throne. Meantime, in the thick darkness, there are not wanting gleams of a better light,—occasional examples of the action of man upon nature with his entire force,—with reason as well as understanding. Such examples are, the traditions of miracles in the earliest antiquity of all nations; the history of Jesus Christ; the achievements of a principle, as in religious and political revolutions, and in the abolition of the slave-trade; the miracles of enthusiasm, as those reported of Swedenborg, Hohenlohe, and the Shakers; many obscure and yet contested facts, now arranged under the name of Animal Magnetism; prayer; eloquence; self-healing; and the wisdom of children. These are examples of Reason's momentary grasp of the sceptre; the exertions of a power which exists not in time or space, but an instantaneous in-streaming causing power. The difference between the actual and the ideal force of man is happily figured by the schoolmen, in saying, that the knowledge of man is an evening knowledge, *vespertina cognitio*, but that of God is a morning knowledge, *matutina cognitio*.

The problem of restoring to the world original and eternal beauty is solved by the redemption of the soul. The ruin or the blank that we see when we look at nature, is in our own eye. The axis of vision is not coincident with the axis of things, and so they appear not transparent but opaque. The reason why the world lacks unity, and lies broken and in heaps, is because man is disunited with himself. He cannot be a naturalist until he satisfies all the demands of the spirit. Love is as much its demand as perception. Indeed, neither can be perfect without the other. In the uttermost meaning of the words, thought is devout, and devotion is thought. Deep calls unto deep. But in actual life, the marriage is not celebrated. There are innocent men who worship God after the tradition of their fathers, but their sense of duty has not yet extended to the use of all their faculties. And there are patient naturalists, but they freeze their subject under the wintry light of the understanding. Is not prayer also a study of truth,—a sally of the soul into the unfound infinite? No man ever prayed heartily without learning something. But when a faithful thinker, resolute to detach every object from personal relations and see it in the light of thought, shall, at the same time, kindle science with the fire of the holiest affections, then will God go forth anew into the creation.

It will not need, when the mind is prepared for study, to search for objects. The invariable mark of wisdom is to see the miraculous in the common. What is a day? What is a year? What is summer? What is woman? What is a child? What is sleep? To our blindness, these things seem unaffecting. We make fables to hide the baldness of the fact and conform it, as we say, to the higher law of the mind. But when the fact is seen under the light of an idea, the gaudy fable fades and shrivels.

We behold the real higher law. To the wise, therefore, a fact is true poetry, and the most beautiful of fables. These wonders are brought to our own door. You also are a man. Man and woman and their social life, poverty, labor, sleep, fear, fortune, are known to you. Learn that none of these things is superficial, but that each phenomenon has its roots in the faculties and affections of the mind. Whilst the abstract question occupies your intellect, nature brings it in the concrete to be solved by your hands. It were a wise inquiry for the closet, to compare, point by point, especially at remarkable crises in life, our daily history with the rise and progress of ideas in the mind.

So shall we come to look at the world with new eyes. It shall answer the endless inquiry of the intellect,—What is truth? and of the affections,—What is good? by yielding itself passive to the educated Will. Then shall come to pass what my poet said: "Nature is not fixed but fluid. Spirit alters, moulds, makes it. The immobility or bruteness of nature is the absence of spirit; to pure spirit it is fluid, it is volatile, it is obedient. Every spirit builds itself a house, and beyond its house a world, and beyond its world a heaven. Know then that the world exists for you. For you is the phenomenon perfect. What we are, that only can we see. All that Adam had, all that Cæsar could, you have and can do. Adam called his house, heaven and earth; Cæsar called his house, Rome; you perhaps call yours, a cobbler's trade; a hundred acres of ploughed land; or a scholar's garret. Yet line for line and point for point your dominion is as great as theirs, though without fine names. Build therefore your own world. As fast as you conform your life to the pure idea in your mind, that will unfold its great proportions. A correspondent revolution in things will attend the influx of the spirit. So fast will disagreeable appearances, swine, spiders, snakes, pests, mad-houses, prisons, enemies, vanish; they are temporary and shall be no more seen. The sordor and filths of nature, the sun shall dry up and the wind exhale. As when the summer comes from the south the snow-banks melt and the face of the earth becomes green before it, so shall the advancing spirit create its ornaments along its path, and carry with it the beauty it visits and the song which enchants it; it shall draw beautiful faces, warm hearts, wise discourse, and heroic acts, around its way, until evil is no more seen. The kingdom of man over nature, which cometh not with observation,—a dominion such as now is beyond his dream of God,—he shall enter without more wonder than the blind man feels who is gradually restored to perfect sight."

1836

THE AMERICAN SCHOLAR

AN ORATION DELIVERED BEFORE THE PHI BETA KAPPA SOCIETY, AT CAMBRIDGE, AUGUST 31, 1837

Mr. President and Gentlemen:

I greet you on the recommencement of our literary year. Our anniversary is one of hope, and, perhaps, not enough of labor. We do not meet for games of strength or skill, for the recitation of histories, tragedies, and odes, like the ancient Greeks; for parliaments of love and poesy, like the Troubadours; nor for the advancement of science, like our contemporaries in the British and European capitals. Thus far, our holiday has been simply a friendly sign of the survival of the love of letters amongst a people too busy to give to letters any more. As such it is precious as the sign of an indestructible instinct. Perhaps the time is already come when it ought to be, and will be, something else; when the sluggard intellect of this continent will look from under its iron lids and fill the postponed expectation of the world with something better than the exertions of mechanical skill. Our day of dependence, our long apprenticeship to the learning of other lands, draws to a close. The millions that around us are rushing into life, cannot always be fed on the sere remains of foreign harvests. Events, actions arise, that must be sung, that will sing themselves. Who can doubt that poetry will revive and lead in a new age, as the star in the constellation Harp, which now flames in our zenith, astronomers announce, shall one day be the pole-star for a thousand years?

In this hope I accept the topic which not only usage but the nature of our association seem to prescribe to this day,—the AMERICAN SCHOLAR. Year by year we come up hither to read one more chapter of his biography. Let us inquire what light new days and events have thrown on his character and his hopes.

It is one of those fables which out of an unknown antiquity convey an unlooked-for wisdom, that the gods, in the beginning, divided Man into men, that he might be more helpful to himself; just as the hand was divided into fingers, the better to answer its end.

The old fable covers a doctrine ever new and sublime; that there is One Man,—present to all particular men only partially, or through one faculty; and that you must take the whole society to find the whole man. Man is not a farmer, or a professor, or an engineer, but he is all. Man is priest, and scholar, and statesman, and producer, and soldier. In the *divided* or social state these functions are parcelled out to individuals, each of whom aims to do his stint of the joint work, whilst each other performs his. The fable implies that the individual, to possess himself, must sometimes return from his own labor to embrace all the other laborers. But, unfortunately, this original unit, this fountain of power, has been so distributed to multitudes, has been so minutely subdivided and peddled out, that it is spilled into drops, and cannot be gathered. The state of society is one in which the members have suffered amputation from the trunk, and strut about so many walking monsters,—a good finger, a neck, a stomach, an elbow, but never a man.

Man is thus metamorphosed into a thing, into many things. The planter, who is Man sent out into the field to gather food, is seldom cheered by any idea of the true dignity of his ministry. He sees his bushel and his cart, and nothing beyond, and sinks into the farmer, instead of Man on the farm. The tradesman scarcely ever gives an ideal worth to his work, but is ridden by the routine of his craft, and the soul is subject to dollars. The priest becomes a form; the attorney a statute-book; the mechanic a machine; the sailor a rope of the ship.

In this distribution of functions the scholar is the delegated intellect. In the right state he is *Man Thinking*. In the degenerate state, when the victim of society, he tends to become a mere thinker, or still worse, the parrot of other men's thinking.

In this view of him, as Man Thinking, the theory of his office is contained. Him Nature solicits with all her placid, all her monitory pictures; him the past instructs; him the future invites. Is not indeed every man a student, and do not all things exist for the student's behoof? And, finally, is not the true scholar the only true master? But the old oracle said, "All things have two handles: beware of the wrong one." In life, too often, the scholar errs with mankind and forfeits his privilege. Let us see him in his school, and consider him in reference to the main influences he receives.

I. The first in time and the first in importance of the influences upon the mind is that of nature. Every day, the sun; and, after sunset, Night and her stars. Ever the winds blow; ever the grass grows. Every day, men and women, conversing —beholding and beholden. The scholar is he of all men whom this spectacle most engages. He must settle its value in his mind. What is nature to him? There is never a beginning, there is never an end, to the inexplicable continuity of this web of God, but always circular power returning into itself. Therein it resembles his own spirit, whose beginning, whose ending, he never can find,—so entire, so boundless. Far too as her splendors shine, system on system shooting like rays, upward, downward, without centre, without circumference,—in the mass and in the particle, Nature hastens to render account of herself to the mind. Classification begins. To the young mind every thing is individual, stands by itself. By and by, it finds how to join two things and see in them one nature; then three, then three thousand; and so, tyrannized over by its own unifying instinct, it goes on tying things together, diminishing anomalies, discovering roots running under ground whereby contrary and remote things cohere and flower out from one stem. It presently learns that since the dawn of history there has been a constant accumulation and classifying of facts. But what is classification but the perceiving that these objects are not chaotic, and are not foreign, but have a law which is also a law of the human mind? The astronomer discovers that geometry, a pure abstraction of the human mind, is the measure of planetary motion. The chemist finds proportions and intelligible method throughout matter; and science is nothing but the finding of analogy, identity, in the most remote parts. The ambitious soul sits down before each refractory fact; one after another reduces all strange constitutions, all new powers, to their class and their law, and goes on forever to animate the last fibre of organization, the outskirts of nature, by insight.

Thus to him, to this schoolboy under the bending dome of day, is suggested that he and it proceed from one root; one is leaf and one is flower; relation, sympathy, stirring in every vein. And what is that root? Is not that the soul of his soul? A thought too bold; a dream too wild. Yet when this spiritual light shall have revealed the law of more earthly natures,—when he has learned to worship the soul, and to see that the natural philosophy that now is, is only the first gropings of its gigantic hand, he shall look forward to an ever expanding knowledge as to a becoming creator. He shall see that nature is the opposite of the soul, answering to it part for part. One is seal and one is print. Its beauty is the beauty of his own mind. Its laws are the laws of his own mind. Nature then becomes to him the measure of his attainments. So much of nature as he is ignorant of, so much of his own mind does he not yet possess. And, in fine, the ancient precept, "Know thyself," and the modern precept, "Study nature," become at last one maxim.

II. The next great influence into the spirit of the scholar is the mind of the Past,—in whatever form, whether of literature, of art, of institutions, that mind is inscribed. Books are the best type of the influence of the past, and perhaps we shall get at the truth,—learn the amount of this influence more conveniently,—by considering their value alone.

The theory of books is noble. The scholar of the first age received into him the world around; brooded thereon; gave it the new arrangement of his own mind, and uttered it again. It came into him life; it went out from him truth. It came to him short-lived actions; it went out from him immortal thoughts. It came to him business; it went from him poetry. It was dead fact; now, it is quick thought. It can stand, and it can go. It now endures, it now flies, it now inspires. Precisely in proportion to the depth of mind from which it issued, so high does it soar, so long does it sing.

Or, I might say, it depends on how far the process had gone, of transmuting life into truth. In proportion to the completeness of the distillation, so will the purity and imperishableness of the product be. But none is quite perfect. As no air-pump can by any means make a perfect vacuum, so neither can any artist entirely exclude the conventional, the local, the perishable from his book, or write a book of pure thought, that shall be as efficient, in all respects, to a remote posterity, as to contemporaries, or rather to the second age. Each age, it is found, must write its own books; or rather, each generation for the next succeeding. The books of an older period will not fit this.

Yet hence arises a grave mischief. The sacredness which attaches to the act of creation, the act of thought, is transferred to the record. The poet chanting was felt to be a divine man: henceforth the chant is divine also. The writer was a just and wise spirit: henceforward it is settled the book is perfect; as love of the hero corrupts into worship of his statue. Instantly the book becomes noxious: the guide is a tyrant. The sluggish and perverted mind of the multitude, slow to open to the incursions of Reason, having once so opened, having once received this book, stands upon it, and makes an outcry if it is disparaged. Colleges are built on it. Books are written on it by thinkers, not by Man Thinking; by men of talent, that is, who start wrong, who set out from accepted dogmas, not from their own sight of principles. Meek young men grow up in libraries, believing it their duty to accept the views which Cicero, which Locke, which Bacon, have given; forgetful that Cicero, Locke, and Bacon were only young men in libraries when they wrote these books.

Hence, instead of Man Thinking, we have the bookworm. Hence the book-learned class, who value books, as such; not as related to nature and the human constitution, but as making a sort of Third Estate with the world and the soul. Hence the restorers of readings, the emendators, the bibliomaniacs of all degrees.

Books are the best of things, well used; abused, among the worst. What is the right use? What is the one end which all means go to effect? They are for nothing but to inspire. I had better never see a book than to be warped by its attraction clean out of my own orbit, and made a satellite instead of a system. The one thing in the world, of value, is the active soul. This every man is entitled to; this every man contains within him, although in almost all men obstructed and as yet unborn. The soul active sees absolute truth and utters truth, or creates. In this action it is genius; not the privilege of here and there a favorite, but the sound estate of every man. In its essence it is progressive. The book, the college, the school of art, the institution of any kind, stop with some past utterance of genius. This is good, say they,—let us hold by this. They pin me down. They look backward and not forward. But genius looks forward: the eyes of man are set in his forehead, not in his hindhead: man hopes: genius creates. Whatever talents may be, if the man create not, the pure efflux of the Deity is not his;—cinders and smoke there may be, but not yet flame. There are creative manners, there are creative actions, and creative words; manners, actions, words, that is, indicative of no custom or authority, but springing spontaneous from the mind's own sense of good and fair.

On the other part, instead of being its own seer, let it receive from another mind its truth, though it were in torrents of light, without periods of solitude, inquest, and self-recovery, and a fatal disservice is done. Genius is always sufficiently the enemy of genius by over-influence. The literature of every nation bears me witness. The English dramatic poets have Shakspearized now for two hundred years.

Undoubtedly there is a right way of reading, so it be sternly subordinated. Man Thinking must not be subdued by his instruments. Books are for the scholar's idle times. When he can read God directly, the hour is too precious to be wasted in other men's transcripts of their readings. But when the intervals of darkness come, as come they must,—when the sun is hid and the stars withdraw their shining,—we repair to the lamps which were kindled by their ray, to guide our steps to the East again, where the dawn is. We hear, that we may speak. The Arabian proverb says, "A fig tree, looking on a fig tree, becometh fruitful."

It is remarkable, the character of the pleasure we derive from the best books. They impress us with the conviction that one nature wrote and the same reads. We read the verses of one of the great English poets, of Chaucer, of Marvell, of Dryden, with the most modern joy,—with a pleasure, I mean, which is in great part caused by the abstraction of all *time* from their verses. There is some awe mixed with the joy of our surprise, when this poet, who lived in some past world, two or three hundred years ago, says that which lies close to my own soul, that which I also had well-nigh thought and said. But for the evidence thence afforded to the philosophical doctrine of the identity of all minds, we should suppose some preëstablished harmony, some foresight of souls that were to be, and some preparation of stores for their future wants, like the fact observed in insects, who lay up food before death for the young grub they shall never see.

I would not be hurried by any love of system, by any exaggeration of instincts, to underrate the Book. We all know, that as the human body can be nourished on any food, though it were boiled grass and the broth of shoes, so the human mind can be fed by any knowledge. And great and heroic men have existed who had almost no other information than by the printed page. I only would say that it needs a strong head to bear that diet. One must be an inventor to read well. As the proverb says, "He that would bring home the wealth of the Indies, must carry out the wealth of the Indies." There is then creative reading as well as creative writing. When the mind is braced by labor and invention, the page of whatever book we read becomes luminous with manifold allusion. Every sentence is doubly significant, and the sense of our author is as broad as the world. We then see, what is always true, that as the seer's hour of vision is short and rare among heavy days and months, so is its record, perchance, the least part of his volume. The discerning will read, in his Plato or Shakspeare, only that least part,—only the authentic utterances of the oracle;—all the rest he rejects, were it never so many times Plato's and Shakspeare's.

Of course there is a portion of reading quite indispensable to a wise man. History and exact science he must learn by laborious reading. Colleges, in like manner, have their indispensable office,—to teach elements. But they can only highly serve us when they aim not to drill, but to create; when they gather from far every ray of various genius to their hospitable halls, and by the concentrated fires, set the hearts of their youth on flame. Thought and knowledge are natures in which apparatus and pretension avail nothing. Gowns and pecuniary foundations, though of towns of gold, can never countervail the least sentence or syllable of wit. Forget this, and our American colleges will recede in their public importance, whilst they grow richer every year.

III. There goes in the world a notion that the scholar should be a recluse, a valetudinarian,—as unfit for any handiwork or public labor as a penknife for an axe. The so-called "practical men" sneer at speculative men, as if, because they speculate or *see*, they could do nothing. I have heard it said that the clergy, —who are always, more universally than any other class, the scholars of their day,—are addressed as women; that the rough, spontaneous conversation of men they do not hear, but only a mincing and diluted speech. They are often virtually disfranchised; and indeed there are advocates for their celibacy. As far as this is true of the studious classes, it is not just and wise. Action is with the scholar subordinate, but it is essential. Without it he is not yet man. Without it thought can never ripen into truth. Whilst the world hangs before the eye as a cloud of beauty, we cannot even see its beauty. Inaction is cowardice, but there can be no scholar without the heroic mind. The preamble of thought, the transition through which it passes from the unconscious to the conscious, is action. Only so much do I know, as I have lived. Instantly we know whose words are loaded with life, and whose not.

The world,—this shadow of the soul, or *other me*,—lies wide around. Its attractions are the keys which unlock my thoughts and make me acquainted with myself. I run eagerly into this resounding tumult. I grasp the hands of those next me, and take my place in the ring to suffer and to work, taught by an instinct that so shall the dumb abyss be vocal with speech. I pierce its order; I dissipate its fear; I dispose of it within the circuit of my expanding life. So much only of life as I know by experience, so much of the wilderness have I vanquished and planted, or so far have I extended my being, my dominion. I do not see how any man can afford, for the sake of his nerves and his nap, to spare any action in which he can partake. It is pearls and rubies to his discourse. Drudgery, calamity, exasperation, want, are instructors in eloquence and wisdom. The true scholar grudges every opportunity of action past by, as a loss of power. It is the raw material out of which the intellect moulds her splendid products. A strange process too, this by which experience is converted into thought, as a mulberry leaf is converted into satin. The manufacture goes forward at all hours.

The actions and events of our childhood and youth are now matters of calmest observation. They lie like fair pictures in the air. Not so with our recent actions,—with the business which we now have in hand. On this we are quite unable to speculate. Our affections as yet circulate through it. We no more feel or know it than we feel the feet, or the hand, or the brain of our body. The new deed is yet a part of life,—remains for a time immersed in our unconscious life. In some contemplative hour it detaches itself from the life like a ripe fruit, to become a thought of the mind. Instantly it is raised, transfigured; the corruptible has put on incorruption. Henceforth it is an object of beauty, however base its origin and neighborhood. Observe too the impossibility of antedating this act. In its grub state, it cannot fly, it cannot shine, it is a dull grub. But suddenly, without observation, the selfsame thing unfurls beautiful wings, and is an angel of wisdom. So is there no fact, no event, in our private history, which shall not, sooner or later, lose its adhesive, inert form, and astonish us by soaring from our body into the empyrean. Cradle and infancy, school and playground, the fear of boys, and dogs, and ferules, the love of little maids and berries, and many another fact that once filled the whole sky, are gone already; friend and relative, profession and party, town and country, nation and world, must also soar and sing.

Of course, he who has put forth his total strength in fit actions has the richest return of wisdom. I will not shut myself out of this globe of action, and transplant an oak into a flowerpot, there to hunger and pine; nor trust the revenue of some single faculty, and exhaust one vein of thought, much like those Savoyards, who, getting their livelihood by carving shepherds, shepherdesses, and smoking Dutchmen, for all Europe, went out one day to the mountain to find stock, and discovered that they had whittled up the last of their pine trees. Authors we have, in numbers, who have written out their vein, and who, moved by a commendable prudence, sail for Greece or Palestine, follow the trapper into the prairie, or ramble round Algiers, to replenish their merchantable stock.

If it were only for a vocabulary, the scholar would be covetous of action. Life is our dictionary. Years are well spent in country labors; in town; in the insight into trades and manufactures; in frank intercourse with many men and women; in science; in art; to the one end of mastering in all their facts a language by which to illustrate and embody our perceptions. I learn immediately from any speaker how much he has already lived, through the poverty or the splendor of his speech. Life lies behind us as the quarry from whence we get tiles and copestones for the masonry of to-day. This is the way to learn grammar. Colleges and books only copy the language which the field and the work-yard made.

But the final value of action, like that of books, and better than books, is that it is a resource. That great principle of Undulation in nature, that shows itself in the inspiring and expiring of the breath; in desire and satiety; in the ebb and flow of the sea; in day and night; in heat and cold; and, as yet more deeply ingrained in every atom and every fluid, is known to us under the name of Polarity,—these "fits of easy transmission and reflection," as Newton called them, are the law of nature because they are the law of spirit.

The mind now thinks, now acts, and each fit reproduces the other. When the artist has exhausted his materials, when the fancy no longer paints, when thoughts are no longer apprehended and books are a weariness,—he has always the resource *to live*. Character is higher than intellect. Thinking is the function. Living is the functionary. The stream retreats to its source. A great soul will be strong to live, as well as strong to think. Does he lack organ or medium to impart his truths? He can still fall back on this elemental force of living them. This is a total act. Thinking is a partial act. Let the grandeur of justice shine in his affairs. Let the beauty of affection cheer his lowly roof. Those "far from fame," who dwell and act with him, will feel the force of his constitution in the doings and passages of the day better than it can be measured by any public and designed display. Time shall teach him that the scholar loses no hour which the man lives. Herein he unfolds the sacred germ of his instinct, screened from influence. What is lost in seemliness is gained in strength. Not out of those on whom systems of education have exhausted their culture, comes the helpful giant to destroy the old or to build the new, but out of unhandselled savage nature; out of terrible Druids and Berserkers come at last Alfred and Shakspeare.

I hear therefore with joy whatever is beginning to be said of the dignity and necessity of labor to every citizen. There is virtue yet in the hoe and the spade, for learned as well as for unlearned hands. And labor is everywhere welcome; always we are invited to work; only be this limitation observed, that a man shall not for the sake of wider activity sacrifice any opinion to the popular judgments and modes of action.

I have now spoken of the education of the scholar by nature, by books, and by action. It remains to say somewhat of his duties.

They are such as become Man Thinking. They may all be comprised in self-trust. The office of the scholar is to cheer, to raise, and to guide men by showing them facts amidst appearances. He plies the slow, unhonored, and unpaid task of observation. Flamsteed and Herschel, in their glazed observatories, may catalogue the stars with the praise of all men, and the results being splendid and useful, honor is sure. But he, in his private observatory, cataloguing obscure and nebulous stars of the human mind, which as yet no man has thought of as such, —watching days and months sometimes for a few facts; correcting still his old records;—must relinquish display and immediate fame. In the long period of his preparation he must betray often an ignorance and shiftlessness in popular arts, incurring the disdain of the able who shoulder him aside. Long he must stammer in his speech; often forego the living for the dead. Worse yet, he must accept—how often!—poverty and solitude. For the ease and pleasure of treading the old road, accepting the fashions, the education, the religion of society, he takes the cross of making his own, and, of course, the self-accusation, the faint heart, the frequent uncertainty and loss of time, which are the nettles and tangling vines in the way of the self-relying and self-directed; and the state of virtual hostility in which he seems to stand to society, and especially to educated society. For all this loss and scorn, what offset? He is to find consolation in exercising the highest functions of human nature. He is one who raises himself from private considerations and breathes and lives on public and illustrious thoughts. He is the world's eye. He is the world's heart. He is to resist the vulgar prosperity that retrogrades ever to barbarism, by preserving and communicating heroic sentiments, noble biographies, melodious verse, and the conclusions of history. Whatsoever oracles the human heart, in all emergencies, in all solemn hours, has uttered as its commentary on the world of actions,— these he shall receive and impart. And whatsoever new verdict Reason from her inviolable seat pronounces on the passing men and events of to-day,—this he shall hear and promulgate.

These being his functions, it becomes him to feel all confidence in himself, and to defer never to the popular cry. He and he only knows the world. The world of any moment is the merest appearance. Some great decorum, some fetish of a government, some ephemeral trade, or war, or man, is cried up by half mankind and cried down by the other half, as if all depended on this particular up or down. The odds are that the whole question is not worth the poorest thought which the scholar has lost in listening to the controversy. Let him not quit his belief that a popgun is a popgun, though the ancient and honorable of the earth affirm it to be the crack of doom. In silence, in steadiness, in severe abstraction, let him hold by himself; add observation to observation, patient of neglect, patient of reproach, and bide his own time,—happy enough if he can satisfy himself alone that this day he has seen something truly. Success treads on every right step. For the instinct is sure, that prompts him to tell his brother what he thinks. He then learns that in going down into the secrets of his own mind he has descended into the secrets of all minds. He learns that he who has mastered any law in his private thoughts, is master to that extent of all men whose language he speaks, and of all into whose language his own can be translated. The poet, in utter solitude remembering his spontaneous thoughts and recording them, is found to have recorded that which men in crowded cities find true for them also. The orator distrusts at first the fitness of his frank confessions, his want of knowledge of the persons he addresses, until he finds that he is the complement of his hearers;—that they drink his words because he fulfils for them their own nature; the deeper he dives into his privatest, secretest presentiment, to his wonder he finds this is the most acceptable, most public, and universally true. The people delight in it; the better part of every man feels, This is my music; this is myself.

In self-trust all the virtues are comprehended. Free should the scholar be,—free and brave. Free even to the definition of freedom, "without any hindrance that does not arise out of his own constitution." Brave; for fear is a thing which a scholar by his very function puts behind him. Fear always springs from ignorance. It is a shame to him if his tranquillity, amid dangerous times, arise from the presumption that like children and women his is a protected class; or if he seek a temporary peace by the diversion of his thoughts from politics or vexed questions, hiding his head like an ostrich in the flowering bushes, peeping into microscopes, and turning rhymes, as a boy whistles to keep his courage up. So is the danger a danger still; so is the fear worse. Manlike let him turn and face it. Let him look into its eye and search its nature, inspect its origin,—see the whelping of this lion,—which lies no great way back; he will then find in himself a perfect comprehension of its nature and extent; he will have made his hands meet on the other side, and can henceforth defy it and pass on superior. The world is his who can see through its pretension. What deafness, what stone-blind custom, what overgrown error you behold is there only by sufferance,—by your sufferance. See it to be a lie, and you have already dealt it its mortal blow.

Yes, we are the cowed,—we the trustless. It is a mischievous notion that we are come late into nature; that the world was finished a long time ago. As the world was plastic and fluid in the hands of God, so it is ever to so much of his attributes as we bring to it. To ignorance and sin, it is flint. They adapt themselves to it as they may; but in proportion as a man has any thing in him divine, the firmament flows before him and takes his signet and form. Not he is great who can alter matter, but he who can alter my state of mind. They are the kings of the world who give the color of their present thought to all nature and all art, and persuade men by the cheerful serenity of their carrying the matter, that this thing which they do is the apple which the ages have desired to pluck, now at last ripe, and inviting nations to the harvest. The great man makes the great thing. Wherever Macdonald sits, there is the head of the table. Linnæus makes botany the most alluring of studies, and wins it from the farmer and the herb-woman; Davy, chemistry; and Cuvier, fossils. The day is always his who works in it with serenity and great aims. The unstable estimates of men crowd to him whose mind is filled with a truth, as the heaped waves of the Atlantic follow the moon.

For this self-trust, the reason is deeper than can be fathomed,—darker than can be enlightened. I might not carry with me the feeling of my audience in stating my own belief. But I have already shown the ground of my hope, in adverting to the doctrine that man is one. I believe man has been wronged; he has wronged himself. He has almost lost the light that can lead him back to his prerogatives. Men are become of no account. Men in history, men in the world of to-day, are bugs, are spawn, and are called "the mass" and "the herd." In a century, in a millennium, one or two men; that is to say, one or two approximations to the right state of every man. All the rest behold in the hero or the poet their own green and crude being,—ripened; yes, and are content to be less, so *that* may attain to its full stature. What a testimony, full of grandeur, full of pity, is borne to the demands of his own nature, by the poor clansman, the poor partisan, who rejoices in the glory of his chief. The poor and the low find some amends to their immense moral capacity, for their acquiescence in a political and social inferiority. They are content to be brushed like flies from the path of a great person, so that justice shall be done by him to that common nature which it is the dearest desire of all to see enlarged and glorified. They sun themselves in the great man's light, and feel it to be their own element. They cast the dignity of man from their downtrod selves upon the shoulders of a hero, and will perish to add one drop of blood to make that great heart beat, those giant sinews combat and conquer. He lives for us, and we live in him.

Men, such as they are, very naturally seek money or power; and power because it is as good as money,—the "spoils," so called, "of office." And why not? for they aspire to the highest, and this, in their sleep-walking, they dream is highest. Wake them and they shall quit the false good and leap to the true, and leave governments to clerks and desks. This revolution is to be wrought by the gradual domestication of the idea of Culture. The main enterprise of the world for splendor, for extent, is the upbuilding of a man. Here are the materials strewn along the ground. The private life of one man shall be a more illustrious monarchy, more formidable to its enemy, more sweet and serene in its influence to its friend, than any kingdom in history. For a man, rightly viewed, comprehendeth the particular natures of all men. Each philosopher, each bard, each actor has only done for me, as by a delegate, what one day I can do for myself. The books which once we valued more than the apple of the eye, we have quite exhausted. What is that but saying that we have come up with the point of view which the universal mind took through the eyes of one scribe; we have been that man, and have passed on. First, one, then another, we drain all cisterns, and waxing greater by all these supplies, we crave a better and more abundant food. The man has never lived that can feed us ever. The human mind cannot be enshrined in a person who shall set a barrier on any one side to this unbounded, unboundable empire. It is one central fire, which, flaming now out of the lips of Etna, lightens the capes of Sicily, and now out of the throat of Vesuvius, illuminates the towers and vineyards of Naples. It is one light which beams out of a thousand stars. It is one soul which animates all men.

But I have dwelt perhaps tediously upon this abstraction of the Scholar. I ought not to delay longer to add what I have to say of nearer reference to the time and to this country.

Historically, there is thought to be a difference in the ideas which predominate over successive epochs, and there are data for marking the genius of the Classic, of the Romantic, and now of the Reflective or Philosophical age. With the views I have intimated of the oneness or the identity of the mind through all individuals, I do not much dwell on these differences. In fact, I believe each individual passes through all three. The boy is a Greek; the youth, romantic; the adult, reflective. I deny not, however, that a revolution in the leading idea may be distinctly enough traced.

Our age is bewailed as the age of Introversion. Must that needs be evil? We, it seems, are critical; we are embarrassed with second thoughts; we cannot enjoy any thing for hankering to know whereof the pleasure consists; we are lined with eyes; we see with our feet; the time is infected with Hamlet's unhappiness,—

"Sicklied o'er with the pale cast of thought."

It is so bad then? Sight is the last thing to be pitied. Would we be blind? Do we fear lest we should outsee nature and God, and drink truth dry? I look upon the discontent of the literary class as a mere announcement of the fact that they find themselves not in the state of mind of their fathers, and regret the coming state as untried; as a boy dreads the water before he has learned that he can swim. If there is any period one would desire to be born in, is it not the age of Revolution; when the old and the new stand side by side and admit of being compared; when the energies of all men are searched by fear and by hope; when the historic glories of the old can be compensated by the rich possibilities of the new era? This time, like all times, is a very good one, if we but know what to do with it.

I read with some joy of the auspicious signs of the coming days, as they glimmer already through poetry and art, through philosophy and science, through church and state.

One of these signs is the fact that the same movement which effected the elevation of what was called the lowest class in the state, assumed in literature a very marked and as benign an aspect. Instead of the sublime and beautiful, the near, the low, the common, was explored and poetized. That which had been negligently trodden under foot by those who were harnessing and provisioning themselves for long journeys into far countries, is suddenly found to be richer than all foreign parts. The literature of the poor, the feelings of the child, the philosophy of the street, the meaning of household life, are the topics of the time. It is a great stride. It is a sign—is it not?—of new vigor when the extremities are made active, when currents of warm life run into the hands and the feet. I ask not for the great, the remote, the romantic; what is doing in Italy or Arabia; what is Greek art, or Provençal minstrelsy; I embrace the common, I explore and sit at the feet of the familiar, the low. Give me insight into to-day, and you may have the antique and future worlds. What would we really know the meaning of? The meal in the firkin; the milk in the pan; the ballad in the street; the news of the boat; the glance of the eye; the form and the gait of the body;—show me the ultimate reason of these matters; show me the sublime presence of the highest spiritual cause lurking, as always it does lurk, in these suburbs and extremities of nature; let me see every trifle bristling with the polarity that ranges it instantly on an eternal law; and the shop, the plough, and the ledger referred to the like cause by which light undulates and poets sing;—and the world lies no longer a dull miscellany and lumber-room, but has form and order; there is no trifle, there is no puzzle, but one design unites and animates the farthest pinnacle and the lowest trench.

This idea has inspired the genius of Goldsmith, Burns, Cowper, and, in a newer time, of Goethe, Wordsworth, and Carlyle. This idea they have differently followed and with various success. In contrast with their writing, the style of Pope, of Johnson, of Gibbon, looks cold and pedantic. This writing is blood-warm. Man is surprised to find that things near are not less beautiful and wondrous than things remote. The near explains the far. The drop is a small ocean. A man is related to all nature. This perception of the worth of the vulgar is fruitful in discoveries. Goethe, in this very thing the most modern of the moderns, has shown us, as none ever did, the genius of the ancients.

There is one man of genius who has done much for this philosophy of life, whose literary value has never yet been rightly estimated;—I mean Emanuel Swedenborg. The most imaginative of men, yet writing with the precision of a mathematician, he endeavored to engraft a purely philosophical Ethics on the popular Christianity of his time. Such an attempt of course must have difficulty which no genius could surmount. But he saw and showed the connection between nature and the affections of the soul. He pierced the emblematic or spiritual character of the visible, audible, tangible world. Especially did his shade-loving muse hover over and interpret the lower parts of nature; he showed the mysterious bond that allies moral evil to the foul material forms, and has given in epical parables a theory of insanity, of beasts, of unclean and fearful things.

Another sign of our times, also marked by an analogous political movement, is the new importance given to the single person. Every thing that tends to insulate the individual,—to surround him with barriers of natural respect, so that each man shall feel the world is his, and man shall treat with man as a sovereign state with a sovereign state,—tends to true union as well as greatness. "I learned," said the melancholy Pestalozzi, "that no man in God's wide earth is either willing or able to help any other man." Help must come from the bosom alone. The scholar is that man who must take up into himself all the ability of the time, all the contributions of the past, all the hopes of the future. He must be an university of knowledges. If there be one lesson more than another which should pierce his ear, it is, The world is nothing, the man is all; in yourself is the law of all nature, and you know not yet how a globule of sap ascends; in yourself slumbers the whole of Reason; it is for you to know all; it is for you to dare all. Mr. President and Gentlemen, this confidence in the unsearched might of man belongs, by all motives, by all prophecy, by all preparation, to the American Scholar. We have listened too long to the courtly muses of Europe. The spirit of the American freeman is already suspected to be timid, imitative, tame. Public and private avarice make the air we breathe thick and fat. The scholar is decent, indolent, complaisant. See already the tragic consequence. The mind of this country, taught to aim at low objects, eats upon itself. There is no work for any but the decorous and the complaisant. Young men of the fairest promise, who begin life upon our shores, inflated by the mountain winds, shined upon by all the stars of God, find the earth below not in unison with these, but are hindered from action by the disgust which the principles on which business is managed inspire, and turn drudges, or die of disgust, some of them suicides. What is the remedy? They did not yet see, and thousands of young men as hopeful now crowding to the barriers for the career do not yet see, that if the single man plant himself indomitably on his instincts, and there abide, the huge world will come round to him. Patience,—patience; with the shades of all the good and great for company; and for solace the perspective of your own infinite life; and for work the study and the communication of principles, the making those instincts prevalent, the conversion of the world. Is it not the chief disgrace in the world, not to be an unit;—not to be reckoned one character;—not to yield that peculiar fruit which each man was created to bear, but to be reckoned in the gross, in the hundred, or the thousand, of the party, the section, to which we belong; and our opinion predicted geographically, as the north, or the south? Not so, brothers and friends—please God, ours shall not be so. We will walk on our own feet; we will work with our own hands; we will speak our own minds. The study of letters shall be no longer a name for pity, for doubt, and for sensual indulgence. The dread of man and the love of man shall be a wall of defence and a wreath of joy around all. A nation of men will for the first time exist, because each believes himself inspired by the Divine Soul which also inspires all men.

1837

THE DIVINITY SCHOOL ADDRESS

DELIVERED BEFORE THE SENIOR CLASS IN DIVINITY COLLEGE, CAMBRIDGE, SUNDAY EVENING, JULY 15, 1838

In this refulgent summer, it has been a luxury to draw the breath of life. The grass grows, the buds burst, the meadow is spotted with fire and gold in the tint of flowers. The air is full of birds, and sweet with the breath of the pine, the balm-of-Gilead, and the new hay. Night brings no gloom to the heart with its welcome shade. Through the transparent darkness the stars pour their almost spiritual rays. Man under them seems a young child, and his huge globe a toy. The cool night bathes the world as with a river, and prepares his eyes again for the crimson dawn. The mystery of nature was never displayed more happily. The corn and the wine have been freely dealt to all creatures, and the never-broken silence with which the old bounty goes forward has not yielded yet one word of explanation. One is constrained to respect the perfection of this world in which our senses converse. How wide; how rich; what invitation from every property it gives to every faculty of man! In its fruitful soils; in its navigable sea; in its mountains of metal and stone; in its forests of all woods; in its animals; in its chemical ingredients; in the powers and path of light, heat, attraction and life, it is well worth the pith and heart of great men to subdue and enjoy it. The planters, the mechanics, the inventors, the astronomers, the builders of cities, and the captains, history delights to honor.

But when the mind opens and reveals the laws which traverse the universe and make things what they are, then shrinks the great world at once into a mere illustration and fable of this mind. What am I? and What is? asks the human spirit with a curiosity new-kindled, but never to be quenched. Behold these outrunning laws, which our imperfect apprehension can see tend this way and that, but not come full circle. Behold these infinite relations, so like, so unlike; many, yet one. I would study, I would know, I would admire forever. These works of thought have been the entertainments of the human spirit in all ages.

A more secret, sweet, and overpowering beauty appears to man when his heart and mind open to the sentiment of virtue. Then he is instructed in what is above him. He learns that his being is without bound; that to the good, to the perfect, he is born, low as he now lies in evil and weakness. That which he venerates is still his own, though he has not realized it yet. *He ought*. He knows the sense of that grand word, though his analysis fails to render account of it. When in innocency or when by intellectual perception he attains to say,—"I love the Right; Truth is beautiful within and without for evermore. Virtue, I am thine; save me; use me; thee will I serve, day and night, in great, in small, that I may be not virtuous, but virtue;"—then is the end of the creation answered, and God is well pleased.

The sentiment of virtue is a reverence and delight in the presence of certain divine laws. It perceives that this homely game of life we play, covers, under what seem foolish details, principles that astonish. The child amidst his baubles is learning the action of light, motion, gravity, muscular force; and in the game of human life, love, fear, justice, appetite, man, and God, interact. These laws refuse to be adequately stated. They will not be written out on paper, or spoken by the tongue. They elude our persevering thought; yet we read them hourly in each other's faces, in each other's actions, in our own remorse. The moral traits which are all globed into every virtuous act and thought, —in speech we must sever, and describe or suggest by painful enumeration of many particulars. Yet, as this sentiment is the essence of all religion, let me guide your eye to the precise objects of the sentiment, by an enumeration of some of those classes of facts in which this element is conspicuous.

The intuition of the moral sentiment is an insight of the perfection of the laws of the soul. These laws execute themselves. They are out of time, out of space, and not subject to circumstance. Thus in the soul of man there is a justice whose retributions are instant and entire. He who does a good deed is instantly ennobled. He who does a mean deed is by the action itself contracted. He who puts off impurity, thereby puts on purity. If a man is at heart just, then in so far is he God; the safety of God, the immortality of God, the majesty of God do enter into that man with justice. If a man dissemble, deceive, he deceives himself, and goes out of acquaintance with his own being. A man in the view of absolute goodness, adores, with total humility. Every step so downward, is a step upward. The man who renounces himself, comes to himself.

See how this rapid intrinsic energy worketh everywhere, righting wrongs, correcting appearances, and bringing up facts to a harmony with thoughts. Its operation in life, though slow to the senses, is at last as sure as in the soul. By it a man is made the Providence to himself, dispensing good to his goodness, and evil to his sin. Character is always known. Thefts never enrich; alms never impoverish; murder will speak out of stone walls. The least admixture of a lie,—for example, the taint of vanity, any attempt to make a good impression, a favorable appearance,—will instantly vitiate the effect. But speak the truth, and all nature and all spirits help you with unexpected furtherance. Speak the truth, and all things alive or brute are vouchers, and the very roots of the grass underground there do seem to stir and move to bear you witness. See again the perfection of the Law as it applies itself to the affections, and becomes the law of society. As we are, so we associate. The good, by affinity, seek the good; the vile, by affinity, the vile. Thus of their own volition, souls proceed into heaven, into hell.

These facts have always suggested to man the sublime creed that the world is not the product of manifold power, but of one will, of one mind; and that one mind is everywhere active, in each ray of the star, in each wavelet of the pool; and whatever opposes that will is everywhere balked and baffled, because things are made so, and not otherwise. Good is positive. Evil is merely privative, not absolute: it is like cold, which is the privation of heat. All evil is so much death or nonentity. Benevolence is absolute and real. So much benevolence as a man hath, so much life hath he. For all things proceed out of this same spirit, which is differently named love, justice, temperance, in its different applications, just as the ocean receives different names on the several shores which it washes. All things proceed out of the same spirit, and all things conspire with it. Whilst a man seeks good ends, he is strong by the whole strength of nature. In so far as he roves from these ends, he bereaves himself of power, of auxiliaries; his being shrinks out of all remote channels, he becomes less and less, a mote, a point, until absolute badness is absolute death.

The perception of this law of laws awakens in the mind a sentiment which we call the religious sentiment, and which makes our highest happiness. Wonderful is its power to charm and to command. It is a mountain air. It is the embalmer of the world. It is myrrh and storax, and chlorine and rosemary. It makes the sky and the hills sublime, and the silent song of the stars is it. By it is the universe made safe and habitable, not by science or power. Thought may work cold and intransitive in things, and find no end or unity; but the dawn of the sentiment of virtue on the heart, gives and is the assurance that Law is sovereign over all natures; and the worlds, time, space, eternity, do seem to break out into joy.

This sentiment is divine and deifying. It is the beatitude of man. It makes him illimitable. Through it, the soul first knows itself. It corrects the capital mistake of the infant man, who seeks to be great by following the great, and hopes to derive advantages *from another*,—by showing the fountain of all good to be in himself, and that he, equally with every man, is an inlet into the deeps of Reason. When he says, "I ought;" when love warms him; when he chooses, warned from on high, the good and great deed; then, deep melodies wander through his soul from Supreme Wisdom.—Then he can worship, and be enlarged by his worship; for he can never go behind this sentiment. In the sublimest flights of the soul, rectitude is never surmounted, love is never outgrown.

This sentiment lies at the foundation of society, and successively creates all forms of worship. The principle of veneration never dies out. Man fallen into superstition, into sensuality, is never quite without the visions of the moral sentiment.

In like manner, all the expressions of this sentiment are sacred and permanent in proportion to their purity. The expressions of this sentiment affect us more than all other compositions. The sentences of the oldest time, which ejaculate this piety, are still fresh and fragrant. This thought dwelled always deepest in the minds of men in the devout and contemplative East; not alone in Palestine, where it reached its purest expression, but in Egypt, in Persia, in India, in China. Europe has always owed to oriental genius its divine impulses. What these holy bards said, all sane men found agreeable and true. And the unique impression of Jesus upon mankind, whose name is not so much written as ploughed into the history of this world, is proof of the subtle virtue of this infusion.

Meantime, whilst the doors of the temple stand open, night and day, before every man, and the oracles of this truth cease never, it is guarded by one stern condition; this, namely; it is an intuition. It cannot be received at second hand. Truly speaking, it is not instruction, but provocation, that I can receive from another soul. What he announces, I must find true in me, or reject; and on his word, or as his second, be he who he may, I can accept nothing. On the contrary, the absence of this primary faith is the presence of degradation. As is the flood, so is the ebb. Let this faith depart, and the very words it spake and the things it made become false and hurtful. Then falls the church, the state, art, letters, life. The doctrine of the divine nature being forgotten, a sickness infects and dwarfs the constitution. Once man was all; now he is an appendage, a nuisance. And because the indwelling Supreme Spirit cannot wholly be got rid of, the doctrine of it suffers this perversion, that the divine nature is attributed to one or two persons, and denied to all the rest, and denied with fury. The doctrine of inspiration is lost; the base doctrine of the majority of voices usurps the place of the doctrine of the soul. Miracles, prophecy, poetry, the ideal life, the holy life, exist as ancient history merely; they are not in the belief, nor in the aspiration of society; but, when suggested, seem ridiculous. Life is comic or pitiful as soon as the high ends of being fade out of sight, and man becomes near-sighted, and can only attend to what addresses the senses.

These general views, which, whilst they are general, none will contest, find abundant illustration in the history of religion, and especially in the history of the Christian church. In that, all of us have had our birth and nurture. The truth contained in that, you, my young friends, are now setting forth to teach. As the Cultus, or established worship of the civilized world, it has great historical interest for us. Of its blessed words, which have been the consolation of humanity, you need not that I should speak. I shall endeavor to discharge my duty to you on this occasion, by pointing out two errors in its administration, which daily appear more gross from the point of view we have just now taken.

Jesus Christ belonged to the true race of prophets. He saw with open eye the mystery of the soul. Drawn by its severe harmony, ravished with its beauty, he lived in it, and had his being there. Alone in all history he estimated the greatness of man. One man was true to what is in you and me. He saw that God incarnates himself in man, and evermore goes forth anew to take possession of his World. He said, in this jubilee of sublime emotion, "I am divine. Through me, God acts; through me, speaks. Would you see God, see me; or see thee, when thou also thinkest as I now think." But what a distortion did his doctrine and memory suffer in the same, in the next, and the following ages! There is no doctrine of the Reason which will bear to be taught by the Understanding. The understanding caught this high chant from the poet's lips, and said, in the next age, "This was Jehovah come down out of heaven. I will kill you, if you say he was a man." The idioms of his language and the figures of his rhetoric have usurped the place of his truth; and churches are not built on his principles, but on his tropes. Christianity became a Mythus, as the poetic teaching of Greece and of Egypt, before. He spoke of miracles; for he felt that man's life was a miracle, and all that man doth, and he knew that this daily miracle shines as the character ascends. But the word Miracle, as pronounced by Christian churches, gives a false impression; it is Monster. It is not one with the blowing clover and the falling rain.

He felt respect for Moses and the prophets, but no unfit tenderness at postponing their initial revelations to the hour and the man that now is; to the eternal revelation in the heart. Thus was he a true man. Having seen that the law in us is commanding, he would not suffer it to be commanded. Boldly, with hand, and heart, and life, he declared it was God. Thus is he, as I think, the only soul in history who has appreciated the worth of man.

1. In this point of view we become sensible of the first defect of historical Christianity. Historical Christianity has fallen into the error that corrupts all attempts to communicate religion. As it appears to us, and as it has appeared for ages, it is not the doctrine of the soul, but an exaggeration of the personal, the positive, the ritual. It has dwelt, it dwells, with noxious exaggeration about the *person* of Jesus. The soul knows no persons. It invites every man to expand to the full circle of the universe, and will have no preferences but those of spontaneous love. But by this eastern monarchy of a Christianity, which indolence and fear have built, the friend of man is made the injurer of man. The manner in which his name is surrounded with expressions which were once sallies of admiration and love, but are now petrified into official titles, kills all generous sympathy and liking. All who hear me, feel that the language that describes Christ to Europe and America is not the style of friendship and enthusiasm to a good and noble heart, but is appropriated and formal,—paints a demigod, as the Orientals or the Greeks would describe Osiris or Apollo. Accept the injurious impositions of our early catechetical instruction, and even honesty and self-denial were but splendid sins, if they did not wear the Christian name. One would rather be

"A pagan, suckled in a creed outworn,"

than to be defrauded of his manly right in coming into nature and finding not names and places, not land and professions, but even virtue and truth foreclosed and monopolized. You shall not be a man even. You shall not own the world; you shall not dare and live after the infinite Law that is in you, and in company with the infinite Beauty which heaven and earth reflect to you in all lovely forms; but you must subordinate your nature to Christ's nature; you must accept our interpretations, and take his portrait as the vulgar draw it.

That is always best which gives me to myself. The sublime is excited in me by the great stoical doctrine, Obey thyself. That which shows God in me, fortifies me. That which shows God out of me, makes me a wart and a wen. There is no longer a necessary reason for my being. Already the long shadows of untimely oblivion creep over me, and I shall decease forever.

The divine bards are the friends of my virtue, of my intellect, of my strength. They admonish me that the gleams which flash across my mind are not mine, but God's; that they had the like, and were not disobedient to the heavenly vision. So I love them. Noble provocations go out from them, inviting me to resist evil; to subdue the world; and to Be. And thus, by his holy thoughts, Jesus serves us, and thus only. To aim to convert a man by miracles is a profanation of the soul. A true conversion, a true Christ, is now, as always, to be made by the reception of beautiful sentiments. It is true that a great and rich soul, like his, falling among the simple, does so preponderate, that, as his did, it names the world. The world seems to them to exist for him, and they have not yet drunk so deeply of his sense as to see that only by coming again to themselves, or to God in themselves, can they grow forevermore. It is a low benefit to give me something; it is a high benefit to enable me to do somewhat of myself. The time is coming when all men will see that the gift of God to the soul is not a vaunting, overpowering, excluding sanctity, but a sweet, natural goodness, a goodness like thine and mine, and that so invites thine and mine to be and to grow.

The injustice of the vulgar tone of preaching is not less flagrant to Jesus than to the souls which it profanes. The preachers do not see that they make his gospel not glad, and shear him of the locks of beauty and the attributes of heaven. When I see a majestic Epaminondas, or Washington; when I see among my contemporaries a true orator, an upright judge, a dear friend; when I vibrate to the melody and fancy of a poem; I see beauty that is to be desired. And so lovely, and with yet more entire consent of my human being, sounds in my ear the severe music of the bards that have sung of the true God in all ages. Now do not degrade the life and dialogues of Christ out of the circle of this charm, by insulation and peculiarity. Let them lie as they befell, alive and warm, part of human life and of the landscape and of the cheerful day.

2. The second defect of the traditionary and limited way of using the mind of Christ is a consequence of the first; this, namely; that the Moral Nature, that Law of laws whose revelations introduce greatness—yea, God himself—into the open soul, is not explored as the fountain of the established teaching in society. Men have come to speak of the revelation as somewhat long ago given and done, as if God were dead. The injury to faith throttles the preacher; and the goodliest of institutions becomes an uncertain and inarticulate voice.

It is very certain that it is the effect of conversation with the beauty of the soul, to beget a desire and need to impart to others the same knowledge and love. If utterance is denied, the thought lies like a burden on the man. Always the seer is a sayer. Somehow his dream is told; somehow he publishes it with solemn joy: sometimes with pencil on canvas, sometimes with chisel on stone, sometimes in towers and aisles of granite, his soul's worship is builded; sometimes in anthems of indefinite music; but clearest and most permanent, in words.

The man enamored of this excellency becomes its priest or poet. The office is coeval with the world. But observe the condition, the spiritual limitation of the office. The spirit only can teach. Not any profane man, not any sensual, not any liar, not any slave can teach, but only he can give, who has; he only can create, who is. The man on whom the soul descends, through whom the soul speaks, alone can teach. Courage, piety, love, wisdom, can teach; and every man can open his door to these angels, and they shall bring him the gift of tongues. But the man who aims to speak as books enable, as synods use, as the fashion guides, and as interest commands, babbles. Let him hush.

To this holy office you propose to devote yourselves. I wish you may feel your call in throbs of desire and hope. The office is the first in the world. It is of that reality that it cannot suffer the deduction of any falsehood. And it is my duty to say to you that the need was never greater of new revelation than now. From the views I have already expressed, you will infer the sad conviction, which I share, I believe, with numbers, of the universal decay and now almost death of faith in society. The soul is not preached. The Church seems to totter to its fall, almost all life extinct. On this occasion, any complaisance would be criminal which told you, whose hope and commission it is to preach the faith of Christ, that the faith of Christ is preached.

It is time that this ill-suppressed murmur of all thoughtful men against the famine of our churches;—this moaning of the heart because it is bereaved of the consolation, the hope, the grandeur that come alone out of the culture of the moral nature,—should be heard through the sleep of indolence, and over the din of routine. This great and perpetual office of the preacher is not discharged. Preaching is the expression of the moral sentiment in application to the duties of life. In how many churches, by how many prophets, tell me, is man made sensible that he is an infinite Soul; that the earth and heavens are passing into his mind; that he is drinking forever the soul of God? Where now sounds the persuasion, that by its very melody imparadises my heart, and so affirms its own origin in heaven? Where shall I hear words such as in elder ages drew men to leave all and follow,—father and mother, house and land, wife and child? Where shall I hear these august laws of moral being so pronounced as to fill my ear, and I feel ennobled by the offer of my uttermost action and passion? The test of the true faith, certainly, should be its power to charm and command the soul, as the laws of nature control the activity of the hands,—so commanding that we find pleasure and honor in obeying. The faith should blend with the light of rising and of setting suns, with the flying cloud, the singing bird, and the breath of flowers. But now the priest's Sabbath has lost the splendor of nature; it is unlovely; we are glad when it is done; we can make, we do make, even sitting in our pews, a far better, holier, sweeter, for ourselves.

Whenever the pulpit is usurped by a formalist, then is the worshipper defrauded and disconsolate. We shrink as soon as the prayers begin, which do not uplift, but smite and offend us. We are fain to wrap our cloaks about us, and secure, as best we can, a solitude that hears not. I once heard a preacher who sorely tempted me to say I would go to church no more. Men go, thought I, where they are wont to go, else had no soul entered the temple in the afternoon. A snow-storm was falling around us. The snow-storm was real, the preacher merely spectral, and the eye felt the sad contrast in looking at him, and then out of the window behind him into the beautiful meteor of the snow. He had lived in vain. He had no one word intimating that he had laughed or wept, was married or in love, had been commended, or cheated, or chagrined. If he had ever lived and acted, we were none the wiser for it. The capital secret of his profession, namely, to convert life into truth, he had not learned. Not one fact in all his experience had he yet imported into his doctrine. This man had ploughed and planted and talked and bought and sold; he had read books; he had eaten and drunken; his head aches, his heart throbs; he smiles and suffers; yet was there not a surmise, a hint, in all the discourse, that he had ever lived at all. Not a line did he draw out of real history. The true preacher can be known by this, that he deals out to the people his life,—life passed through the fire of thought. But of the bad preacher, it could not be told from his sermon what age of the world he fell in; whether he had a father or a child; whether he was a freeholder or a pauper; whether he was a citizen or a countryman; or any other fact of his biography. It seemed strange that the people should come to church. It seemed as if their houses were very unentertaining, that they should prefer this thoughtless clamor. It shows that there is a commanding attraction in the moral sentiment, that can lend a faint tint of light to dulness and ignorance coming in its name and place. The good hearer is sure he has been touched sometimes; is sure there is somewhat to be reached, and some word that can reach it. When he listens to these vain words, he comforts himself by their relation to his remembrance of better hours, and so they clatter and echo unchallenged.

I am not ignorant that when we preach unworthily, it is not always quite in vain. There is a good ear, in some men, that draws supplies to virtue out of very indifferent nutriment. There is poetic truth concealed in all the commonplaces of prayer and of sermons, and though foolishly spoken, they may be wisely heard; for each is some select expression that broke out in a moment of piety from some stricken or jubilant soul, and its excellency made it remembered. The prayers and even the dogmas of our church are like the zodiac of Denderah and the astronomical monuments of the Hindoos, wholly insulated from anything now extant in the life and business of the people. They mark the height to which the waters once rose. But this docility is a check upon the mischief from the good and devout. In a large portion of the community, the religious service gives rise to quite other thoughts and emotions. We need not chide the negligent servant. We are struck with pity, rather, at the swift retribution of his sloth. Alas for the unhappy man that is called to stand in the pulpit, and *not* give bread of life. Everything that befalls, accuses him. Would he ask contributions for the missions, foreign or domestic? Instantly his face is suffused with shame, to propose to his parish that they should send money a hundred or a thousand miles, to furnish such poor fare as they have at home and would do well to go the hundred or the thousand miles to escape. Would he urge people to a godly way of living;—and can he ask a fellow-creature to come to Sabbath meetings, when he and they all know what is the poor uttermost they can hope for therein? Will he invite them privately to the Lord's Supper? He dares not. If no heart warm this rite, the hollow, dry, creaking formality is too plain, than that he can face a man of wit and energy and put the invitation without terror. In the street, what has he to say to the bold village blasphemer? The village blasphemer sees fear in the face, form, and gait of the minister.

Let me not taint the sincerity of this plea by any oversight of the claims of good men. I know and honor the purity and strict conscience of numbers of the clergy. What life the public worship retains, it owes to the scattered company of pious men, who minister here and there in the churches, and who, sometimes accepting with too great tenderness the tenet of the elders, have not accepted from others, but from their own heart, the genuine impulses of virtue, and so still command our love and awe, to the sanctity of character. Moreover, the exceptions are not so much to be found in a few eminent preachers, as in the better hours, the truer inspirations of all,—nay, in the sincere moments of every man. But, with whatever exception, it is still true that tradition characterizes the preaching of this country; that it comes out of the memory, and not out of the soul; that it aims at what is usual, and not at what is necessary and eternal; that thus historical Christianity destroys the power of preaching, by withdrawing it from the exploration of the moral nature of man; where the sublime is, where are the resources of astonishment and power. What a cruel injustice it is to that Law, the joy of the whole earth, which alone can make thought dear and rich; that Law whose fatal sureness the astronomical orbits poorly emulate;—that it is travestied and depreciated, that it is behooted and behowled, and not a trait, not a word of it articulated. The pulpit in losing sight of this Law, loses its reason, and gropes after it knows not what. And for want of this culture the soul of the community is sick and faithless. It wants nothing so much as a stern, high, stoical, Christian discipline, to make it know itself and the divinity that speaks through it. Now man is ashamed of himself; he skulks and sneaks through the world, to be tolerated, to be pitied, and scarcely in a thousand years does any man dare to be wise and good, and so draw after him the tears and blessings of his kind.

Certainly there have been periods when, from the inactivity of the intellect on certain truths, a greater faith was possible in names and persons. The Puritans in England and America found in the Christ of the Catholic Church and in the dogmas inherited from Rome, scope for their austere piety and their longings for civil freedom. But their creed is passing away, and none arises in its room. I think no man can go with his thoughts about him into one of our churches, without feeling that what hold the public worship had on men is gone, or going. It has lost its grasp on the affection of the good and the fear of the bad. In the country, neighborhoods, half parishes are *signing off*, to use the local term. It is already beginning to indicate character and religion to withdraw from the religious meetings. I have heard a devout person, who prized the Sabbath, say in bitterness of heart, "On Sundays, it seems wicked to go to church." And the motive that holds the best there is now only a hope and a waiting. What was once a mere circumstance, that the best and the worst men in the parish, the poor and the rich, the learned and the ignorant, young and old, should meet one day as fellows in one house, in sign of an equal right in the soul, has come to be a paramount motive for going thither.

My friends, in these two errors, I think, I find the causes of a decaying church and a wasting unbelief. And what greater calamity can fall upon a nation than the loss of worship? Then all things go to decay. Genius leaves the temple to haunt the senate or the market. Literature becomes frivolous. Science is cold. The eye of youth is not lighted by the hope of other worlds, and age is without honor. Society lives to trifles, and when men die we do not mention them.

And now, my brothers, you will ask, What in these desponding days can be done by us? The remedy is already declared in the ground of our complaint of the Church. We have contrasted the Church with the Soul. In the soul then let the redemption be sought. Wherever a man comes, there comes revolution. The old is for slaves. When a man comes, all books are legible, all things transparent, all religions are forms. He is religious. Man is the wonderworker. He is seen amid miracles. All men bless and curse. He saith yea and nay, only. The stationariness of religion; the assumption that the age of inspiration is past, that the Bible is closed; the fear of degrading the character of Jesus by representing him as a man;—indicate with sufficient clearness the falsehood of our theology. It is the office of a true teacher to show us that God is, not was; that He speaketh, not spake. The true Christianity,—a faith like Christ's in the infinitude of man,—is lost. None believeth in the soul of man, but only in some man or person old and departed. Ah me! no man goeth alone. All men go in flocks to this saint or that poet, avoiding the God who seeth in secret. They cannot see in secret; they love to be blind in public. They think society wiser than their soul, and know not that one soul, and their soul, is wiser than the whole world. See how nations and races flit by on the sea of time and leave no ripple to tell where they floated or sunk, and one good soul shall make the name of Moses, or of Zeno, or of Zoroaster, reverend forever. None assayeth the stern ambition to be the Self of the nation and of nature, but each would be an easy secondary to some Christian scheme, or sectarian connection, or some eminent man. Once leave your own knowledge of God, your own sentiment, and take secondary knowledge, as St. Paul's, or George Fox's, or Swedenborg's, and you get wide from God with every year this secondary form lasts, and if, as now, for centuries,—the chasm yawns to that breadth, that men can scarcely be convinced there is in them anything divine.

Let me admonish you, first of all, to go alone; to refuse the good models, even those which are sacred in the imagination of men, and dare to love God without mediator or veil. Friends enough you shall find who will hold up to your emulation Wesleys and Oberlins, Saints and Prophets. Thank God for these good men, but say, "I also am a man." Imitation cannot go above its model. The imitator dooms himself to hopeless mediocrity. The inventor did it because it was natural to him, and so in him it has a charm. In the imitator something else is natural, and he bereaves himself of his own beauty, to come short of another man's.

Yourself a newborn bard of the Holy Ghost, cast behind you all conformity, and acquaint men at first hand with Deity. Look to it first and only, that fashion, custom, authority, pleasure, and money, are nothing to you,—are not bandages over your eyes, that you cannot see,—but live with the privilege of the immeasurable mind. Not too anxious to visit periodically all families and each family in your parish connection,—when you meet one of these men or women, be to them a divine man; be to them thought and virtue; let their timid aspirations find in you a friend; let their trampled instincts be genially tempted out in your atmosphere; let their doubts know that you have doubted, and their wonder feel that you have wondered. By trusting your own heart, you shall gain more confidence in other men. For all our penny-wisdom, for all our soul-destroying slavery to habit, it is not to be doubted that all men have sublime thoughts; that all men value the few real hours of life; they love to be heard; they love to be caught up into the vision of principles. We mark with light in the memory the few interviews we have had, in the dreary years of routine and of sin, with souls that made our souls wiser; that spoke what we thought; that told us what we knew; that gave us leave to be what we inly were. Discharge to men the priestly office, and, present or absent, you shall be followed with their love as by an angel.

And, to this end, let us not aim at common degrees of merit. Can we not leave, to such as love it, the virtue that glitters for the commendation of society, and ourselves pierce the deep solitudes of absolute ability and worth? We easily come up to the standard of goodness in society. Society's praise can be cheaply secured, and almost all men are content with those easy merits; but the instant effect of conversing with God will be to put them away. There are persons who are not actors, not speakers, but influences; persons too great for fame, for display; who disdain eloquence; to whom all we call art and artist, seems too nearly allied to show and by-ends, to the exaggeration of the finite and selfish, and loss of the universal. The orators, the poets, the commanders encroach on us only as fair women do, by our allowance and homage. Slight them by preoccupation of mind, slight them, as you can well afford to do, by high and universal aims, and they instantly feel that you have right, and that it is in lower places that they must shine. They also feel your right; for they with you are open to the influx of the all-knowing Spirit, which annihilates before its broad noon the little shades and gradations of intelligence in the compositions we call wiser and wisest.

In such high communion let us study the grand strokes of rectitude: a bold benevolence, an independence of friends, so that not the unjust wishes of those who love us shall impair our freedom, but we shall resist for truth's sake the freest flow of kindness, and appeal to sympathies far in advance; and,—what is the highest form in which we know this beautiful element,—a certain solidity of merit, that has nothing to do with opinion, and which is so essentially and manifestly virtue, that it is taken for granted that the right, the brave, the generous step will be taken by it, and nobody thinks of commending it. You would compliment a coxcomb doing a good act, but you would not praise an angel. The silence that accepts merit as the most natural thing in the world, is the highest applause. Such souls, when they appear, are the Imperial Guard of Virtue, the perpetual reserve, the dictators of fortune. One needs not praise their courage,—they are the heart and soul of nature. O my friends, there are resources in us on which we have not drawn. There are men who rise refreshed on hearing a threat; men to whom a crisis which intimidates and paralyzes the majority,—demanding not the faculties of prudence and thrift, but comprehension, immovableness, the readiness of sacrifice,—comes graceful and beloved as a bride. Napoleon said of Massena, that he was not himself until the battle began to go against him; then, when the dead began to fall in ranks around him, awoke his powers of combination, and he put on terror and victory as a robe. So it is in rugged crises, in unweariable endurance, and in aims which put sympathy out of question, that the angel is shown. But these are heights that we can scarce remember and look up to without contrition and shame. Let us thank God that such things exist.

And now let us do what we can to rekindle the smouldering, nigh quenched fire on the altar. The evils of the church that now is are manifest. The question returns, What shall we do?

I confess, all attempts to project and establish a Cultus with new rites and forms, seem to me vain. Faith makes us and not we it, and faith makes its own forms. All attempts to contrive a system are as cold as the new worship introduced by the French to the goddess of Reason,—to-day, pasteboard and filigree, and ending to-morrow in madness and murder. Rather let the breath of new life be breathed by you through the forms already existing. For if once you are alive, you shall find they shall become plastic and new. The remedy to their deformity is first, soul, and second, soul, and evermore, soul. A whole popedom of forms one pulsation of virtue can uplift and vivify. Two inestimable advantages Christianity has given us; first the Sabbath, the jubilee of the whole world, whose light dawns welcome alike into the closet of the philosopher, into the garret of toil, and into prison-cells, and everywhere suggests, even to the vile, the dignity of spiritual being. Let it stand forevermore, a temple, which new love, new faith, new sight shall restore to more than its first splendor to mankind. And secondly, the institution of preaching,—the speech of man to men,—essentially the most flexible of all organs, of all forms. What hinders that now, everywhere, in pulpits, in lecture-rooms, in houses, in fields, wherever the invitation of men or your own occasions lead you, you speak the very truth, as your life and conscience teach it, and cheer the waiting, fainting hearts of men with new hope and new revelation?

I look for the hour when that supreme Beauty which ravished the souls of those Eastern men, and chiefly of those Hebrews, and through their lips spoke oracles to all time, shall speak in the West also. The Hebrew and Greek Scriptures contain immortal sentences, that have been bread of life to millions. But they have no epical integrity; are fragmentary; are not shown in their order to the intellect. I look for the new Teacher that shall follow so far those shining laws that he shall see them come full circle; shall see their rounding complete grace; shall see the world to be the mirror of the soul; shall see the identity of the law of gravitation with purity of heart; and shall show that the Ought, that Duty, is one thing with Science, with Beauty, and with Joy.

1838

SELF-RELIANCE

"Ne te quæsiveris extra."

"Man is his own star; and the soul that can
Render an honest and a perfect man
Commands all light, all influence, all fate;
Nothing to him falls early or too late.
Our acts our angels are, or good or ill,
Our fatal shadows that walk by us still."

Epilogue to Beaumont and
Fletcher's *Honest Man's Fortune*

Cast the bantling on the rocks,
Suckle him with the she-wolf's teat,
Wintered with the hawk and fox,
Power and speed be hands and feet.

I read the other day some verses written by an eminent painter which were original and not conventional. The soul always hears an admonition in such lines, let the subject be what it may. The sentiment they instil is of more value than any thought they may contain. To believe your own thought, to believe that what is true for you in your private heart is true for all men,—that is genius. Speak your latent conviction, and it shall be the universal sense; for the inmost in due time becomes the outmost, and our first thought is rendered back to us by the trumpets of the Last Judgment. Familiar as the voice of the mind is to each, the highest merit we ascribe to Moses, Plato and Milton is that they set at naught books and traditions, and spoke not what men, but what *they* thought. A man should learn to detect and watch that gleam of light which flashes across his mind from within, more than the lustre of the firmament of bards and sages. Yet he dismisses without notice his thought, because it is his. In every work of genius we recognize our own rejected thoughts; they come back to us with a certain alienated majesty. Great works of art have no more affecting lesson for us than this. They teach us to abide by our spontaneous impression with good-humored inflexibility then most when the whole cry of voices is on the other side. Else to-morrow a stranger will say with masterly good sense precisely what we have thought and felt all the time, and we shall be forced to take with shame our own opinion from another.

There is a time in every man's education when he arrives at the conviction that envy is ignorance; that imitation is suicide; that he must take himself for better for worse as his portion; that though the wide universe is full of good, no kernel of nourishing corn can come to him but through his toil bestowed on that plot of ground which is given to him to till. The power which resides in him is new in nature, and none but he knows what that is which he can do, nor does he know until he has tried. Not for nothing one face, one character, one fact, makes much impression on him, and another none. This sculpture in the memory is not without preëstablished harmony. The eye was placed where one ray should fall, that it might testify of that particular ray. We but half express ourselves, and are ashamed of that divine idea which each of us represents. It may be safely trusted as proportionate and of good issues, so it be faithfully imparted, but God will not have his work made manifest by cowards. A man is relieved and gay when he has put his heart into his work and done his best; but what he has said or done otherwise shall give him no peace. It is a deliverance which does not deliver. In the attempt his genius deserts him; no muse befriends; no invention, no hope.

Trust thyself: every heart vibrates to that iron string. Accept the place the divine providence has found for you, the society of your contemporaries, the connection of events. Great men have always done so, and confided themselves childlike to the genius of their age, betraying their perception that the absolutely trustworthy was seated at their heart, working through their hands, predominating in all their being. And we are now men, and must accept in the highest mind the same transcendent destiny; and not minors and invalids in a protected corner, not cowards fleeing before a revolution, but guides, redeemers and benefactors, obeying the Almighty effort and advancing on Chaos and the Dark.

What pretty oracles nature yields us on this text in the face and behavior of children, babes, and even brutes! That divided and rebel mind, that distrust of a sentiment because our arithmetic has computed the strength and means opposed to our purpose, these have not. Their mind being whole, their eye is as yet unconquered, and when we look in their faces we are disconcerted. Infancy conforms to nobody; all conform to it; so that one babe commonly makes four or five out of the adults who prattle and play to it. So God has armed youth and puberty and manhood no less with its own piquancy and charm, and made it enviable and gracious and its claims not to be put by, if it will stand by itself. Do not think the youth has no force, because he cannot speak to you and me. Hark! in the next room his voice is sufficiently clear and emphatic. It seems he knows how to speak to his contemporaries. Bashful or bold then, he will know how to make us seniors very unnecessary.

The nonchalance of boys who are sure of a dinner, and would disdain as much as a lord to do or say aught to conciliate one, is the healthy attitude of human nature. A boy is in the parlor what the pit is in the playhouse; independent, irresponsible, looking out from his corner on such people and facts as pass by, he tries and sentences them on their merits, in the swift, summary way of boys, as good, bad, interesting, silly, eloquent, troublesome. He cumbers himself never about consequences, about interests; he gives an independent, genuine verdict. You must court him; he does not court you. But the man is as it were clapped into jail by his consciousness. As soon as he has once acted or spoken with *éclat* he is a committed person, watched by the sympathy or the hatred of hundreds, whose affections must now enter into his account. There is no Lethe for this. Ah, that he could pass again into his neutrality! Who can thus avoid all pledges and, having observed, observe again from the same unaffected, unbiased, unbribable, unaffrighted innocence,—must always be formidable. He would utter opinions on all passing affairs, which being seen to be not private but necessary, would sink like darts into the ear of men and put them in fear.

These are the voices which we hear in solitude, but they grow faint and inaudible as we enter into the world. Society everywhere is in conspiracy against the manhood of every one of its members. Society is a joint-stock company, in which the members agree, for the better securing of his bread to each shareholder, to surrender the liberty and culture of the eater. The virtue in most request is conformity. Self-reliance is its aversion. It loves not realities and creators, but names and customs.

Whoso would be a man, must be a nonconformist. He who would gather immortal palms must not be hindered by the name of goodness, but must explore if it be goodness. Nothing is at last sacred but the integrity of your own mind. Absolve you to yourself, and you shall have the suffrage of the world. I remember an answer which when quite young I was prompted to make to a valued adviser who was wont to importune me with the dear old doctrines of the church. On my saying, "What have I to do with the sacredness of traditions, if I live wholly from within?" my friend suggested,—"But these impulses may be from below, not from above." I replied, "They do not seem to me to be such; but if I am the Devil's child, I will live then from the Devil." No law can be sacred to me but that of my nature. Good and bad are but names very readily transferable to that or this; the only right is what is after my constitution; the only wrong what is against it. A man is to carry himself in the presence of all opposition as if every thing were titular and ephemeral but he. I am ashamed to think how easily we capitulate to badges and names, to large societies and dead institutions. Every decent and well-spoken individual affects and sways me more than is right. I ought to go upright and vital, and speak the rude truth in all ways. If malice and vanity wear the coat of philanthropy, shall that pass? If an angry bigot assumes this bountiful cause of Abolition, and comes to me with his last news from Barbadoes, why should I not say to him, "Go love thy infant; love thy wood-chopper; be good-natured and modest; have that grace; and never varnish your hard, uncharitable ambition with this incredible tenderness for black folk a thousand miles off. Thy love afar is spite at home." Rough and graceless would be such greeting, but truth is handsomer than the affectation of love. Your goodness must have some edge to it,—else it is none. The doctrine of hatred must be preached, as the counteraction of the doctrine of love, when that pules and whines. I shun father and mother and wife and brother when my genius calls me. I would write on the lintels of the door-post, *Whim*. I hope it is somewhat better than whim at last, but we cannot spend the day in explanation. Expect me not to show cause why I seek or why I exclude company. Then again, do not tell me, as a good man did to-day, of my obligation to put all poor men in good situations. Are they *my* poor? I tell thee, thou foolish philanthropist, that I grudge the dollar, the dime, the cent I give to such men as do not belong to me and to whom I do not belong. There is a class of persons to whom by all spiritual affinity I am bought and sold; for them I will go to prison if need be; but your miscellaneous popular charities; the education at college of fools; the building of meeting-houses to the vain end to which many now stand; alms to sots, and the thousand-fold Relief Societies;—though I confess with shame I sometimes succumb and give the dollar, it is a wicked dollar, which by and by I shall have the manhood to withhold.

Virtues are, in the popular estimate, rather the exception than the rule. There is the man *and* his virtues. Men do what is called a good action, as some piece of courage or charity, much as they would pay a fine in expiation of daily non-appearance on parade. Their works are done as an apology or extenuation of their living in the world,—as invalids and the insane pay a high board. Their virtues are penances. I do not wish to expiate, but to live. My life is for itself and not for a spectacle. I much prefer that it should be of a lower strain, so it be genuine and equal, than that it should be glittering and unsteady. I wish it to be sound and sweet, and not to need diet and bleeding. I ask primary evidence that you are a man, and refuse this appeal from the man to his actions. I know that for myself it makes no difference whether I do or forbear those actions which are reckoned excellent. I cannot consent to pay for a privilege where I have intrinsic right. Few and mean as my gifts may be, I actually am, and do not need for my own assurance or the assurance of my fellows any secondary testimony.

What I must do is all that concerns me, not what the people think. This rule, equally arduous in actual and in intellectual life, may serve for the whole distinction between greatness and meanness. It is the harder because you will always find those who think they know what is your duty better than you know it. It is easy in the world to live after the world's opinion; it is easy in solitude to live after our own; but the great man is he who in the midst of the crowd keeps with perfect sweetness the independence of solitude.

The objection to conforming to usages that have become dead to you is that it scatters your force. It loses your time and blurs the impression of your character. If you maintain a dead church, contribute to a dead Bible-society, vote with a great party either for the government or against it, spread your table like base housekeepers,—under all these screens I have difficulty to detect the precise man you are: and of course so much force is withdrawn from your proper life. But do your work, and I shall know you. Do your work, and you shall reinforce yourself. A man must consider what a blind-man's-buff is this game of conformity. If I know your sect I anticipate your argument. I hear a preacher announce for his text and topic the expediency of one of the institutions of his church. Do I not know beforehand that not possibly can he say a new and spontaneous word? Do I not know that with all this ostentation of examining the grounds of the institution he will do no such thing? Do I not know that he is pledged to himself not to look but at one side, the permitted side, not as a man, but as a parish minister? He is a retained attorney, and these airs of the bench are the emptiest affectation. Well, most men have bound their eyes with one or another handkerchief, and attached themselves to some one of these communities of opinion. This conformity makes them not false in a few particulars, authors of a few lies, but false in all particulars. Their every truth is not quite true. Their two is not the real two, their four not the real four; so that every word they say chagrins us and we know not where to begin to set them right. Meantime nature is not slow to equip us in the prison-uniform of the party to which we adhere. We come to wear one cut of face and figure, and acquire by degrees the gentlest asinine expression. There is a mortifying experience in particular, which does not fail to wreak itself also in the general history; I mean "the foolish face of praise," the forced smile which we put on in company where we do not feel at ease, in answer to conversation which does not interest us. The muscles, not spontaneously moved but moved by a low usurping wilfulness, grow tight about the outline of the face, with the most disagreeable sensation.

For nonconformity the world whips you with its displeasure. And therefore a man must know how to estimate a sour face. The by-standers look askance on him in the public street or in the friend's parlor. If this aversion had its origin in contempt and resistance like his own he might well go home with a sad countenance; but the sour faces of the multitude, like their sweet faces, have no deep cause, but are put on and off as the wind blows and a newspaper directs. Yet is the discontent of the multitude more formidable than that of the senate and the college. It is easy enough for a firm man who knows the world to brook the rage of the cultivated classes. Their rage is decorous and prudent, for they are timid, as being very vulnerable themselves. But when to their feminine rage the indignation of the people is added, when the ignorant and the poor are aroused, when the unintelligent brute force that lies at the bottom of society is made to growl and mow, it needs the habit of magnanimity and religion to treat it godlike as a trifle of no concernment.

The other terror that scares us from self-trust is our consistency; a reverence for our past act or word because the eyes of others have no other data for computing our orbit than our past acts, and we are loth to disappoint them.

But why should you keep your head over your shoulder? Why drag about this corpse of your memory, lest you contradict somewhat you have stated in this or that public place?

Suppose you should contradict yourself; what then? It seems to be a rule of wisdom never to rely on your memory alone, scarcely even in acts of pure memory, but to bring the past for judgment into the thousand-eyed present, and live ever in a new day. In your metaphysics you have denied personality to the Deity, yet when the devout motions of the soul come, yield to them heart and life, though they should clothe God with shape and color. Leave your theory, as Joseph his coat in the hand of the harlot, and flee.

A foolish consistency is the hobgoblin of little minds, adored by little statesmen and philosophers and divines. With consistency a great soul has simply nothing to do. He may as well concern himself with his shadow on the wall. Speak what you think now in hard words and to-morrow speak what to-morrow thinks in hard words again, though it contradict every thing you said to-day.—"Ah, so you shall be sure to be misunderstood."—Is it so bad then to be misunderstood? Pythagoras was misunderstood, and Socrates, and Jesus, and Luther, and Copernicus, and Galileo, and Newton, and every pure and wise spirit that ever took flesh. To be great is to be misunderstood.

I suppose no man can violate his nature. All the sallies of his will are rounded in by the law of his being, as the inequalities of Andes and Himmaleh are insignificant in the curve of the sphere. Nor does it matter how you gauge and try him. A character is like an acrostic or Alexandrian stanza;—read it forward, backward, or across, it still spells the same thing. In this pleasing contrite wood-life which God allows me, let me record day by day my honest thought without prospect or retrospect, and, I cannot doubt, it will be found symmetrical, though I mean it not and see it not. My book should smell of pines and resound with the hum of insects. The swallow over my window should interweave that thread or straw he carries in his bill into my web also. We pass for what we are. Character teaches above our wills. Men imagine that they communicate their virtue or vice only by overt actions, and do not see that virtue or vice emit a breath every moment.

There will be an agreement in whatever variety of actions,

so they be each honest and natural in their hour. For of one will, the actions will be harmonious, however unlike they seem. These varieties are lost sight of at a little distance, at a little height of thought. One tendency unites them all. The voyage of the best ship is a zigzag line of a hundred tacks. See the line from a sufficient distance, and it strengthens itself to the average tendency. Your genuine action will explain itself and will explain your other genuine actions. Your conformity explains nothing. Act singly, and what you have already done singly will justify you now. Greatness appeals to the future. If I can be firm enough to-day to do right and scorn eyes, I must have done so much right before as to defend me now. Be it how it will, do right now. Always scorn appearances and you always may. The force of character is cumulative. All the foregone days of virtue work their health into this. What makes the majesty of the heroes of the senate and the field, which so fills the imagination? The consciousness of a train of great days and victories behind. They shed a united light on the advancing actor. He is attended as by a visible escort of angels. That is it which throws thunder into Chatham's voice, and dignity into Washington's port, and America into Adams's eye. Honor is venerable to us because it is no ephemera. It is always ancient virtue. We worship it to-day because it is not of to-day. We love it and pay it homage because it is not a trap for our love and homage, but is self-dependent, self-derived, and therefore of an old immaculate pedigree, even if shown in a young person.

I hope in these days we have heard the last of conformity and consistency. Let the words be gazetted and ridiculous henceforward. Instead of the gong for dinner, let us hear a whistle from the Spartan fife. Let us never bow and apologize more. A great man is coming to eat at my house. I do not wish to please him; I wish that he should wish to please me. I will stand here for humanity, and though I would make it kind, I would make it true. Let us affront and reprimand the smooth mediocrity and squalid contentment of the times, and hurl in the face of custom and trade and office, the fact which is the upshot of all history, that there is a great responsible Thinker and Actor working wherever a man works; that a true man belongs to no other time or place, but is the centre of things. Where he is, there is nature. He measures you and all men and all events. Ordinarily, every body in society reminds us of somewhat else, or of some other person. Character, reality, reminds you of nothing else; it takes place of the whole creation. The man must be so much that he must make all circumstances indifferent. Every true man is a cause, a country, and an age; requires infinite spaces and numbers and time fully to accomplish his design;—and posterity seem to follow his steps as a train of clients. A man Cæsar is born, and for ages after we have a Roman Empire. Christ is born, and millions of minds so grow and cleave to his genius that he is confounded with virtue and the possible of man. An institution is the lengthened shadow of one man; as, Monachism, of the Hermit Antony; the Reformation, of Luther; Quakerism, of Fox; Methodism, of Wesley; Abolition, of Clarkson. Scipio, Milton called "the height of Rome;" and all history resolves itself very easily into the biography of a few stout and earnest persons.

Let a man then know his worth, and keep things under his feet. Let him not peep or steal, or skulk up and down with the air of a charity-boy, a bastard, or an interloper in the world which exists for him. But the man in the street, finding no worth in himself which corresponds to the force which built a tower or sculptured a marble god, feels poor when he looks on these. To him a palace, a statue, or a costly book have an alien and forbidding air, much like a gay equipage, and seem to say like that, "Who are you, Sir?" Yet they all are his, suitors for his notice, petitioners to his faculties that they will come out and take possession. The picture waits for my verdict; it is not to command me, but I am to settle its claims to praise. That popular fable of the sot who was picked up dead-drunk in the street, carried to the duke's house, washed and dressed and laid in the duke's bed, and, on his waking, treated with all obsequious ceremony like the duke, and assured that he had been insane, owes its popularity to the fact that it symbolizes so well the state of man, who is in the world a sort of sot, but now and then wakes up, exercises his reason and finds himself a true prince.

Our reading is mendicant and sycophantic. In history our imagination plays us false. Kingdom and lordship, power and estate, are a gaudier vocabulary than private John and Edward in a small house and common day's work; but the things of life are the same to both; the sum total of both is the same. Why all this deference to Alfred and Scanderbeg and Gustavus? Suppose they were virtuous; did they wear out virtue? As great a stake depends on your private act to-day as followed their public and renowned steps. When private men shall act with original views, the lustre will be transferred from the actions of kings to those of gentlemen.

The world has been instructed by its kings, who have so magnetized the eyes of nations. It has been taught by this colossal symbol the mutual reverence that is due from man to man. The joyful loyalty with which men have everywhere suffered the king, the noble, or the great proprietor to walk among them by a law of his own, make his own scale of men and things and reverse theirs, pay for benefits not with money but with honor, and represent the law in his person, was the hieroglyphic by which they obscurely signified their consciousness of their own right and comeliness, the right of every man.

The magnetism which all original action exerts is explained when we inquire the reason of self-trust. Who is the Trustee? What is the aboriginal Self, on which a universal reliance may be grounded? What is the nature and power of that science-baffling star, without parallax, without calculable elements, which shoots a ray of beauty even into trivial and impure actions, if the least mark of independence appear? The inquiry leads us to that source, at once the essence of genius, of virtue, and of life, which we call Spontaneity or Instinct. We denote this primary wisdom as Intuition, whilst all later teachings are tuitions. In that deep force, the last fact behind which analysis cannot go, all things find their common origin. For the sense of being which in calm hours arises, we know not how, in the soul, is not diverse from things, from space, from light, from time, from man, but one with them and proceeds obviously from the same source whence their life and being also proceed. We first share the life by which things exist and afterwards see them as appearances in nature and forget that we have shared their cause. Here is the fountain of action and of thought. Here are the lungs of that inspiration which giveth man wisdom and which cannot be denied without impiety and atheism. We lie in the lap of immense intelligence, which makes us receivers of its truth and organs of its activity. When we discern justice, when we discern truth, we do nothing of ourselves, but allow a passage to its beams. If we ask whence this comes, if we seek to pry into the soul that causes, all philosophy is at fault. Its presence or its absence is all we can affirm. Every man discriminates between the voluntary acts of his mind and his involuntary perceptions, and knows that to his involuntary perceptions a perfect faith is due. He may err in the expression of them, but he knows that these things are so, like day and night, not to be disputed. My wilful actions and acquisitions are but roving;—the idlest reverie, the faintest native emotion, command my curiosity and respect. Thoughtless people contradict as readily the statement of perceptions as of opinions, or rather much more readily; for they do not distinguish between perception and notion. They fancy that I choose to see this or that thing. But perception is not whimsical, but fatal. If I see a trait, my children will see it after me, and in course of time all mankind,—although it may chance that no one has seen it before me. For my perception of it is as much a fact as the sun.

The relations of the soul to the divine spirit are so pure that it is profane to seek to interpose helps. It must be that when God speaketh he should communicate, not one thing, but all things; should fill the world with his voice; should scatter forth light, nature, time, souls, from the centre of the present thought; and new date and new create the whole. Whenever a mind is simple and receives a divine wisdom, old things pass away,—means, teachers, texts, temples fall; it lives now, and absorbs past and future into the present hour. All things are made sacred by relation to it,—one as much as another. All things are dissolved to their centre by their cause, and in the universal miracle petty and particular miracles disappear. If therefore a man claims to know and speak of God and carries you backward to the phraseology of some old mouldered nation in another country, in another world, believe him not. Is the acorn better than the oak which is its fulness and completion? Is the parent better than the child into whom he has cast his ripened being? Whence then this worship of the past? The centuries are conspirators against the sanity and authority of the soul. Time and space are but physiological colors which the eye makes, but the soul is light: where it is, is day; where it was, is night; and history is an impertinence and an injury if it be any thing more than a cheerful apologue or parable of my being and becoming.

Man is timid and apologetic; he is no longer upright; he dares not say "I think," "I am," but quotes some saint or sage. He is ashamed before the blade of grass or the blowing rose. These roses under my window make no reference to former roses or to better ones; they are for what they are; they exist with God to-day. There is no time to them. There is simply the rose; it is perfect in every moment of its existence. Before a leaf-bud has burst, its whole life acts; in the full-blown flower there is no more; in the leafless root there is no less. Its nature is satisfied and it satisfies nature in all moments alike. But man postpones or remembers; he does not live in the present, but with reverted eye laments the past, or, heedless of the riches that surround him, stands on tiptoe to foresee the future. He cannot be happy and strong until he too lives with nature in the present, above time.

This should be plain enough. Yet see what strong intellects dare not yet hear God himself unless he speak the phraseology of I know not what David, or Jeremiah, or Paul. We shall not always set so great a price on a few texts, on a few lives. We are like children who repeat by rote the sentences of grandames and tutors, and, as they grow older, of the men of talents and character they chance to see,—painfully recollecting the exact words they spoke; afterwards, when they come into the point of view which those had who uttered these sayings, they understand them and are willing to let the words go; for at any time they can use words as good when occasion comes. If we live truly, we shall see truly. It is as easy for the strong man to be strong, as it is for the weak to be weak. When we have new perception, we shall gladly disburden the memory of its hoarded treasures as old rubbish. When a man lives with God, his voice shall be as sweet as the murmur of the brook and the rustle of the corn.

And now at last the highest truth on this subject remains unsaid; probably cannot be said; for all that we say is the far-off remembering of the intuition. That thought by what I can now nearest approach to say it, is this. When good is near you, when you have life in yourself, it is not by any known or accustomed way; you shall not discern the footprints of any other; you shall not see the face of man; you shall not hear any name;—the way, the thought, the good, shall be wholly strange and new. It shall exclude example and experience. You take the way from man, not to man. All persons that ever existed are its forgotten ministers. Fear and hope are alike beneath it. There is somewhat low even in hope. In the hour of vision there is nothing that can be called gratitude, nor properly joy. The soul raised over passion beholds identity and eternal causation, perceives the self-existence of Truth and Right, and calms itself with knowing that all things go well. Vast spaces of nature, the Atlantic Ocean, the South Sea; long intervals of time, years, centuries, are of no account. This which I think and feel underlay every former state of life and circumstances, as it does underlie my present, and what is called life and what is called death.

Life only avails, not the having lived. Power ceases in the instant of repose; it resides in the moment of transition from a past to a new state, in the shooting of the gulf, in the darting to an aim. This one fact the world hates; that the soul *becomes;* for that forever degrades the past, turns all riches to poverty, all reputation to a shame, confounds the saint with the rogue, shoves Jesus and Judas equally aside. Why then do we prate of self-reliance? Inasmuch as the soul is present there will be power not confident but agent. To talk of reliance is a poor external way of speaking. Speak rather of that which relies because it works and is. Who has more obedience than I masters me, though he should not raise his finger. Round him I must revolve by the gravitation of spirits. We fancy it rhetoric when we speak of eminent virtue. We do not yet see that virtue is Height, and that a man or a company of men, plastic and permeable to principles, by the law of nature must overpower and ride all cities, nations, kings, rich men, poets, who are not.

This is the ultimate fact which we so quickly reach on this, as on every topic, the resolution of all into the ever-blessed ONE. Self-existence is the attribute of the Supreme Cause, and it constitutes the measure of good by the degree in which it enters into all lower forms. All things real are so by so much virtue as they contain. Commerce, husbandry, hunting, whaling, war, eloquence, personal weight, are somewhat, and engage my respect as examples of its presence and impure action. I see the same law working in nature for conservation and growth. Power is, in nature, the essential measure of right. Nature suffers nothing to remain in her kingdoms which cannot help itself. The genesis and maturation of a planet, its poise and orbit, the bended tree recovering itself from the strong wind, the vital resources of every animal and vegetable, are demonstrations of the self-sufficing and therefore self-relying soul.

Thus all concentrates: let us not rove; let us sit at home with the cause. Let us stun and astonish the intruding rabble of men and books and institutions by a simple declaration of the divine fact. Bid the invaders take the shoes from off their feet, for God is here within. Let our simplicity judge them, and our docility to our own law demonstrate the poverty of nature and fortune beside our native riches.

But now we are a mob. Man does not stand in awe of man, nor is his genius admonished to stay at home, to put itself in communication with the internal ocean, but it goes abroad to beg a cup of water of the urns of other men. We must go alone. I like the silent church before the service begins, better than any preaching. How far off, how cool, how chaste the persons look, begirt each one with a precinct or sanctuary! So let us always sit. Why should we assume the faults of our friend, or wife, or father, or child, because they sit around our hearth, or are said to have the same blood? All men have my blood and I all men's. Not for that will I adopt their petulance or folly, even to the extent of being ashamed of it. But your isolation must not be mechanical, but spiritual, that is, must be elevation. At times the whole world seems to be in conspiracy to importune you with emphatic trifles. Friend, client, child, sickness, fear, want, charity, all knock at once at thy closet door and say,—"Come out unto us." But keep thy state; come not into their confusion. The power men possess to annoy me I give them by a weak curiosity. No man can come near me but through my act. "What we love that we have, but by desire we bereave ourselves of the love."

If we cannot at once rise to the sanctities of obedience and faith, let us at least resist our temptations; let us enter into the state of war and wake Thor and Woden, courage and constancy, in our Saxon breasts. This is to be done in our smooth times by speaking the truth. Check this lying hospitality and lying affection. Live no longer to the expectation of these deceived and deceiving people with whom we converse. Say to them, "O father, O mother, O wife, O brother, O friend, I have lived with you after appearances hitherto. Henceforward I am the truth's. Be it known unto you that henceforward I obey no law less than the eternal law. I will have no covenants but proximities. I shall endeavor to nourish my parents, to support my family, to be the chaste husband of one wife,—but these relations I must fill after a new and unprecedented way. I appeal from your customs. I must be myself. I cannot break myself any longer for you, or you. If you can love me for what I am, we shall be the happier. If you cannot, I will still seek to deserve that you should. I will not hide my tastes or aversions. I will so trust that what is deep is holy, that I will do strongly before the sun and moon whatever inly rejoices me and the heart appoints. If you are noble, I will love you; if you are not, I will not hurt you and myself by hypocritical attentions. If you are true, but not in the same truth with me, cleave to your companions; I will seek my own. I do this not selfishly but humbly and truly. It is alike your interest, and mine, and all men's, however long we have dwelt in lies, to live in truth. Does this sound harsh to-day? You will soon love what is dictated by your nature as well as mine, and if we follow the truth it will bring us out safe at last."—But so may you give these friends pain. Yes, but I cannot sell my liberty and my power, to save their sensibility. Besides, all persons have their moments of reason, when they look out into the region of absolute truth; then will they justify me and do the same thing.

The populace think that your rejection of popular standards is a rejection of all standard, and mere antinomianism; and the bold sensualist will use the name of philosophy to gild his crimes. But the law of consciousness abides. There are two confessionals, in one or the other of which we must be shriven. You may fulfil your round of duties by clearing yourself in the *direct*, or in the *reflex* way. Consider whether you have satisfied your relations to father, mother, cousin, neighbor, town, cat and dog—whether any of these can upbraid you. But I may also neglect this reflex standard and absolve me to myself. I have my own stern claims and perfect circle. It denies the name of duty to many offices that are called duties. But if I can discharge its debts it enables me to dispense with the popular code. If any one imagines that this law is lax, let him keep its commandment one day.

And truly it demands something godlike in him who has cast off the common motives of humanity and has ventured to trust himself for a taskmaster. High be his heart, faithful his will, clear his sight, that he may in good earnest be doctrine, society, law, to himself, that a simple purpose may be to him as strong as iron necessity is to others!

If any man consider the present aspects of what is called by distinction *society*, he will see the need of these ethics. The sinew and heart of man seem to be drawn out, and we are become timorous, desponding whimperers. We are afraid of truth, afraid of fortune, afraid of death, and afraid of each other. Our age yields no great and perfect persons. We want men and women who shall renovate life and our social state, but we see that most natures are insolvent, cannot satisfy their own wants, have an ambition out of all proportion to their practical force and do lean and beg day and night continually. Our housekeeping is mendicant, our arts, our occupations, our marriages, our religion we have not chosen, but society has chosen for us. We are parlor soldiers. We shun the rugged battle of fate, where strength is born.

If our young men miscarry in their first enterprises they lose all heart. If the young merchant fails, men say he is *ruined.* If the finest genius studies at one of our colleges and is not installed in an office within one year afterwards in the cities or suburbs of Boston or New York, it seems to his friends and to himself that he is right in being disheartened and in complaining the rest of his life. A sturdy lad from New Hampshire or Vermont, who in turn tries all the professions, who *teams it, farms it, peddles,* keeps a school, preaches, edits a newspaper, goes to Congress, buys a township, and so forth, in successive years, and always like a cat falls on his feet, is worth a hundred of these city dolls. He walks abreast with his days and feels no shame in not "studying a profession," for he does not postpone his life, but lives already. He has not one chance, but a hundred chances. Let a Stoic open the resources of man and tell men they are not leaning willows, but can and must detach themselves; that with the exercise of self-trust, new powers shall appear; that a man is the word made flesh, born to shed healing to the nations; that he should be ashamed of our compassion, and that the moment he acts from himself, tossing the laws, the books, idolatries and customs out of the window, we pity him no more but thank and revere him;—and that teacher shall restore the life of man to splendor and make his name dear to all history.

It is easy to see that a greater self-reliance must work a revolution in all the offices and relations of men; in their religion; in their education; in their pursuits; their modes of living; their association; in their property; in their speculative views.

1. In what prayers do men allow themselves! That which they call a holy office is not so much as brave and manly. Prayer looks abroad and asks for some foreign addition to come through some foreign virtue, and loses itself in endless mazes

of natural and supernatural, and mediatorial and miraculous. Prayer that craves a particular commodity, anything less than all good, is vicious. Prayer is the contemplation of the facts of life from the highest point of view. It is the soliloquy of a beholding and jubilant soul. It is the spirit of God pronouncing his works good. But prayer as a means to effect a private end is meanness and theft. It supposes dualism and not unity in nature and consciousness. As soon as the man is at one with God, he will not beg. He will then see prayer in all action. The prayer of the farmer kneeling in his field to weed it, the prayer of the rower kneeling with the stroke of his oar, are true prayers heard throughout nature, though for cheap ends. Caratach, in Fletcher's "Bonduca," when admonished to inquire the mind of the god Audate, replies,—

> "His hidden meaning lies in our endeavors;
> Our valors are our best gods."

Another sort of false prayers are our regrets. Discontent is the want of self-reliance: it is infirmity of will. Regret calamities if you can thereby help the sufferer; if not, attend your own work and already the evil begins to be repaired. Our sympathy is just as base. We come to them who weep foolishly and sit down and cry for company, instead of imparting to them truth and health in rough electric shocks, putting them once more in communication with their own reason. The secret of fortune is joy in our hands. Welcome evermore to gods and men is the self-helping man. For him all doors are flung wide; him all tongues greet, all honors crown, all eyes follow with desire. Our love goes out to him and embraces him because he did not need it. We solicitously and apologetically caress and celebrate him because he held on his way and scorned our disapprobation. The gods love him because men hated him. "To the persevering mortal," said Zoroaster, "the blessed Immortals are swift."

As men's prayers are a disease of the will, so are their creeds a disease of the intellect. They say with those foolish Israelites, "Let not God speak to us, lest we die. Speak thou, speak any man with us, and we will obey." Everywhere I am hindered of meeting God in my brother, because he has shut his own temple doors and recites fables merely of his brother's, or his brother's brother's God. Every new mind is a new classification. If it prove a mind of uncommon activity and power, a Locke, a Lavoisier, a Hutton, a Bentham, a Fourier, it imposes its classification on other men, and lo! a new system. In proportion to the depth of the thought, and so to the number of the objects it touches and brings within reach of the pupil, is his complacency. But chiefly is this apparent in creeds and churches, which are also classifications of some powerful mind acting on the elemental thought of duty and man's relation to the Highest. Such is Calvinism, Quakerism, Swedenborgism. The pupil takes the same delight in subordinating every thing to the new terminology as a girl who has just learned botany in seeing a new earth and new seasons thereby. It will happen for a time that the pupil will find his intellectual power has grown by the study of his master's mind. But in all unbalanced minds the classification is idolized, passes for the end and not for a speedily exhaustible means, so that the walls of the system blend to their eye in the remote horizon with the walls of the universe; the luminaries of heaven seem to them hung on the arch their master built. They cannot imagine how you aliens have any right to see,—how you can see; "It must be somehow that you stole the light from us." They do not yet perceive that light, unsystematic, indomitable, will break into any cabin, even into theirs. Let them chirp awhile and call it their own. If they are honest and do well, presently their neat new pinfold will be too strait and low, will crack, will lean, will rot and vanish, and the immortal light, all young and joyful, million-orbed, million-colored, will beam over the universe as on the first morning.

2. It is for want of self-culture that the superstition of Travelling, whose idols are Italy, England, Egypt, retains its fascination for all educated Americans. They who made England, Italy, or Greece venerable in the imagination, did so by sticking fast where they were, like an axis of the earth. In manly hours we feel that duty is our place. The soul is no traveller; the wise

man stays at home, and when his necessities, his duties, on any occasion call him from his house, or into foreign lands, he is at home still and shall make men sensible by the expression of his countenance that he goes, the missionary of wisdom and virtue, and visits cities and men like a sovereign and not like an interloper or a valet.

I have no churlish objection to the circumnavigation of the globe for the purposes of art, of study, and benevolence, so that the man is first domesticated, or does not go abroad with the hope of finding somewhat greater than he knows. He who travels to be amused, or to get somewhat which he does not carry, travels away from himself, and grows old even in youth among old things. In Thebes, in Palmyra, his will and mind have become old and dilapidated as they. He carries ruins to ruins.

Travelling is a fool's paradise. Our first journeys discover to us the indifference of places. At home I dream that at Naples, at Rome, I can be intoxicated with beauty and lose my sadness. I pack my trunk, embrace my friends, embark on the sea and at last wake up in Naples, and there beside me is the stern fact, the sad self, unrelenting, identical, that I fled from. I seek the Vatican and the palaces. I affect to be intoxicated with sights and suggestions, but I am not intoxicated. My giant goes with me wherever I go.

3. But the rage of travelling is a symptom of a deeper unsoundness affecting the whole intellectual action. The intellect is vagabond, and our system of education fosters restlessness. Our minds travel when our bodies are forced to stay at home. We imitate; and what is imitation but the travelling of the mind? Our houses are built with foreign taste; our shelves are garnished with foreign ornaments; our opinions, our tastes, our faculties lean, and follow the Past and the Distant. The soul created the arts wherever they have flourished. It was in his own mind that the artist sought his model. It was an application of his own thought to the thing to be done and the conditions to be observed. And why need we copy the Doric or the Gothic model? Beauty, convenience, grandeur of thought and quaint expression are as near to us as to any, and if the American artist will

study with hope and love the precise thing to be done by him, considering the climate, the soil, the length of the day, the wants of the people, the habit and form of the government, he will create a house in which all these will find themselves fitted, and taste and sentiment will be satisfied also.

Insist on yourself; never imitate. Your own gift you can present every moment with the cumulative force of a whole life's cultivation; but of the adopted talent of another you have only an extemporaneous half possession. That which each can do best, none but his Maker can teach him. No man yet knows what it is, nor can, till that person has exhibited it. Where is the master who could have taught Shakspeare? Where is the master who could have instructed Franklin, or Washington, or Bacon, or Newton? Every great man is a unique. The Scipionism of Scipio is precisely that part he could not borrow. Shakspeare will never be made by the study of Shakspeare. Do that which is assigned you, and you cannot hope too much or dare too much. There is at this moment for you an utterance brave and grand as that of the colossal chisel of Phidias, or trowel of the Egyptians, or the pen of Moses or Dante, but different from all these. Not possibly will the soul, all rich, all eloquent, with thousand-cloven tongue, deign to repeat itself; but if you can hear what these patriarchs say, surely you can reply to them in the same pitch of voice; for the ear and the tongue are two organs of one nature. Abide in the simple and noble regions of thy life, obey thy heart, and thou shalt reproduce the Foreworld again.

4. As our Religion, our Education, our Art look abroad, so does our spirit of society. All men plume themselves on the improvement of society, and no man improves.

Society never advances. It recedes as fast on one side as it gains on the other. It undergoes continual changes; it is barbarous, it is civilized, it is christianized, it is rich, it is scientific; but this change is not amelioration. For every thing that is given something is taken. Society acquires new arts and loses old instincts. What a contrast between the well-clad, reading, writing, thinking American, with a watch, a pencil and a bill of exchange in his pocket, and the naked New Zealander, whose property is a club, a spear, a mat and an undivided twentieth of a shed to sleep under! But compare the health of the two men and you shall see that the white man has lost his aboriginal strength. If the traveller tell us truly, strike the savage with a broad-axe and in a day or two the flesh shall unite and heal as if you struck the blow into soft pitch, and the same blow shall send the white to his grave.

The civilized man has built a coach, but has lost the use of his feet. He is supported on crutches, but lacks so much support of muscle. He has a fine Geneva watch, but he fails of the skill to tell the hour by the sun. A Greenwich nautical almanac he has, and so being sure of the information when he wants it, the man in the street does not know a star in the sky. The solstice he does not observe; the equinox he knows as little; and the whole bright calendar of the year is without a dial in his mind. His note-books impair his memory; his libraries overload his wit; the insurance-office increases the number of accidents; and it may be a question whether machinery does not encumber; whether we have not lost by refinement some energy, by a Christianity, entrenched in establishments and forms, some vigor of wild virtue. For every Stoic was a Stoic; but in Christendom where is the Christian?

There is no more deviation in the moral standard than in the standard of height or bulk. No greater men are now than ever were. A singular equality may be observed between the great men of the first and of the last ages; nor can all the science, art, religion, and philosophy of the nineteenth century avail to educate greater men than Plutarch's heroes, three or four and twenty centuries ago. Not in time is the race progressive. Phocion, Socrates, Anaxagoras, Diogenes, are great men, but they leave no class. He who is really of their class will not be called by their name, but will be his own man, and in his turn the founder of a sect. The arts and inventions of each period are only its costume and do not invigorate men. The harm of the improved machinery may compensate its good. Hudson and Behring accomplished so much in their fishing-boats as to astonish Parry and Franklin, whose equipment exhausted the resources of science and art. Galileo, with an opera-glass, discovered a more splendid series of celestial phenomena than any one since. Columbus found the New World in an undecked boat. It is curious to see the periodical disuse and perishing of means and machinery which were introduced with loud laudation a few years or centuries before. The great genius returns to essential man. We reckoned the improvements of the art of war among the triumphs of science, and yet Napoleon conquered Europe by the bivouac, which consisted of falling back on naked valor and disencumbering it of all aids. The Emperor held it impossible to make a perfect army, says Las Cases, "without abolishing our arms, magazines, commissaries and carriages, until, in imitation of the Roman custom, the soldier should receive his supply of corn, grind it in his hand-mill and bake his bread himself."

Society is a wave. The wave moves onward, but the water of which it is composed does not. The same particle does not rise from the valley to the ridge. Its unity is only phenomenal. The persons who make up a nation to-day, next year die, and their experience dies with them.

And so the reliance on Property, including the reliance on governments which protect it, is the want of self-reliance. Men have looked away from themselves and at things so long that they have come to esteem the religious, learned and civil institutions as guards of property, and they deprecate assaults on these, because they feel them to be assaults on property. They measure their esteem of each other by what each has, and not by what each is. But a cultivated man becomes ashamed of his property, out of new respect for his nature. Especially he hates what he has if he see that it is accidental,—came to him by inheritance, or gift, or crime; then he feels that it is not having; it does not belong to him, has no root in him and merely lies there because no revolution or no robber takes it away. But that which a man is, does always by necessity acquire; and what the man acquires, is living property, which does not wait the beck of rulers, or mobs, or revolutions, or fire, or storm, or bankruptcies, but perpetually renews itself wherever the man breathes. "Thy lot or portion of life," said the Caliph Ali, "is seeking after thee; therefore be at rest from seeking after it." Our dependence on these foreign goods leads us to our slavish respect for numbers. The political parties meet in numerous conventions; the greater the concourse and with each new uproar of announcement, The delegation from Essex! The Democrats from New Hampshire! The Whigs of Maine! the young patriot feels himself stronger than before by a new thousand of eyes and arms. In like manner the reformers summon conventions and vote and resolve in multitude. Not so, O friends! will the God deign to enter and inhabit you, but by a method precisely the reverse. It is only as a man puts off all foreign support and stands alone that I see him to be strong and to prevail. He is weaker by every recruit to his banner. Is not a man better than a town? Ask nothing of men, and, in the endless mutation, thou only firm column must presently appear the upholder of all that surrounds thee. He who knows that power is inborn, that he is weak because he has looked for good out of him and elsewhere, and, so perceiving, throws himself unhesitatingly on his thought, instantly rights himself, stands in the erect position, commands his limbs, works miracles; just as a man who stands on his feet is stronger than a man who stands on his head.

So use all that is called Fortune. Most men gamble with her, and gain all, and lose all, as her wheel rolls. But do thou leave as unlawful these winnings, and deal with Cause and Effect, the chancellors of God. In the Will work and acquire, and thou hast chained the wheel of Chance, and shall sit hereafter out of fear from her rotations. A political victory, a rise of rents, the recovery of your sick or the return of your absent friend, or some other favorable event raises your spirits, and you think good days are preparing for you. Do not believe it. Nothing can bring you peace but yourself. Nothing can bring you peace but the triumph of principles.

1841

COMPENSATION

The wings of Time are black and white,
Pied with morning and with night.
Mountain tall and ocean deep
Trembling balance duly keep.
In changing moon, in tidal wave,
Glows the feud of Want and Have.
Gauge of more and less through space
Electric star and pencil plays.
The lonely Earth amid the balls
That hurry through the eternal halls,
A makeweight flying to the void,
Supplemental asteroid,
Or compensatory spark,
Shoots across the neutral Dark.

Man's the elm, and Wealth the vine,
Stanch and strong the tendrils twine:
Though the frail ringlets thee deceive,
None from its stock that vine can reave.
Fear not, then, thou child infirm,
There's no god dare wrong a worm.
Laurel crowns cleave to deserts
And power to him who power exerts;
Hast not thy share? On wingèd feet,
Lo! it rushes thee to meet;
And all that Nature made thy own,
Floating in air or pent in stone,
Will rive the hills and swim the sea
And, like thy shadow, follow thee.

Ever since I was a boy I have wished to write a discourse on Compensation; for it seemed to me when very young that on this subject life was ahead of theology and the people knew more than the preachers taught. The documents too from which the doctrine is to be drawn, charmed my fancy by their endless variety, and lay always before me, even in sleep; for they are the tools in our hands, the bread in our basket, the transactions of the street, the farm and the dwelling-house; greetings, relations, debts and credits, the influence of character, the nature and endowment of all men. It seemed to me also that in it might be shown men a ray of divinity, the present action of the soul of this world, clean from all vestige of tradition; and so the heart of man might be bathed by an inundation of eternal love, conversing with that which he knows was always and always must be, because it really is now. It appeared moreover that if this doctrine could be stated in terms with any resemblance to those bright intuitions in which this truth is sometimes revealed to us, it would be a star in many dark hours and crooked passages in our journey, that would not suffer us to lose our way.

I was lately confirmed in these desires by hearing a sermon at church. The preacher, a man esteemed for his orthodoxy, unfolded in the ordinary manner the doctrine of the Last Judgment. He assumed that judgment is not executed in this world; that the wicked are successful; that the good are miserable; and then urged from reason and from Scripture a compensation to be made to both parties in the next life. No offence appeared to be taken by the congregation at this doctrine. As far as I could observe when the meeting broke up they separated without remark on the sermon.

Yet what was the import of this teaching? What did the preacher mean by saying that the good are miserable in the present life? Was it that houses and lands, offices, wine, horses, dress, luxury, are had by unprincipled men, whilst the saints are poor and despised; and that a compensation is to be made to these last hereafter, by giving them the like gratifications another day,—bank-stock and doubloons, venison and champagne? This must be the compensation intended; for what else? Is it that they are to have leave to pray and praise? to love and serve men? Why, that they can do now. The legitimate inference the disciple would draw was,—"We are to have *such* a good time as the sinners have now;"—or, to push it to its extreme import,—"You sin now, we shall sin by and by; we would sin now, if we could; not being successful we expect our revenge to-morrow."

The fallacy lay in the immense concession that the bad are successful; that justice is not done now. The blindness of the preacher consisted in deferring to the base estimate of the market of what constitutes a manly success, instead of confronting and convicting the world from the truth; announcing the presence of the soul; the omnipotence of the will; and so establishing the standard of good and ill, of success and falsehood.

I find a similar base tone in the popular religious works of the day and the same doctrines assumed by the literary men when occasionally they treat the related topics. I think that our popular theology has gained in decorum, and not in principle, over the superstitions it has displaced. But men are better than their theology. Their daily life gives it the lie. Every ingenuous and aspiring soul leaves the doctrine behind him in his own experience, and all men feel sometimes the falsehood which they cannot demonstrate. For men are wiser than they know. That which they hear in schools and pulpits without afterthought, if said in conversation would probably be questioned in silence. If a man dogmatize in a mixed company on Providence and the divine laws, he is answered by a silence which conveys well enough to an observer the dissatisfaction of the hearer, but his incapacity to make his own statement.

I shall attempt in this and the following chapter* to record some facts that indicate the path of the law of Compensation; happy beyond my expectation if I shall truly draw the smallest arc of this circle.

Polarity, or action and reaction, we meet in every part of nature; in darkness and light; in heat and cold; in the ebb and flow of waters; in male and female; in the inspiration and expiration of plants and animals; in the equation of quantity and quality in the fluids of the animal body; in the systole and diastole of the heart; in the undulations of fluids and of sound; in the centrifugal and centripetal gravity; in electricity,

* The reference here is to the essay, "Spiritual Laws," which immediately followed in *Essays, First Series*.

galvanism, and chemical affinity. Superinduce magnetism at one end of a needle, the opposite magnetism takes place at the other end. If the south attracts, the north repels. To empty here, you must condense there. An inevitable dualism bisects nature, so that each thing is a half, and suggests another thing to make it whole; as, spirit, matter; man, woman; odd, even; subjective, objective; in, out; upper, under; motion, rest; yea, nay.

Whilst the world is thus dual, so is every one of its parts. The entire system of things gets represented in every particle. There is somewhat that resembles the ebb and flow of the sea, day and night, man and woman, in a single needle of the pine, in a kernel of corn, in each individual of every animal tribe. The reaction, so grand in the elements, is repeated within these small boundaries. For example, in the animal kingdom the physiologist has observed that no creatures are favorites, but a certain compensation balances every gift and every defect. A surplusage given to one part is paid out of a reduction from another part of the same creature. If the head and neck are enlarged, the trunk and extremities are cut short.

The theory of the mechanic forces is another example. What we gain in power is lost in time, and the converse. The periodic or compensating errors of the planets is another instance. The influences of climate and soil in political history are another. The cold climate invigorates. The barren soil does not breed fevers, crocodiles, tigers or scorpions.

The same dualism underlies the nature and condition of man. Every excess causes a defect; every defect an excess. Every sweet hath its sour; every evil its good. Every faculty which is a receiver of pleasure has an equal penalty put on its abuse. It is to answer for its moderation with its life. For every grain of wit there is a grain of folly. For every thing you have missed, you have gained something else; and for every thing you gain, you lose something. If riches increase, they are increased that use them. If the gatherer gathers too much, Nature takes out of the man what she puts into his chest; swells the estate, but kills the owner. Nature hates monopolies and exceptions. The waves of the sea do not more speedily seek a level from their loftiest tossing than the varieties of condition tend to equalize themselves. There is always some levelling circumstance that puts down the overbearing, the strong, the rich, the fortunate, substantially on the same ground with all others. Is a man too strong and fierce for society and by temper and position a bad citizen,—a morose ruffian, with a dash of the pirate in him?—Nature sends him a troop of pretty sons and daughters who are getting along in the dame's classes at the village school, and love and fear for them smooths his grim scowl to courtesy. Thus she contrives to intenerate the granite and felspar, takes the boar out and puts the lamb in and keeps her balance true.

The farmer imagines power and place are fine things. But the President has paid dear for his White House. It has commonly cost him all his peace, and the best of his manly attributes. To preserve for a short time so conspicuous an appearance before the world, he is content to eat dust before the real masters who stand erect behind the throne. Or do men desire the more substantial and permanent grandeur of genius? Neither has this an immunity. He who by force of will or of thought is great and overlooks thousands, has the charges of that eminence. With every influx of light comes new danger. Has he light? he must bear witness to the light, and always outrun that sympathy which gives him such keen satisfaction, by his fidelity to new revelations of the incessant soul. He must hate father and mother, wife and child. Has he all that the world loves and admires and covets?—he must cast behind him their admiration, and afflict them by faithfulness to his truth, and become a byword and a hissing.

This law writes the laws of cities and nations. It is in vain to build or plot or combine against it. Things refuse to be mismanaged long. *Res nolunt diu male administrari.* Though no checks to a new evil appear, the checks exist, and will appear. If the government is cruel, the governor's life is not safe. If you tax too high, the revenue will yield nothing. If you make the criminal code sanguinary, juries will not convict. If the law is too mild, private vengeance comes in. If the government is a terrific democracy, the pressure is resisted by an over-charge of energy in the citizen, and life glows with a fiercer flame. The true life and satisfactions of man seem to elude the utmost rigors or felicities of condition and to establish themselves with great indifferency under all varieties of circumstances. Under all governments the influence of character remains the same,—in Turkey and in New England about alike. Under the primeval despots of Egypt, history honestly confesses that man must have been as free as culture could make him.

These appearances indicate the fact that the universe is represented in every one of its particles. Every thing in nature contains all the powers of nature. Every thing is made of one hidden stuff; as the naturalist sees one type under every metamorphosis, and regards a horse as a running man, a fish as a swimming man, a bird as a flying man, a tree as a rooted man. Each new form repeats not only the main character of the type, but part for part all the details, all the aims, furtherances, hindrances, energies, and whole system of every other. Every occupation, trade, art, transaction, is a compend of the world and a correlative of every other. Each one is an entire emblem of human life; of its good and ill, its trials, its enemies, its course and its end. And each one must somehow accommodate the whole man and recite all his destiny.

The world globes itself in a drop of dew. The microscope cannot find the animalcule which is less perfect for being little. Eyes, ears, taste, smell, motion, resistance, appetite, and organs of reproduction that take hold on eternity,—all find room to consist in the small creature. So do we put our life into every act. The true doctrine of omnipresence is that God reappears with all his parts in every moss and cobweb. The value of the universe contrives to throw itself into every point. If the good is there, so is the evil; if the affinity, so the repulsion; if the force, so the limitation.

Thus is the universe alive. All things are moral. That soul which within us is a sentiment, outside of us is a law. We feel its inspiration; but there in history we can see its fatal strength. "It is in the world, and the world was made by it." Justice is not postponed. A perfect equity adjusts its balance in all parts of life. Ἀεὶ γὰρ εὖ πίπτουσιν οἱ Διὸς κύβοι,—The dice of God are always loaded. The world looks like a multiplication-table, or a mathematical equation, which, turn it how you will, balances itself. Take what figure you will, its exact value, nor more nor less, still returns to you. Every secret is told, every crime is punished, every virtue rewarded, every wrong redressed, in silence and certainty. What we call retribution is the universal necessity by which the whole appears wherever a part appears. If you see smoke, there must be fire. If you see a hand or a limb, you know that the trunk to which it belongs is there behind.

Every act rewards itself, or in other words integrates itself, in a twofold manner; first in the thing, or in real nature; and secondly in the circumstance, or in apparent nature. Men call the circumstance the retribution. The causal retribution is in the thing and is seen by the soul. The retribution in the circumstance is seen by the understanding; it is inseparable from the thing, but is often spread over a long time and so does not become distinct until after many years. The specific stripes may follow late after the offence, but they follow because they accompany it. Crime and punishment grow out of one stem. Punishment is a fruit that unsuspected ripens within the flower of the pleasure which concealed it. Cause and effect, means and ends, seed and fruit, cannot be severed; for the effect already blooms in the cause, the end preëxists in the means, the fruit in the seed.

Whilst thus the world will be whole and refuses to be disparted, we seek to act partially, to sunder, to appropriate; for example,—to gratify the senses we sever the pleasure of the senses from the needs of the character. The ingenuity of man has always been dedicated to the solution of one problem,—how to detach the sensual sweet, the sensual strong, the sensual bright, etc., from the moral sweet, the moral deep, the moral fair; that is, again, to contrive to cut clean off this upper surface so thin as to leave it bottomless; to get a *one end*, without an *other end*. The soul says, "Eat;" the body would feast. The soul says, "The man and woman shall be one flesh and one soul;" the body would join the flesh only. The soul says, "Have dominion over all things to the ends of virtue;" the body would have the power over things to its own ends.

The soul strives amain to live and work through all things. It would be the only fact. All things shall be added unto it,—power, pleasure, knowledge, beauty. The particular man aims to be somebody; to set up for himself; to truck and higgle for a private good; and, in particulars, to ride that he may ride; to dress that he may be dressed; to eat that he may eat; and to govern, that he may be seen. Men seek to be great; they would have offices, wealth, power, and fame. They think that to be great is to possess one side of nature,—the sweet, without the other side, the bitter.

This dividing and detaching is steadily counteracted. Up to this day it must be owned no projector has had the smallest success. The parted water reunites behind our hand. Pleasure is taken out of pleasant things, profit out of profitable things, power out of strong things, as soon as we seek to separate them from the whole. We can no more halve things and get the sensual good, by itself, than we can get an inside that shall have no outside, or a light without a shadow. "Drive out Nature with a fork, she comes running back."

Life invests itself with inevitable conditions, which the unwise seek to dodge, which one and another brags that he does not know, that they do not touch him;—but the brag is on his lips, the conditions are in his soul. If he escapes them in one part they attack him in another more vital part. If he has escaped them in form and in the appearance, it is because he has resisted his life and fled from himself, and the retribution is so much death. So signal is the failure of all attempts to make this separation of the good from the tax, that the experiment would not be tried,—since to try it is to be mad,—but for the circumstance that when the disease began in the will, of rebellion and separation, the intellect is at once infected, so that the man ceases to see God whole in each object, but is able to see the sensual allurement of an object and not see the sensual hurt;

he sees the mermaid's head but not the dragon's tail, and thinks he can cut off that which he would have from that which he would not have. "How secret art thou who dwellest in the highest heavens in silence, O thou only great God, sprinkling with an unwearied providence certain penal blindnesses upon such as have unbridled desires!"

The human soul is true to these facts in the painting of fable, of history, of law, of proverbs, of conversation. It finds a tongue in literature unawares. Thus the Greeks called Jupiter, Supreme Mind; but having traditionally ascribed to him many base actions, they involuntarily made amends to reason by tying up the hands of so bad a god. He is made as helpless as a king of England. Prometheus knows one secret which Jove must bargain for; Minerva, another. He cannot get his own thunders; Minerva keeps the key of them:—

"Of all the gods, I only know the keys
That ope the solid doors within whose vaults
His thunders sleep."

A plain confession of the in-working of the All and of its moral aim. The Indian mythology ends in the same ethics; and it would seem impossible for any fable to be invented and get any currency which was not moral. Aurora forgot to ask youth for her lover, and though Tithonus is immortal, he is old. Achilles is not quite invulnerable; the sacred waters did not wash the heel by which Thetis held him. Siegfried, in the Nibelungen, is not quite immortal, for a leaf fell on his back whilst he was bathing in the dragon's blood, and that spot which it covered is mortal. And so it must be. There is a crack in every thing God has made. It would seem there is always this vindictive circumstance stealing in at unawares even into the wild poesy in which the human fancy attempted to make bold holiday and to shake itself free of the old laws,—this back-stroke, this kick of the gun, certifying that the law is fatal; that in nature nothing can be given, all things are sold.

This is that ancient doctrine of Nemesis, who keeps watch in the universe and lets no offence go unchastised. The Furies, they said, are attendants on justice, and if the sun in heaven should transgress his path they would punish him. The poets related that stone walls and iron swords and leathern thongs had an occult sympathy with the wrongs of their owners; that the belt which Ajax gave Hector dragged the Trojan hero over the field at the wheels of the car of Achilles, and the sword which Hector gave Ajax was that on whose point Ajax fell. They recorded that when the Thasians erected a statue to Theagenes, a victor in the games, one of his rivals went to it by night and endeavored to throw it down by repeated blows, until at last he moved it from its pedestal and was crushed to death beneath its fall.

This voice of fable has in it somewhat divine. It came from thought above the will of the writer. That is the best part of each writer which has nothing private in it; that which he does not know; that which flowed out of his constitution and not from his too active invention; that which in the study of a single artist you might not easily find, but in the study of many you would abstract as the spirit of them all. Phidias it is not, but the work of man in that early Hellenic world that I would know. The name and circumstance of Phidias, however convenient for history, embarrass when we come to the highest criticism. We are to see that which man was tending to do in a given period, and was hindered, or, if you will, modified in doing, by the interfering volitions of Phidias, of Dante, of Shakspeare, the organ whereby man at the moment wrought.

Still more striking is the expression of this fact in the proverbs of all nations, which are always the literature of reason, or the statements of an absolute truth without qualification. Proverbs, like the sacred books of each nation, are the sanctuary of the intuitions. That which the droning world, chained to appearances, will not allow the realist to say in his own words, it will suffer him to say in proverbs without contradiction. And this law of laws, which the pulpit, the senate and the college deny, is hourly preached in all markets and workshops by flights of proverbs, whose teaching is as true and as omnipresent as that of birds and flies.

All things are double, one against another.—Tit for tat; an eye for an eye; a tooth for a tooth; blood for blood; measure for measure; love for love.—Give, and it shall be given you.—He that watereth shall be watered himself.—What will you have? quoth God; pay for it and take it.—Nothing venture, nothing have.—Thou shalt be paid exactly for what thou hast done, no more, no less.—Who doth not work shall not eat.—Harm watch, harm catch.—Curses always recoil on the head of him who imprecates them.—If you put a chain around the neck of a slave, the other end fastens itself around your own.—Bad counsel confounds the adviser.—The Devil is an ass.

It is thus written, because it is thus in life. Our action is overmastered and characterized above our will by the law of nature. We aim at a petty end quite aside from the public good, but our act arranges itself by irresistible magnetism in a line with the poles of the world.

A man cannot speak but he judges himself. With his will or against his will he draws his portrait to the eye of his companions by every word. Every opinion reacts on him who utters it. It is a thread-ball thrown at a mark, but the other end remains in the thrower's bag. Or rather it is a harpoon hurled at the whale, unwinding, as it flies, a coil of cord in the boat, and, if the harpoon is not good, or not well thrown, it will go nigh to cut the steersman in twain or to sink the boat.

You cannot do wrong without suffering wrong. "No man had ever a point of pride that was not injurious to him," said Burke. The exclusive in fashionable life does not see that he excludes himself from enjoyment, in the attempt to appropriate it. The exclusionist in religion does not see that he shuts the door of heaven on himself, in striving to shut out others. Treat men as pawns and ninepins and you shall suffer as well as they. If you leave out their heart, you shall lose your own. The senses would make things of all persons; of women, of children, of the poor. The vulgar proverb, "I will get it from his purse or get it from his skin," is sound philosophy.

All infractions of love and equity in our social relations are speedily punished. They are punished by fear. Whilst I stand in simple relations to my fellow-man, I have no displeasure in meeting him. We meet as water meets water, or as two currents of air mix, with perfect diffusion and interpenetration of nature. But as soon as there is any departure from simplicity and attempt at halfness, or good for me that is not good for him, my neighbor feels the wrong; he shrinks from me as far as I have shrunk from him; his eyes no longer seek mine; there is war between us; there is hate in him and fear in me.

All the old abuses in society, universal and particular, all unjust accumulations of property and power, are avenged in the same manner. Fear is an instructor of great sagacity and the herald of all revolutions. One thing he teaches, that there is rottenness where he appears. He is a carrion crow, and though you see not well what he hovers for, there is death somewhere. Our property is timid, our laws are timid, our cultivated classes are timid. Fear for ages has boded and mowed and gibbered over government and property. That obscene bird is not there for nothing. He indicates great wrongs which must be revised.

Of the like nature is that expectation of change which instantly follows the suspension of our voluntary activity. The terror of cloudless noon, the emerald of Polycrates, the awe of prosperity, the instinct which leads every generous soul to impose on itself tasks of a noble asceticism and vicarious virtue, are the tremblings of the balance of justice through the heart and mind of man.

Experienced men of the world know very well that it is best to pay scot and lot as they go along, and that a man often pays dear for a small frugality. The borrower runs in his own debt. Has a man gained any thing who has received a hundred favors and rendered none? Has he gained by borrowing, through indolence or cunning, his neighbor's wares, or horses, or money? There arises on the deed the instant acknowledgment of benefit on the one part and of debt on the other; that is, of superiority and inferiority. The transaction remains in the memory of himself and his neighbor; and every new transaction alters according to its nature their relation to each other. He may soon come to see that he had better have broken his own bones than to have ridden in his neighbor's coach, and that "the highest price he can pay for a thing is to ask for it."

A wise man will extend this lesson to all parts of life, and know that it is the part of prudence to face every claimant and pay every just demand on your time, your talents, or your heart. Always pay; for first or last you must pay your entire debt. Persons and events may stand for a time between you and justice, but it is only a postponement. You must pay at last your own debt. If you are wise you will dread a prosperity which only loads you with more. Benefit is the end of nature. But for every benefit which you receive, a tax is levied. He is great who confers the most benefits. He is base,—and that is the one base thing in the universe,—to receive favors and render none. In the order of nature we cannot render benefits to those from whom we receive them, or only seldom. But the benefit we receive must be rendered again, line for line, deed for deed, cent for cent, to somebody. Beware of too much good staying in your hand. It will fast corrupt and worm worms. Pay it away quickly in some sort.

Labor is watched over by the same pitiless laws. Cheapest, say the prudent, is the dearest labor. What we buy in a broom, a mat, a wagon, a knife, is some application of good sense to a common want. It is best to pay in your land a skilful gardener, or to buy good sense applied to gardening; in your sailor, good sense applied to navigation; in the house, good sense applied to cooking, sewing, serving; in your agent, good sense applied to accounts and affairs. So do you multiply your presence, or spread yourself throughout your estate. But because of the dual constitution of things, in labor as in life there can be no cheating. The thief steals from himself. The swindler swindles himself. For the real price of labor is knowledge and virtue, whereof wealth and credit are signs. These signs, like paper money, may be counterfeited or stolen, but that which they represent, namely, knowledge and virtue, cannot be counterfeited or stolen. These ends of labor cannot be answered but by real exertions of the mind, and in obedience to pure motives. The cheat, the defaulter, the gambler, cannot extort the knowledge of material and moral nature which his honest care and pains yield to the operative. The law of nature is, Do the thing, and you shall have the power; but they who do not the thing have not the power.

Human labor, through all its forms, from the sharpening of a stake to the construction of a city or an epic, is one immense illustration of the perfect compensation of the universe. The absolute balance of Give and Take, the doctrine that every thing has its price,—and if that price is not paid, not that thing but something else is obtained, and that it is impossible to get any thing without its price,—is not less sublime in the columns of a ledger than in the budgets of states, in the laws of light and darkness, in all the action and reaction of nature. I cannot doubt that the high laws which each man sees implicated in those processes with which he is conversant, the stern ethics which sparkle on his chisel-edge, which are measured out by his plumb and foot-rule, which stand as manifest in the footing of the shop-bill as in the history of a state,—do recommend to him his trade, and though seldom named, exalt his business to his imagination.

The league between virtue and nature engages all things to assume a hostile front to vice. The beautiful laws and substances of the world persecute and whip the traitor. He finds that things are arranged for truth and benefit, but there is no den in the wide world to hide a rogue. Commit a crime, and the earth is made of glass. Commit a crime, and it seems as if a coat of snow fell on the ground, such as reveals in the woods the track of every partridge and fox and squirrel and mole. You cannot recall the spoken word, you cannot wipe out the foot-track, you cannot draw up the ladder, so as to leave no inlet or clew. Some damning circumstance always transpires. The laws and substances of nature,—water, snow, wind, gravitation,—become penalties to the thief.

On the other hand the law holds with equal sureness for all right action. Love, and you shall be loved. All love is mathematically just, as much as the two sides of an algebraic equation. The good man has absolute good, which like fire turns every thing to its own nature, so that you cannot do him any harm; but as the royal armies sent against Napoleon, when he approached cast down their colors and from enemies became friends, so disasters of all kinds, as sickness, offence, poverty, prove benefactors:—

> "Winds blow and waters roll
> Strength to the brave and power and deity,
> Yet in themselves are nothing."

The good are befriended even by weakness and defect. As no man had ever a point of pride that was not injurious to him, so no man had ever a defect that was not somewhere made useful to him. The stag in the fable admired his horns and blamed his feet, but when the hunter came, his feet saved him, and afterwards, caught in the thicket, his horns destroyed him. Every man in his lifetime needs to thank his faults. As no man thoroughly understands a truth until he has contended against it, so no man has a thorough acquaintance with the hindrances or talents of men until he has suffered from the one and seen the triumph of the other over his own want of the same. Has he a defect of temper that unfits him to live in society? Thereby he is driven to entertain himself alone and acquire habits of self-help; and thus, like the wounded oyster, he mends his shell with pearl.

Our strength grows out of our weakness. The indignation which arms itself with secret forces does not awaken until we are pricked and stung and sorely assailed. A great man is always willing to be little. Whilst he sits on the cushion of advantages, he goes to sleep. When he is pushed, tormented, defeated, he has a chance to learn something; he has been put on his wits, on his manhood; he has gained facts; learns his ignorance; is cured of the insanity of conceit; has got moderation and real skill. The wise man throws himself on the side of his assailants. It is more his interest than it is theirs to find his weak point. The wound cicatrizes and falls off from him like a dead skin and when they would triumph, lo! he has passed on invulnerable. Blame is safer than praise. I hate to be defended in a newspaper. As long as all that is said is said against me, I feel a certain assurance of success. But as soon as honeyed words of praise are spoken for me I feel as one that lies unprotected before his enemies. In general, every evil to which we do not succumb is a benefactor. As the Sandwich Islander believes that the strength and valor of the enemy he kills passes into himself, so we gain the strength of the temptation we resist.

The same guards which protect us from disaster, defect and enmity, defend us, if we will, from selfishness and fraud. Bolts and bars are not the best of our institutions, nor is shrewdness in trade a mark of wisdom. Men suffer all their life long under the foolish superstition that they can be cheated. But it is as impossible for a man to be cheated by any one but himself, as for a thing to be and not to be at the same time. There is a third silent party to all our bargains. The nature and soul of things takes on itself the guaranty of the fulfilment of every contract, so that honest service cannot come to loss. If you serve an ungrateful master, serve him the more. Put God in your debt. Every stroke shall be repaid. The longer the payment is withholden, the better for you; for compound interest on compound interest is the rate and usage of this exchequer.

The history of persecution is a history of endeavors to cheat nature, to make water run up hill, to twist a rope of sand. It makes no difference whether the actors be many or one, a tyrant or a mob. A mob is a society of bodies voluntarily bereaving themselves of reason and traversing its work. The mob is man voluntarily descending to the nature of the beast. Its fit hour of activity is night. Its actions are insane, like its whole constitution. It persecutes a principle; it would whip a right; it would tar and feather justice, by inflicting fire and outrage upon the houses and persons of those who have these. It resembles the prank of boys, who run with fire-engines to put out the ruddy aurora streaming to the stars. The inviolate spirit turns their spite against the wrongdoers. The martyr cannot be dishonored. Every lash inflicted is a tongue of fame; every prison a more illustrious abode; every burned book or house enlightens the world; every suppressed or expunged word reverberates through the earth from side to side. Hours of sanity and consideration are always arriving to communities, as to individuals, when the truth is seen and the martyrs are justified.

Thus do all things preach the indifferency of circumstances. The man is all. Every thing has two sides, a good and an evil. Every advantage has its tax. I learn to be content. But the doctrine of compensation is not the doctrine of indifferency. The thoughtless say, on hearing these representations,—What boots it to do well? there is one event to good and evil; if I gain any good I must pay for it; if I lose any good I gain some other; all actions are indifferent.

There is a deeper fact in the soul than compensation, to wit, its own nature. The soul is not a compensation, but a life. The soul *is*. Under all this running sea of circumstance, whose waters ebb and flow with perfect balance, lies the aboriginal abyss of real Being. Essence, or God, is not a relation or a part, but the whole. Being is the vast affirmative, excluding negation, self-balanced, and swallowing up all relations, parts and times within itself. Nature, truth, virtue, are the influx from thence. Vice is the absence or departure of the same. Nothing, Falsehood, may indeed stand as the great Night or shade on which as a background the living universe paints itself forth, but no fact is begotten by it; it cannot work, for it is not. It cannot work any good; it cannot work any harm. It is harm inasmuch as it is worse not to be than to be.

We feel defrauded of the retribution due to evil acts, because the criminal adheres to his vice and contumacy and does not come to a crisis or judgment anywhere in visible nature. There is no stunning confutation of his nonsense before men and angels. Has he therefore outwitted the law? Inasmuch as he carries the malignity and the lie with him he so far deceases from nature. In some manner there will be a demonstration of the wrong to the understanding also; but, should we not see it, this deadly deduction makes square the eternal account.

Neither can it be said, on the other hand, that the gain of

rectitude must be bought by any loss. There is no penalty to virtue; no penalty to wisdom; they are proper additions of being. In a virtuous action I properly *am;* in a virtuous act I add to the world; I plant into deserts conquered from Chaos and Nothing and see the darkness receding on the limits of the horizon. There can be no excess to love, none to knowledge, none to beauty, when these attributes are considered in the purest sense. The soul refuses limits, and always affirms an Optimism, never a Pessimism.

His life is a progress, and not a station. His instinct is trust. Our instinct uses "more" and "less" in application to man, of the *presence of the soul*, and not of its absence; the brave man is greater than the coward; the true, the benevolent, the wise, is more a man and not less, than the fool and knave. There is no tax on the good of virtue, for that is the incoming of God himself, or absolute existence, without any comparative. Material good has its tax, and if it came without desert or sweat, has no root in me, and the next wind will blow it away. But all the good of nature is the soul's, and may be had if paid for in nature's lawful coin, that is, by labor which the heart and the head allow. I no longer wish to meet a good I do not earn, for example to find a pot of buried gold, knowing that it brings with it new burdens. I do not wish more external goods,—neither possessions, nor honors, nor powers, nor persons. The gain is apparent; the tax is certain. But there is no tax on the knowledge that the compensation exists and that it is not desirable to dig up treasure. Herein I rejoice with a serene eternal peace. I contract the boundaries of possible mischief. I learn the wisdom of St. Bernard,—"Nothing can work me damage except myself; the harm that I sustain I carry about with me, and never am a real sufferer but by my own fault."

In the nature of the soul is the compensation for the inequalities of condition. The radical tragedy of nature seems to be the distinction of More and Less. How can Less not feel the pain; how not feel indignation or malevolence towards More? Look at those who have less faculty, and one feels sad and knows not well what to make of it. He almost shuns their eye; he fears they will upbraid God. What should they do? It seems a great injustice. But see the facts nearly and these mountainous inequalities vanish. Love reduces them as the sun melts the iceberg in the sea. The heart and soul of all men being one, this bitterness of *His* and *Mine* ceases. His is mine. I am my brother and my brother is me. If I feel overshadowed and outdone by great neighbors, I can yet love; I can still receive; and he that loveth maketh his own the grandeur he loves. Thereby I make the discovery that my brother is my guardian, acting for me with the friendliest designs, and the estate I so admired and envied is my own. It is the nature of the soul to appropriate all things. Jesus and Shakspeare are fragments of the soul, and by love I conquer and incorporate them in my own conscious domain. His virtue,—is not that mine? His wit,—if it cannot be made mine, it is not wit.

Such also is the natural history of calamity. The changes which break up at short intervals the prosperity of men are advertisements of a nature whose law is growth. Every soul is by this intrinsic necessity quitting its whole system of things, its friends and home and laws and faith, as the shellfish crawls out of its beautiful but stony case, because it no longer admits of its growth, and slowly forms a new house. In proportion to the vigor of the individual these revolutions are frequent, until in some happier mind they are incessant and all worldly relations hang very loosely about him, becoming as it were a transparent fluid membrane through which the living form is seen, and not, as in most men, an indurated heterogeneous fabric of many dates and of no settled character, in which the man is imprisoned. Then there can be enlargement, and the man of to-day scarcely recognizes the man of yesterday. And such should be the outward biography of man in time, a putting off of dead circumstances day by day, as he renews his raiment day by day. But to us, in our lapsed estate, resting, not advancing, resisting, not coöperating with the divine expansion, this growth comes by shocks.

We cannot part with our friends. We cannot let our angels go. We do not see that they only go out that archangels may come in. We are idolators of the old. We do not believe in the riches of the soul, in its proper eternity and omnipresence. We do not believe there is any force in to-day to rival or recreate that beautiful yesterday. We linger in the ruins of the old tent where once we had bread and shelter and organs, nor believe that the spirit can feed, cover, and nerve us again. We cannot again find aught so dear, so sweet, so graceful. But we sit and weep in vain. The voice of the Almighty saith, "Up and onward for evermore!" We cannot stay amid the ruins. Neither will we rely on the new; and so we walk ever with reverted eyes, like those monsters who look backwards.

And yet the compensations of calamity are made apparent to the understanding also, after long intervals of time. A fever, a mutilation, a cruel disappointment, a loss of wealth, a loss of friends, seems at the moment unpaid loss, and unpayable. But the sure years reveal the deep remedial force that underlies all facts. The death of a dear friend, wife, brother, lover, which seemed nothing but privation, somewhat later assumes the aspect of a guide or genius; for it commonly operates revolutions in our way of life, terminates an epoch of infancy or of youth which was waiting to be closed, breaks up a wonted occupation, or a household, or style of living, and allows the formation of new ones more friendly to the growth of character. It permits or constrains the formation of new acquaintances and the reception of new influences that prove of the first importance to the next years; and the man or woman who would have remained a sunny garden-flower, with no room for its roots and too much sunshine for its head, by the falling of the walls and the neglect of the gardener is made the banian of the forest, yielding shade and fruit to wide neighborhoods of men.

1841

THE OVER-SOUL

"But souls that of his own good life partake,
He loves as his own self; dear as his eye
They are to Him: He'll never them forsake:
When they shall die, then God himself shall die:
They live, they live in blest eternity."

—HENRY MORE

Space is ample, east and west,
But two cannot go abreast,
Cannot travel in it two:
Yonder masterful cuckoo
Crowds every egg out of the nest,
Quick or dead, except its own;
A spell is laid on sod and stone,
Night and Day 've been tampered with,
Every quality and pith
Surcharged and sultry with a power
That works its will on age and hour.

There is a difference between one and another hour of life in their authority and subsequent effect. Our faith comes in moments; our vice is habitual. Yet there is a depth in those brief moments which constrains us to ascribe more reality to them than to all other experiences. For this reason the argument which is always forthcoming to silence those who conceive extraordinary hopes of man, namely the appeal to experience, is for ever invalid and vain. We give up the past to the objector, and yet we hope. He must explain this hope. We grant that human life is mean, but how did we find out that it was mean? What is the ground of this uneasiness of ours; of this old discontent? What is the universal sense of want and ignorance, but the fine innuendo by which the soul makes its enormous claim? Why do men feel that the natural history of man has never been written, but he is always leaving behind what you have said of him, and it becomes old, and books of metaphysics worthless? The philosophy of six thousand years has not searched the chambers and magazines of the soul. In its experiments there has always remained, in the last analysis, a residuum it could not resolve. Man is a stream whose source is hidden. Our being is descending into us from we know not whence. The most exact calculator has no prescience that somewhat incalculable may not balk the very next moment. I am constrained every moment to acknowledge a higher origin for events than the will I call mine.

As with events, so is it with thoughts. When I watch that flowing river, which, out of regions I see not, pours for a season its streams into me, I see that I am a pensioner; not a cause but a surprised spectator of this ethereal water; that I desire and look up and put myself in the attitude of reception, but from some alien energy the visions come.

The Supreme Critic on the errors of the past and the present, and the only prophet of that which must be, is that great nature in which we rest as the earth lies in the soft arms of the atmosphere; that Unity, that Over-Soul, within which every man's particular being is contained and made one with all other; that common heart of which all sincere conversation is the worship, to which all right action is submission; that over-powering reality which confutes our tricks and talents, and constrains every one to pass for what he is, and to speak from his character and not from his tongue, and which evermore tends to pass into our thought and hand and become wisdom and virtue and power and beauty. We live in succession, in division, in parts, in particles. Meantime within man is the soul of the whole; the wise silence; the universal beauty, to which every part and particle is equally related; the eternal ONE. And this deep power in which we exist and whose beatitude is all accessible to us, is not only self-sufficing and perfect in every hour, but the act of seeing and the thing seen, the seer and the spectacle, the subject and the object, are one. We see the world piece by piece, as the sun, the moon, the animal, the tree; but the whole, of which these are the shining parts, is the soul. Only by the vision of that Wisdom can the horoscope of the ages be read, and by falling back on our better thoughts, by yielding to the spirit of prophecy which is innate in every man, we can know what it saith. Every man's words who speaks from that life must sound vain to those who do not dwell in the same thought on their own part. I dare not speak for it. My words do not carry its august sense; they fall short and cold. Only itself can inspire whom it will, and behold! their speech shall be lyrical, and sweet, and universal as the rising of the wind. Yet I desire, even by profane words, if I may not use sacred, to indicate the heaven of this deity and to report what hints I have collected of the transcendent simplicity and energy of the Highest Law.

If we consider what happens in conversation, in reveries, in remorse, in times of passion, in surprises, in the instructions of dreams, wherein often we see ourselves in masquerade,—the droll disguises only magnifying and enhancing a real element and forcing it on our distant notice,—we shall catch many hints that will broaden and lighten into knowledge of the secret of nature. All goes to show that the soul in man is not an organ, but animates and exercises all the organs; is not a function, like the power of memory, of calculation, of comparison, but uses these as hands and feet; is not a faculty, but a light; is not the intellect or the will, but the master of the intellect and the will; is the background of our being, in which they lie,—an immensity not possessed and that cannot be possessed. From within or from behind, a light shines through us upon things and makes us aware that we are nothing, but the light is all. A man is the façade of a temple wherein all wisdom and all good abide. What we commonly call man, the eating, drinking, planting, counting man, does not, as we know him, represent himself, but misrepresents himself. Him we do not respect, but the soul, whose organ he is, would he let it appear through his action, would make our knees bend. When it breathes through his intellect, it is genius; when it breathes through his will, it is virtue; when it flows through his affection, it is love. And the blindness of the intellect begins when it would be something of itself. The weakness of the will begins when the individual would be something of himself. All reform aims in some one particular to let the soul have its way through us; in other words, to engage us to obey.

Of this pure nature every man is at some time sensible. Language cannot paint it with his colors. It is too subtile. It is undefinable, unmeasurable; but we know that it pervades and contains us. We know that all spiritual being is in man. A wise old proverb says, "God comes to see us without bell;" that is, as there is no screen or ceiling between our heads and the infinite heavens, so is there no bar or wall in the soul, where man, the effect, ceases, and God, the cause, begins. The walls are taken away. We lie open on one side to the deeps of spiritual nature, to the attributes of God. Justice we see and know, Love, Freedom, Power. These natures no man ever got above, but they tower over us, and most in the moment when our interests tempt us to wound them.

The sovereignty of this nature whereof we speak is made known by its independency of those limitations which circumscribe us on every hand. The soul circumscribes all things. As I have said, it contradicts all experience. In like manner it abolishes time and space. The influence of the senses has in most men overpowered the mind to that degree that the walls of time and space have come to look real and insurmountable; and to speak with levity of these limits is, in the world, the sign of insanity. Yet time and space are but inverse measures of the force of the soul. The spirit sports with time,—

> "Can crowd eternity into an hour,
> Or stretch an hour to eternity."

We are often made to feel that there is another youth and age than that which is measured from the year of our natural birth. Some thoughts always find us young, and keep us so. Such a thought is the love of the universal and eternal beauty. Every man parts from that contemplation with the feeling that it rather belongs to ages than to mortal life. The least activity of the intellectual powers redeems us in a degree from the conditions of time. In sickness, in languor, give us a strain of poetry or a profound sentence, and we are refreshed; or produce a volume of Plato or Shakspeare, or remind us of their names, and instantly we come into a feeling of longevity. See how the deep divine thought reduces centuries and millenniums, and makes itself present through all ages. Is the teaching of Christ less effective now than it was when first his mouth was opened? The emphasis of facts and persons in my thought has nothing to do with time. And so always the soul's scale is one, the scale of the senses and the understanding is another. Before the revelations of the soul, Time, Space and Nature shrink away. In common speech we refer all things to time, as we habitually refer the immensely sundered stars to one concave sphere. And so we say that the Judgment is distant or near, that the Millennium approaches, that a day of certain political, moral, social reforms is at hand, and the like, when we mean that in the nature of things one of the facts we contemplate is external and fugitive, and the other is permanent and connate with the soul. The things we now esteem fixed shall, one by one, detach themselves like ripe fruit from our experience, and fall. The wind shall blow them none knows whither. The landscape, the figures, Boston, London, are facts as fugitive as any institution past, or any whiff of mist or smoke, and so is society, and so is the world. The soul looketh steadily forwards, creating a world before her, leaving worlds behind her. She has no dates, nor rites, nor persons, nor specialties nor men. The soul knows only the soul; the web of events is the flowing robe in which she is clothed.

After its own law and not by arithmetic is the rate of its progress to be computed. The soul's advances are not made by gradation, such as can be represented by motion in a straight line, but rather by ascension of state, such as can be represented by metamorphosis,—from the egg to the worm, from the worm to the fly. The growths of genius are of a certain *total* character, that does not advance the elect individual first over John, then Adam, then Richard, and give to each the pain of discovered inferiority,—but by every throe of growth the man expands there where he works, passing, at each pulsation, classes, populations, of men. With each divine impulse the mind rends the thin rinds of the visible and finite, and comes out into eternity, and inspires and expires its air. It converses with truths that have always been spoken in the world, and becomes conscious of a closer sympathy with Zeno and Arrian than with persons in the house.

This is the law of moral and of mental gain. The simple rise as by specific levity not into a particular virtue, but into the region of all the virtues. They are in the spirit which contains them all. The soul requires purity, but purity is not it; requires justice, but justice is not that; requires beneficence, but is somewhat better; so that there is a kind of descent and accommodation felt when we leave speaking of moral nature to urge a virtue which it enjoins. To the well-born child all the virtues are natural, and not painfully acquired. Speak to his heart, and the man becomes suddenly virtuous.

Within the same sentiment is the germ of intellectual growth, which obeys the same law. Those who are capable of humility, of justice, of love, of aspiration, stand already on a platform that commands the sciences and arts, speech and poetry, action and grace. For whoso dwells in this moral beatitude already anticipates those special powers which men prize so highly. The lover has no talent, no skill, which passes for quite nothing with his enamored maiden, however little she may possess of related faculty; and the heart which abandons itself to the Supreme Mind finds itself related to all its works, and will travel a royal road to particular knowledges and powers. In ascending to this primary and aboriginal sentiment we have come from our remote station on the circumference instantaneously to the centre of the world, where, as in the closet of God, we see causes, and anticipate the universe, which is but a slow effect.

One mode of the divine teaching is the incarnation of the spirit in a form,—in forms, like my own. I live in society; with persons who answer to thoughts in my own mind, or express a certain obedience to the great instincts to which I live. I see its presence to them. I am certified of a common nature; and these other souls, these separated selves, draw me as nothing else can. They stir in me the new emotions we call passion; of love, hatred, fear, admiration, pity; thence come conversation, competition, persuasion, cities and war. Persons are supplementary to the primary teaching of the soul. In youth we are mad for persons. Childhood and youth see all the world in them. But the larger experience of man discovers the identical nature appearing through them all. Persons themselves acquaint us with the impersonal. In all conversation between two persons tacit reference is made, as to a third party, to a common nature. That third party or common nature is not social; it is impersonal; is God. And so in groups where debate is earnest, and especially on high questions, the company become aware that the thought rises to an equal level in all bosoms, that all have a spiritual property in what was said, as well as the sayer. They all become wiser than they were. It arches over them like a temple, this unity of thought in which every heart beats with nobler sense of power and duty, and thinks and acts with unusual solemnity. All are conscious of attaining to a higher self-possession. It shines for all. There is a certain wisdom of humanity which is common to the greatest men with the lowest, and which our ordinary education often labors to silence and obstruct. The mind is one, and the best minds, who love truth for its own sake, think much less of property in truth. They accept it thankfully everywhere, and do not label or stamp it with any man's name, for it is theirs long beforehand, and from eternity. The learned and the studious of thought have no monopoly of wisdom. Their violence of direction in some degree disqualifies them to think truly. We owe many valuable observations to people who are not very acute or profound, and who say the thing without effort which we want and have long been hunting in vain. The action of the soul is oftener in that which is felt and left unsaid than in that which is said in any conversation. It broods over every society, and they unconsciously seek for it in each other. We know better than we do. We do not yet possess ourselves, and we know at the same time that we are much more. I feel the same truth how often in my trivial conversation with my neighbors, that somewhat higher in each of us overlooks this by-play, and Jove nods to Jove from behind each of us.

Men descend to meet. In their habitual and mean service to the world, for which they forsake their native nobleness, they resemble those Arabian sheiks who dwell in mean houses and affect an external poverty, to escape the rapacity of the Pacha, and reserve all their display of wealth for their interior and guarded retirements.

As it is present in all persons, so it is in every period of life. It is adult already in the infant man. In my dealing with my child, my Latin and Greek, my accomplishments and my money stead me nothing; but as much soul as I have avails. If I am wilful, he sets his will against mine, one for one, and leaves me, if I please, the degradation of beating him by my superiority of strength. But if I renounce my will and act for the soul, setting that up as umpire between us two, out of his young eyes looks the same soul; he reveres and loves with me.

The soul is the perceiver and revealer of truth. We know truth when we see it, let sceptic and scoffer say what they choose. Foolish people ask you, when you have spoken what they do not wish to hear, "How do you know it is truth, and not an error of your own?" We know truth when we see it, from opinion, as we know when we are awake that we are awake. It was a grand sentence of Emanuel Swedenborg, which would alone indicate the greatness of that man's perception,—"It is no proof of a man's understanding to be able to affirm whatever he pleases; but to be able to discern that what is true is true, and that what is false is false,—this is the mark and character of intelligence." In the book I read, the good thought returns to me, as every truth will, the image of the whole soul. To the bad thought which I find in it, the same soul becomes a discerning, separating sword, and lops it away. We are wiser than we know. If we will not interfere with our thought, but will act entirely, or see how the thing stands in God, we know the particular thing, and every thing, and every man. For the Maker of all things and all persons stands behind us and casts his dread omniscience through us over things.

But beyond this recognition of its own in particular passages of the individual's experience, it also reveals truth. And here we should seek to reinforce ourselves by its very presence, and to speak with a worthier, loftier strain of that advent. For the soul's communication of truth is the highest event in nature, since it then does not give somewhat from itself, but it gives itself, or passes into and becomes that man whom it enlightens; or in proportion to that truth he receives, it takes him to itself.

We distinguish the announcements of the soul, its manifestations of its own nature, by the term *Revelation*. These are always attended by the emotion of the sublime. For this communication is an influx of the Divine mind into our mind. It is an ebb of the individual rivulet before the flowing surges of the sea of life. Every distinct apprehension of this central commandment agitates men with awe and delight. A thrill passes through all men at the reception of new truth, or at the performance of a great action, which comes out of the heart of nature. In these communications the power to see is not separated from the will to do, but the insight proceeds from obedience, and the obedience proceeds from a joyful perception. Every moment when the individual feels himself invaded by it is memorable. By the necessity of our constitution a certain enthusiasm attends the individual's consciousness of that divine presence. The character and duration of this enthusiasm vary with the state of the individual, from an ecstasy and trance and prophetic inspiration,—which is its rarer appearance,—to the faintest glow of virtuous emotion, in which form it warms, like our household fires, all the families and associations of men, and makes society possible. A certain tendency to insanity has always attended the opening of the religious sense in men, as if they had been "blasted with excess of light." The trances of Socrates, the "union" of Plotinus, the vision of Porphyry, the conversion of Paul, the aurora of Behmen, the convulsions of George Fox and his Quakers, the illumination of Swedenborg, are of this kind. What was in the case of these remarkable persons a ravishment, has, in innumerable instances in common life, been exhibited in less striking manner. Everywhere the history of religion betrays a tendency to enthusiasm. The rapture of the Moravian and Quietist; the opening of the eternal sense of the Word, in the language of the New Jerusalem Church; the *revival* of the Calvinistic churches; the *experiences* of the Methodists, are varying forms of that shudder of awe and delight with which the individual soul always mingles with the universal soul.

The nature of these revelations is the same; they are perceptions of the absolute law. They are solutions of the soul's own questions. They do not answer the questions which the understanding asks. The soul answers never by words, but by the thing itself that is inquired after.

Revelation is the disclosure of the soul. The popular notion of a revelation is that it is a telling of fortunes. In past oracles of the soul the understanding seeks to find answers to sensual questions, and undertakes to tell from God how long men shall exist, what their hands shall do and who shall be their company, adding names and dates and places. But we must pick no locks. We must check this low curiosity. An answer in words is delusive; it is really no answer to the questions you ask. Do not require a description of the countries towards which you sail. The description does not describe them to you, and to-morrow you arrive there and know them by inhabiting them. Men ask concerning the immortality of the soul, the employments of heaven, the state of the sinner, and so forth. They even dream that Jesus has left replies to precisely these interrogatories. Never a moment did that sublime spirit speak in their *patois*. To truth, justice, love, the attributes of the soul, the idea of immutableness is essentially associated. Jesus, living in these moral sentiments, heedless of sensual fortunes, heeding only the manifestations of these, never made the separation of the idea of duration from the essence of these attributes, nor uttered a syllable concerning the duration of the soul. It was left to his disciples to sever duration from the moral elements, and to teach the immortality of the soul as a doctrine, and maintain it by evidences. The moment the doctrine of the immortality is separately taught, man is already fallen. In the flowing of love, in the adoration of humility, there is no question of continuance.

No inspired man ever asks this question or condescends to these evidences. For the soul is true to itself, and the man in whom it is shed abroad cannot wander from the present, which is infinite, to a future which would be finite.

These questions which we lust to ask about the future are a confession of sin. God has no answer for them. No answer in words can reply to a question of things. It is not in an arbitrary "decree of God," but in the nature of man, that a veil shuts down on the facts of to-morrow; for the soul will not have us read any other cipher than that of cause and effect. By this veil which curtains events it instructs the children of men to live in to-day. The only mode of obtaining an answer to these questions of the senses is to forego all low curiosity, and, accepting the tide of being which floats us into the secret of nature, work and live, work and live, and all unawares the advancing soul has built and forged for itself a new condition, and the question and the answer are one.

By the same fire, vital, consecrating, celestial, which burns until it shall dissolve all things into the waves and surges of an ocean of light, we see and know each other, and what spirit each is of. Who can tell the grounds of his knowledge of the character of the several individuals in his circle of friends? No man. Yet their acts and words do not disappoint him. In that man, though he knew no ill of him, he put no trust. In that other, though they had seldom met, authentic signs had yet passed, to signify that he might be trusted as one who had an interest in his own character. We know each other very well,—which of us has been just to himself and whether that which we teach or behold is only an aspiration or is our honest effort also.

We are all discerners of spirits. That diagnosis lies aloft in our life or unconscious power. The intercourse of society, its trade, its religion, its friendships, its quarrels, is one wide judicial investigation of character. In full court, or in small committee, or confronted face to face, accuser and accused, men offer themselves to be judged. Against their will they exhibit those decisive trifles by which character is read. But who judges?

and what? Not our understanding. We do not read them by learning or craft. No; the wisdom of the wise man consists herein, that he does not judge them; he lets them judge themselves and merely reads and records their own verdict.

By virtue of this inevitable nature, private will is overpowered, and, maugre our efforts or our imperfections, your genius will speak from you, and mine from me. That which we are, we shall teach, not voluntarily but involuntarily. Thoughts come into our minds by avenues which we never left open, and thoughts go out of our minds through avenues which we never voluntarily opened. Character teaches over our head. The infallible index of true progress is found in the tone the man takes. Neither his age, nor his breeding, nor company, nor books, nor actions, nor talents, nor all together can hinder him from being deferential to a higher spirit than his own. If he have not found his home in God, his manners, his forms of speech, the turn of his sentences, the build, shall I say, of all his opinions will involuntarily confess it, let him brave it out how he will. If he have found his centre, the Deity will shine through him, through all the disguises of ignorance, of ungenial temperament, of unfavorable circumstance. The tone of seeking is one, and the tone of having is another.

The great distinction between teachers sacred or literary,—between poets like Herbert, and poets like Pope,—between philosophers like Spinoza, Kant and Coleridge, and philosophers like Locke, Paley, Mackintosh and Stewart,—between men of the world who are reckoned accomplished talkers, and here and there a fervent mystic, prophesying half insane under the infinitude of his thought,—is that one class speak *from within*, or from experience, as parties and possessors of the fact; and the other class *from without*, as spectators merely, or perhaps as acquainted with the fact on the evidence of third persons. It is of no use to preach to me from without. I can do that too easily myself. Jesus speaks always from within, and in a degree that transcends all others. In that is the miracle. I believe beforehand that it ought so to be. All men stand continually in the expectation of the appearance of such a teacher. But if a man do not speak from within the veil, where the word is one with that it tells of, let him lowly confess it.

The same Omniscience flows into the intellect and makes what we call genius. Much of the wisdom of the world is not wisdom, and the most illuminated class of men are no doubt superior to literary fame, and are not writers. Among the multitude of scholars and authors we feel no hallowing presence; we are sensible of a knack and skill rather than of inspiration; they have a light and know not whence it comes and call it their own; their talent is some exaggerated faculty, some overgrown member, so that their strength is a disease. In these instances the intellectual gifts do not make the impression of virtue, but almost of vice; and we feel that a man's talents stand in the way of his advancement in truth. But genius is religious. It is a larger imbibing of the common heart. It is not anomalous, but more like and not less like other men. There is in all great poets a wisdom of humanity which is superior to any talents they exercise. The author, the wit, the partisan, the fine gentleman, does not take place of the man. Humanity shines in Homer, in Chaucer, in Spenser, in Shakspeare, in Milton. They are content with truth. They use the positive degree. They seem frigid and phlegmatic to those who have been spiced with the frantic passion and violent coloring of inferior but popular writers. For they are poets by the free course which they allow to the informing soul, which through their eyes beholds again and blesses the things which it hath made. The soul is superior to its knowledge, wiser than any of its works. The great poet makes us feel our own wealth, and then we think less of his compositions. His best communication to our mind is to teach us to despise all he has done. Shakspeare carries us to such a lofty strain of intelligent activity as to suggest a wealth which beggars his own; and we then feel that the splendid works which he has created, and which in other hours we extol as a sort of self-existent poetry, take no stronger hold of real nature than the shadow of a passing traveller on the rock. The inspiration which uttered itself in Hamlet and Lear could utter things as good from day to day for ever. Why then should I make account of Hamlet and Lear, as if we had not the soul from which they fell as syllables from the tongue?

This energy does not descend into individual life on any other condition than entire possession. It comes to the lowly and simple; it comes to whomsoever will put off what is foreign and proud; it comes as insight; it comes as serenity and grandeur. When we see those whom it inhabits, we are apprised of new degrees of greatness. From that inspiration the man comes back with a changed tone. He does not talk with men with an eye to their opinion. He tries them. It requires of us to be plain and true. The vain traveller attempts to embellish his life by quoting my lord and the prince and the countess, who thus said or did to *him*. The ambitious vulgar show you their spoons and brooches and rings, and preserve their cards and compliments. The more cultivated, in their account of their own experience, cull out the pleasing, poetic circumstance,—the visit to Rome, the man of genius they saw, the brilliant friend they know; still further on perhaps the gorgeous landscape, the mountain lights, the mountain thoughts they enjoyed yesterday,—and so seek to throw a romantic color over their life. But the soul that ascends to worship the great God is plain and true; has no rose-color, no fine friends, no chivalry, no adventures; does not want admiration; dwells in the hour that now is, in the earnest experience of the common day,—by reason of the present moment and the mere trifle having become porous to thought and bibulous of the sea of light.

Converse with a mind that is grandly simple, and literature looks like word-catching. The simplest utterances are worthiest to be written, yet are they so cheap and so things of course, that in the infinite riches of the soul it is like gathering a few pebbles off the ground, or bottling a little air in a phial, when the whole earth and the whole atmosphere are ours. Nothing can pass there, or make you one of the circle, but the casting aside your trappings and dealing man to man in naked truth, plain confession and omniscient affirmation.

Souls such as these treat you as gods would, walk as gods in the earth, accepting without any admiration your wit, your bounty, your virtue even,—say rather your act of duty, for your virtue they own as their proper blood, royal as themselves, and over-royal, and the father of the gods. But what rebuke their plain fraternal bearing casts on the mutual flattery with which authors solace each other and wound themselves! These flatter not. I do not wonder that these men go to see Cromwell and Christina and Charles the Second and James the First and the Grand Turk. For they are, in their own elevation, the fellows of kings, and must feel the servile tone of conversation in the world. They must always be a godsend to princes, for they confront them, a king to a king, without ducking or concession, and give a high nature the refreshment and satisfaction of resistance, of plain humanity, of even companionship and of new ideas. They leave them wiser and superior men. Souls like these make us feel that sincerity is more excellent than flattery. Deal so plainly with man and woman as to constrain the utmost sincerity and destroy all hope of trifling with you. It is the highest compliment you can pay. Their "highest praising," said Milton, "is not flattery, and their plainest advice is a kind of praising."

Ineffable is the union of man and God in every act of the soul. The simplest person who in his integrity worships God, becomes God; yet for ever and ever the influx of this better and universal self is new and unsearchable. It inspires awe and astonishment. How dear, how soothing to man, arises the idea of God, peopling the lonely place, effacing the scars of our mistakes and disappointments! When we have broken our god of tradition and ceased from our god of rhetoric, then may God fire the heart with his presence. It is the doubling of the heart itself, nay, the infinite enlargement of the heart with a power of growth to a new infinity on every side. It inspires in man an infallible trust. He has not the conviction, but the sight, that the best is the true, and may in that thought easily dismiss all particular uncertainties and fears, and adjourn to the sure revelation of time the solution of his private riddles. He is sure that his welfare is dear to the heart of being. In the presence of law to his mind he is overflowed with a reliance so universal that it sweeps away all cherished hopes and the most stable projects of mortal condition in its flood. He believes that he cannot escape from his good. The things that are really for thee gravitate to thee. You are running to seek your friend. Let your feet run, but your mind need not. If you do not find him, will you not acquiesce that it is best you should not find him? for there is a power, which, as it is in you, is in him also, and could therefore very well bring you together, if it were for the best. You are preparing with eagerness to go and render a service to which your talent and your taste invite you, the love of men and the hope of fame. Has it not occurred to you that you have no right to go, unless you are equally willing to be prevented from going? O, believe, as thou livest, that every sound that is spoken over the round world, which thou oughtest to hear, will vibrate on thine ear! Every proverb, every book, every by-word that belongs to thee for aid or comfort, shall surely come home through open or winding passages. Every friend whom not thy fantastic will but the great and tender heart in thee craveth, shall lock thee in his embrace. And this because the heart in thee is the heart of all; not a valve, not a wall, not an intersection is there anywhere in nature, but one blood rolls uninterruptedly an endless circulation through all men, as the water of the globe is all one sea, and, truly seen, its tide is one.

Let man then learn the revelation of all nature and all thought to his heart; this, namely; that the Highest dwells with him; that the sources of nature are in his own mind, if the sentiment of duty is there. But if he would know what the great God speaketh, he must "go into his closet and shut the door," as Jesus said. God will not make himself manifest to cowards. He must greatly listen to himself, withdrawing himself from all the accents of other men's devotion. Even their prayers are hurtful to him, until he have made his own. Our religion vulgarly stands on numbers of believers. Whenever the appeal is made,—no matter how indirectly,—to numbers, proclamation is then and there made that religion is not. He that finds God a sweet enveloping thought to him never counts his company. When I sit in that presence, who shall dare to come in? When I rest in perfect humility, when I burn with pure love, what can Calvin or Swedenborg say?

It makes no difference whether the appeal is to numbers or to one. The faith that stands on authority is not faith. The reliance on authority measures the decline of religion, the withdrawal of the soul. The position men have given to Jesus, now for many centuries of history, is a position of authority. It characterizes themselves. It cannot alter the eternal facts. Great is the soul, and plain. It is no flatterer, it is no follower; it never appeals from itself. It believes in itself. Before the immense possibilities of man all mere experience, all past biography, however spotless and sainted, shrinks away. Before that heaven which our presentiments foreshow us, we cannot easily praise any form of life we have seen or read of. We not only affirm that we have few great men, but, absolutely speaking, that we have none; that we have no history, no record of any character or mode of living that entirely contents us. The saints and demigods whom history worships we are constrained to accept with a grain of allowance. Though in our lonely hours we draw a new strength out of their memory, yet, pressed on our attention, as they are by the thoughtless and customary, they fatigue and invade. The soul gives itself, alone, original and pure, to the Lonely, Original and Pure, who, on that condition, gladly inhabits, leads and speaks through it. Then is it glad, young and nimble. It is not wise, but it sees through all things. It is not called religious, but it is innocent. It calls the light its own, and feels that the grass grows and the stone falls by a law inferior to, and dependent on, its nature. Behold, it saith, I am born into the great, the universal mind. I, the imperfect, adore my own Perfect. I am somehow receptive of the great soul, and thereby I do overlook the sun and the stars and feel them to be the fair accidents and effects which change and pass. More and more the surges of everlasting nature enter into me, and I become public and human in my regards and actions. So come I to live in thoughts and act with energies which are immortal. Thus revering the soul, and learning, as the ancient said, that "its beauty is immense," man will come to see that the world is the perennial miracle which the soul worketh, and be less astonished at particular wonders; he will learn that there is no profane history; that all history is sacred; that the universe is represented in an atom, in a moment of time. He will weave no longer a spotted life of shreds and patches, but he will live with a divine unity. He will cease from what is base and frivolous in his life and be content with all places and with any service he can render. He will calmly front the morrow in the negligency of that trust which carries God with it and so hath already the whole future in the bottom of the heart.

1841

THE YOUNG AMERICAN

A LECTURE READ BEFORE THE MERCANTILE LIBRARY ASSOCIATION, BOSTON, FEBRUARY 7, 1844

GENTLEMEN:

It is remarkable that our people have their intellectual culture from one country and their duties from another. This false state of things is newly in a way to be corrected. America is beginning to assert herself to the senses and to the imagination of her children, and Europe is receding in the same degree. This their reaction on education gives a new importance to the internal improvements and to the politics of the country. Who has not been stimulated to reflection by the facilities now in progress of construction for travel and the transportation of goods in the United States?

This rage of road building is beneficent for America, where vast distance is so main a consideration in our domestic politics and trade, inasmuch as the great political promise of the invention is to hold the Union staunch, whose days seemed already numbered by the mere inconvenience of transporting representatives, judges, and officers across such tedious distances of land and water. Not only is distance annihilated, but when, as now, the locomotive and the steamboat, like enormous shuttles, shoot every day across the thousand various threads of national descent and employment and bind them fast in one web, an hourly assimilation goes forward, and there is no danger that local peculiarities and hostilities should be preserved.

1. But I hasten to speak of the utility of these improvements in creating an American sentiment. An unlooked-for consequence of the railroad is the increased acquaintance it has given the American people with the boundless resources of their own soil. If this invention has reduced England to a third of its size, by bringing people so much nearer, in this country it has given a new celerity to *time*, or anticipated by fifty years the planting of tracts of land, the choice of water privileges, the working of mines, and other natural advantages. Railroad iron is a magi-

cian's rod, in its power to evoke the sleeping energies of land and water.

The railroad is but one arrow in our quiver, though it has great value as a sort of yard-stick and surveyor's line. The bountiful continent is ours, state on state, and territory on territory, to the waves of the Pacific sea;

> "Our garden is the immeasurable earth,
> The heaven's blue pillars are Medea's house.

The task of surveying, planting, and building upon this immense tract requires an education and a sentiment commensurate thereto. A consciousness of this fact is beginning to take the place of the purely trading spirit and education which sprang up whilst all the population lived on the fringe of sea-coast. And even on the coast, prudent men have begun to see that every American should be educated with a view to the values of land. The arts of engineering and of architecture are studied; scientific agriculture is an object of growing attention; the mineral riches are explored; limestone, coal, slate, and iron; and the value of timber-lands is enhanced.

Columbus alleged as a reason for seeking a continent in the West, that the harmony of nature required a great tract of land in the western hemisphere, to balance the known extent of land in the eastern; and it now appears that we must estimate the native values of this broad region to redress the balance of our own judgments, and appreciate the advantages opened to the human race in this country which is our fortunate home. The land is the appointed remedy for whatever is false and fantastic in our culture. The continent we inhabit is to be physic and food for our mind, as well as our body. The land, with its tranquillizing, sanative influences, is to repair the errors of a scholastic and traditional education, and bring us into just relations with men and things.

The habit of living in the presence of these invitations of natural wealth is not inoperative; and this habit, combined with the moral sentiment which, in the recent years, has interrogated every institution, usage, and law, has naturally given a strong direction to the wishes and aims of active young men, to withdraw from cities and cultivate the soil. This inclination has appeared in the most unlooked-for quarters, in men supposed to be absorbed in business, and in those connected with the liberal professions. And since the walks of trade were crowded, whilst that of agriculture cannot easily be, inasmuch as the farmer who is not wanted by others can yet grow his own bread, whilst the manufacturer or the trader, who is not wanted, cannot,—this seemed a happy tendency. For beside all the moral benefit which we may expect from the farmer's profession, when a man enters it considerately; this promised the conquering of the soil, plenty, and beyond this the adorning of the country with every advantage and ornament which labor, ingenuity, and affection for a man's home could suggest.

Meantime, with cheap land, and the pacific disposition of the people, everything invites to the arts of agriculture, of gardening, and domestic architecture. Public gardens, on the scale of such plantations in Europe and Asia, are now unknown to us. There is no feature of the old countries that strikes an American with more agreeable surprise than the beautiful gardens of Europe; such as the Boboli in Florence, the Villa Borghese in Rome, the Villa d' Este in Tivoli, the gardens at Munich and at Frankfort on the Main: works easily imitated here, and which might well make the land dear to the citizen, and inflame patriotism. It is the fine art which is left for us, now that sculpture, painting, and religious and civil architecture have become effete, and have passed into second childhood. We have twenty degrees of latitude wherein to choose a seat, and the new modes of travelling enlarge the opportunity of selection, by making it easy to cultivate very distant tracts and yet remain in strict intercourse with the centres of trade and population. And the whole force of all the arts goes to facilitate the decoration of lands and dwellings. A garden has this advantage, that it makes it indifferent where you live. A well-laid garden makes the face of the country of no account; let that be low or high, grand or mean, you have made a beautiful abode worthy of man. If the landscape is pleasing, the garden shows it,—if tame, it excludes it.

A little grove, which any farmer can find or cause to grow near his house, will in a few years make cataracts and chains of mountains quite unnecessary to his scenery; and he is so contented with his alleys, woodlands, orchards and river, that Niagara, and the Notch of the White Hills, and Nantasket Beach, are superfluities. And yet the selection of a fit house-lot has the same advantage over an indifferent one, as the selection to a given employment of a man who has a genius for that work. In the last case the culture of years will never make the most painstaking apprentice his equal: no more will gardening give the advantage of a happy site to a house in a hole or on a pinnacle. In America we have hitherto little to boast in this kind. The cities drain the country of the best part of its population: the flower of the youth, of both sexes, goes into the towns, and the country is cultivated by a so much inferior class. The land,—travel a whole day together,—looks poverty-stricken, and the buildings plain and poor. In Europe, where society has an aristocratic structure, the land is full of men of the best stock and the best culture, whose interest and pride it is to remain half the year on their estates, and to fill them with every convenience and ornament. Of course these make model farms, and model architecture, and are a constant education to the eye of the surrounding population. Whatever events in progress shall go to disgust men with cities and infuse into them the passion for country life and country pleasures, will render a service to the whole face of this continent, and will further the most poetic of all the occupations of real life, the bringing out by art the native but hidden graces of the landscape.

I look on such improvements also as directly tending to endear the land to the inhabitant. Any relation to the land, the habit of tilling it, or mining it, or even hunting on it, generates the feeling of patriotism. He who keeps shop on it, or he who merely uses it as a support to his desk and ledger, or to his manufactory, values it less. The vast majority of the people of this country live by the land, and carry its quality in their manners and opinions. We in the Atlantic states, by position, have been commercial, and have, as I said, imbibed easily an European culture. Luckily for us, now that steam has narrowed the Atlantic to a strait, the nervous, rocky West is intruding a new and continental element into the national mind, and we shall yet have an American genius. How much better when the whole land is a garden, and the people have grown up in the bowers of a paradise. Without looking then to those extraordinary social influences which are now acting in precisely this direction, but only at what is inevitably doing around us, I think we must regard the *land* as a commanding and increasing power on the citizen, the sanative and Americanizing influence, which promises to disclose new virtues for ages to come.

2. In the second place, the uprise and culmination of the new and anti-feudal power of Commerce is the political fact of most significance to the American at this hour.

We cannot look on the freedom of this country, in connexion with its youth, without a presentiment that here shall laws and institutions exist on some scale of proportion to the majesty of nature. To men legislating for the area betwixt the two oceans, betwixt the snows and the tropics, somewhat of the gravity of nature will infuse itself into the code. A heterogeneous population crowding on all ships from all corners of the world to the great gates of North America, namely Boston, New York, and New Orleans, and thence proceeding inward to the prairie and the mountains, and quickly contributing their private thought to the public opinion, their toll to the treasury, and their vote to the election, it cannot be doubted that the legislation of this country should become more catholic and cosmopolitan than that of any other. It seems so easy for America to inspire and express the most expansive and humane spirit; new-born, free, healthful, strong, the land of the laborer, of the democrat, of the philanthropist, of the believer, of the saint, she should speak for the human race. It is the country of the Future. From Washington, proverbially "the city of magnificent distances," through all its cities, states, and territories, it is a country of beginnings, of projects, of designs, of expectations.

Gentlemen, there is a sublime and friendly Destiny by which the human race is guided,—the race never dying, the individual never spared,—to results affecting masses and ages. Men are narrow and selfish, but the Genius or Destiny is not narrow, but beneficent. It is not discovered in their calculated and voluntary activity, but in what befalls, with or without their design. Only what is inevitable interests us, and it turns out that love and good are inevitable, and in the course of things. That Genius has infused itself into nature. It indicates itself by a small excess of good, a small balance in brute facts always favorable to the side of reason. All the facts in any part of nature shall be tabulated and the results shall indicate the same security and benefit; so slight as to be hardly observable, and yet it is there. The sphere is flattened at the poles and swelled at the equator; a form flowing necessarily from the fluid state, yet *the* form, the mathematician assures us, required to prevent the protuberances of the continent, or even of lesser mountains cast up at any time by earthquakes, from continually deranging the axis of the earth. The census of the population is found to keep an invariable equality in the sexes, with a trifling predominance in favor of the male, as if to counterbalance the necessarily increased exposure of male life in war, navigation, and other accidents. Remark the unceasing effort throughout nature at somewhat better than the actual creatures: *amelioration in nature*, which alone permits and authorizes amelioration in mankind. The population of the world is a conditional population; these are not the best, but the best that could live in the existing state of soils, gases, animals and morals: the best that could *yet* live; there shall be a better, please God. This Genius or Destiny is of the sternest administration, though rumors exist of its secret tenderness. It may be styled a cruel kindness, serving the whole even to the ruin of the member; a terrible communist, reserving all profits to the community, without dividend to individuals. Its law is, you shall have everything as a member, nothing to yourself. For Nature is the noblest engineer, yet uses a grinding economy, working up all that is wasted to-day into to-morrow's creation;—not a superfluous grain of sand, for all the ostentation she makes of expense and public works. It is because Nature thus saves and uses, laboring for the general, that we poor particulars are so crushed and straitened, and find it so hard to live. She flung us out in her plenty, but we cannot shed a hair or a paring of a nail but instantly she snatches at the shred and appropriates it to the general stock. Our condition is like that of the poor wolves: if one of the flock wound himself or so much as limp, the rest eat him up incontinently.

That serene Power interposes the check upon the caprices and officiousness of our wills. Its charity is not our charity. One of its agents is our will, but that which expresses itself in our will is stronger than our will. We are very forward to help it, but it will not be accelerated. It resists our meddling, eleemosynary contrivances. We devise sumptuary and relief laws, but the principle of population is always reducing wages to the lowest pittance on which human life can be sustained. We legislate against forestalling and monopoly; we would have a common granary for the poor; but the selfishness which hoards the corn for high prices is the preventive of famine; and the law of self-preservation is surer policy than any legislation can be. We concoct eleemosynary systems, and it turns out that our charity increases pauperism. We inflate our paper currency, we repair commerce with unlimited credit, and are presently visited with unlimited bankruptcy.

It is easy to see that the existing generation are conspiring with a beneficence which in its working for coming generations, sacrifices the passing one; which infatuates the most selfish men to act against their private interest for the public welfare. We build railroads, we know not for what or for whom; but one thing is certain, that we who build will receive the very smallest share of benefit. Benefit will accrue, they are essential to the country, but that will be felt not until we are no longer countrymen. We do the like in all matters:—

> "Man's heart the Almighty to the Future set
> By secret and inviolable springs."

We plant trees, we build stone houses, we redeem the waste, we make prospective laws, we found colleges and hospitals, for remote generations. We should be mortified to learn that the little benefit we chanced in our own persons to receive was the utmost they would yield.

The history of commerce is the record of this beneficent tendency. The patriarchal form of government readily becomes despotic, as each person may see in his own family. Fathers wish to be fathers of the minds of their children, and behold with impatience a new character and way of thinking presuming to show itself in their own son or daughter. This feeling, which all their love and pride in the powers of their children cannot subdue, becomes petulance and tyranny when the head of the clan, the emperor of an empire, deals with the same difference of opinion in his subjects. Difference of opinion is the one crime which kings never forgive. An empire is an immense egotism. "I am the State," said the French Louis. When a French ambassador mentioned to Paul of Russia that a man of consequence in St. Petersburg was interesting himself in some matter, the Czar interrupted him,—"There is no man of consequence in this empire but he with whom I am actually speaking; and so long only as I am speaking to him is he of any consequence." And the Emperor Nicholas is reported to have said to his council, "The age is embarrassed with new opinions; rely on me, gentlemen, I shall oppose an iron will to the progress of liberal opinions."

It is easy to see that this patriarchal or family management gets to be rather troublesome to all but the papa; the sceptre comes to be a crow-bar. And this unpleasant egotism, Feudalism opposes and finally destroys. The king is compelled to call in the aid of his brothers and cousins and remote relations, to help him keep his overgrown house in order; and this club of noblemen always come at last to have a will of their own; they combine to brave the sovereign, and call in the aid of the people. Each chief attaches as many followers as he can, by kindness, maintenance, and gifts; and as long as war lasts, the nobles, who must be soldiers, rule very well. But when peace comes, the nobles prove very whimsical and uncomfortable masters; their frolics turn out to be insulting and degrading to the commoner. Feudalism grew to be a bandit and brigand.

Meantime Trade had begun to appear: Trade, a plant which grows wherever there is peace, as soon as there is peace, and as long as there is peace. The luxury and necessity of the noble fostered it. And as quickly as men go to foreign parts in ships or caravans, a new order of things springs up; new command takes place, new servants and new masters. Their information, their wealth, their correspondence, have made them quite other men than left their native shore. *They* are nobles now, and by another patent than the king's. Feudalism had been good, had broken the power of the kings, and had some good traits of its own; but it had grown mischievous, it was time for it to die, and as they say of dying people, all its faults came out. Trade was the strong man that broke it down and raised a new and unknown power in its place. It is a new agent in the world, and one of great function; it is a very intellectual force. This displaces physical strength, and instals computation, combination, information, science, in its room. It calls out all force of a certain kind that slumbered in the former dynasties. It is now in the midst of its career. Feudalism is not ended yet. Our governments still partake largely of that element. Trade goes to make the governments insignificant, and to bring every kind of faculty of every individual that can in any manner serve any person, *on sale*. Instead of a huge Army and Navy and Executive Departments, it converts Government into an Intelligence-Office, where every man may find what he wishes to buy, and expose what he has to sell; not only produce and manufactures, but art, skill, and intellectual and moral values. This is the good and this the evil of trade, that it would put everything into market; talent, beauty, virtue, and man himself.

The philosopher and lover of man have much harm to say of trade; but the historian will see that trade was the principle of Liberty; that trade planted America and destroyed Feudalism; that it makes peace and keeps peace, and it will abolish slavery. We complain of its oppression of the poor, and of its building up a new aristocracy on the ruins of the aristocracy it destroyed. But the aristocracy of trade has no permanence, is not entailed, was the result of toil and talent, the result of merit of some kind, and is continually falling, like the waves of the sea, before new claims of the same sort. Trade is an instrument in the hands of that friendly Power which works for us in our own despite. We design it thus and thus; it turns out otherwise and far better. This beneficent tendency, omnipotent without violence, exists and works. Every line of history inspires a confidence that we shall not go far wrong; that things mend. That is the moral of all we learn, that it warrants Hope, the prolific mother of reforms. Our part is plainly not to throw ourselves across the track, to block improvement and sit till we are stone, but to watch the uprise of successive mornings, and to conspire with the new works of new days. Government has been a fossil; it should be a plant. I conceive that the office of statute law should be to express and not to impede the mind of mankind. New thoughts, new things. Trade was one instrument, but Trade is also but for a time, and must give way to somewhat broader and better, whose signs are already dawning in the sky.

3. I pass to speak of the signs of that which is the sequel of trade.

In consequence of the revolution in the state of society wrought by trade, Government in our times is beginning to wear a clumsy and cumbrous appearance. We have already seen our way to shorter methods. The time is full of good signs. Some of them shall ripen to fruit. All this beneficent socialism is a friendly omen, and the swelling cry of voices for the education of the people indicates that Government has other offices than those of banker and executioner. Witness the new movements in the civilized world, the Communism of France, Germany, and Switzerland; the Trades' Unions, the English League against the Corn Laws; and the whole *Industrial Statistics*, so called. In Paris, the blouse, the badge of the operative, has begun to make its appearance in the *salons*. Witness too the spectacle of three Communities which have within a very short time sprung up within this Commonwealth, besides several others undertaken by citizens of Massachusetts within the territory of other States. These proceeded from a variety of motives, from an impatience of many usages in common life, from a wish for greater freedom than the manners and opinions of society permitted, but in great part from a feeling that the true offices of the State, the State had let fall to the ground; that in the scramble of parties for the public purse, the main duties of government were omitted,—the duty to instruct the ignorant, to supply the poor with work and with good guidance. These communists preferred the agricultural life as the most favorable condition for human culture; but they thought that the farm, as we manage it, did not satisfy the right ambition of man. The farmer, after sacrificing pleasure, taste, freedom, thought, love, to his work, turns out often a bankrupt, like the merchant. This result might well seem astounding. All this drudgery, from cock-crowing to starlight, for all these years, to end in mortgages and the auctioneer's flag, and removing from bad to worse. It is time to have the thing looked into, and with a sifting criticism ascertained who is the fool. It seemed a great deal worse, because the farmer is living in the same town with men who pretend to know exactly what he wants. On one side is agricultural chemistry, coolly exposing the nonsense of our spendthrift agriculture and ruinous expense of manures, and offering, by means of a teaspoonful of artificial guano, to turn a sandbank into corn; and on the other, the farmer, not only eager for the information, but with bad crops and in debt and bankruptcy, for want of it. Here are Etzlers and mechanical projectors, who, with the Fourierists, undoubtingly affirm that the smallest union would make every man rich;—and, on the other side, a multitude of poor men and women seeking work, and who cannot find enough to pay their board. The science is confident, and surely the poverty is real. If any means could be found to bring these two together!

This was one design of the projectors of the Associations which are now making their first feeble experiments. They were founded in love and in labor. They proposed, as you know, that all men should take a part in the manual toil, and proposed to amend the condition of men by substituting harmonious for hostile industry. It was a noble thought of Fourier, which gives a favorable idea of his system, to distinguish in his

Phalanx a class as the Sacred Band, by whom whatever duties were disagreeable and likely to be omitted, were to be assumed.

At least an economical success seemed certain for the enterprise, and that agricultural association must, sooner or later, fix the price of bread, and drive single farmers into association in self-defence; as the great commercial and manufacturing companies had already done. The Community is only the continuation of the same movement which made the joint-stock companies for manufactures, mining, insurance, banking, and so forth. It has turned out cheaper to make calico by companies; and it is proposed to plant corn and to bake bread by companies.

Undoubtedly, abundant mistakes will be made by these first adventurers, which will draw ridicule on their schemes. I think for example that they exaggerate the importance of a favorite project of theirs, that of paying talent and labor at one rate, paying all sorts of service at one rate, say ten cents the hour. They have paid it so; but not an instant would a dime remain a dime. In one hand it became an eagle as it fell, and in another hand a copper cent. For the whole value of the dime is in knowing what to do with it. One man buys with it a land-title of an Indian, and makes his posterity princes; or buys corn enough to feed the world; or pen, ink, and paper, or a painter's brush, by which he can communicate himself to the human race as if he were fire; and the other buys barley candy. Money is of no value; it cannot spend itself. All depends on the skill of the spender. Whether too the objection almost universally felt by such women in the community as were mothers, to an associate life, to a common table, and a common nursery, etc., setting a higher value on the private family, with poverty, than on an association with wealth, will not prove insuperable, remains to be determined.

But the Communities aimed at a higher success in securing to all their members an equal and thorough education. And on the whole one may say that aims so generous and so forced on them by the times, will not be relinquished, even if these attempts fail, but will be prosecuted until they succeed.

This is the value of the Communities; not what they have done, but the revolution which they indicate as on the way. Yes, Government must educate the poor man. Look across the country from any hill-side around us and the landscape seems to crave Government. The actual differences of men must be acknowledged, and met with love and wisdom. These rising grounds which command the champaign below, seem to ask for lords, true lords, *land*-lords, who understand the land and its uses and the applicabilities of men, and whose government would be what it should, namely mediation between want and supply. How gladly would each citizen pay a commission for the support and continuation of good guidance. None should be a governor who has not a talent for governing. Now many people have a native skill for carving out business for many hands; a genius for the disposition of affairs; and are never happier than when difficult practical questions, which embarrass other men, are to be solved. All lies in light before them; they are in their element. Could any means be contrived to appoint only these! There really seems a progress towards such a state of things in which this work shall be done by these natural workmen; and this, not certainly through any increased discretion shown by the citizens at elections, but by the gradual contempt into which official government falls, and the increasing disposition of private adventurers to assume its fallen functions. Thus the national Post Office is likely to go into disuse before the private telegraph and the express companies. The currency threatens to fall entirely into private hands. Justice is continually administered more and more by private reference, and not by litigation. We have feudal governments in a commercial age. It would be but an easy extension of our commercial system, to pay a private emperor a fee for services, as we pay an architect, an engineer, or a lawyer. If any man has a talent for righting wrong, for administering difficult affairs, for counselling poor farmers how to turn their estates to good husbandry, for combining a hundred private enterprises to a general benefit, let him in the county-town, or in Court Street, put up his sign-board, Mr. Smith, *Governor*, Mr. Johnson, *Working king*.

How can our young men complain of the poverty of things in New England, and not feel that poverty as a demand on their charity to make New England rich? Where is he who seeing a thousand men useless and unhappy, and making the whole region forlorn by their inaction, and conscious himself of possessing the faculty they want, does not hear his call to go and be their king?

We must have kings, and we must have nobles. Nature provides such in every society,—only let us have the real instead of the titular. Let us have our leading and our inspiration from the best. In every society some men are born to rule and some to advise. Let the powers be well directed, directed by love, and they would everywhere be greeted with joy and honor. The chief is the chief all the world over, only not his cap and his plume. It is only their dislike of the pretender, which makes men sometimes unjust to the accomplished man. If society were transparent, the noble would everywhere be gladly received and accredited, and would not be asked for his day's work, but would be felt as benefit, inasmuch as he was noble. That were his duty and stint,—to keep himself pure and purifying, the leaven of his nation. I think I see place and duties for a nobleman in every society; but it is not to drink wine and ride in a fine coach, but to guide and adorn life for the multitude by forethought, by elegant studies, by perseverance, self-devotion, and the remembrance of the humble old friend, by making his life secretly beautiful.

I call upon you, young men, to obey your heart and be the nobility of this land. In every age of the world there has been a leading nation, one of a more generous sentiment, whose eminent citizens were willing to stand for the interests of general justice and humanity, at the risk of being called, by the men of the moment, chimerical and fantastic. Which should be that nation but these States? Which should lead that movement, if not New England? Who should lead the leaders, but the Young American? The people, and the world, are now suffering from the want of religion and honor in its public mind. In America, out-of-doors all seems a market; in-doors an air-tight stove of conventionalism. Every body who comes into our houses savors of these habits; the men, of the market; the women, of the custom. I find no expression in our state papers or legislative debate, in our lyceums or churches, especially in our newspapers, of a high national feeling, no lofty counsels that rightfully stir the blood. I speak of those organs which can be presumed to speak a popular sense. They recommend conventional virtues, whatever will earn and preserve property; always the capitalist; the college, the church, the hospital, the theatre, the hotel, the road, the ship of the capitalist,—whatever goes to secure, adorn, enlarge these is good; what jeopardizes any of these is damnable. The "opposition" papers, so called, are on the same side. They attack the great capitalist, but with the aim to make a capitalist of the poor man. The opposition is against those who have money, from those who wish to have money. But who announces to us in journal, or in pulpit, or in the street, the secret of heroism?

> "Man alone
> Can perform the impossible."

I shall not need to go into an enumeration of our national defects and vices which require this Order of Censors in the State. I might not set down our most proclaimed offences as the worst. It is not often the worst trait that occasions the loudest outcry. Men complain of their suffering, and not of the crime. I fear little from the bad effect of Repudiation; I do not fear that it will spread. Stealing is a suicidal business; you cannot repudiate but once. But the bold face and tardy repentance permitted to this local mischief reveal a public mind so preoccupied with the love of gain that the common sentiment of indignation at fraud does not act with its natural force. The more need of a withdrawal from the crowd, and a resort to the fountain of right, by the brave. The timidity of our public opinion is our disease, or, shall I say, the publicness of opinion, the absence of private opinion. Good nature is plentiful, but we want justice, with heart of steel, to fight down the proud. The private mind has the access to the totality of goodness and truth that it may be a balance to a corrupt society; and to stand for the private verdict against popular clamor is the office of the noble. If a humane measure is propounded in behalf of the slave, or of the Irishman, or the Catholic, or for the succor of the poor; that sentiment, that project, will have the homage of the hero. That is his nobility, his oath of knighthood, to succor the helpless and oppressed; always to throw himself on the side of weakness, of youth, of hope; on the liberal, on the expansive side, never on the defensive, the conserving, the timorous, the lock-and-bolt system. More than our good-will we may not be able to give. We have our own affairs, our own genius, which chains each to his proper work. We cannot give our life to the cause of the debtor, of the slave, or the pauper, as another is doing; but to one thing we are bound, not to blaspheme the sentiment and the work of that man, not to throw stumbling-blocks in the way of the abolitionist, the philanthropist; as the organs of influence and opinion are swift to do. It is for us to confide in the beneficent Supreme Power, and not to rely on our money, and on the state because it is the guard of money. At this moment, the terror of old people and of vicious people is lest the Union of these states be destroyed: as if the Union had any other real basis than the good pleasure of a majority of the citizens to be united. But the wise and just man will always feel that he stands on his own feet; that he imparts strength to the State, not receives security from it; and that if all went down, he and such as he would quite easily combine in a new and better constitution. Every great and memorable community has consisted of formidable individuals, who, like the Roman or the Spartan, lent his own spirit to the State and made it great. Yet only by the supernatural is a man strong; nothing is so weak as an egotist. Nothing is mightier than we, when we are vehicles of a truth before which the State and the individual are alike ephemeral.

Gentlemen, the development of our American internal resources, the extension to the utmost of the commercial system, and the appearance of new moral causes which are to modify the State, are giving an aspect of greatness to the Future, which the imagination fears to open. One thing is plain for all men of common sense and common conscience, that here, here in America, is the home of man. After all the deductions which are to be made for our pitiful politics, which stake every gravest national question on the silly die whether James or whether Robert shall sit in the chair and hold the purse; after all the deduction is made for our frivolities and insanities, there still remains an organic simplicity and liberty, which, when it loses its balance, redresses itself presently, which offers opportunity to the human mind not known in any other region.

It is true, the public mind wants self-respect. We are full of vanity, of which the most signal proof is our sensitiveness to foreign and especially English censure. One cause of this is our immense reading, and that reading chiefly confined to the productions of the English press. It is also true that to imaginative persons in this country there is somewhat bare and bald in our short history and unsettled wilderness. They ask, who would live in a new country that can live in an old? and it is not strange that our youths and maidens should burn to see the picturesque extremes of an antiquated country. But it is one thing to visit the Pyramids, and another to wish to live there. Would they like tithes to the clergy, and sevenths to the government, and Horse-Guards, and licensed press, and grief when a child is born, and threatening, starved weavers, and a pauperism now constituting one thirteenth of the population? Instead of the open future expanding here before the eye of every boy to vastness, would they like the closing in of the future to a narrow slit of sky, and that fast contracting to be no future? One thing for instance, the beauties of aristocracy, we commend to the study of the travelling American. The English, the most conservative people this side of India, are not sensible of the restraint, but an American would seriously resent it. The aristocracy, incorporated by law and education, degrades life for the unprivileged classes. It is a questionable compensation to the embittered feeling of a proud commoner, the reflection that a fop, who, by the magic of title, paralyzes his arm and plucks from him half the graces and rights of a man, is himself also an aspirant excluded with the same ruthlessness from higher circles, since there is no end to the wheels within wheels of this spiral heaven. Something may be pardoned to the spirit of loyalty when it becomes fantastic; and something to the imagination, for the baldest life is symbolic. Philip II. of Spain rated his ambassador for neglecting serious affairs in Italy, whilst he debated some point of honor with the French ambassador; "You have left a business of importance for a ceremony." The ambassador replied, "Your Majesty's self is but a ceremony." In the East, where the religious sentiment comes in to the support of the aristocracy, and in the Romish church also, there is a grain of sweetness in the tyranny; but in England, the fact seems to me intolerable, what is commonly affirmed, that such is the transcendent honor accorded to wealth and birth, that no man of letters, be his eminence what it may, is received into the best society, except as a lion and a show. The English have many virtues, many advantages, and the proudest history of the world; but they need all and more than all the resources of the past to indemnify a heroic gentleman in that country for the mortifications prepared for him by the system of society, and which seem to impose the alternative to resist or to avoid it. That there are mitigations and practical alleviations to this rigor, is not an excuse for the rule. Commanding worth and personal power must sit crowned in all companies, nor will extraordinary persons be slighted or affronted in any company of civilized men. But the system is an invasion of the sentiment of justice and the native rights of men, which however decorated, must lessen the value of English citizenship. It is for Englishmen to consider, not for us; we only say, Let us live in America, too thankful for our want of feudal institutions. Our houses and towns are like mosses and lichens, so slight and new; but youth is a fault of which we shall daily mend. This land too is as old as the Flood, and wants no ornament or privilege which nature could bestow. Here stars, here woods, here hills, here animals, here men abound, and the vast tendencies concur of a new order. If only the men are employed in conspiring with the designs of the Spirit who led us hither and is leading us still, we shall quickly enough advance out of all hearing of others' censures, out of all regrets of our own, into a new and more excellent social state than history has recorded.

1844

EXPERIENCE

The lords of life, the lords of life,—
I saw them pass,
In their own guise,
Like and unlike,
Portly and grim,
Use and Surprise,
Surface and Dream,
Succession swift, and spectral Wrong,
Temperament without a tongue,
And the inventor of the game
Omnipresent without name;—
Some to see, some to be guessed,
They marched from east to west:
Little man, least of all,
Among the legs of his guardians tall,
Walked about with puzzled look:—
Him by the hand dear Nature took;
Dearest Nature, strong and kind,
Whispered, "Darling, never mind!
To-morrow they will wear another face,
The founder thou! these are thy race!"

Where do we find ourselves? In a series of which we do not know the extremes, and believe that it has none. We wake and find ourselves on a stair; there are stairs below us, which we seem to have ascended; there are stairs above us, many a one, which go upward and out of sight. But the Genius which according to the old belief stands at the door by which we enter, and gives us the lethe to drink, that we may tell no tales, mixed the cup too strongly, and we cannot shake off the lethargy now at noonday. Sleep lingers all our lifetime about our eyes, as night hovers all day in the boughs of the fir-tree. All things swim and glitter. Our life is not so much threatened as our perception. Ghostlike we glide through nature, and should not know our place again. Did our birth fall in some fit of indigence and frugality in nature, that she was so sparing of her fire and so liberal of her earth that it appears to us that we lack the affirmative principle, and though we have health and reason, yet we have no superfluity of spirit for new creation? We have enough to live and bring the year about, but not an ounce to impart or to invest. Ah that our Genius were a little more of a genius! We are like millers on the lower levels of a stream, when the factories above them have exhausted the water. We too fancy that the upper people must have raised their dams.

If any of us knew what we were doing, or where we are going, then when we think we best know! We do not know to-day whether we are busy or idle. In times when we thought ourselves indolent, we have afterwards discovered that much was accomplished and much was begun in us. All our days are so unprofitable while they pass, that 't is wonderful where or when we ever got anything of this which we call wisdom, poetry, virtue. We never got it on any dated calendar day. Some heavenly days must have been intercalated somewhere, like those that Hermes won with dice of the Moon, that Osiris might be born. It is said all martyrdoms looked mean when they were suffered. Every ship is a romantic object, except that we sail in. Embark, and the romance quits our vessel and hangs on every other sail in the horizon. Our life looks trivial, and we shun to record it. Men seem to have learned of the horizon the art of perpetual retreating and reference. "Yonder uplands are rich pasturage, and my neighbor has fertile meadow, but my field," says the querulous farmer, "only holds the world together." I quote another man's saying; unluckily that other withdraws himself in the same way, and quotes me. 'T is the trick of nature thus to degrade to-day; a good deal of buzz, and somewhere a result slipped magically in. Every roof is agreeable to the eye until it is lifted; then we find tragedy and moaning women and hard-eyed husbands and deluges of lethe, and the men ask, "What's the news?" as if the old were so bad. How many individuals can we count in society? how many actions? how many opinions? So much of our time is preparation, so much is routine, and so much retrospect, that the pith of each man's genius contracts itself to a very few hours. The history of literature—take the net result of Tiraboschi, Warton, or Schlegel—is a sum of very few ideas and of very few original tales; all the rest being variation of these. So in this great society wide lying around us, a critical analysis would find very few spontaneous actions. It is almost all custom and gross sense. There are even few opinions, and these seem organic in the speakers, and do not disturb the universal necessity.

What opium is instilled into all disaster! It shows formidable as we approach it, but there is at last no rough rasping friction, but the most slippery sliding surfaces; we fall soft on a thought; *Ate Dea* is gentle,—

"Over men's heads walking aloft,
With tender feet treading so soft."

People grieve and bemoan themselves, but it is not half so bad with them as they say. There are moods in which we court suffering, in the hope that here at least we shall find reality, sharp peaks and edges of truth. But it turns out to be scene-painting and counterfeit. The only thing grief has taught me is to know how shallow it is. That, like all the rest, plays about the surface, and never introduces me into the reality, for contact with which we would even pay the costly price of sons and lovers. Was it Boscovich who found out that bodies never come in contact? Well, souls never touch their objects. An innavigable sea washes with silent waves between us and the things we aim at and converse with. Grief too will make us idealists. In the death of my son, now more than two years ago, I seem to have lost a beautiful estate,—no more. I cannot get it nearer to me. If to-morrow I should be informed of the bankruptcy of my principal debtors, the loss of my property would be a great inconvenience to me, perhaps, for many years; but it would leave me as it found me,—neither better nor worse. So is it with this calamity; it does not touch me; something which I fancied was a part of me, which could not be torn away without tearing me nor enlarged without enriching me, falls off from me and leaves no scar. It was caducous. I grieve that grief can teach me nothing, nor carry me one step into real nature. The Indian who was laid under a curse that the wind should not blow on him, nor water flow to him, nor fire burn him, is a type of us all. The dearest events are summer-rain, and we the Para coats that shed every drop. Nothing is left us now but death. We look to that with a grim satisfaction, saying, There at least is reality that will not dodge us.

I take this evanescence and lubricity of all objects, which lets them slip through our fingers then when we clutch hardest, to be the most unhandsome part of our condition. Nature does not like to be observed, and likes that we should be her fools and playmates. We may have the sphere for our cricket-ball, but not a berry for our philosophy. Direct strokes she never gave us power to make; all our blows glance, all our hits are accidents. Our relations to each other are oblique and casual.

Dream delivers us to dream, and there is no end to illusion. Life is a train of moods like a string of beads, and as we pass through them they prove to be many-colored lenses which paint the world their own hue, and each shows only what lies in its focus. From the mountain you see the mountain. We animate what we can, and we see only what we animate. Nature and books belong to the eyes that see them. It depends on the mood of the man whether he shall see the sunset or the fine poem. There are always sunsets, and there is always genius; but only a few hours so serene that we can relish nature or criticism. The more or less depends on structure or temperament. Temperament is the iron wire on which the beads are strung. Of what use is fortune or talent to a cold and defective nature? Who cares what sensibility or discrimination a man has at some time shown, if he falls asleep in his chair? or if he laugh and giggle? or if he apologize? or is infected with egotism? or thinks of his dollar? or cannot go by food? or has gotten a child in his boyhood? Of what use is genius, if the organ is too convex or too concave and cannot find a focal distance within the actual horizon of human life? Of what use, if the brain is too cold or too hot, and the man does not care enough for results to stimulate him to experiment, and hold him up in it? or if the web is too finely woven, too irritable by pleasure and pain, so that life stagnates from too much reception without due outlet? Of what use to make heroic vows of amendment, if the same old law-breaker is to keep them? What cheer can the religious sentiment yield, when that is suspected to be secretly dependent on the seasons of the year and the state of the blood? I knew a witty physician who found the creed in the biliary duct, and used to affirm that if there was disease in the liver, the man became a Calvinist, and if that organ was sound, he became a Unitarian. Very mortifying is the reluctant experience that some unfriendly excess or imbecility neutralizes the promise of genius. We see young men who owe us a new world, so readily and lavishly they promise, but they never acquit the debt; they die young and dodge the account; or if they live they lose themselves in the crowd.

Temperament also enters fully into the system of illusions and shuts us in a prison of glass which we cannot see. There is an optical illusion about every person we meet. In truth they are all creatures of given temperament, which will appear in a given character, whose boundaries they will never pass; but we look at them, they seem alive, and we presume there is impulse in them. In the moment it seems impulse; in the year, in the lifetime, it turns out to be a certain uniform tune which the revolving barrel of the music-box must play. Men resist the conclusion in the morning, but adopt it as the evening wears on, that temper prevails over everything of time, place and condition, and is inconsumable in the flames of religion. Some modifications the moral sentiment avails to impose, but the individual texture holds its dominion, if not to bias the moral judgments, yet to fix the measure of activity and of enjoyment.

I thus express the law as it is read from the platform of ordinary life, but must not leave it without noticing the capital exception. For temperament is a power which no man willingly hears any one praise but himself. On the platform of physics we cannot resist the contracting influences of so-called science. Temperament puts all divinity to rout. I know the mental proclivity of physicians. I hear the chuckle of the phrenologists. Theoretic kidnappers and slave-drivers, they esteem each man the victim of another, who winds him round his finger by knowing the law of his being; and, by such cheap signboards as the color of his beard or the slope of his occiput, reads the inventory of his fortunes and character. The grossest ignorance does not disgust like this impudent knowingness. The physicians say they are not materialists; but they are:—Spirit is matter reduced to an extreme thinness: O *so* thin!—But the definition of *spiritual* should be, *that which is its own evidence*. What notions do they attach to love! what to religion! One would not willingly pronounce these words in their hearing, and give them the occasion to profane them. I saw a gracious gentleman who adapts his conversation to the form of the head of the man he talks with! I had fancied that the value of life lay in its inscrutable possibilities; in the fact that I never know, in addressing myself to a new individual, what may befall me. I carry the keys of my castle in my hand, ready to throw them at the feet of my lord, whenever and in what disguise soever he shall appear. I know he is in the neighborhood, hidden among vagabonds. Shall I preclude my future by taking a high seat and kindly adapting my conversation to the shape of heads? When I come to that, the doctors shall buy me for a cent.—"But, sir, medical history; the report to the Institute; the proven facts!"—I distrust the facts and the inferences. Temperament is the veto or limitation-power in the constitution, very justly applied to restrain an opposite excess in the constitution, but absurdly offered as a bar to original equity. When virtue is in presence, all subordinate powers sleep. On its own level, or in view of nature, temperament is final. I see not, if one be once caught in this trap of so-called sciences, any escape for the man from the links of the chain of physical necessity. Given such an embryo, such a history must follow. On this platform one lives in a sty of sensualism, and would soon come to suicide. But it is impossible that the creative power should exclude itself. Into every intelligence there is a door which is never closed, through which the creator passes. The intellect, seeker of absolute truth, or the heart, lover of absolute good, intervenes for our succor, and at one whisper of these high powers we awake from ineffectual struggles with this nightmare. We hurl it into its own hell, and cannot again contract ourselves to so base a state.

The secret of the illusoriness is in the necessity of a succession of moods or objects. Gladly we would anchor, but the anchorage is quicksand. This onward trick of nature is too strong for us: *Pero si muove*. When at night I look at the moon and stars, I seem stationary, and they to hurry. Our love of the real draws us to permanence, but health of body consists in circulation, and sanity of mind in variety or facility of association. We need change of objects. Dedication to one thought is quickly odious. We house with the insane, and must humor them; then conversation dies out. Once I took such delight in Montaigne that I thought I should not need any other book; before that, in Shakspeare; then in Plutarch; then in Plotinus; at one time in Bacon; afterwards in Goethe; even in Bettine; but now I turn the pages of either of them languidly, whilst I still cherish their genius. So with pictures; each will bear an emphasis of attention once, which it cannot retain, though we fain would continue to be pleased in that manner. How strongly I have felt of pictures that when you have seen one well, you must take your leave of it; you shall never see it again. I have had good lessons from pictures which I have since seen without emotion or remark. A deduction must be made from the opinion which even the wise express on a new book or occurrence. Their opinion gives me tidings of their mood, and some vague guess at the new fact, but is nowise to be trusted as the lasting relation between that intellect and that thing. The child asks, "Mamma, why don't I like the story as well as when you told it me yesterday?" Alas! child, it is even so with the oldest cherubim of knowledge. But will it answer thy question to say, Because thou wert born to a whole and this story is a particular? The reason of the pain this discovery causes us (and we make it late in respect to works of art and intellect) is the plaint of tragedy which murmurs from it in regard to persons, to friendship and love.

That immobility and absence of elasticity which we find in the arts, we find with more pain in the artist. There is no power of expansion in men. Our friends early appear to us as representatives of certain ideas which they never pass or exceed. They stand on the brink of the ocean of thought and power, but they never take the single step that would bring them there. A man is like a bit of Labrador spar, which has no lustre as you turn it in your hand until you come to a particular angle; then it shows deep and beautiful colors. There is no adaptation or universal applicability in men, but each has his special talent, and the mastery of successful men consists in adroitly keeping themselves where and when that turn shall be oftenest to be practised. We do what we must, and call it by the best names we can, and would fain have the praise of having intended the result which ensues. I cannot recall any form of man who is not superfluous sometimes. But is not this pitiful? Life is not worth the taking, to do tricks in.

Of course it needs the whole society to give the symmetry we seek. The party-colored wheel must revolve very fast to appear white. Something is earned too by conversing with so much folly and defect. In fine, whoever loses, we are always of the gaining party. Divinity is behind our failures and follies also. The plays of children are nonsense, but very educative nonsense. So it is with the largest and solemnest things, with commerce, government, church, marriage, and so with the history of every man's bread, and the ways by which he is to come by it. Like a bird which alights nowhere, but hops perpetually from bough to bough, is the Power which abides in no man and in no woman, but for a moment speaks from this one, and for another moment from that one.

But what help from these fineries or pedantries? What help from thought? Life is not dialectics. We, I think, in these times, have had lessons enough of the futility of criticism. Our young people have thought and written much on labor and reform, and for all that they have written, neither the world nor themselves have got on a step. Intellectual tasting of life will not supersede muscular activity. If a man should consider the nicety of the passage of a piece of bread down his throat, he would starve. At Education Farm the noblest theory of life sat on the noblest figures of young men and maidens, quite powerless and melancholy. It would not rake or pitch a ton of hay; it would not rub down a horse; and the men and maidens it left pale and hungry. A political orator wittily compared our party promises to western roads, which opened stately enough, with planted trees on either side to tempt the traveller, but soon became narrow and narrower and ended in a squirrel-track and ran up a tree. So does culture with us; it ends in headache. Unspeakably sad and barren does life look to those who a few months ago were dazzled with the splendor of the promise of the times. "There is now no longer any right course of action nor any self-devotion left among the Iranis." Objections and criticism we have had our fill of. There are objections to every course of life and action, and the practical wisdom infers an indifferency, from the omnipresence of objection. The whole frame of things preaches indifferency. Do not craze yourself with thinking, but go about your business anywhere. Life is not intellectual or critical, but sturdy. Its chief good is for well-mixed people who can enjoy what they find, without question. Nature hates peeping, and our mothers speak her very sense when they say, "Children, eat your victuals, and say no more of it." To fill the hour,—that is happiness; to fill the hour and leave no crevice for a repentance or an approval. We live amid surfaces, and the true art of life is to skate well on them. Under the oldest mouldiest conventions a man of native force prospers just as well as in the newest world, and that by skill of handling and treatment. He can take hold anywhere. Life itself is a mixture of power and form, and will not bear the least excess of either. To finish the moment, to find the journey's end in every step of the road, to live the greatest number of good hours, is wisdom. It is not the part of men, but of fanatics, or of mathematicians if you will, to say that, the shortness of life considered, it is not worth caring whether for so short a duration we were sprawling in want or sitting high. Since our office is with moments, let us husband them. Five minutes of to-day are worth as much to me as five minutes in the next millennium. Let us be poised, and wise, and our own, to-day. Let us treat the men and women well; treat them as if they were real; perhaps they are. Men live in their fancy, like drunkards whose hands are too soft and tremulous for successful labor. It is a tempest of fancies, and the only ballast I know is a respect to the present hour. Without any shadow of doubt, amidst this vertigo of shows and politics, I settle myself ever the firmer in the creed that we should not postpone and refer and wish, but do broad justice where we are, by whomsoever we deal with, accepting our actual companions and circumstances, however humble or odious, as the mystic officials to whom the universe has delegated its whole pleasure for us. If these are mean and malignant, their contentment, which is the last victory of justice, is a more satisfying echo to the heart than the voice of poets and the casual sympathy of admirable persons. I think that however a thoughtful man may suffer from the defects and absurdities of his company, he cannot without affectation deny to any set of men and women a sensibility to extraordinary merit. The coarse and frivolous have an instinct of superiority, if they have not a sympathy, and honor it in their blind capricious way with sincere homage.

The fine young people despise life, but in me, and in such as with me are free from dyspepsia, and to whom a day is a sound and solid good, it is a great excess of politeness to look scornful and to cry for company. I am grown by sympathy a little eager and sentimental, but leave me alone and I should relish every hour and what it brought me, the potluck of the day, as heartily as the oldest gossip in the bar-room. I am thankful for small mercies. I compared notes with one of my friends who expects everything of the universe and is disappointed when anything is less than the best, and I found that I begin at the other extreme, expecting nothing, and am always full of thanks for moderate goods. I accept the clangor and jangle of contrary tendencies. I find my account in sots and bores also. They give a reality to the circumjacent picture which such a vanishing meteorous appearance can ill spare. In the morning I awake and find the old world, wife, babes and mother, Concord and Boston, the dear old spiritual world and even the dear old devil not far off. If we will take the good we find, asking no questions, we shall have heaping measures. The great gifts are not got by analysis. Everything good is on the highway. The middle region of our being is the temperate zone. We may climb into the thin and cold realm of pure geometry and lifeless science, or sink into that of sensation. Between these extremes is the equator of life, of thought, of spirit, of poetry,—a narrow belt. Moreover, in popular experience everything good is on the highway. A collector peeps into all the picture-shops of Europe for a landscape of Poussin, a crayon-sketch of Salvator; but the Transfiguration, the Last Judgment, the Communion of Saint Jerome, and what are as transcendent as these, are on the walls of the Vatican, the Uffizi, or the Louvre, where every footman may see them; to say nothing of Nature's pictures in every street, of sunsets and sunrises every day, and the sculpture of the human body never absent. A collector recently bought at public auction, in London, for one hundred and fifty-seven guineas, an autograph of Shakspeare; but for nothing a school-boy can read Hamlet and can detect secrets of highest concernment yet unpublished therein. I think I will never read any but the commonest books,—the Bible, Homer, Dante, Shakspeare and Milton. Then we are impatient of so public a life and planet, and run hither and thither for nooks and secrets. The imagination delights in the woodcraft of Indians, trappers and bee-hunters. We fancy that we are strangers, and not so intimately domesticated in the planet as the wild man and the wild beast and bird. But the exclusion reaches them also; reaches the climbing, flying, gliding, feathered and four-footed man. Fox and woodchuck, hawk and snipe and bittern, when nearly seen, have no more root in the deep world than man, and are just such superficial tenants of the globe. Then the new molecular philosophy shows astronomical interspaces betwixt atom and atom, shows that the world is all outside; it has no inside.

The mid-world is best. Nature, as we know her, is no saint.

The lights of the church, the ascetics, Gentoos and corn-eaters, she does not distinguish by any favor. She comes eating and drinking and sinning. Her darlings, the great, the strong, the beautiful, are not children of our law; do not come out of the Sunday School, nor weigh their food, nor punctually keep the commandments. If we will be strong with her strength we must not harbor such disconsolate consciences, borrowed too from the consciences of other nations. We must set up the strong present tense against all the rumors of wrath, past or to come. So many things are unsettled which it is of the first importance to settle;—and, pending their settlement, we will do as we do. Whilst the debate goes forward on the equity of commerce, and will not be closed for a century or two, New and Old England may keep shop. Law of copyright and international copyright is to be discussed, and in the interim we will sell our books for the most we can. Expediency of literature, reason of literature, lawfulness of writing down a thought, is questioned; much is to say on both sides, and, while the fight waxes hot, thou, dearest scholar, stick to thy foolish task, add a line every hour, and between whiles add a line. Right to hold land, right of property, is disputed, and the conventions convene, and before the vote is taken, dig away in your garden, and spend your earnings as a waif or godsend to all serene and beautiful purposes. Life itself is a bubble and a scepticism, and a sleep within a sleep. Grant it, and as much more as they will,—but thou, God's darling! heed thy private dream; thou wilt not be missed in the scorning and scepticism; there are enough of them; stay there in thy closet and toil until the rest are agreed what to do about it. Thy sickness, they say, and thy puny habit require that thou do this or avoid that, but know that thy life is a flitting state, a tent for a night, and do thou, sick or well, finish that stint. Thou art sick, but shalt not be worse, and the universe, which holds thee dear, shall be the better.

Human life is made up of the two elements, power and form, and the proportion must be invariably kept if we would have it sweet and sound. Each of these elements in excess makes a mischief as hurtful as its defect. Everything runs to excess; every good quality is noxious if unmixed, and, to carry the danger to the edge of ruin, nature causes each man's peculiarity to superabound. Here, among the farms, we adduce the scholars as examples of this treachery. They are nature's victims of expression. You who see the artist, the orator, the poet, too near, and find their life no more excellent than that of mechanics or farmers, and themselves victims of partiality, very hollow and haggard, and pronounce them failures, not heroes, but quacks,—conclude very reasonably that these arts are not for man, but are disease. Yet nature will not bear you out. Irresistible nature made men such, and makes legions more of such, every day. You love the boy reading in a book, gazing at a drawing or a cast; yet what are these millions who read and behold, but incipient writers and sculptors? Add a little more of that quality which now reads and sees, and they will seize the pen and chisel. And if one remembers how innocently he began to be an artist, he perceives that nature joined with his enemy. A man is a golden impossibility. The line he must walk is a hair's breadth. The wise through excess of wisdom is made a fool.

How easily, if fate would suffer it, we might keep forever these beautiful limits, and adjust ourselves, once for all, to the perfect calculation of the kingdom of known cause and effect. In the street and in the newspapers, life appears so plain a business that manly resolution and adherence to the multiplication-table through all weathers will insure success. But ah! presently comes a day, or is it only a half-hour, with its angel-whispering,—which discomfits the conclusions of nations and of years! To-morrow again every thing looks real and angular, the habitual standards are reinstated, common-sense is as rare as genius,—is the basis of genius, and experience is hands and feet to every enterprise;—and yet, he who should do his business on this understanding would be quickly bankrupt. Power keeps quite another road than the turnpikes of choice and will; namely the subterranean and invisible tunnels and channels of life. It is ridiculous that we are diplomatists, and doctors, and considerate people; there are no dupes like these. Life is a series of surprises, and would not be worth taking or keeping if it were not. God delights to isolate us every day, and hide from us the past and the future. We would look about us, but with grand politeness he draws down before us an impenetrable screen of purest sky, and another behind us of purest sky. "You will not remember," he seems to say, "and you will not expect." All good conversation, manners and action come from a spontaneity which forgets usages and makes the moment great. Nature hates calculators; her methods are saltatory and impulsive. Man lives by pulses; our organic movements are such; and the chemical and ethereal agents are undulatory and alternate; and the mind goes antagonizing on, and never prospers but by fits. We thrive by casualties. Our chief experiences have been casual. The most attractive class of people are those who are powerful obliquely and not by the direct stroke; men of genius, but not yet accredited; one gets the cheer of their light without paying too great a tax. Theirs is the beauty of the bird or the morning light, and not of art. In the thought of genius there is always a surprise; and the moral sentiment is well called "the newness," for it is never other; as new to the oldest intelligence as to the young child;—"the kingdom that cometh without observation." In like manner, for practical success, there must not be too much design. A man will not be observed in doing that which he can do best. There is a certain magic about his properest action which stupefies your powers of observation, so that though it is done before you, you wist not of it. The art of life has a pudency, and will not be exposed. Every man is an impossibility until he is born; every thing impossible until we see a success. The ardors of piety agree at last with the coldest scepticism,—that nothing is of us or our works,—that all is of God. Nature will not spare us the smallest leaf of laurel. All writing comes by the grace of God, and all doing and having. I would gladly be moral and keep due metes and bounds, which I dearly love, and allow the most to the will of man; but I have set my heart on honesty in this chapter, and I can see nothing at last, in success or failure, than more or less of vital force supplied from the Eternal. The results of life are uncalculated and uncalculable. The years teach much which the days never know.

The persons who compose our company converse, and come and go, and design and execute many things, and somewhat comes of it all, but an unlooked-for result. The individual is always mistaken. He designed many things, and drew in other persons as coadjutors, quarrelled with some or all, blundered much, and something is done; all are a little advanced, but the individual is always mistaken. It turns out somewhat new and very unlike what he promised himself.

The ancients, struck with this irreducibleness of the elements of human life to calculation, exalted Chance into a divinity; but that is to stay too long at the spark, which glitters truly at one point, but the universe is warm with the latency of the same fire. The miracle of life which will not be expounded but will remain a miracle, introduces a new element. In the growth of the embryo, Sir Everard Home I think noticed that the evolution was not from one central point, but coactive from three or more points. Life has no memory. That which proceeds in succession might be remembered, but that which is coexistent, or ejaculated from a deeper cause, as yet far from being conscious, knows not its own tendency. So is it with us, now sceptical or without unity, because immersed in forms and effects all seeming to be of equal yet hostile value, and now religious, whilst in the reception of spiritual law. Bear with these distractions, with this coetaneous growth of the parts; they will one day be *members*, and obey one will. On that one will, on that secret cause, they nail our attention and hope. Life is hereby melted into an expectation or a religion. Underneath the inharmonious and trivial particulars, is a musical perfection; the Ideal journeying always with us, the heaven without rent or seam. Do but observe the mode of our illumination. When I converse with a profound mind, or if at any time being alone I have good thoughts, I do not at once arrive at satisfactions, as when, being thirsty, I drink water; or go to the fire, being cold; no! but I am at first apprised of my vicinity to a new and excellent region of life. By persisting to read or to think, this region gives further sign of itself, as it were in flashes of light, in sudden discoveries of its profound beauty and repose, as if the clouds that covered it parted at intervals and showed the approaching traveller the inland mountains, with the tranquil eternal meadows spread at their base, whereon flocks graze and shepherds pipe and dance. But every insight from this realm of thought is felt as initial, and promises a sequel. I do not make it; I arrive there, and behold what was there already. I make! O no! I clap my hands in infantine joy and amazement before the first opening to me of this august magnificence, old with the love and homage of innumerable ages, young with the life of life, the sunbright Mecca of the desert. And what a future it opens! I feel a new heart beating with the love of the new beauty. I am ready to die out of nature and be born again into this new yet unapproachable America I have found in the West:—

> "Since neither now nor yesterday began
> These thoughts, which have been ever, nor yet can
> A man be found who their first entrance knew."

If I have described life as a flux of moods, I must now add that there is that in us which changes not and which ranks all sensations and states of mind. The consciousness in each man is a sliding scale, which identifies him now with the First Cause, and now with the flesh of his body; life above life, in infinite degrees. The sentiment from which it sprung determines the dignity of any deed, and the question ever is, not what you have done or forborne, but at whose command you have done or forborne it.

Fortune, Minerva, Muse, Holy Ghost,—these are quaint names, too narrow to cover this unbounded substance. The baffled intellect must still kneel before this cause, which refuses to be named,—ineffable cause, which every fine genius has essayed to represent by some emphatic symbol, as, Thales by water, Anaximenes by air, Anaxagoras by (*Νοῦς*) thought, Zoroaster by fire, Jesus and the moderns by love; and the metaphor of each has become a national religion. The Chinese Mencius has not been the least successful in his generalization.

"I fully understand language," he said, "and nourish well my vast-flowing vigor."—"I beg to ask what you call vast-flowing vigor?" said his companion. "The explanation," replied Mencius, "is difficult. This vigor is supremely great, and in the highest degree unbending. Nourish it correctly and do it no injury, and it will fill up the vacancy between heaven and earth. This vigor accords with and assists justice and reason, and leaves no hunger."—In our more correct writing we give to this generalization the name of Being, and thereby confess that we have arrived as far as we can go. Suffice it for the joy of the universe that we have not arrived at a wall, but at interminable oceans. Our life seems not present so much as prospective; not for the affairs on which it is wasted, but as a hint of this vast-flowing vigor. Most of life seems to be mere advertisement of faculty; information is given us not to sell ourselves cheap; that we are very great. So, in particulars, our greatness is always in a tendency or direction, not in an action. It is for us to believe in the rule, not in the exception. The noble are thus known from the ignoble. So in accepting the leading of the sentiments, it is not what we believe concerning the immortality of the soul or the like, but *the universal impulse to believe*, that is the material circumstance and is the principal fact in the history of the globe. Shall we describe this cause as that which works directly? The spirit is not helpless or needful of mediate organs. It has plentiful powers and direct effects. I am explained without explaining, I am felt without acting, and where I am not. Therefore all just persons are satisfied with their own praise. They refuse to explain themselves, and are content that new actions should do them that office. They believe that we communicate without speech and above speech, and that no right action of ours is quite unaffecting to our friends, at whatever distance; for the influence of action is not to be measured by miles. Why should I fret myself because a circumstance has occurred which hinders my presence where I was expected? If I am not at the meeting, my presence where I am should be as useful to the commonwealth of friendship and wisdom, as would be my presence in that place. I exert the same quality of power in all places. Thus journeys the mighty Ideal before us; it never was known to fall into the rear. No man ever came to an experience which was satiating, but his good is tidings of a better. Onward and onward! In liberated moments we know that a new picture of life and duty is already possible; the elements already exist in many minds around you of a doctrine of life which shall transcend any written record we have. The new statement will comprise the scepticisms as well as the faiths of society, and out of unbeliefs a creed shall be formed. For scepticisms are not gratuitous or lawless, but are limitations of the affirmative statement, and the new philosophy must take them in and make affirmations outside of them, just as much as it must include the oldest beliefs.

It is very unhappy, but too late to be helped, the discovery we have made that we exist. That discovery is called the Fall of Man. Ever afterwards we suspect our instruments. We have learned that we do not see directly, but mediately, and that we have no means of correcting these colored and distorting lenses which we are, or of computing the amount of their errors. Perhaps these subject-lenses have a creative power; perhaps there are no objects. Once we lived in what we saw; now, the rapaciousness of this new power, which threatens to absorb all things, engages us. Nature, art, persons, letters, religions, objects, successively tumble in, and God is but one of its ideas. Nature and literature are subjective phenomena; every evil and every good thing is a shadow which we cast. The street is full of humiliations to the proud. As the fop contrived to dress his bailiffs in his livery and make them wait on his guests at table, so the chagrins which the bad heart gives off as bubbles, at once take form as ladies and gentlemen in the street, shopmen or bar-keepers in hotels, and threaten or insult whatever is threatenable and insultable in us. 'T is the same with our idolatries. People forget that it is the eye which makes the horizon, and the rounding mind's eye which makes this or that man a type or representative of humanity, with the name of hero or saint. Jesus, the "providential man," is a good man on whom many people are agreed that these optical laws shall take effect. By love on one part and by forbearance to press objection on the other part, it is for a time settled that we will look at him in the center of the horizon, and ascribe to him the properties that will attach to any man so seen. But the longest love or aversion has a speedy term. The great and crescive self, rooted in absolute nature, supplants all relative existence and ruins the kingdom of mortal friendship and love. Marriage (in what is called the spiritual world) is impossible, because of the inequality between every subject and every object. The subject is the receiver of Godhead, and at every comparison must feel his being enhanced by that cryptic might. Though not in energy, yet by presence, this magazine of substance cannot be otherwise than felt; nor can any force of intellect attribute to the object the proper deity which sleeps or wakes forever in every subject. Never can love make consciousness and ascription equal in force. There will be the same gulf between every me and thee as between the original and the picture. The universe is the bride of the soul. All private sympathy is partial. Two human beings are like globes, which can touch only in a point, and whilst they remain in contact all other points of each of the spheres are inert; their turn must also come, and the longer a particular union lasts the more energy of appetency the parts not in union acquire.

Life will be imaged, but cannot be divided nor doubled. Any invasion of its unity would be chaos. The soul is not twin-born but the only begotten, and though revealing itself as child in time, child in appearance, is of a fatal and universal power, admitting no co-life. Every day, every act betrays the ill-concealed deity. We believe in ourselves as we do not believe in others. We permit all things to ourselves, and that which we call sin in others is experiment for us. It is an instance of our faith in ourselves that men never speak of crime as lightly as they think; or every man thinks a latitude safe for himself which is nowise to be indulged to another. The act looks very differently on the inside and on the outside; in its quality and in its consequences. Murder in the murderer is no such ruinous thought as poets and romancers will have it; it does not unsettle him or fright him from his ordinary notice of trifles; it is an act quite easy to be contemplated; but in its sequel it turns out to be a horrible jangle and confounding of all relations. Especially the crimes that spring from love seem right and fair from the actor's point of view, but when acted are found destructive of society. No man at last believes that he can be lost, or that the crime in him is as black as in the felon. Because the intellect qualifies in our own case the moral judgments. For there is no crime to the intellect. That is antinomian or hypernomian, and judges law as well as fact. "It is worse than a crime, it is a blunder," said Napoleon, speaking the language of the intellect. To it, the world is a problem in mathematics or the science of quantity, and it leaves out praise and blame and all weak emotions. All stealing is comparative. If you come to absolutes, pray who does not steal? Saints are sad, because they behold sin (even when they speculate) from the point of view of the conscience, and not of the intellect; a confusion of thought. Sin, seen from the thought, is a diminution, or *less;* seen from the conscience or will, it is pravity or *bad.* The intellect names it shade, absence of light, and no essence. The conscience must feel it as essence, essential evil. This it is not; it has an objective existence, but no subjective.

Thus inevitably does the universe wear our color, and every object fall successively into the subject itself. The subject exists, the subject enlarges; all things sooner or later fall into place. As I am, so I see; use what language we will, we can never say anything but what we are; Hermes, Cadmus, Columbus, Newton, Bonaparte, are the mind's ministers. Instead of feeling a poverty when we encounter a great man, let us treat the newcomer like a travelling geologist who passes through our estate and shows us good slate, or limestone, or anthracite, in our brush pasture. The partial action of each strong mind in one direction is a telescope for the objects on which it is pointed. But every other part of knowledge is to be pushed to the same extravagance, ere the soul attains her due sphericity. Do you see that kitten chasing so prettily her own tail? If you could look with her eyes you might see her surrounded with hundreds of figures performing complex dramas, with tragic and comic issues, long conversations, many characters, many ups and downs of fate,—and meantime it is only puss and her tail. How long before our masquerade will end its noise of tambourines, laughter and shouting, and we shall find it was a solitary performance? A subject and an object,—it takes so much to make the galvanic circuit complete, but magnitude adds nothing. What imports it whether it is Kepler and the sphere, Columbus and America, a reader and his book, or puss with her tail?

It is true that all the muses and love and religion hate these developments, and will find a way to punish the chemist who publishes in the parlor the secrets of the laboratory. And we cannot say too little of our constitutional necessity of seeing things under private aspects, or saturated with our humors. And yet is the God the native of these bleak rocks. That need makes in morals the capital virtue of self-trust. We must hold hard to this poverty, however scandalous, and by more vigorous self-recoveries, after the sallies of action, possess our axis more firmly. The life of truth is cold and so far mournful; but it is not the slave of tears, contritions and perturbations. It does not attempt another's work, nor adopt another's facts. It is a main lesson of wisdom to know your own from another's. I have learned that I cannot dispose of other people's facts; but I possess such a key to my own as persuades me, against all their denials, that they also have a key to theirs. A sympathetic person is placed in the dilemma of a swimmer among drowning men, who all catch at him, and if he give so much as a leg or a finger they will drown him. They wish to be saved from the mischiefs of their vices, but not from their vices. Charity would be wasted on this poor waiting on the symptoms. A wise and hardy physician will say, *Come out of that*, as the first condition of advice.

In this our talking America we are ruined by our good nature and listening on all sides. This compliance takes away the power of being greatly useful. A man should not be able to look other than directly and forthright. A preoccupied attention is the only answer to the importunate frivolity of other people; an attention, and to an aim which makes their wants frivolous. This is a divine answer, and leaves no appeal and no hard thoughts. In Flaxman's drawing of the Eumenides of Æschylus, Orestes supplicates Apollo, whilst the Furies sleep on the threshold. The face of the god expresses a shade of regret and compassion, but is calm with the conviction of the irreconcilableness of the two spheres. He is born into other politics, into the eternal and beautiful. The man at his feet asks for his interest in turmoils of the earth, into which his nature cannot enter. And the Eumenides there lying express pictorially this disparity. The god is surcharged with his divine destiny.

Illusion, Temperament, Succession, Surface, Surprise, Reality, Subjectiveness,—these are threads on the loom of time, these are the lords of life. I dare not assume to give their order, but I name them as I find them in my way. I know better than to claim any completeness for my picture. I am a fragment, and this is a fragment of me. I can very confidently announce one or another law, which throws itself into relief and form, but I am too young yet by some ages to compile a code. I gossip for my hour concerning the eternal politics. I have seen many fair pictures not in vain. A wonderful time I have lived in. I am not the novice I was fourteen, nor yet seven years ago. Let who will ask, Where is the fruit? I find a private fruit sufficient. This is a fruit,—that I should not ask for a rash effect from meditations, counsels and the hiving of truths. I should feel it pitiful to demand a result on this town and county, an overt effect on the instant month and year. The effect is deep and secular as the cause. It works on periods in which mortal life-time is lost. All I know is reception; I am and I have: but I do not get, and when I have fancied I had gotten anything, I found I did not. I worship with wonder the great Fortune. My reception has been so large, that I am not annoyed by receiving this or that superabundantly. I say to the Genius, if he will pardon the proverb, *In for a mill, in for a million.* When I receive a new gift, I do not macerate my body to make the account square, for if I should die I could not make the account square. The benefit overran the merit the first day, and has overrun the merit ever since. The merit itself, so-called, I reckon part of the receiving.

Also that hankering after an overt or practical effect seems to me an apostasy. In good earnest I am willing to spare this most unnecessary deal of doing. Life wears to me a visionary face. Hardest roughest action is visionary also. It is but a choice between soft and turbulent dreams. People disparage knowing and the intellectual life, and urge doing. I am very content with knowing, if only I could know. That is an august entertainment, and would suffice me a great while. To know a little would be worth the expense of this world. I hear always the law of Adrastia, "that every soul which had acquired any truth, should be safe from harm until another period."

I know that the world I converse with in the city and in the farms, is not the world I *think*. I observe that difference, and shall observe it. One day I shall know the value and law of this discrepance. But I have not found that much was gained by manipular attempts to realize the world of thought. Many eager persons successively make an experiment in this way, and make themselves ridiculous. They acquire democratic manners, they foam at the mouth, they hate and deny. Worse, I observe that in the history of mankind there is never a solitary example of success,—taking their own tests of success. I say this polemically, or in reply to the inquiry, Why not realize your world? But far be from me the despair which prejudges the law by a paltry empiricism;—since there never was a right endeavor but it succeeded. Patience and patience, we shall win at the last. We must be very suspicious of the deceptions of the element of time. It takes a good deal of time to eat or to sleep, or to earn a hundred dollars, and a very little time to entertain a hope and an insight which becomes the light of our life. We dress our garden, eat our dinners, discuss the household with our wives, and these things make no impression, are forgotten next week; but, in the solitude to which every man is always returning, he has a sanity and revelations which in his passage into new worlds he will carry with him. Never mind the ridicule, never mind the defeat; up again, old heart!—it seems to say,—there is victory yet for all justice; and the true romance which the world exists to realize will be the transformation of genius into practical power.

1844

POLITICS

Gold and iron are good
To buy iron and gold;
All earth's fleece and food
For their like are sold.
Boded Merlin wise,
Proved Napoleon great,—
Nor kind nor coinage buys
Aught above its rate.
Fear, Craft and Avarice
Cannot rear a State.
Out of dust to build
What is more than dust,—
Walls Amphion piled
Phœbus stablish must.
When the Muses nine
With the Virtues meet,
Find to their design
An Atlantic seat,
By green orchard boughs
Fended from the heat,
Where the statesman ploughs
Furrow for the wheat;
When the Church is social worth,
When the state-house is the hearth,
Then the perfect State is come,
The republican at home.

In dealing with the State we ought to remember that its institutions are not aboriginal, though they existed before we were born; that they are not superior to the citizen; that every one of them was once the act of a single man; every law and usage was a man's expedient to meet a particular case; that they all are imitable, all alterable; we may make as good, we may make better. Society is an illusion to the young citizen. It lies before him in rigid repose, with certain names, men and institutions rooted like oak-trees to the centre, round which all arrange themselves the best they can. But the old statesman knows that society is fluid; there are no such roots and centres, but any particle may suddenly become the centre of the movement and compel the system to gyrate round it; as every man of strong will, like Pisistratus or Cromwell, does for a time, and every man of truth, like Plato or Paul, does forever. But politics rest on necessary foundations, and cannot be treated with levity. Republics abound in young civilians who believe that the laws make the city, that grave modifications of the policy and modes of living and employments of the population, that commerce, education and religion may be voted in or out; and that any measure, though it were absurd, may be imposed on a people if only you can get sufficient voices to make it a law. But the wise know that foolish legislation is a rope of sand which perishes in the twisting; that the State must follow and not lead the character and progress of the citizen; the strongest usurper is quickly got rid of; and they only who build on Ideas, build for eternity; and that the form of government which prevails is the expression of what cultivation exists in the population which permits it. The law is only a memorandum. We are superstitious, and esteem the statute somewhat: so much life as it has in the character of living men is its force. The statute stands there to say, Yesterday we agreed so and so, but how feel ye this article to-day? Our statute is a currency which we stamp with our own portrait: it soon becomes unrecognizable, and in process of time will return to the mint. Nature is not democratic, nor limited-monarchical, but despotic, and will not be fooled or abated of any jot of her authority by the pertest of her sons; and as fast as the public mind is opened to more intelligence, the code is seen to be brute and stammering. It speaks not articulately, and must be made to. Meantime the education of the general mind never stops. The reveries of the true and simple are prophetic. What the tender poetic youth dreams, and prays, and paints to-day, but shuns the ridicule of saying aloud, shall presently be the resolutions of public bodies; then shall be carried as grievance and bill of rights through conflict and war, and then shall be triumphant law and establishment for a hundred years, until it gives place in turn to new prayers and pictures. The history of the State sketches in coarse outline the progress of thought, and follows at a distance the delicacy of culture and of aspiration.

The theory of politics which has possessed the mind of men, and which they have expressed the best they could in their laws and in their revolutions, considers persons and property as the two objects for whose protection government exists. Of persons, all have equal rights, in virtue of being identical in nature. This interest of course with its whole power demands a democracy. Whilst the rights of all as persons are equal, in virtue of their access to reason, their rights in property are very unequal. One man owns his clothes, and another owns a county. This accident, depending primarily on the skill and virtue of the parties, of which there is every degree, and secondarily on patrimony, falls unequally, and its rights of course are unequal. Personal rights, universally the same, demand a government framed on the ratio of the census; property demands a government framed on the ratio of owners and of owning. Laban, who has flocks and herds, wishes them looked after by an officer on the frontiers, lest the Midianites shall drive them off; and pays a tax to that end. Jacob has no flocks or herds and no fear of the Midianites, and pays no tax to the officer. It seemed fit that Laban and Jacob should have equal rights to elect the officer who is to defend their persons, but that Laban and not Jacob should elect the officer who is to guard the sheep and cattle. And if question arise whether additional officers or watch-towers should be provided, must not Laban and Isaac, and those who must sell part of their herds to buy protection for the rest, judge better of this, and with more right, than Jacob, who, because he is a youth and a traveller, eats their bread and not his own?

In the earliest society the proprietors made their own wealth, and so long as it comes to the owners in the direct way, no other opinion would arise in any equitable community than that property should make the law for property, and persons the law for persons.

But property passes through donation or inheritance to those who do not create it. Gift, in one case, makes it as really the new owner's, as labor made it the first owner's: in the other case, of patrimony, the law makes an ownership which will be valid in each man's view according to the estimate which he sets on the public tranquillity.

It was not, however, found easy to embody the readily admitted principle that property should make law for property, and persons for persons; since persons and property mixed themselves in every transaction. At last it seemed settled that the rightful distinction was that the proprietors should have more elective franchise than non-proprietors, on the Spartan principle of "calling that which is just, equal; not that which is equal, just."

That principle no longer looks so self-evident as it appeared in former times, partly because doubts have arisen whether too much weight had not been allowed in the laws to property, and such a structure given to our usages as allowed the rich to encroach on the poor, and to keep them poor; but mainly because there is an instinctive sense, however obscure and yet inarticulate, that the whole constitution of property, on its present tenures, is injurious, and its influence on persons deteriorating and degrading; that truly the only interest for the consideration of the State is persons; that property will always follow persons; that the highest end of government is the culture of men; and that if men can be educated, the institutions will share their improvement and the moral sentiment will write the law of the land.

If it be not easy to settle the equity of this question, the peril is less when we take note of our natural defences. We are kept by better guards than the vigilance of such magistrates as we commonly elect. Society always consists in greatest part of young and foolish persons. The old, who have seen through the hypocrisy of courts and statesmen, die and leave no wisdom to their sons. They believe their own newspaper, as their fathers did at their age. With such an ignorant and deceivable majority, States would soon run to ruin, but that there are limitations beyond which the folly and ambition of governors cannot go. Things have their laws, as well as men; and things refuse to be trifled with. Property will be protected. Corn will not grow unless it is planted and manured; but the farmer will not plant or hoe it unless the chances are a hundred to one that he will cut and harvest it. Under any forms, persons and property must and will have their just sway. They exert their power, as steadily as matter its attraction. Cover up a pound of earth never so cunningly, divide and subdivide it; melt it to liquid, convert it to gas; it will always weigh a pound; it will always attract and resist other matter by the full virtue of one pound weight:—and the attributes of a person, his wit and his moral energy, will exercise, under any law or extinguishing tyranny, their proper force,—if not overtly, then covertly; if not for the law, then against it; if not wholesomely, then poisonously; with right, or by might.

The boundaries of personal influence it is impossible to fix, as persons are organs of moral or supernatural force. Under the dominion of an idea which possesses the minds of multitudes, as civil freedom, or the religious sentiment, the powers of persons are no longer subjects of calculation. A nation of men unanimously bent on freedom or conquest can easily confound the arithmetic of statists, and achieve extravagant actions out of all proportion to their means; as the Greeks, the Saracens, the Swiss, the Americans, and the French have done.

In like manner to every particle of property belongs its own attraction. A cent is the representative of a certain quantity of corn or other commodity. Its value is in the necessities of the animal man. It is so much warmth, so much bread, so much water, so much land. The law may do what it will with the owner of property; its just power will still attach to the cent. The law may in a mad freak say that all shall have power except the owners of property; they shall have no vote. Nevertheless, by a higher law, the property will, year after year, write every statute that respects property. The non-proprietor will be the scribe of the proprietor. What the owners wish to do, the whole power of property will do, either through the law or else in defiance of it. Of course I speak of all the property, not merely of the great estates. When the rich are outvoted, as frequently happens, it is the joint treasury of the poor which exceeds their accumulations. Every man owns something, if it is only a cow, or a wheelbarrow, or his arms, and so has that property to dispose of.

The same necessity which secures the rights of person and property against the malignity or folly of the magistrate, determines the form and methods of governing, which are proper to each nation and to its habit of thought, and nowise transferable to other states of society. In this country we are very vain of our political institutions, which are singular in this, that they sprung, within the memory of living men, from the character and condition of the people, which they still express with sufficient fidelity,—and we ostentatiously prefer them to any other in history. They are not better, but only fitter for us. We may be wise in asserting the advantage in modern times of the democratic form, but to other states of society, in which religion consecrated the monarchical, that and not this was expedient. Democracy is better for us, because the religious sentiment of the present time accords better with it. Born democrats, we are nowise qualified to judge of monarchy, which, to our fathers living in the monarchical idea, was also relatively right. But our institutions, though in coincidence with the spirit of the age, have not any exemption from the practical defects which have discredited other forms. Every actual State is corrupt. Good men must not obey the laws too well. What satire on government can equal the severity of censure conveyed in the word *politic*, which now for ages has signified *cunning*, intimating that the State is a trick?

The same benign necessity and the same practical abuse appear in the parties, into which each State divides itself, of opponents and defenders of the administration of the government. Parties are also founded on instincts, and have better guides to their own humble aims than the sagacity of their leaders. They have nothing perverse in their origin, but rudely mark some real and lasting relation. We might as wisely reprove the east wind or the frost, as a political party, whose members, for the most part, could give no account of their position, but stand for the defence of those interests in which they find themselves. Our quarrel with them begins when they quit this deep natural ground at the bidding of some leader, and obeying personal considerations, throw themselves into the maintenance and defence of points nowise belonging to their system. A party is perpetually corrupted by personality. Whilst we absolve the association from dishonesty, we cannot extend the same charity to their leaders. They reap the rewards of the docility and zeal of the masses which they direct. Ordinarily our parties are parties of circumstance, and not of principle; as the planting interest in conflict with the commercial; the party of capitalists and that of operatives: parties which are identical in their moral character, and which can easily change ground with each other in the support of many of their measures. Parties of principle, as, religious sects, or the party of free-trade, of universal suffrage, of abolition of slavery, of abolition of capital punishment, degenerate into personalities, or would inspire enthusiasm. The vice of our leading parties in this country (which may be cited as a fair specimen of these societies of opinion) is that they do not plant themselves on the deep and necessary grounds to which they are respectively entitled, but lash themselves to fury in the carrying of some local and momentary measure, nowise useful to the commonwealth. Of the two great parties which at this hour almost share the nation between them, I should say that one has the best cause, and the other contains the best men. The philosopher, the poet, or the religious man, will of course wish to cast his vote with the democrat, for free-trade, for wide suffrage, for the abolition of legal cruelties in the penal code, and for facilitating in every manner the access of the young and the poor to the sources of wealth and power. But he can rarely accept the persons whom the so-called popular party propose to him as representatives of these liberalities. They have not at heart the ends which give to the name of democracy what hope and virtue are in it. The spirit of our American radicalism is destructive and aimless: it is not loving; it has no ulterior and divine ends, but is destructive only out of hatred and selfishness. On the other side, the conservative party, composed of the most moderate, able and cultivated part of the population, is timid, and merely defensive of property. It vindicates no right, it aspires to no real good, it brands no crime, it proposes no generous policy; it does not build, nor write, nor cherish the arts, nor foster religion, nor establish schools, nor encourage science, nor emancipate the slave, nor befriend the poor, or the Indian, or the immigrant. From neither party, when in power, has the world any benefit to expect in science, art, or humanity, at all commensurate with the resources of the nation.

I do not for these defects despair of our republic. We are not at the mercy of any waves of chance. In the strife of ferocious parties, human nature always finds itself cherished; as the children of the convicts at Botany Bay are found to have as healthy a moral sentiment as other children. Citizens of feudal states are alarmed at our democratic institutions lapsing into anarchy, and the older and more cautious among ourselves are learning from Europeans to look with some terror at our turbulent freedom. It is said that in our license of construing the Constitution, and in the despotism of public opinion, we have no anchor; and one foreign observer thinks he has found the safeguard in the sanctity of Marriage among us; and another thinks he has found it in our Calvinism. Fisher Ames expressed the popular security more wisely, when he compared a monarchy and a republic, saying that a monarchy is a merchantman, which sails well, but will sometimes strike on a rock and go to the bottom; whilst a republic is a raft, which would never sink, but then your feet are always in water. No forms can have any dangerous importance whilst we are befriended by the laws of things. It makes no difference how many tons' weight of atmosphere presses on our heads, so long as the same pressure resists it within the lungs. Augment the mass a thousand fold, it cannot begin to crush us, as long as reaction is equal to action. The fact of two poles, of two forces, centripetal and centrifugal, is universal, and each force by its own activity develops the other. Wild liberty develops iron conscience. Want of liberty, by strengthening law and decorum, stupefies conscience. "Lynch-law" prevails only where there is greater hardihood and self-subsistency in the leaders. A mob cannot be a permanency; everybody's interest requires that it should not exist, and only justice satisfies all.

We must trust infinitely to the beneficent necessity which shines through all laws. Human nature expresses itself in them as characteristically as in statues, or songs, or railroads; and an abstract of the codes of nations would be a transcript of the common conscience. Governments have their origin in the moral identity of men. Reason for one is seen to be reason for another, and for every other. There is a middle measure which satisfies all parties, be they never so many or so resolute for their own. Every man finds a sanction for his simplest claims and deeds, in decisions of his own mind, which he calls Truth and Holiness. In these decisions all the citizens find a perfect agreement, and only in these; not in what is good to eat, good to wear, good use of time, or what amount of land or of public aid each is entitled to claim. This truth and justice men presently endeavor to make application of to the measuring of land, the apportionment of service, the protection of life and property. Their first endeavors, no doubt, are very awkward. Yet absolute right is the first governor; or, every government is an impure theocracy. The idea after which each community is aiming to make and mend its law, is the will of the wise man. The wise man it cannot find in nature, and it makes awkward but earnest efforts to secure his government by contrivance; as by causing the entire people to give their voices on every measure; or by a double choice to get the representation of the whole; or by a selection of the best citizens; or to secure the advantages of efficiency and internal peace by confiding the government to one, who may himself select his agents. All forms of government symbolize an immortal government, common to all dynasties and independent of numbers, perfect where two men exist, perfect where there is only one man.

Every man's nature is a sufficient advertisement to him of the character of his fellows. My right and my wrong is their right and their wrong. Whilst I do what is fit for me, and abstain from what is unfit, my neighbor and I shall often agree in our means, and work together for a time to one end. But whenever I find my dominion over myself not sufficient for me, and undertake the direction of him also, I overstep the truth, and come into false relations to him. I may have so much more skill or strength than he that he cannot express adequately his sense of wrong, but it is a lie, and hurts like a lie both him and me. Love and nature cannot maintain the assumption; it must be executed by a practical lie, namely by force. This undertaking for another is the blunder which stands in colossal ugliness in the governments of the world. It is the same thing in numbers, as in a pair, only not quite so intelligible. I can see well enough a great difference between my setting myself down to a self-control, and my going to make somebody else act after my views; but when a quarter of the human race assume to tell me what I must do, I may be too much disturbed by the circumstances to see so clearly the absurdity of their command. Therefore all public ends look vague and quixotic beside private ones. For any laws but those which men make for themselves are laughable. If I put myself in the place of my child, and we stand in one thought and see that things are thus or thus, that perception is law for him and me. We are both there, both act. But if, without carrying him into the thought, I look over into his plot, and, guessing how it is with him, ordain this or that, he will never obey me. This is the history of governments,—one man does something which is to bind another. A man who cannot be acquainted with me, taxes me; looking from afar at me ordains that a part of my labor shall go to this or that whimsical end,—not as I, but as he happens to fancy. Behold the consequence. Of all debts men are least willing to pay the taxes. What a satire is this on government! Everywhere they think they get their money's worth, except for these.

Hence the less government we have the better,—the fewer laws, and the less confided power. The antidote to this abuse of formal government is the influence of private character, the growth of the Individual; the appearance of the principal to supersede the proxy; the appearance of the wise man; of whom the existing government is, it must be owned, but a shabby imitation. That which all things tend to educe; which freedom, cultivation, intercourse, revolutions, go to form and deliver, is character; that is the end of Nature, to reach unto this coronation of her king. To educate the wise man the State exists, and with the appearance of the wise man the State expires. The appearance of character makes the State unnecessary. The wise man is the State. He needs no army, fort, or navy,—he loves men too well; no bribe, or feast, or palace, to draw friends to him; no vantage ground, no favorable circumstance. He needs no library, for he has not done thinking; no church, for he is a prophet; no statute-book, for he has the lawgiver; no money, for he is value; no road, for he is at home where he is; no experience, for the life of the creator shoots through him, and looks from his eyes. He has no personal friends, for he who has the spell to draw the prayer and the piety of all men unto him needs not husband and educate a few to share with him a select and poetic life. His relation to men is angelic; his memory is myrrh to them; his presence, frankincense and flowers.

We think our civilization near its meridian, but we are yet only at the cock-crowing and the morning star. In our barbarous society the influence of character is in its infancy. As a political power, as the rightful lord who is to tumble all rulers from their chairs, its presence is hardly yet suspected. Malthus and Ricardo quite omit it; the Annual Register is silent; in the Conversations' Lexicon it is not set down; the President's Message, the Queen's Speech, have not mentioned it; and yet it is never nothing. Every thought which genius and piety throw into the world, alters the world. The gladiators in the lists of power feel, through all their frocks of force and simulation, the presence of worth. I think the very strife of trade and ambition is confession of this divinity; and successes in those fields are the poor amends, the fig-leaf with which the shamed soul attempts to hide its nakedness. I find the like unwilling homage in all quarters. It is because we know how much is due from us that we are impatient to show some petty talent as a substitute for worth. We are haunted by a conscience of this right to grandeur of character, and are false to it. But each of us has some talent, can do somewhat useful, or graceful, or formidable, or amusing, or lucrative. That we do, as an apology to others and to ourselves for not reaching the mark of a good and equal life. But it does not satisfy *us*, whilst we thrust it on the notice of our companions. It may throw dust in their eyes, but does not smooth our own brow, or give us the tranquillity of the strong when we walk abroad. We do penance as we go. Our talent is a sort of expiation, and we are constrained to reflect on our splendid moment with a certain humiliation, as somewhat too fine, and not as one act of many acts, a fair expression of our permanent energy. Most persons of ability meet in society with a kind of tacit appeal. Each seems to say, "I am not all here." Senators and presidents have climbed so high with pain enough, not because they think the place specially agreeable, but as an apology for real worth, and to vindicate their manhood in our eyes. This conspicuous chair is their compensation to themselves for being of a poor, cold, hard nature. They must do what they can. Like one class of forest animals, they have nothing but a prehensile tail; climb they must, or crawl. If a man found himself so rich-natured that he could enter into strict relations with the best persons and make life serene around him by the dignity and sweetness of his behavior, could he afford to circumvent the favor of the caucus and the press, and covet relations so hollow and pompous as those of a politician? Surely nobody would be a charlatan who could afford to be sincere.

The tendencies of the times favor the idea of self-government, and leave the individual, for all code, to the rewards and penalties of his own constitution; which work with more energy than we believe whilst we depend on artificial restraints. The movement in this direction has been very marked in modern history. Much has been blind and discreditable, but the nature of the revolution is not affected by the vices of the revolters; for this is a purely moral force. It was never adopted by any party in history, neither can be. It separates the individual from all party, and unites him at the same time to the race. It promises a recognition of higher rights than those of personal freedom, or the security of property. A man has a right to be employed, to be trusted, to be loved, to be revered. The power of love, as the basis of a State, has never been tried. We must not imagine that all things are lapsing into confusion if every tender protestant be not compelled to bear his part in certain social conventions; nor doubt that roads can be built, letters carried, and the fruit of labor secured, when the government of force is at an end. Are our methods now so excellent that all competition is hopeless? could not a nation of friends even devise better ways? On the other hand, let not the most conservative and timid fear anything from a premature surrender of the bayonet and the system of force. For, according to the order of nature, which is quite superior to our will, it stands thus; there will always be a government of force where men are selfish; and when they are pure enough to abjure the code of force they will be wise enough to see how these public ends of the post-office, of the highway, of commerce and the exchange of property, of museums and libraries, of institutions of art and science can be answered.

We live in a very low state of the world, and pay unwilling tribute to governments founded on force. There is not, among the most religious and instructed men of the most religious and civil nations, a reliance on the moral sentiment and a sufficient belief in the unity of things, to persuade them that society can be maintained without artificial restraints, as well as the solar system; or that the private citizen might be reasonable and a good neighbor, without the hint of a jail or a confiscation. What is strange too, there never was in any man sufficient faith in the power of rectitude to inspire him with the broad design of renovating the State on the principle of right and love. All those who have pretended this design have been partial reformers, and have admitted in some manner the supremacy of the bad State. I do not call to mind a single human being who has steadily denied the authority of the laws, on the simple ground of his own moral nature. Such designs, full of genius and full of faith as they are, are not entertained except avowedly as air-pictures. If the individual who exhibits them dare to think them practicable, he disgusts scholars and churchmen; and men of talent and women of superior sentiments cannot hide their contempt. Not the less does nature continue to fill the heart of youth with suggestions of this enthusiasm, and there are now men,—if indeed I can speak in the plural number,—more exactly, I will say, I have just been conversing with one man, to whom no weight of adverse experience will make it for a moment appear impossible that thousands of human beings might exercise towards each other the grandest and simplest sentiments, as well as a knot of friends, or a pair of lovers.

1844

THE POET

A moody child and wildly wise
Pursued the game with joyful eyes,
Which chose, like meteors, their way,
And rived the dark with private ray:
They overleapt the horizon's edge,
Searched with Apollo's privilege;
Through man, and woman, and sea, and star
Saw the dance of nature forward far;
Through worlds, and races, and terms, and times
Saw musical order, and pairing rhymes.

Olympian bards who sung
Divine ideas below,
Which always find us young,
And always keep us so.

Those who are esteemed umpires of taste are often persons who have acquired some knowledge of admired pictures or sculptures, and have an inclination for whatever is elegant; but if you inquire whether they are beautiful souls, and whether their own acts are like fair pictures, you learn that they are selfish and sensual. Their cultivation is local, as if you should rub a log of dry wood in one spot to produce fire, all the rest remaining cold. Their knowledge of the fine arts is some study of rules and particulars, or some limited judgment of color or form, which is exercised for amusement or for show. It is a proof of the shallowness of the doctrine of beauty as it lies in the minds of our amateurs, that men seem to have lost the perception of the instant dependence of form upon soul. There is no doctrine of forms in our philosophy. We were put into our bodies, as fire is put into a pan to be carried about; but there is no accurate adjustment between the spirit and the organ, much less is the latter the germination of the former. So in regard to other forms, the intellectual men do not believe in any essential dependence of the material world on thought and volition.

Theologians think it a pretty air-castle to talk of the spiritual meaning of a ship or a cloud, of a city or a contract, but they prefer to come again to the solid ground of historical evidence; and even the poets are contented with a civil and conformed manner of living, and to write poems from the fancy, at a safe distance from their own experience. But the highest minds of the world have never ceased to explore the double meaning, or shall I say the quadruple or the centuple or much more manifold meaning, of every sensuous fact; Orpheus, Empedocles, Heraclitus, Plato, Plutarch, Dante, Swedenborg, and the masters of sculpture, picture and poetry. For we are not pans and barrows, nor even porters of the fire and torch-bearers, but children of the fire, made of it, and only the same divinity transmuted and at two or three removes, when we know least about it. And this hidden truth, that the fountains whence all this river of Time and its creatures floweth are intrinsically ideal and beautiful, draws us to the consideration of the nature and functions of the Poet, or the man of Beauty; to the means and materials he uses, and to the general aspect of the art in the present time.

The breadth of the problem is great, for the poet is representative. He stands among partial men for the complete man, and apprises us not of his wealth, but of the common wealth. The young man reveres men of genius, because, to speak truly, they are more himself than he is. They receive of the soul as he also receives, but they more. Nature enhances her beauty, to the eye of loving men, from their belief that the poet is beholding her shows at the same time. He is isolated among his contemporaries by truth and by his art, but with this consolation in his pursuits, that they will draw all men sooner or later. For all men live by truth and stand in need of expression. In love, in art, in avarice, in politics, in labor, in games, we study to utter our painful secret. The man is only half himself, the other half is his expression.

Notwithstanding this necessity to be published, adequate expression is rare. I know not how it is that we need an interpreter, but the great majority of men seem to be minors, who have not yet come into possession of their own, or mutes, who cannot report the conversation they have had with nature. There is no man who does not anticipate a supersensual utility in the sun and stars, earth and water. These stand and wait to render him a peculiar service. But there is some obstruction or some excess of phlegm in our constitution, which does not suffer them to yield the due effect. Too feeble fall the impressions of nature on us to make us artists. Every touch should thrill. Every man should be so much an artist that he could report in conversation what had befallen him. Yet, in our experience, the rays or appulses have sufficient force to arrive at the senses, but not enough to reach the quick and compel the reproduction of themselves in speech. The poet is the person in whom these powers are in balance, the man without impediment, who sees and handles that which others dream of, traverses the whole scale of experience, and is representative of man, in virtue of being the largest power to receive and to impart.

For the Universe has three children, born at one time, which reappear under different names in every system of thought, whether they be called cause, operation and effect; or, more poetically, Jove, Pluto, Neptune; or, theologically, the Father, the Spirit and the Son; but which we will call here the Knower, the Doer and the Sayer. These stand respectively for the love of truth, for the love of good, and for the love of beauty. These three are equal. Each is that which he is, essentially, so that he cannot be surmounted or analyzed, and each of these three has the power of the others latent in him and his own, patent.

The poet is the sayer, the namer, and represents beauty. He is a sovereign, and stands on the centre. For the world is not painted or adorned, but is from the beginning beautiful; and God has not made some beautiful things, but Beauty is the creator of the universe. Therefore the poet is not any permissive potentate, but is emperor in his own right. Criticism is infested with a cant of materialism, which assumes that manual skill and activity is the first merit of all men, and disparages such as say and do not, overlooking the fact that some men, namely poets, are natural sayers, sent into the world to the end of expression, and confounds them with those whose province is action but who quit it to imitate the sayers. But Homer's words are as costly and admirable to Homer as Agamemnon's victories are to Agamemnon. The poet does not wait for the hero or the sage, but, as they act and think primarily, so he writes primarily what will and must be spoken, reckoning the others, though primaries also, yet, in respect to him, secondaries and servants; as sitters or models in the studio of a painter, or as assistants who bring building-materials to an architect.

For poetry was all written before time was, and whenever we are so finely organized that we can penetrate into that region where the air is music, we hear those primal warblings and attempt to write them down, but we lose ever and anon a word or a verse and substitute something of our own, and thus miswrite the poem. The men of more delicate ear write down these cadences more faithfully, and these transcripts, though imperfect, become the songs of the nations. For nature is as truly beautiful as it is good, or as it is reasonable, and must as much appear as it must be done, or be known. Words and deeds are quite indifferent modes of the divine energy. Words are also actions, and actions are a kind of words.

The sign and credentials of the poet are that he announces that which no man foretold. He is the true and only doctor; he knows and tells; he is the only teller of news, for he was present and privy to the appearance which he describes. He is a beholder of ideas and an utterer of the necessary and causal. For we do not speak now of men of poetical talents, or of industry and skill in metre, but of the true poet. I took part in a conversation the other day concerning a recent writer of lyrics, a man of subtle mind, whose head appeared to be a music-box of delicate tunes and rhythms, and whose skill and command of language we could not sufficiently praise. But when the question arose whether he was not only a lyrist but a poet, we were obliged to confess that he is plainly a contemporary, not an eternal man. He does not stand out of our low limitations, like a Chimborazo under the line, running up from a torrid base through all the climates of the globe, with belts of the herbage of every latitude on its high and mottled sides; but this genius is the landscape-garden of a modern house, adorned with fountains and statues, with well-bred men and women standing and sitting in the walks and terraces. We hear, through all the varied music, the ground-tone of conventional life. Our poets are men of talents who sing, and not the children of music. The argument is secondary, the finish of the verses is primary.

For it is not metres, but a metre-making argument that makes a poem,—a thought so passionate and alive that like the spirit of a plant or an animal it has an architecture of its own, and adorns nature with a new thing. The thought and the form are equal in the order of time, but in the order of genesis the thought is prior to the form. The poet has a new thought; he has a whole new experience to unfold; he will tell us how it was with him, and all men will be the richer in his fortune. For the experience of each new age requires a new confession, and the world seems always waiting for its poet. I remember when I was young how much I was moved one morning by tidings that genius had appeared in a youth who sat near me at table. He had left his work and gone rambling none knew whither, and had written hundreds of lines, but could not tell whether that which was in him was therein told; he could tell nothing but that all was changed,—man, beast, heaven, earth and sea. How gladly we listened! how credulous! Society seemed to be compromised. We sat in the aurora of a sunrise which was to put out all the stars. Boston seemed to be at twice the distance it had the night before, or was much farther than that. Rome,—what was Rome? Plutarch and Shakspeare were in the yellow leaf, and Homer no more should be heard of. It is much to know that poetry has been written this very day, under this very roof, by your side. What! that wonderful spirit has not expired! These stony moments are still sparkling and animated! I had fancied that the oracles were all silent, and nature had spent her fires; and behold! all night, from every pore, these fine auroras have been streaming. Every one has some interest in the advent of the poet, and no one knows how much it may concern him. We know that the secret of the world is profound, but who or what shall be our interpreter, we know not. A mountain ramble, a new style of face, a new person, may put the key into our hands. Of course the value of genius to us is in the veracity of its report. Talent may frolic and juggle; genius realizes and adds. Mankind in good earnest have availed so far in understanding themselves and their work, that the foremost watchman on the peak announces his news. It is the truest word ever spoken, and the phrase will be the fittest, most musical, and the unerring voice of the world for that time.

All that we call sacred history attests that the birth of a poet is the principal event in chronology. Man, never so often deceived, still watches for the arrival of a brother who can hold him steady to a truth until he has made it his own. With what joy I begin to read a poem which I confide in as an inspiration! And now my chains are to be broken; I shall mount above these clouds and opaque airs in which I live,—opaque, though they seem transparent,—and from the heaven of truth I shall see and comprehend my relations. That will reconcile me to life and renovate nature, to see trifles animated by a tendency, and to know what I am doing. Life will no more be a noise; now I shall see men and women, and know the signs by which they may be discerned from fools and satans. This day shall be better than my birthday: then I became an animal; now I am invited into the science of the real. Such is the hope, but the fruition is postponed. Oftener it falls that this winged man, who will carry me into the heaven, whirls me into mists, then leaps and frisks about with me as it were from cloud to cloud, still affirming that he is bound heavenward; and I, being myself a novice, am slow in perceiving that he does not know the way into the heavens, and is merely bent that I should admire his skill to rise like a fowl or a flying fish, a little way from the ground or the water; but the all-piercing, all-feeding and ocular air of heaven that man shall never inhabit. I tumble down again soon into my old nooks, and lead the life of exaggerations as before, and have lost my faith in the possibility of any guide who can lead me thither where I would be.

But, leaving these victims of vanity, let us, with new hope, observe how nature, by worthier impulses, has insured the poet's fidelity to his office of announcement and affirming, namely by the beauty of things, which becomes a new and higher beauty when expressed. Nature offers all her creatures to him as a picture-language. Being used as a type, a second wonderful value appears in the object, far better than its old value; as the carpenter's stretched cord, if you hold your ear close enough, is musical in the breeze. "Things more excellent than every image," says Jamblichus, "are expressed through images." Things admit of being used as symbols because nature is a symbol, in the whole, and in every part. Every line we can draw in the sand has expression; and there is no body without its spirit or genius. All form is an effect of character; all condition, of the quality of the life; all harmony, of health; and for this reason a perception of beauty should be sympathetic, or proper only to the good. The beautiful rests on the foundations of the necessary. The soul makes the body, as the wise Spenser teaches:—

"So every spirit, as it is more pure,
And hath in it the more of heavenly light,
So it the fairer body doth procure
To habit in, and it more fairly dight,
With cheerful grace and amiable sight.
For, of the soul, the body form doth take,
For soul is form, and doth the body make."

Here we find ourselves suddenly not in a critical speculation but in a holy place, and should go very warily and reverently. We stand before the secret of the world, there where Being passes into Appearance and Unity into Variety.

The Universe is the externization of the soul. Wherever the life is, that bursts into appearance around it. Our science is sensual, and therefore superficial. The earth and the heavenly bodies, physics and chemistry, we sensually treat, as if they were self-existent; but these are the retinue of that Being we have. "The mighty heaven," said Proclus, "exhibits, in its transfigurations, clear images of the splendor of intellectual perceptions; being moved in conjunction with the unapparent periods of intellectual natures." Therefore science always goes abreast with the just elevation of the man, keeping step with religion and metaphysics; or the state of science is an index of our self-knowledge. Since every thing in nature answers to a moral power, if any phenomenon remains brute and dark it is because the corresponding faculty in the observer is not yet active.

No wonder then, if these waters be so deep, that we hover over them with a religious regard. The beauty of the fable proves the importance of the sense; to the poet, and to all others; or, if you please, every man is so far a poet as to be susceptible of these enchantments of nature; for all men have the thoughts whereof the universe is the celebration. I find that the fascination resides in the symbol. Who loves nature? Who does not? Is it only poets, and men of leisure and cultivation, who live with her? No; but also hunters, farmers, grooms and butchers, though they express their affection in their choice of life and not in their choice of words. The writer wonders what the coachman or the hunter values in riding, in horses and dogs. It is not superficial qualities. When you talk with him he holds these at as slight a rate as you. His worship is sympathetic; he has no definitions, but he is commanded in nature by the living power which he feels to be there present. No imitation or playing of these things would content him; he loves the earnest of the north wind, of rain, of stone and wood and iron. A beauty not explicable is dearer than a beauty which we can see to the end of. It is nature the symbol, nature certifying the supernatural, body overflowed by life which he worships with coarse but sincere rites.

The inwardness and mystery of this attachment drive men of every class to the use of emblems. The schools of poets and philosophers are not more intoxicated with their symbols than the populace with theirs. In our political parties, compute the power of badges and emblems. See the great ball which they roll from Baltimore to Bunker Hill! In the political processions, Lowell goes in a loom, and Lynn in a shoe, and Salem in a ship. Witness the cider-barrel, the log-cabin, the hickory-stick, the palmetto, and all the cognizances of party. See the power of national emblems. Some stars, lilies, leopards, a crescent, a lion, an eagle, or other figure which came into credit God knows how, on an old rag of bunting, blowing in the wind on a fort at the ends of the earth, shall make the blood tingle under the rudest or the most conventional exterior. The people fancy they hate poetry, and they are all poets and mystics!

Beyond this universality of the symbolic language, we are apprised of the divineness of this superior use of things, whereby the world is a temple whose walls are covered with emblems, pictures and commandments of the Deity,—in this, that there is no fact in nature which does not carry the whole sense of nature; and the distinctions which we make in events and in affairs, of low and high, honest and base, disappear when nature is used as a symbol. Thought makes everything fit for use. The vocabulary of an omniscient man would embrace words and images excluded from polite conversation. What would be base, or even obscene, to the obscene, becomes illustrious, spoken in a new connection of thought. The piety of the Hebrew prophets purges their grossness. The circumcision is an example of the power of poetry to raise the low and offensive. Small and mean things serve as well as great symbols. The meaner the type by which a law is expressed, the more pungent it is, and the more lasting in the memories of men; just as we choose the smallest box or case in which any needful utensil can be carried. Bare lists of words are found suggestive to an imaginative and excited mind; as it is related of Lord Chatham that he was accustomed to read in Bailey's Dictionary when he was preparing to speak in Parliament. The poorest experience is rich enough for all the purposes of expressing thought. Why covet a knowledge of new facts? Day and night, house and garden, a few books, a few actions, serve us as well as would all trades and all spectacles. We are far from having exhausted the significance of the few symbols we use. We can come to use them yet with a terrible simplicity. It does not need that a poem should be long. Every word was once a poem. Every new relation is a new word. Also we use defects and deformities to a sacred purpose, so expressing our sense that the evils of the world are such only to the evil eye. In the old mythology, mythologists observe, defects are ascribed to divine natures, as lameness to Vulcan, blindness to Cupid, and the like,—to signify exuberances.

For as it is dislocation and detachment from the life of God that makes things ugly, the poet, who re-attaches things to nature and the Whole,—re-attaching even artificial things and violation of nature, to nature, by a deeper insight,—disposes very easily of the most disagreeable facts. Readers of poetry see the factory-village and the railway, and fancy that the poetry of the landscape is broken up by these; for these works of art are not yet consecrated in their reading; but the poet sees them fall within the great Order not less than the beehive or the spider's geometrical web. Nature adopts them very fast into her vital circles, and the gliding train of cars she loves like her own. Besides, in a centred mind, it signifies nothing how many mechanical inventions you exhibit. Though you add millions, and never so surprising, the fact of mechanics has not gained a grain's weight. The spiritual fact remains unalterable, by many or by few particulars; as no mountain is of any appreciable height to break the curve of the sphere. A shrewd country-boy goes to the city for the first time, and the complacent citizen is not satisfied with his little wonder. It is not that he does not see all the fine houses and know that he never saw such before, but he disposes of them as easily as the poet finds place for the railway. The chief value of the new fact is to enhance the great and constant fact of Life, which can dwarf any and every circumstance, and to which the belt of wampum and the commerce of America are alike.

The world being thus put under the mind for verb and

noun, the poet is he who can articulate it. For though life is great, and fascinates and absorbs; and though all men are intelligent of the symbols through which it is named; yet they cannot originally use them. We are symbols and inhabit symbols; workmen, work, and tools, words and things, birth and death, all are emblems; but we sympathize with the symbols, and being infatuated with the economical uses of things, we do not know that they are thoughts. The poet, by an ulterior intellectual perception, gives them a power which makes their old use forgotten, and puts eyes and a tongue into every dumb and inanimate object. He perceives the independence of the thought on the symbol, the stability of the thought, the accidency and fugacity of the symbol. As the eyes of Lyncæus were said to see through the earth, so the poet turns the world to glass, and shows us all things in their right series and procession. For through that better perception he stands one step nearer to things, and sees the flowing or metamorphosis; perceives that thought is multiform; that within the form of every creature is a force impelling it to ascend into a higher form; and following with his eyes the life, uses the forms which express that life, and so his speech flows with the flowing of nature. All the facts of the animal economy, sex, nutriment, gestation, birth, growth, are symbols of the passage of the world into the soul of man, to suffer there a change and reappear a new and higher fact. He uses forms according to the life, and not according to the form. This is true science. The poet alone knows astronomy, chemistry, vegetation and animation, for he does not stop at these facts, but employs them as signs. He knows why the plain or meadow of space was strown with these flowers we call suns and moons and stars; why the great deep is adorned with animals, with men, and gods; for in every word he speaks he rides on them as the horses of thought.

By virtue of this science the poet is the Namer or Language-maker, naming things sometimes after their appearance, sometimes after their essence, and giving to every one its own name and not another's, thereby rejoicing the intellect, which delights in detachment or boundary. The poets made all the words, and therefore language is the archives of history, and, if we must say it, a sort of tomb of the muses. For though the origin of most of our words is forgotten, each word was at first a stroke of genius, and obtained currency because for the moment it symbolized the world to the first speaker and to the hearer. The etymologist finds the deadest word to have been once a brilliant picture. Language is fossil poetry. As the limestone of the continent consists of infinite masses of the shells of animalcules, so language is made up of images or tropes, which now, in their secondary use, have long ceased to remind us of their poetic origin. But the poet names the thing because he sees it, or comes one step nearer to it than any other. This expression or naming is not art, but a second nature, grown out of the first, as a leaf out of a tree. What we call nature is a certain self-regulated motion or change; and nature does all things by her own hands, and does not leave another to baptize her but baptizes herself; and this through the metamorphosis again. I remember that a certain poet described it to me thus:—

Genius is the activity which repairs the decays of things, whether wholly or partly of a material and finite kind. Nature, through all her kingdoms, insures herself. Nobody cares for planting the poor fungus; so she shakes down from the gills of one agaric countless spores, any one of which, being preserved, transmits new billions of spores to-morrow or next day. The new agaric of this hour has a chance which the old one had not. This atom of seed is thrown into a new place, not subject to the accidents which destroyed its parent two rods off. She makes a man; and having brought him to ripe age, she will no longer run the risk of losing this wonder at a blow, but she detaches from him a new self, that the kind may be safe from accidents to which the individual is exposed. So when the soul of the poet has come to ripeness of thought, she detaches and sends away from it its poems or songs,—a fearless, sleepless, deathless progeny, which is not exposed to the accidents of the weary kingdom of time; a fearless, vivacious offspring, clad with wings (such was the virtue of the soul out of which they came) which carry them fast and far, and infix them irrecoverably into the hearts of men. These wings are the beauty of the poet's soul. The songs, thus flying immortal from their mortal parent, are pursued by clamorous flights of censures, which swarm in far greater numbers and threaten to devour them; but these last are not winged. At the end of a very short leap they fall plump down and rot, having received from the souls out of which they came no beautiful wings. But the melodies of the poet ascend and leap and pierce into the deeps of infinite time.

So far the bard taught me, using his freer speech. But nature has a higher end, in the production of new individuals, than security, namely *ascension*, or the passage of the soul into higher forms. I knew in my younger days the sculptor who made the statue of the youth which stands in the public garden. He was, as I remember, unable to tell directly what made him happy or unhappy, but by wonderful indirections he could tell. He rose one day, according to his habit, before the dawn, and saw the morning break, grand as the eternity out of which it came, and for many days after, he strove to express this tranquillity, and lo! his chisel had fashioned out of marble the form of a beautiful youth, Phosphorus, whose aspect is such that it is said all persons who look on it become silent. The poet also resigns himself to his mood, and that thought which agitated him is expressed, but *alter idem*, in a manner totally new. The expression is organic, or the new type which things themselves take when liberated. As, in the sun, objects paint their images on the retina of the eye, so they, sharing the aspiration of the whole universe, tend to paint a far more delicate copy of their essence in his mind. Like the metamorphosis of things into higher organic forms is their change into melodies. Over everything stands its dæmon or soul, and, as the form of the thing is reflected by the eye, so the soul of the thing is reflected by a melody. The sea, the mountain-ridge, Niagara, and every flower-bed, pre-exist, or super-exist, in pre-cantations, which sail like odors in the air, and when any man goes by with an ear sufficiently fine, he overhears them and endeavors to write down the notes without diluting or depraving them. And herein is the legitimation of criticism, in the mind's faith that the poems are a corrupt version of some text in nature with which they ought to be made to tally. A rhyme in one of our sonnets should not be less pleasing than the iterated nodes of a seashell, or the resembling difference of a group of flowers. The pairing of the birds is an idyl, not tedious as our idyls are; a tempest is a rough ode, without falsehood or rant; a summer, with its harvest sown, reaped and stored, is an epic song, subordinating how many admirably executed parts. Why should not the symmetry and truth that modulate these, glide into our spirits, and we participate the invention of nature?

This insight, which expresses itself by what is called Imagination, is a very high sort of seeing, which does not come by study, but by the intellect being where and what it sees; by sharing the path or circuit of things through forms, and so making them translucid to others. The path of things is silent. Will they suffer a speaker to go with them? A spy they will not suffer; a lover, a poet, is the transcendency of their own nature,—him they will suffer. The condition of true naming, on the poet's part, is his resigning himself to the divine *aura* which breathes through forms, and accompanying that.

It is a secret which every intellectual man quickly learns, that beyond the energy of his possessed and conscious intellect he is capable of a new energy (as of an intellect doubled on itself), by abandonment to the nature of things; that beside his privacy of power as an individual man, there is a great public power on which he can draw, by unlocking, at all risks, his human doors, and suffering the ethereal tides to roll and circulate through him; then he is caught up into the life of the Universe, his speech is thunder, his thought is law, and his words are universally intelligible as the plants and animals. The poet knows that he speaks adequately then only when he speaks somewhat wildly, or "with the flower of the mind;" not with the intellect used as an organ, but with the intellect released from all service and suffered to take its direction from its celestial life; or as the

ancients were wont to express themselves, not with intellect alone but with the intellect inebriated by nectar. As the traveller who has lost his way throws his reins on his horse's neck and trusts to the instinct of the animal to find his road, so must we do with the divine animal who carries us through this world. For if in any manner we can stimulate this instinct, new passages are opened for us into nature; the mind flows into and through things hardest and highest, and the metamorphosis is possible.

This is the reason why bards love wine, mead, narcotics, coffee, tea, opium, the fumes of sandalwood and tobacco, or whatever other procurers of animal exhilaration. All men avail themselves of such means as they can, to add this extraordinary power to their normal powers; and to this end they prize conversation, music, pictures, sculpture, dancing, theatres, travelling, war, mobs, fires, gaming, politics, or love, or science, or animal intoxication,—which are several coarser or finer *quasi*-mechanical substitutes for the true nectar, which is the ravishment of the intellect by coming nearer to the fact. These are auxiliaries to the centrifugal tendency of a man, to his passage out into free space, and they help him to escape the custody of that body in which he is pent up, and of that jail-yard of individual relations in which he is enclosed. Hence a great number of such as were professionally expressers of Beauty, as painters, poets, musicians and actors, have been more than others wont to lead a life of pleasure and indulgence; all but the few who received the true nectar; and, as it was a spurious mode of attaining freedom, as it was an emancipation not into the heavens but into the freedom of baser places, they were punished for that advantage they won, by a dissipation and deterioration. But never can any advantage be taken of nature by a trick. The spirit of the world, the great calm presence of the Creator, comes not forth to the sorceries of opium or of wine. The sublime vision comes to the pure and simple soul in a clean and chaste body. That is not an inspiration, which we owe to narcotics, but some counterfeit excitement and fury. Milton says that the lyric poet may drink wine and live generously, but the epic poet, he who shall sing of the gods and their descent unto men, must drink water out of a wooden bowl. For poetry is not "Devil's wine," but God's wine. It is with this as it is with toys. We fill the hands and nurseries of our children with all manner of dolls, drums and horses; withdrawing their eyes from the plain face and sufficing objects of nature, the sun and moon, the animals, the water and stones, which should be their toys. So the poet's habit of living should be set on a key so low that the common influences should delight him. His cheerfulness should be the gift of the sunlight; the air should suffice for his inspiration, and he should be tipsy with water. That spirit which suffices quiet hearts, which seems to come forth to such from every dry knoll of sere grass, from every pine stump and half-imbedded stone on which the dull March sun shines, comes forth to the poor and hungry, and such as are of simple taste. If thou fill thy brain with Boston and New York, with fashion and covetousness, and wilt stimulate thy jaded senses with wine and French coffee, thou shalt find no radiance of wisdom in the lonely waste of the pine woods.

If the imagination intoxicates the poet, it is not inactive in other men. The metamorphosis excites in the beholder an emotion of joy. The use of symbols has a certain power of emancipation and exhilaration for all men. We seem to be touched by a wand which makes us dance and run about happily, like children. We are like persons who come out of a cave or cellar into the open air. This is the effect on us of tropes, fables, oracles and all poetic forms. Poets are thus liberating gods. Men have really got a new sense, and found within their world another world, or nest of worlds; for, the metamorphosis once seen, we divine that it does not stop. I will not now consider how much this makes the charm of algebra and the mathematics, which also have their tropes, but it is felt in every definition; as when Aristotle defines *space* to be an immovable vessel in which things are contained;—or when Plato defines a *line* to be a flowing point; or *figure* to be a bound of solid; and many the like. What a joyful sense of freedom we have when Vitruvius announces the old opinion of artists that no architect can build any house well who does not know something of anatomy. When Socrates, in Charmides, tells us that the soul is cured of its maladies by certain incantations, and that these incantations are beautiful reasons, from which temperance is generated in souls; when Plato calls the world an animal, and Timæus affirms that the plants also are animals; or affirms a man to be a heavenly tree, growing with his root, which is his head, upward; and, as George Chapman, following him, writes,

> "So in our tree of man, whose nervie root
> Springs in his top;"—

when Orpheus speaks of hoariness as "that white flower which marks extreme old age;" when Proclus calls the universe the statue of the intellect; when Chaucer, in his praise of "Gentilesse," compares good blood in mean condition to fire, which, though carried to the darkest house betwixt this and the mount of Caucasus, will yet hold its natural office and burn as bright as if twenty thousand men did it behold; when John saw, in the Apocalypse, the ruin of the world through evil, and the stars fall from heaven as the fig tree casteth her untimely fruit; when Æsop reports the whole catalogue of common daily relations through the masquerade of birds and beasts;—we take the cheerful hint of the immortality of our essence and its versatile habit and escapes, as when the gypsies say of themselves "it is in vain to hang them, they cannot die."

The poets are thus liberating gods. The ancient British bards had for the title of their order, "Those who are free throughout the world." They are free, and they make free. An imaginative book renders us much more service at first, by stimulating us through its tropes, than afterward when we arrive at the precise sense of the author. I think nothing is of any value in books excepting the transcendental and extraordinary. If a man is inflamed and carried away by his thought, to that degree that he forgets the authors and the public and heeds only this one dream which holds him like an insanity, let me read his paper, and you may have all the arguments and histories and criticism. All the value which attaches to Pythagoras,

Paracelsus, Cornelius Agrippa, Cardan, Kepler, Swedenborg, Schelling, Oken, or any other who introduces questionable facts into his cosmogony, as angels, devils, magic, astrology, palmistry, mesmerism, and so on, is the certificate we have of departure from routine, and that here is a new witness. That also is the best success in conversation, the magic of liberty, which puts the world like a ball in our hands. How cheap even the liberty then seems; how mean to study, when an emotion communicates to the intellect the power to sap and upheave nature; how great the perspective! nations, times, systems, enter and disappear like threads in tapestry of large figure and many colors; dream delivers us to dream, and while the drunkenness lasts we will sell our bed, our philosophy, our religion, in our opulence.

There is good reason why we should prize this liberation. The fate of the poor shepherd, who, blinded and lost in the snow-storm, perishes in a drift within a few feet of his cottage door, is an emblem of the state of man. On the brink of the waters of life and truth, we are miserably dying. The inaccessibleness of every thought but that we are in, is wonderful. What if you come near to it; you are as remote when you are nearest as when you are farthest. Every thought is also a prison; every heaven is also a prison. Therefore we love the poet, the inventor, who in any form, whether in an ode or in an action or in looks and behavior, has yielded us a new thought. He unlocks our chains and admits us to a new scene.

This emancipation is dear to all men, and the power to impart it, as it must come from greater depth and scope of thought, is a measure of intellect. Therefore all books of the imagination endure, all which ascend to that truth that the writer sees nature beneath him, and uses it as his exponent. Every verse or sentence possessing this virtue will take care of its own immortality. The religions of the world are the ejaculations of a few imaginative men.

But the quality of the imagination is to flow, and not to freeze. The poet did not stop at the color or the form, but read their meaning; neither may he rest in this meaning, but he makes the same objects exponents of his new thought. Here is the difference betwixt the poet and the mystic, that the last nails a symbol to one sense, which was a true sense for a moment, but soon becomes old and false. For all symbols are fluxional; all language is vehicular and transitive, and is good, as ferries and horses are, for conveyance, not as farms and houses are, for homestead. Mysticism consists in the mistake of an accidental and individual symbol for an universal one. The morning-redness happens to be the favorite meteor to the eyes of Jacob Behmen, and comes to stand to him for truth and faith; and, he believes, should stand for the same realities to every reader. But the first reader prefers as naturally the symbol of a mother and child, or a gardener and his bulb, or a jeweller polishing a gem. Either of these, or of a myriad more, are equally good to the person to whom they are significant. Only they must be held lightly, and be very willingly translated into the equivalent terms which others use. And the mystic must be steadily told,—All that you say is just as true without the tedious use of that symbol as with it. Let us have a little algebra, instead of this trite rhetoric,—universal signs, instead of these village symbols,—and we shall both be gainers. The history of hierarchies seems to show that all religious error consisted in making the symbol too stark and solid, and was at last nothing but an excess of the organ of language.

Swedenborg, of all men in the recent ages, stands eminently for the translator of nature into thought. I do not know the man in history to whom things stood so uniformly for words. Before him the metamorphosis continually plays. Everything on which his eye rests, obeys the impulses of moral nature. The figs become grapes whilst he eats them. When some of his angels affirmed a truth, the laurel twig which they held blossomed in their hands. The noise which at a distance appeared like gnashing and thumping, on coming nearer was found to be the voice of disputants. The men in one of his visions, seen in heavenly light, appeared like dragons, and seemed in darkness; but to each other they appeared as men, and when the light from heaven shone into their cabin, they complained of the darkness, and were compelled to shut the window that they might see.

There was this perception in him which makes the poet or seer an object of awe and terror, namely that the same man or society of men may wear one aspect to themselves and their companions, and a different aspect to higher intelligences. Certain priests, whom he describes as conversing very learnedly together, appeared to the children who were at some distance, like dead horses; and many the like misappearances. And instantly the mind inquires whether these fishes under the bridge, yonder oxen in the pasture, those dogs in the yard, are immutably fishes, oxen and dogs, or only so appear to me, and perchance to themselves appear upright men; and whether I appear as a man to all eyes. The Brahmins and Pythagoras propounded the same question, and if any poet has witnessed the transformation he doubtless found it in harmony with various experiences. We have all seen changes as considerable in wheat and caterpillars. He is the poet and shall draw us with love and terror, who sees through the flowing vest the firm nature, and can declare it.

I look in vain for the poet whom I describe. We do not with sufficient plainness or sufficient profoundness address ourselves to life, nor dare we chaunt our own times and social circumstance. If we filled the day with bravery, we should not shrink from celebrating it. Time and nature yield us many gifts, but not yet the timely man, the new religion, the reconciler, whom all things await. Dante's praise is that he dared to write his autobiography in colossal cipher, or into universality. We have yet had no genius in America, with tyrannous eye, which knew the value of our incomparable materials, and saw, in the barbarism and materialism of the times, another carnival of the same gods whose picture he so much admires in Homer; then in the Middle Age; then in Calvinism. Banks and tariffs, the newspaper and caucus, Methodism and Unitarianism, are flat and dull to dull people, but rest on the same foundations of wonder as the town of Troy and the temple of Delphi, and are as swiftly passing away. Our log-rolling, our stumps and their politics, our fisheries, our Negroes and Indians, our boats and our repudiations, the wrath of rogues and the pusillanimity of honest men, the northern trade, the southern planting, the western clearing, Oregon and Texas, are yet unsung. Yet America is a poem in our eyes; its ample geography dazzles the imagination, and it will not wait long for metres. If I have not found that excellent combination of gifts in my countrymen which I seek, neither could I aid myself to fix the idea of the poet by reading now and then in Chalmers's collection of five centuries of English poets. These are wits more than poets, though there have been poets among them. But when we adhere to the ideal of the poet, we have our difficulties even with Milton and Homer. Milton is too literary, and Homer too literal and historical.

But I am not wise enough for a national criticism, and must use the old largeness a little longer, to discharge my errand from the muse to the poet concerning his art.

Art is the path of the creator to his work. The paths or methods are ideal and eternal, though few men ever see them; not the artist himself for years, or for a lifetime, unless he come into the conditions. The painter, the sculptor, the composer, the epic rhapsodist, the orator, all partake one desire, namely to express themselves symmetrically and abundantly, not dwarfishly and fragmentarily. They found or put themselves in certain conditions, as, the painter and sculptor before some impressive human figures; the orator into the assembly of the people; and the others in such scenes as each has found exciting to his intellect; and each presently feels the new desire. He hears a voice, he sees a beckoning. Then he is apprised, with wonder, what herds of dæmons hem him in. He can no more rest; he says, with the old painter, "By God it is in me and must go forth of me." He pursues a beauty, half seen, which flies before him. The poet pours out verses in every solitude. Most of the things he says are conventional, no doubt; but by and by he says something which is original and beautiful. That charms him. He would say nothing else but such things. In our way of talking we say "That is yours, this is mine;" but the poet knows well that it is not his; that it is as strange and beautiful to him as to you; he would fain hear the like eloquence at length. Once having tasted this immortal ichor, he cannot have enough of it, and as an admirable creative power exists in these intellections, it is of the last importance that these things get spoken. What a little of all we know is said! What drops of all the sea of our science are baled up! and by what accident it is that these are exposed, when so many secrets sleep in nature! Hence the necessity of speech and song; hence these throbs and heart-beatings in the orator, at the door of the assembly, to the end namely that thought may be ejaculated as Logos, or Word.

Doubt not, O poet, but persist. Say "It is in me, and shall out." Stand there, balked and dumb, stuttering and stammering, hissed and hooted, stand and strive, until at last rage draw out of thee that *dream*-power which every night shows thee is thine own; a power transcending all limit and privacy, and by virtue of which a man is the conductor of the whole river of electricity. Nothing walks, or creeps, or grows, or exists, which must not in turn arise and walk before him as exponent of his meaning. Comes he to that power, his genius is no longer exhaustible. All the creatures by pairs and by tribes pour into his mind as into a Noah's ark, to come forth again to people a new world. This is like the stock of air for our respiration or for the combustion of our fireplace; not a measure of gallons, but the entire atmosphere if wanted. And therefore the rich poets, as Homer, Chaucer, Shakspeare, and Raphael, have obviously no limits to their works except the limits of their lifetime, and resemble a mirror carried through the street, ready to render an image of every created thing.

O poet! a new nobility is conferred in groves and pastures, and not in castles or by the sword-blade any longer. The conditions are hard, but equal. Thou shalt leave the world, and know the muse only. Thou shalt not know any longer the times, customs, graces, politics, or opinions of men, but shalt take all from the muse. For the time of towns is tolled from the world by funereal chimes, but in nature the universal hours are counted by succeeding tribes of animals and plants, and by growth of joy on joy. God wills also that thou abdicate a manifold and duplex life, and that thou be content that others speak for thee. Others shall be thy gentlemen and shall represent all courtesy and worldly life for thee; others shall do the great and resounding actions also. Thou shalt lie close hid with nature, and canst not be afforded to the Capitol or the Exchange. The world is full of renunciations and apprenticeships, and this is thine; thou must pass for a fool and a churl for a long season. This is the screen and sheath in which Pan has protected his well-beloved flower, and thou shalt be known only to thine own, and they shall console thee with tenderest love. And thou shalt not be able to rehearse the names of thy friends in thy verse, for an old shame before the holy ideal. And this is the reward; that the ideal shall be real to thee, and the impressions of the actual world shall fall like summer rain, copious, but not troublesome to thy invulnerable essence. Thou shalt have the whole land for thy park and manor, the sea for thy bath and navigation, without tax and without envy; the woods and the rivers thou shalt own, and thou shalt possess that wherein others are only tenants and boarders. Thou true land-lord! sea-lord! air-lord! Wherever snow falls or water flows or birds fly, wherever day and night meet in twilight, wherever the blue heaven is hung by clouds or sown with stars, wherever are forms with transparent boundaries, wherever are outlets into celestial space, wherever is danger, and awe, and love,—there is Beauty, plenteous as rain, shed for thee, and though thou shouldst walk the world over, thou shalt not be able to find a condition inopportune or ignoble.

1844

PLATO; OR, THE PHILOSOPHER

Among secular books, Plato only is entitled to Omar's fanatical compliment to the Koran, when he said, "Burn the libraries; for their value is in this book." These sentences contain the culture of nations; these are the corner-stone of schools; these are the fountain-head of literatures. A discipline it is in logic, arithmetic, taste, symmetry, poetry, language, rhetoric, ontology, morals or practical wisdom. There was never such range of speculation. Out of Plato come all things that are still written and debated among men of thought. Great havoc makes he among our originalities. We have reached the mountain from which all these drift boulders were detached. The Bible of the learned for twenty-two hundred years, every brisk young man who says in succession fine things to each reluctant generation,—Boethius, Rabelais, Erasmus, Bruno, Locke, Rousseau, Alfieri, Coleridge,—is some reader of Plato, translating into the vernacular, wittily, his good things. Even the men of grander proportion suffer some deduction from the misfortune (shall I say?) of coming after this exhausting generalizer. St. Augustine, Copernicus, Newton, Behmen, Swedenborg, Goethe, are likewise his debtors and must say after him. For it is fair to credit the broadest generalizer with all the particulars deducible from his thesis.

Plato is philosophy, and philosophy, Plato,—at once the glory and the shame of mankind, since neither Saxon nor Roman have availed to add any idea to his categories. No wife, no children had he, and the thinkers of all civilized nations are his posterity and are tinged with his mind. How many great men Nature is incessantly sending up out of night, to be *his men*,—Platonists! the Alexandrians, a constellation of genius; the Elizabethans, not less; Sir Thomas More, Henry More, John Hales, John Smith, Lord Bacon, Jeremy Taylor, Ralph Cudworth, Sydenham, Thomas Taylor; Marcilius Ficinus and Picus Mirandola. Calvinism is in his Phædo: Christianity is in it. Mahometanism draws all its philosophy, in its handbook of morals, the Akhlak-y-Jalaly, from him. Mysticism finds in Plato all its texts. This citizen of a town in Greece is no villager nor patriot. An Englishman reads and says, "how English!" a German,—"how Teutonic!" an Italian,—"how Roman and how Greek!" As they say that Helen of Argos had that universal beauty that every body felt related to her, so Plato seems to a reader in New England an American genius. His broad humanity transcends all sectional lines.

This range of Plato instructs us what to think of the vexed question concerning his reputed works,—what are genuine, what spurious. It is singular that wherever we find a man higher by a whole head than any of his contemporaries, it is sure to come into doubt what are his real works. Thus Homer, Plato, Raffaelle, Shakspeare. For these men magnetize their contemporaries, so that their companions can do for them what they can never do for themselves; and the great man does thus live in several bodies, and write, or paint or act, by many hands; and after some time it is not easy to say what is the authentic work of the master and what is only of his school.

Plato, too, like every great man, consumed his own times. What is a great man but one of great affinities, who takes up into himself all arts, sciences, all knowables, as his food? He can spare nothing; he can dispose of every thing, What is not good for virtue, is good for knowledge. Hence his contemporaries tax him with plagiarism. But the inventor only knows how to borrow; and society is glad to forget the innumerable laborers who ministered to this architect, and reserves all its gratitude for him. When we are praising Plato, it seems we are praising quotations from Solon and Sophron and Philolaus. Be it so. Every book is a quotation; and every house is a quotation out of all forests and mines and stone quarries; and every man is a quotation from all his ancestors. And this grasping inventor puts all nations under contribution.

Plato absorbed the learning of his times,—Philolaus, Timæus, Heraclitus, Parmenides, and what else; then his master, Socrates; and finding himself still capable of a larger synthesis,—beyond all example then or since,—he travelled into Italy, to gain what

Pythagoras had for him; then into Egypt, and perhaps still farther East, to import the other element, which Europe wanted, into the European mind. This breadth entitles him to stand as the representative of philosophy. He says, in the Republic, "Such a genius as philosophers must of necessity have, is wont but seldom in all its parts to meet in one man, but its different parts generally spring up in different persons." Every man who would do anything well, must come to it from a higher ground. A philosopher must be more than a philosopher. Plato is clothed with the powers of a poet, stands upon the highest place of the poet, and (though I doubt he wanted the decisive gift of lyric expression), mainly is not a poet because he chose to use the poetic gift to an ulterior purpose.

Great geniuses have the shortest biographies. Their cousins can tell you nothing about them. They lived in their writings, and so their house and street life was trivial and commonplace. If you would know their tastes and complexions, the most admiring of their readers most resembles them. Plato especially has no external biography. If he had lover, wife, or children, we hear nothing of them. He ground them all into paint. As a good chimney burns its smoke, so a philosopher converts the value of all his fortunes into his intellectual performances.

He was born 427 B. C., about the time of the death of Pericles; was of patrician connection in his times and city, and is said to have had an early inclination for war, but, in his twentieth year, meeting with Socrates, was easily dissuaded from this pursuit and remained for ten years his scholar, until the death of Socrates. He then went to Megara, accepted the invitations of Dion and of Dionysius to the court of Sicily, and went thither three times, though very capriciously treated. He travelled into Italy; then into Egypt, where he stayed a long time; some say three,—some say thirteen years. It is said he went farther, into Babylonia: this is uncertain. Returning to Athens, he gave lessons in the Academy to those whom his fame drew thither; and died, as we have received it, in the act of writing, at eighty-one years.

But the biography of Plato is interior. We are to account

for the supreme elevation of this man in the intellectual history of our race,—how it happens that in proportion to the culture of men they become his scholars; that, as our Jewish Bible has implanted itself in the table-talk and household life of every man and woman in the European and American nations, so the writings of Plato have preoccupied every school of learning, every lover of thought, every church, every poet,—making it impossible to think, on certain levels, except through him. He stands between the truth and every man's mind, and has almost impressed language and the primary forms of thought, with his name and seal. I am struck, in reading him, with the extreme modernness of his style and spirit. Here is the germ of that Europe we know so well, in its long history of arts and arms; here are all its traits, already discernible in the mind of Plato,—and in none before him. It has spread itself since into a hundred histories, but has added no new element. This perpetual modernness is the measure of merit in every work of art; since the author of it was not misled by any thing short-lived or local, but abode by real and abiding traits. How Plato came thus to be Europe, and philosophy, and almost literature, is the problem for us to solve.

This could not have happened without a sound, sincere and catholic man, able to honor, at the same time, the ideal, or laws of the mind, and fate, or the order of nature. The first period of a nation, as of an individual, is the period of unconscious strength. Children cry, scream and stamp with fury, unable to express their desires. As soon as they can speak and tell their want and the reason of it, they become gentle. In adult life, whilst the perceptions are obtuse, men and women talk vehemently and superlatively, blunder and quarrel: their manners are full of desperation; their speech is full of oaths. As soon as, with culture, things have cleared up a little, and they see them no longer in lumps and masses but accurately distributed, they desist from that weak vehemence and explain their meaning in detail. If the tongue had not been framed for articulation, man would still be a beast in the forest. The same weakness and want, on a higher plane, occurs daily in the education of ardent young men and women. "Ah! you don't understand me; I have never met with any one who comprehends me:" and they sigh and weep, write verses and walk alone,—fault of power to express their precise meaning. In a month or two, through the favor of their good genius, they meet some one so related as to assist their volcanic estate, and, good communication being once established, they are thenceforward good citizens. It is ever thus. The progress is to accuracy, to skill, to truth, from blind force.

There is a moment in the history of every nation, when, proceeding out of this brute youth, the perceptive powers reach their ripeness and have not yet become microscopic: so that man, at that instant, extends across the entire scale, and, with his feet still planted on the immense forces of night, converses by his eyes and brain with solar and stellar creation. That is the moment of adult health, the culmination of power.

Such is the history of Europe, in all points; and such in philosophy. Its early records, almost perished, are of the immigrations from Asia, bringing with them the dreams of barbarians; a confusion of crude notions of morals and of natural philosophy, gradually subsiding through the partial insight of single teachers.

Before Pericles came the Seven Wise Masters, and we have the beginnings of geometry, metaphysics and ethics: then the partialists,—deducing the origin of things from flux or water, or from air, or from fire, or from mind. All mix with these causes mythologic pictures. At last comes Plato, the distributor, who needs no barbaric paint, or tattoo, or whooping; for he can define. He leaves with Asia the vast and superlative; he is the arrival of accuracy and intelligence. "He shall be as a god to me, who can rightly divide and define."

This defining is philosophy. Philosophy is the account which the human mind gives to itself of the constitution of the world. Two cardinal facts lie forever at the base; the one, and the two. —1. Unity, or Identity; and, 2. Variety. We unite all things by perceiving the law which pervades them; by perceiving the superficial differences and the profound resemblances. But every mental act,—this very perception of identity or oneness, recognizes the difference of things. Oneness and otherness. It is impossible to speak or to think without embracing both.

The mind is urged to ask for one cause of many effects; then for the cause of that; and again the cause, diving still into the profound: self-assured that it shall arrive at an absolute and sufficient one,—a one that shall be all. "In the midst of the sun is the light, in the midst of the light is truth, and in the midst of truth is the imperishable being," say the Vedas. All philosophy, of East and West, has the same centripetence. Urged by an opposite necessity, the mind returns from the one to that which is not one, but other or many; from cause to effect; and affirms the necessary existence of variety, the self-existence of both, as each is involved in the other. These strictly-blended elements it is the problem of thought to separate and to reconcile. Their existence is mutually contradictory and exclusive; and each so fast slides into the other that we can never say what is one, and what it is not. The Proteus is as nimble in the highest as in the lowest grounds; when we contemplate the one, the true, the good,—as in the surfaces and extremities of matter.

In all nations there are minds which incline to dwell in the conception of the fundamental Unity. The raptures of prayer and ecstasy of devotion lose all being in one Being. This tendency finds its highest expression in the religious writings of the East, and chiefly in the Indian Scriptures, in the Vedas, the Bhagavat Geeta, and the Vishnu Purana. Those writings contain little else than this idea, and they rise to pure and sublime strains in celebrating it.

The Same, the Same: friend and foe are of one stuff; the ploughman, the plough and the furrow are of one stuff; and the stuff is such and so much that the variations of form are unimportant. "You are fit" (says the supreme Krishna to a sage) "to apprehend that you are not distinct from me. That which I am, thou art, and that also is this world, with its gods and heroes and mankind. Men contemplate distinctions, because they are stupefied with ignorance." "The words *I* and *mine* constitute ignorance. What is the great end of all, you shall now learn from me. It is soul,—one in all bodies, pervading, uniform, perfect, preëminent over nature, exempt from birth, growth and decay, omnipresent, made up of true knowledge, independent, unconnected with unrealities, with name, species and the rest, in time past, present and to come. The knowledge that this spirit, which is essentially one, is in one's own and in all other bodies, is the wisdom of one who knows the unity of things. As one diffusive air, passing through the perforations of a flute, is distinguished as the notes of a scale, so the nature of the Great Spirit is single, though its forms be manifold, arising from the consequences of acts. When the difference of the investing form, as that of god or the rest, is destroyed, there is no distinction." "The whole world is but a manifestation of Vishnu, who is identical with all things, and is to be regarded by the wise as not differing from, but as the same as themselves. I neither am going nor coming; nor is my dwelling in any one place; nor art thou, thou; nor are others, others; nor am I, I." As if he had said, "All is for the soul, and the soul is Vishnu; and animals and stars are transient paintings; and light is whitewash; and durations are deceptive; and form is imprisonment; and heaven itself a decoy." That which the soul seeks is resolution into being above form, out of Tartarus and out of heaven,—liberation from nature.

If speculation tends thus to a terrific unity, in which all things are absorbed, action tends directly backwards to diversity. The first is the course or gravitation of mind; the second is the power of nature. Nature is the manifold. The unity absorbs, and melts or reduces. Nature opens and creates. These two principles reappear and interpenetrate all things, all thought; the one, the many. One is being; the other, intellect: one is necessity; the other, freedom: one, rest; the other, motion: one, power; the other, distribution: one, strength; the other, pleasure: one, consciousness; the other, definition: one, genius; the other, talent: one, earnestness; the other, knowledge: one, possession; the other, trade: one, caste; the other, culture: one, king; the other, democracy: and, if we dare carry these generalizations a step higher, and name the last tendency of both, we might say, that the end of the one is escape from organization,—pure science; and the end of the other is the highest instrumentality, or use of means, or executive deity.

Each student adheres, by temperament and by habit, to the first or to the second of these gods of the mind. By religion, he tends to unity; by intellect, or by the senses, to the many. A too rapid unification, and an excessive appliance to parts and particulars, are the twin dangers of speculation.

To this partiality the history of nations corresponded. The country of unity, of immovable institutions, the seat of a philosophy delighting in abstractions, of men faithful in doctrine and in practice to the idea of a deaf, unimplorable, immense fate, is Asia; and it realizes this faith in the social institution of caste. On the other side, the genius of Europe is active and creative: it resists caste by culture; its philosophy was a discipline; it is a land of arts, inventions, trade, freedom. If the East loved infinity, the West delighted in boundaries.

European civility is the triumph of talent, the extension of system, the sharpened understanding, adaptive skill, delight in forms, delight in manifestation, in comprehensible results. Pericles, Athens, Greece, had been working in this element with the joy of genius not yet chilled by any foresight of the detriment of an excess. They saw before them no sinister political economy; no ominous Malthus; no Paris or London; no pitiless subdivision of classes,—the doom of the pin-makers, the doom of the weavers, of dressers, of stockingers, of carders, of spinners, of colliers; no Ireland; no Indian caste, superinduced by the efforts of Europe to throw it off. The understanding was in its health and prime. Art was in its splendid novelty. They cut the Pentelican marble as if it were snow, and their perfect works in architecture and sculpture seemed things of course, not more difficult than the completion of a new ship at the Medford yards, or new mills at Lowell. These things are in course, and may be taken for granted. The Roman legion, Byzantine legislation, English trade, the saloons of Versailles, the cafés of Paris, the steam-mill, steamboat, steam-coach, may all be seen in perspective; the town-meeting, the ballot-box, the newspaper and cheap press.

Meantime, Plato, in Egypt and in Eastern pilgrimages, imbibed the idea of one Deity, in which all things are absorbed. The unity of Asia and the detail of Europe; the infinitude of the Asiatic soul and the defining, result-loving, machine-making, surface-seeking, opera-going Europe,—Plato came to join, and, by contact, to enhance the energy of each. The excellence of Europe and Asia are in his brain. Metaphysics and natural philosophy expressed the genius of Europe; he substructs the religion of Asia, as the base.

In short, a balanced soul was born, perceptive of the two elements. It is as easy to be great as to be small. The reason why we do not at once believe in admirable souls is because they are not in our experience. In actual life, they are so rare as to be incredible; but primarily there is not only no presumption against them, but the strongest presumption in favor of their appearance. But whether voices were heard in the sky, or not; whether his mother or his father dreamed that the infant man-child was the son of Apollo; whether a swarm of bees settled on his lips, or not;—a man who could see two sides of a thing was born. The wonderful synthesis so familiar in nature; the upper and the under side of the medal of Jove; the union of impossibilities, which reappears in every object; its real and its ideal power,—was now also transferred entire to the consciousness of a man.

The balanced soul came. If he loved abstract truth, he saved himself by propounding the most popular of all principles, the absolute good, which rules rulers, and judges the judge. If he made transcendental distinctions, he fortified himself by drawing all his illustrations from sources disdained by orators and polite conversers; from mares and puppies; from pitchers and soup-ladles; from cooks and criers; the shops of potters, horse-doctors, butchers and fishmongers. He cannot forgive in himself a partiality, but is resolved that the two poles of thought shall appear in his statement. His argument and his sentence are self-poised and spherical. The two poles appear; yes, and become two hands, to grasp and appropriate their own.

Every great artist has been such by synthesis. Our strength is transitional, alternating; or, shall I say, a thread of two strands. The sea-shore, sea seen from shore, shore seen from sea; the taste of two metals in contact; and our enlarged powers at the approach and at the departure of a friend; the experience of poetic creativeness, which is not found in staying at home, nor yet in travelling, but in transitions from one to the other, which must therefore be adroitly managed to present as much transitional surface as possible; this command of two elements must explain the power and the charm of Plato. Art expresses the one or the same by the different. Thought seeks to know unity in unity; poetry to show it by variety; that is, always by an object or symbol. Plato keeps the two vases, one of æther and one of pigment, at his side, and invariably uses both. Things added to things, as statistics, civil history, are inventories. Things used as language are inexhaustibly attractive. Plato turns incessantly the obverse and the reverse of the medal of Jove.

To take an example:—the physical philosophers had sketched each his theory of the world; the theory of atoms, of fire, of flux, of spirit; theories mechanical and chemical in their genius. Plato, a master of mathematics, studious of all natural laws and causes, feels these, as second causes, to be no theories of the world but bare inventories and lists. To the study of nature he therefore prefixes the dogma,—"Let us declare the cause which led the Supreme Ordainer to produce and compose the universe. He was good; and he who is good has no kind of envy. Exempt from envy, he wished that all things should be as much as possible like himself. Whosoever, taught by wise men, shall admit this as the prime cause of the origin and foundation of the world, will be in the truth." "All things are for the sake of the good, and it is the cause of every thing beautiful." This dogma animates and impersonates his philosophy.

The synthesis which makes the character of his mind appears in all his talents. Where there is great compass of wit, we usually find excellencies that combine easily in the living man, but in description appear incompatible. The mind of Plato is not to be exhibited by a Chinese catalogue, but is to be apprehended by an original mind in the exercise of its original power. In him the freest abandonment is united with the precision of a geometer. His daring imagination gives him the more solid grasp of facts; as the birds of highest flight have the strongest alar bones. His patrician polish, his intrinsic elegance, edged by an irony so subtle that it stings and paralyzes, adorn the soundest health and strength of frame. According to the old sentence, "If Jove should descend to the earth, he would speak in the style of Plato."

With this palatial air there is, for the direct aim of several of his works and running through the tenor of them all, a certain earnestness, which mounts, in the Republic and in the Phædo, to piety. He has been charged with feigning sickness at the time of the death of Socrates. But the anecdotes that have come down from the times attest his manly interference before the people in his master's behalf, since even the savage cry of the assembly to Plato is preserved; and the indignation towards popular government, in many of his pieces, expresses a personal exasperation. He has a probity, a native reverence for justice and honor, and a humanity which makes him tender for the superstitions of the people. Add to this, he believes that poetry, prophecy and the high insight are from a wisdom of which man is not master; that the gods never philosophize, but by a celestial mania these miracles are accomplished. Horsed on these winged steeds, he sweeps the dim regions, visits worlds which flesh cannot enter; he saw the souls in pain, he hears the doom of the judge, he beholds the penal metempsychosis, the Fates, with the rock and shears, and hears the intoxicating hum of their spindle.

But his circumspection never forsook him. One would say he had read the inscription on the gates of Busyrane,—"Be bold;" and on the second gate,—"Be bold, be bold, and evermore be bold;" and then again had paused well at the third gate, —"Be not too bold." His strength is like the momentum of a falling planet, and his discretion the return of its due and perfect curve,—so excellent is his Greek love of boundary and his skill in definition. In reading logarithms one is not more secure than in following Plato in his flights. Nothing can be colder than his head, when the lightnings of his imagination are playing in the sky. He has finished his thinking before he brings it to the reader, and he abounds in the surprises of a literary master. He has that opulence which furnishes, at every turn, the precise weapon he needs. As the rich man wears no more garments, drives no more horses, sits in no more chambers than the poor, —but has that one dress, or equipage, or instrument, which is fit for the hour and the need; so Plato, in his plenty, is never restricted, but has the fit word. There is indeed no weapon in all the armory of wit which he did not possess and use,—epic, analysis, mania, intuition, music, satire and irony, down to the customary and polite. His illustrations are poetry and his jests illustrations. Socrates' profession of obstetric art is good philosophy; and his finding that word "cookery," and "adulatory art," for rhetoric, in the Gorgias, does us a substantial service still. No orator can measure in effect with him who can give good nicknames.

What moderation and understatement and checking his thunder in mid volley! He has good-naturedly furnished the courtier and citizen with all that can be said against the schools. "For philosophy is an elegant thing, if any one modestly meddles with it; but if he is conversant with it more than is becoming, it corrupts the man." He could well afford to be generous, —he, who from the sunlike centrality and reach of his vision, had a faith without cloud. Such as his perception, was his speech: he plays with the doubt and makes the most of it: he paints and quibbles; and by and by comes a sentence that moves the sea and land. The admirable earnest comes not only at intervals, in the perfect yes and no of the dialogue, but in bursts of light. "I, therefore, Callicles, am persuaded by these accounts, and consider how I may exhibit my soul before the judge in a healthy condition. Wherefore, disregarding the honors that most men value, and looking to the truth, I shall endeavor in reality to live as virtuously as I can; and when I die, to die so. And I invite all other men, to the utmost of my power; and you too I in turn invite to this contest, which, I affirm, surpasses all contests here."

He is a great average man; one who, to the best thinking, adds a proportion and equality in his faculties, so that men see in him their own dreams and glimpses made available and made to pass for what they are. A great common-sense is his warrant and qualification to be the world's interpreter. He has reason, as all the philosophic and poetic class have: but he has also what they have not,—this strong solving sense to reconcile his poetry with the appearances of the world, and build a bridge from the streets of cities to the Atlantis. He omits never this graduation, but slopes his thought, however picturesque the precipice on one side, to an access from the plain. He never writes in ecstasy, or catches us up into poetic raptures.

Plato apprehended the cardinal facts. He could prostrate himself on the earth and cover his eyes whilst he adored that which cannot be numbered, or gauged, or known, or named: that of which every thing can be affirmed and denied: that "which is entity and nonentity." He called it super-essential. He even stood ready, as in the Parmenides, to demonstrate that it was so,—that this Being exceeded the limits of intellect. No man ever more fully acknowledged the Ineffable. Having paid his homage, as for the human race, to the Illimitable, he then stood erect, and for the human race affirmed, "And yet things are knowable!"—that is, the Asia in his mind was first heartily honored,—the ocean of love and power, before form, before will, before knowledge, the Same, the Good, the One; and now, refreshed and empowered by this worship, the instinct of Europe, namely, culture, returns; and he cries, "Yet things are knowable!" They are knowable, because being from one, things correspond. There is a scale; and the correspondence of heaven to earth, of matter to mind, of the part to the whole, is our guide. As there is a science of stars, called astronomy; a science of quantities, called mathematics; a science of qualities, called chemistry; so there is a science of sciences,—I call it Dialectic,—which is the Intellect discriminating the false and the true. It rests on the observation of identity and diversity; for to judge is to unite to an object the notion which belongs to it. The sciences, even the best,—mathematics and astronomy,—are like sportsmen, who seize whatever prey offers, even without being able to make any use of it. Dialectic must teach the use of them. "This is of that rank that no intellectual man will enter on any study for its own sake, but only with a view to advance himself in that one sole science which embraces all."

"The essence or peculiarity of man is to comprehend a whole; or that which in the diversity of sensations can be comprised under a rational unity." "The soul which has never perceived the truth, cannot pass into the human form." I announce to men the Intellect. I announce the good of being interpenetrated by the mind that made nature: this benefit, namely, that it can understand nature, which it made and maketh. Nature is good, but intellect is better: as the law-giver is before the law-receiver. I give you joy, O sons of men! that truth is altogether wholesome; that we have hope to search out what might be the very self of everything. The misery of man is to be baulked of the sight of essence and to be stuffed with conjectures; but the supreme good is reality; the supreme beauty is reality; and all virtue and all felicity depend on this science of the real: for courage is nothing else than knowledge; the fairest fortune that can befall man is to be guided by his dæmon to that which is truly his own. This also is the essence of justice,—to attend every one his own: nay, the notion of virtue is not to be arrived at except through direct contemplation of the divine essence. Courage then! for "the persuasion that we must search that which we do not know, will render us, beyond comparison, better, braver and more industrious than if we thought it impossible to discover what we do not know, and useless to search for it." He secures a position not to be commanded, by his passion for reality; valuing philosophy only as it is the pleasure of conversing with real being.

Thus, full of the genius of Europe, he said, *Culture*. He saw the institutions of Sparta and recognized, more genially one would say than any since, the hope of education. He delighted in every accomplishment, in every graceful and useful and truthful performance; above all in the splendors of genius and intellectual achievement. "The whole of life, O Socrates," said Glauco, "is, with the wise, the measure of hearing such discourses as these." What a price he sets on the feats of talent, on the powers of Pericles, of Isocrates, of Parmenides! What price above price on the talents themselves! He called the several faculties, gods, in his beautiful personation. What value he gives to the art of gymnastic in education; what to geometry; what to music; what to astronomy, whose appeasing and medicinal power he celebrates! In the Timæus he indicates the highest employment of the eyes. "By us it is asserted that God invented and bestowed sight on us for this purpose,—that on surveying the circles of intelligence in the heavens, we might properly employ those of our own minds, which, though disturbed when compared with the others that are uniform, are still allied to their circulations; and that having thus learned, and being naturally possessed of a correct reasoning faculty, we might, by imitating the uniform revolutions of divinity, set right our own wanderings and blunders." And in the Republic,—"By each of these disciplines a certain organ of the soul is both purified and reanimated which is blinded and buried by studies of another kind; an organ better worth saving than ten thousand eyes, since truth is perceived by this alone."

He said, Culture; but he first admitted its basis, and gave immeasurably the first place to advantages of nature. His patrician tastes laid stress on the distinctions of birth. In the doctrine of the organic character and disposition is the origin of caste. "Such as were fit to govern, into their composition the informing Deity mingled gold; into the military, silver; iron and brass for husbandmen and artificers." The East confirms itself, in all ages, in this faith. The Koran is explicit on this point of caste. "Men have their metal, as of gold and silver. Those of you who were the worthy ones in the state of ignorance, will be the worthy ones in the state of faith, as soon as you embrace it." Plato was not less firm. "Of the five orders of things, only four can be taught to the generality of men."

In the Republic he insists on the temperaments of the youth, as first of the first.

A happier example of the stress laid on nature is in the dialogue with the young Theages, who wishes to receive lessons from Socrates. Socrates declares that if some have grown wise by associating with him, no thanks are due to him; but, simply, whilst they were with him they grew wise, not because of him; he pretends not to know the way of it. "It is adverse to many, nor can those be benefited by associating with me whom the Dæmon opposes; so that it is not possible for me to live with these. With many however he does not prevent me from conversing, who yet are not at all benefited by associating with me. Such, O Theages, is the association with me; for, if it pleases the God, you will make great and rapid proficiency: you will not, if he does not please. Judge whether it is not safer to be instructed by some one of those who have power over the benefit which they impart to men, than by me, who benefit or not, just as it may happen." As if he had said, "I have no system. I cannot be answerable for you. You will be what you must. If there is love between us, inconceivably delicious and profitable will our intercourse be; if not, your time is lost and you will only annoy me. I shall seem to you stupid, and the reputation I have, false. Quite above us, beyond the will of you or me, is this secret affinity or repulsion laid. All my good is magnetic, and I educate, not by lessons, but by going about my business."

He said, Culture; he said, Nature; and he failed not to add, "There is also the divine." There is no thought in any mind but it quickly tends to convert itself into a power and organizes a huge instrumentality of means. Plato, lover of limits, loved the illimitable, saw the enlargement and nobility which come from truth itself and good itself, and attempted as if on the part of the human intellect, once for all to do it adequate homage,—homage fit for the immense soul to receive, and yet homage becoming the intellect to render. He said then, "Our faculties run out into infinity, and return to us thence. We can define but a little way; but here is a fact which will not be skipped, and which to shut our eyes upon is suicide. All things are in a scale; and, begin where we will, ascend and ascend. All things are symbolical; and what we call results are beginnings."

A key to the method and completeness of Plato is his twice bisected line. After he has illustrated the relation between the absolute good and true and the forms of the intelligible world, he says: "Let there be a line cut in two unequal parts. Cut again each of these two main parts,—one representing the visible, the other the intelligible world,—and let these two new sections represent the bright part and the dark part of each of these worlds. You will have, for one of the sections of the visible world, images, that is, both shadows and reflections;—for the other section, the objects of these images, that is plants, animals, and the works of art and nature. Then divide the intelligible world in like manner; the one section will be of opinions and hypotheses, and the other section of truths." To these four sections, the four operations of the soul correspond,—conjecture, faith, understanding, reason. As every pool reflects the image of the sun, so every thought and thing restores us an image and creature of the supreme Good. The universe is perforated by a million channels for his activity. All things mount and mount.

All his thought has this ascension; in Phædrus, teaching that beauty is the most lovely of all things, exciting hilarity and shedding desire and confidence through the universe wherever it enters, and it enters in some degree into all things:—but that there is another, which is as much more beautiful than beauty as beauty is than chaos; namely wisdom, which our wonderful organ of sight cannot reach unto, but which, could it be seen, would ravish us with its perfect reality. He has the same regard to it as the source of excellence in works of art. When an artificer, he says, in the fabrication of any work, looks to that which always subsists according *to the same;* and, employing a model of this kind, expresses its idea and power in his work,—it must follow that his production should be beautiful. But when he beholds that which is born and dies, it will be far from beautiful.

Thus ever: the Banquet is a teaching in the same spirit, familiar now to all the poetry and to all the sermons of the world, that the love of the sexes is initial, and symbolizes at a distance the passion of the soul for that immense lake of beauty it exists to seek. This faith in the Divinity is never out of mind, and constitutes the ground of all his dogmas. Body cannot teach wisdom;—God only. In the same mind he constantly affirms that virtue cannot be taught; that it is not a science, but an inspiration; that the greatest goods are produced to us through mania and are assigned to us by a divine gift.

This leads me to that central figure which he has established in his Academy as the organ through which every considered opinion shall be announced, and whose biography he has likewise so labored that the historic facts are lost in the light of Plato's mind. Socrates and Plato are the double star which the most powerful instruments will not entirely separate. Socrates again, in his traits and genius, is the best example of that synthesis which constitutes Plato's extraordinary power. Socrates, a man of humble stem, but honest enough; of the commonest history; of a personal homeliness so remarkable as to be a cause of wit in others:—the rather that his broad good nature and exquisite taste for a joke invited the sally, which was sure to be paid. The players personated him on the stage; the potters copied his ugly face on their stone jugs. He was a cool fellow, adding to his humor a perfect temper and a knowledge of his man, be he who he might whom he talked with, which laid the companion open to certain defeat in any debate,—and in debate he immoderately delighted. The young men are prodigiously fond of him and invite him to their feasts, whither he goes for conversation. He can drink, too; has the strongest head in Athens; and after leaving the whole party under the table, goes away as if nothing had happened, to begin new dialogues with somebody that is sober. In short, he was what our country-people call *an old one.*

He affected a good many citizen-like tastes, was monstrously fond of Athens, hated trees, never willingly went beyond the walls, knew the old characters, valued the bores and philistines, thought every thing in Athens a little better than anything in any other place. He was plain as a Quaker in habit and speech, affected low phrases, and illustrations from cocks and quails, soup-pans and sycamore-spoons, grooms and farriers, and unnamable offices,—especially if he talked with any superfine person. He had a Franklin-like wisdom. Thus he showed one who was afraid to go on foot to Olympia, that it was no more than his daily walk within doors, if continuously extended, would easily reach.

Plain old uncle as he was, with his great ears, an immense talker,—the rumor ran that on one or two occasions, in the war with Bœotia, he had shown a determination which had covered the retreat of a troop; and there was some story that under cover of folly, he had, in the city government, when one day he chanced to hold a seat there, evinced a courage in opposing singly the popular voice, which had well-nigh ruined him. He is very poor; but then he is hardy as a soldier, and can live on a few olives; usually, in the strictest sense, on bread and water, except when entertained by his friends. His necessary expenses were exceedingly small, and no one could live as he did. He wore no under garment; his upper garment was the same for summer and winter, and he went barefooted; and it is said that to procure the pleasure, which he loves, of talking at his ease all day with the most elegant and cultivated young men, he will now and then return to his shop and carve statues, good or bad, for sale. However that be, it is certain that he had grown to delight in nothing else than this conversation; and that, under his hypocritical pretence of knowing nothing, he attacks and brings down all the fine speakers, all the fine philosophers of Athens, whether natives or strangers from Asia Minor and the islands. Nobody can refuse to talk with him, he is so honest and really curious to know; a man who was willingly confuted if he did not speak the truth, and who willingly confuted others asserting what was false; and not less pleased when confuted than when confuting; for he thought not any evil happened to men of such a magnitude as false opinion respecting the just and unjust. A pitiless disputant, who knows nothing, but the bounds of whose conquering intelligence no man had ever reached; whose temper was imperturbable; whose dreadful logic was always leisurely and sportive; so careless and ignorant as to disarm the wariest and draw them, in the pleasantest manner, into horrible doubts and confusion. But he always knew the way out; knew it, yet would not tell it. No escape; he drives them to terrible choices by his dilemmas, and tosses the Hippiases and Gorgiases with their grand reputations, as a boy tosses his balls. The tyrannous realist!—Meno has discoursed a thousand times, at length, on virtue, before many companies, and very well, as it appeared to him; but at this moment he cannot even tell what it is,—this cramp-fish of a Socrates has so bewitched him.

This hard-headed humorist, whose strange conceits, drollery and *bonhommie* diverted the young patricians, whilst the rumor of his sayings and quibbles gets abroad every day, turns out, in the sequel, to have a probity as invincible as his logic, and to be either insane, or at least, under cover of this play, enthusiastic in his religion. When accused before the judges of subverting the popular creed, he affirms the immortality of the soul, the future reward and punishment; and refusing to recant, in a caprice of the popular government was condemned to die, and sent to the prison. Socrates entered the prison and took away all ignominy from the place, which could not be a prison whilst he was there. Crito bribed the jailer; but Socrates would not go out by treachery. "Whatever inconvenience ensue, nothing is to be preferred before justice. These things I hear like pipes and drums, whose sound makes me deaf to every thing you say." The fame of this prison, the fame of the discourses there and the drinking of the hemlock are one of the most precious passages in the history of the world.

The rare coincidence, in one ugly body, of the droll and the martyr, the keen street and market debater with the sweetest saint known to any history at that time, had forcibly struck the mind of Plato, so capacious of these contrasts; and the figure of Socrates by a necessity placed itself in the foreground of the scene, as the fittest dispenser of the intellectual treasures he had to communicate. It was a rare fortune that this Æsop of the mob and this robed scholar should meet, to make each other immortal in their mutual faculty. The strange synthesis in the character of Socrates capped the synthesis in the mind of Plato. Moreover by this means he was able, in the direct way and without envy to avail himself of the wit and weight of Socrates, to which unquestionably his own debt was great; and these derived again their principal advantage from the perfect art of Plato.

It remains to say that the defect of Plato in power is only that which results inevitably from his quality. He is intellectual in his aim; and therefore, in expression, literary. Mounting into heaven, diving into the pit, expounding the laws of the state, the passion of love, the remorse of crime, the hope of the parting soul,—he is literary, and never otherwise. It is almost the sole deduction from the merit of Plato that his writings have not,—what is no doubt incident to this regnancy of intellect in his work,—the vital authority which the screams of prophets and the sermons of unlettered Arabs and Jews possess. There is an interval; and to cohesion, contact is necessary.

I know not what can be said in reply to this criticism but that we have come to a fact in the nature of things: an oak is not an orange. The qualities of sugar remain with sugar, and those of salt with salt.

In the second place, he has not a system. The dearest defenders and disciples are at fault. He attempted a theory of the universe, and his theory is not complete or self-evident. One man thinks he means this, and another that; he has said one thing in one place, and the reverse of it in another place. He is charged with having failed to make the transition from ideas to matter. Here is the world, sound as a nut, perfect, not the smallest piece of chaos left, never a stitch nor an end, not a mark of haste, or botching, or second thought; but the theory of the world is a thing of shreds and patches.

The longest wave is quickly lost in the sea. Plato would willingly have a Platonism, a known and accurate expression for the world, and it should be accurate. It shall be the world passed through the mind of Plato,—nothing less. Every atom shall have the Platonic tinge; every atom, every relation or quality you knew before, you shall know again and find here, but now ordered; not nature, but art. And you shall feel that Alexander indeed overran, with men and horses, some countries of the planet; but countries, and things of which countries are made, elements, planet itself, laws of planet and of men, have passed through this man as bread into his body, and become no longer bread, but body: so all this mammoth morsel has become Plato. He has clapped copyright on the world. This is the ambition of individualism. But the mouthful proves too large. *Boa constrictor* has good will to eat it, but he is foiled. He falls abroad in the attempt; and biting, gets strangled: the bitten world holds the biter fast by his own teeth. There he perishes: unconquered nature lives on and forgets him. So it fares with all: so must it fare with Plato. In view of eternal nature, Plato turns out to be philosophical exercitations. He argues on this side and on that. The acutest German, the lovingest disciple, could never tell what Platonism was; indeed, admirable texts can be quoted on both sides of every great question from him.

These things we are forced to say if we must consider the effort of Plato or of any philosopher to dispose of nature,—which will not be disposed of. No power of genius has ever yet had the smallest success in explaining existence. The perfect enigma remains. But there is an injustice in assuming this ambition for Plato. Let us not seem to treat with flippancy his venerable name. Men, in proportion to their intellect, have admitted his transcendent claims. The way to know him is to compare him, not with nature, but with other men. How many ages have gone by, and he remains unapproached! A chief structure of human wit, like Karnac, or the mediæval cathedrals, or the Etrurian remains, it requires all the breath of human faculty to know it. I think it is trueliest seen when seen with the most respect. His sense deepens, his merits multiply, with study. When we say, Here is a fine collection of fables; or when we praise the style, or the common sense, or arithmetic, we speak as boys, and much of our impatient criticism of the dialectic, I suspect, is no better.

The criticism is like our impatience of miles, when we are in a hurry; but it is still best that a mile should have seventeen hundred and sixty yards. The great-eyed Plato proportioned the lights and shades after the genius of our life.

1845 1850

NAPOLEON; OR, THE MAN OF THE WORLD

Among the eminent persons of the nineteenth century, Bonaparte is far the best known and the most powerful; and owes his predominance to the fidelity with which he expresses the tone of thought and belief, the aims of the masses of active and cultivated men. It is Swedenborg's theory that every organ is made up of homogeneous particles; or as it is sometimes expressed, every whole is made of similars; that is, the lungs are composed of infinitely small lungs; the liver, of infinitely small livers; the kidney, of little kidneys, etc. Following this analogy, if any man is found to carry with him the power and affections of vast numbers, if Napoleon is France, if Napoleon is Europe, it is because the people whom he sways are little Napoleons.

In our society there is a standing antagonism between the conservative and the democratic classes; between those who have made their fortunes, and the young and the poor who have fortunes to make; between the interests of dead labor,—that is, the labor of hands long ago still in the grave, which labor is now entombed in money stocks, or in land and buildings owned by idle capitalists,—and the interests of living labor, which seeks to possess itself of land and buildings and money stocks. The first class is timid, selfish, illiberal, hating innovation, and continually losing numbers by death. The second class is selfish also, encroaching, bold, self-relying, always outnumbering the other and recruiting its numbers every hour by births. It desires to keep open every avenue to the competition of all, and to multiply avenues: the class of business men in America, in England, in France and throughout Europe; the class of industry and skill. Napoleon is its representative. The instinct of active, brave, able men, throughout the middle class every where, has pointed out Napoleon as the incarnate Democrat. He had their virtues and their vices; above all, he had their spirit or aim. That tendency is material, pointing at a sensual success and employing the richest and most various means to that end; conversant with mechanical powers, highly intellectual, widely and accurately learned and skilful, but subordinating all intellectual and spiritual forces into means to a material success. To be the rich man, is the end. "God has granted," says the Koran, "to every people a prophet in its own tongue." Paris and London and New York, the spirit of commerce, of money and material power, were also to have their prophet; and Bonaparte was qualified and sent.

Every one of the million readers of anecdotes or memoirs or lives of Napoleon, delights in the page, because he studies in it his own history. Napoleon is thoroughly modern, and, at the highest point of his fortunes, has the very spirit of the newspapers. He is no saint,—to use his own word, "no capuchin," and he is no hero, in the high sense. The man in the street finds in him the qualities and powers of other men in the street. He finds him, like himself, by birth a citizen, who, by very intelligible merits, arrived at such a commanding position that he could indulge all those tastes which the common man possesses but is obliged to conceal and deny: good society, good books, fast travelling, dress, dinners, servants without number, personal weight, the execution of his ideas, the standing in the attitude of a benefactor to all persons about him, the refined enjoyments of pictures, statues, music, palaces and conventional honors,—precisely what is agreeable to the heart of every man in the nineteenth century, this powerful man possessed.

It is true that a man of Napoleon's truth of adaptation to the mind of the masses around him, becomes not merely representative but actually a monopolizer and usurper of other minds. Thus Mirabeau plagiarized every good thought, every good word that was spoken in France. Dumont relates that he sat in the gallery of the Convention and heard Mirabeau make a speech. It struck Dumont that he could fit it with a peroration, which he wrote in pencil immediately, and showed it to Lord Elgin, who sat by him. Lord Elgin approved it, and Dumont, in the evening, showed it to Mirabeau. Mirabeau read it, pronounced it admirable, and declared he would incorporate it into his harangue to-morrow, to the Assembly. "It is impossible," said Dumont, "as, unfortunately, I have shown it to Lord Elgin." "If you have shown it to Lord Elgin and to fifty persons beside, I shall still speak it to-morrow:" and he did speak it, with much effect, at the next day's session. For Mirabeau, with his overpowering personality, felt that these things which his presence inspired were as much his own as if he had said them, and that his adoption of them gave them their weight. Much more absolute and centralizing was the successor to Mirabeau's popularity and to much more than his predominance in France. Indeed, a man of Napoleon's stamp almost ceases to have a private speech and opinion. He is so largely receptive, and is so placed, that he comes to be a bureau for all the intelligence, wit and power of the age and country. He gains the battle; he makes the code; he makes the system of weights and measures; he levels the Alps; he builds the road. All distinguished engineers, savans, statists, report to him: so likewise do all good heads in every kind: he adopts the best measures, sets his stamp on them, and not these alone, but on every happy and memorable expression. Every sentence spoken by Napoleon and every line of his writing, deserves reading, as it is the sense of France.

Bonaparte was the idol of common men because he had in transcendent degree the qualities and powers of common men. There is a certain satisfaction in coming down to the lowest ground of politics, for we get rid of cant and hypocrisy. Bonaparte wrought, in common with that great class he represented, for power and wealth,—but Bonaparte, specially, without any scruple as to the means. All the sentiments which embarrass men's pursuit of these objects, he set aside. The sentiments were for women and children. Fontanes, in 1804, expressed Napoleon's own sense, when in behalf of the Senate he addressed him,—"Sire, the desire of perfection is the worst disease that ever afflicted the human mind." The advocates of liberty and of progress are "ideologists;"—a word of contempt often in his mouth;—"Necker is an ideologist:" "Lafayette is an ideologist."

An Italian proverb, too well known, declares that "if you would succeed, you must not be too good." It is an advantage, within certain limits, to have renounced the dominion of the sentiments of piety, gratitude and generosity; since what was an impassable bar to us, and still is to others, becomes a convenient weapon for our purposes; just as the river which was a formidable barrier, winter transforms into the smoothest of roads.

Napoleon renounced, once for all, sentiments and affections, and would help himself with his hands and his head. With him is no miracle and no magic. He is a worker in brass, in iron, in wood, in earth, in roads, in buildings, in money and in troops, and a very consistent and wise master-workman. He is never weak and literary, but acts with the solidity and the precision of natural agents. He has not lost his native sense and sympathy with things. Men give way before such a man, as before natural events. To be sure there are men enough who are immersed in things, as farmers, smiths, sailors and mechanics generally; and we know how real and solid such men appear in the presence of scholars and grammarians: but these men ordinarily lack the power of arrangement, and are like hands without a head. But Bonaparte superadded to this mineral and animal force, insight and generalization, so that men saw in him combined the natural and the intellectual power, as if the sea and land had taken flesh and begun to cipher. Therefore the land and sea seem to presuppose him. He came unto his own and they received him. This ciphering operative knows what he is working with and what is the product. He knew the properties of gold and iron, of wheels and ships, of troops and diplomatists, and required that each should do after its kind.

The art of war was the game in which he exerted his arithmetic. It consisted, according to him, in having always more forces than the enemy, on the point where the enemy is attacked, or where he attacks: and his whole talent is strained by endless manœuvre and evolution, to march always on the enemy at an angle, and destroy his forces in detail. It is obvious that a very small force, skilfully and rapidly manœuvring so as always to bring two men against one at the point of engagement, will be an overmatch for a much larger body of men.

The times, his constitution and his early circumstances combined to develop this pattern democrat. He had the virtues of his class and the conditions for their activity. That common-sense which no sooner respects any end than it finds the means to effect it; the delight in the use of means; in the choice, simplification and combining of means; the directness and thoroughness of his work; the prudence with which all was seen and the energy with which all was done, make him the natural organ and head of what I may almost call, from its extent, the *modern* party.

Nature must have far the greatest share in every success, and so in his. Such a man was wanted, and such a man was born; a man of stone and iron, capable of sitting on horseback sixteen or seventeen hours, of going many days together without rest or food except by snatches, and with the speed and spring of a tiger in action; a man not embarrassed by any scruples; compact, instant, selfish, prudent, and of a perception which did not suffer itself to be baulked or misled by any pretences of others, or any superstition or any heat or haste of his own. "My hand of iron," he said, "was not at the extremity of my arm, it was immediately connected with my head." He respected the power of nature and fortune, and ascribed to it his superiority, instead of valuing himself, like inferior men, on his opinionativeness, and waging war with nature. His favorite rhetoric lay in allusion to his star; and he pleased himself, as well as the people, when he styled himself the "Child of Destiny." "They charge me," he said "with the commission of great crimes: men of my stamp do not commit crimes. Nothing has been more simple than my elevation, 'tis in vain to ascribe it to intrigue or crime; it was owing to the peculiarity of the times and to my reputation of having fought well against the enemies of my country. I have always marched with the opinion of great masses and with events. Of what use then would crimes be to me?" Again he said, speaking of his son, "My son can not replace me; I could not replace myself. I am the creature of circumstances."

He had a directness of action never before combined with so much comprehension. He is a realist, terrific to all talkers and confused truth-obscuring persons. He sees where the matter hinges, throws himself on the precise point of resistance, and slights all other considerations. He is strong in the right manner, namely by insight. He never blundered into victory, but won his battles in his head before he won them on the field. His principal means are in himself. He asks counsel of no other. In 1796 he writes to the Directory: "I have conducted the campaign without consulting any one. I should have done no good if I had been under the necessity of conforming to the notions of another person. I have gained some advantages over superior forces and when totally destitute of every thing, because, in the persuasion that your confidence was reposed in me, my actions were as prompt as my thoughts."

History is full, down to this day, of the imbecility of kings and governors. They are a class of persons much to be pitied, for they know not what they should do. The weavers strike for bread, and the king and his ministers, knowing not what to do, meet them with bayonets. But Napoleon understood his business. Here was a man who in each moment and emergency knew what to do next. It is an immense comfort and refreshment to the spirits, not only of kings, but of citizens. Few men have any next; they live from hand to mouth, without plan, and are ever at the end of their line, and after each action wait for an impulse from abroad. Napoleon had been the first man of the world, if his ends had been purely public. As he is, he inspires confidence and vigor by the extraordinary unity of his action. He is firm, sure, self-denying, self-postponing, sacrificing every thing,—money, troops, generals, and his own safety also, to his aim; not misled, like common adventurers, by the splendor of his own means. "Incidents ought not to govern policy," he said, "but policy, incidents." "To be hurried away by every event is to have no political system at all." His victories were only so many doors, and he never for a moment lost sight of his way onward, in the dazzle and uproar of the present circumstance. He knew what to do, and he flew to his mark. He would shorten a straight line to come at his object. Horrible anecdotes may no doubt be collected from his history, of the price at which he bought his successes; but he must not therefore be set down as cruel, but only as one who knew no impediment to his will; not bloodthirsty, not cruel,—but woe to what thing or person stood in his way! Not bloodthirsty, but not sparing of blood,—and pitiless. He saw only the object: the obstacle must give way. "Sire, General Clarke can not combine with General Junot, for the dreadful fire of the Austrian battery."—"Let him carry the battery."—"Sire, every regiment that approaches the heavy artillery is sacrificed: Sire, what orders?"—"Forward, forward!" Seruzier, a colonel of artillery, gives, in his "Military Memoirs," the following sketch of a scene after the battle of Austerlitz.—"At the moment in which the Russian army was making its retreat, painfully, but in good order, on the ice of the lake, the Emperor Napoleon came riding at full speed toward the artillery. 'You are losing time,' he cried; 'fire upon those masses; they must be engulfed: fire upon the ice!' The order remained unexecuted for ten minutes. In vain several officers and myself were placed on the slope of a hill to produce the effect: their balls and mine rolled upon the ice without breaking it up. Seeing that, I tried a simple method of elevating light howitzers. The almost perpendicular fall of the heavy projectiles produced the desired effect. My method was immediately followed by the adjoining batteries, and in less than no time we buried" some "thousands of Russians and Austrians under the waters of the lake."

In the plenitude of his resources, every obstacle seemed to vanish. "There shall be no Alps," he said; and he built his perfect roads, climbing by graded galleries their steepest precipices, until Italy was as open to Paris as any town in France. He laid his bones to, and wrought for his crown. Having decided what was to be done, he did that with might and main. He put out all his strength. He risked everything and spared nothing, neither ammunition, nor money, nor troops, nor generals, nor himself.

We like to see every thing do its office after its kind, whether it be a milch-cow or a rattle-snake; and if fighting be the best mode of adjusting national differences, (as large majorities of men seem to agree,) certainly Bonaparte was right in making it thorough. The grand principle of war, he said, was that an army ought always to be ready, by day and by night and at all hours, to make all the resistance it is capable of making. He never economized his ammunition, but, on a hostile position, rained a torrent of iron,—shells, balls, grape-shot,—to annihilate all defence. On any point of resistance he concentrated squadron on squadron in overwhelming numbers until it was swept out of existence. To a regiment of horse-chasseurs at Lobenstein, two days before the battle of Jena, Napoleon said, "My lads, you must not fear death; when soldiers brave death, they drive him into the enemy's ranks." In the fury of assault, he no more spared himself. He went to the edge of his possibility. It is plain that in Italy he did what he could, and all that he could. He came, several times, within an inch of ruin; and his own person was all but lost. He was flung into the marsh at Arcola. The Austrians were between him and his troops, in the *mêlée*, and he was brought off with desperate efforts. At Lonato, and at other places, he was on the point of being taken prisoner. He fought sixty battles. He had never enough. Each victory was a new weapon. "My power would fall, were I not to support it by new achievements. Conquest has made me what I am, and conquest must maintain me." He felt, with every wise man, that as much life is needed for conservation as for creation. We are always in peril, always in a bad plight, just on the edge of destruction and only to be saved by invention and courage.

This vigor was guarded and tempered by the coldest prudence and punctuality. A thunderbolt in the attack, he was found invulnerable in his intrenchments. His very attack was never the inspiration of courage, but the result of calculation. His idea of the best defence consists in being still the attacking party. "My ambition," he says, "was great, but was of a cold nature." In one of his conversations with Las Cases, he remarked, "As to moral courage, I have rarely met with the two-o'clock-in-the-morning kind: I mean unprepared courage; that which is necessary on an unexpected occasion, and which, in spite of the most unforeseen events, leaves full freedom of judgment and decision:" and he did not hesitate to declare that he was himself eminently endowed with this two-o'clock-in-the-morning courage, and that he had met with few persons equal to himself in this respect.

Every thing depended on the nicety of his combinations, and the stars were not more punctual than his arithmetic. His personal attention descended to the smallest particulars. "At Montebello, I ordered Kellermann to attack with eight hundred horse, and with these he separated the six thousand Hungarian grenadiers, before the very eyes of the Austrian cavalry. This cavalry was half a league off and required a quarter of an hour to arrive on the field of action, and I have observed that it is always these quarters of an hour that decide the fate of a battle." "Before he fought a battle, Bonaparte thought little about what he should do in case of success, but a great deal about what he should do in case of a reverse of fortune." The same prudence and good sense mark all his behavior. His instructions to his secretary at the Tuileries are worth remembering. "During the night, enter my chamber as seldom as possible. Do not awake me when you have any good news to communicate; with that there is no hurry. But when you bring bad news, rouse me instantly, for then there is not a moment to be lost." It was a whimsical economy of the same kind which dictated his practice, when general in Italy, in regard to his burdensome correspondence. He directed Bourrienne to leave all letters unopened for three weeks, and then observed with satisfaction how large a part of the correspondence had thus disposed of itself and no longer required an answer. His achievement of business was immense, and enlarges the known powers of man. There have been many working kings, from Ulysses to William of Orange, but none who accomplished a tithe of this man's performance.

To these gifts of nature, Napoleon added the advantage of having been born to a private and humble fortune. In his later days he had the weakness of wishing to add to his crowns and badges the prescription of aristocracy; but he knew his debt to his austere education, and made no secret of his contempt for the born kings, and for "the hereditary asses," as he coarsely styled the Bourbons. He said that "in their exile they had learned nothing, and forgot nothing." Bonaparte had passed through all the degrees of military service, but also was citizen before he was emperor, and so has the key to citizenship. His remarks and estimates discover the information and justness of measurement of the middle class. Those who had to deal with him found that he was not to be imposed upon, but could cipher as well as another man. This appears in all parts of his Memoirs, dictated at St. Helena. When the expenses of the empress, of his household, of his palaces, had accumulated great debts, Napoleon examined the bills of the creditors himself, detected overcharges and errors, and reduced the claims by considerable sums.

His grand weapon, namely the millions whom he directed, he owed to the representative character which clothed him. He interests us as he stands for France and for Europe; and he exists as captain and king only as far as the Revolution, or the interest of the industrious masses, found an organ and a leader in him. In the social interests, he knew the meaning and value of labor, and threw himself naturally on that side. I like an incident mentioned by one of his biographers at St. Helena. "When walking with Mrs. Balcombe, some servants, carrying heavy boxes, passed by on the road, and Mrs. Balcombe desired them, in rather an angry tone, to keep back. Napoleon interfered, saying, 'Respect the burden, Madam.'" In the time of the empire he directed attention to the improvement and embellishment of the markets of the capital. "The market-place," he said, "is the Louvre of the common people." The principal works that have survived him are his magnificent roads. He filled the troops with his spirit, and a sort of freedom and companionship grew up between him and them, which the forms of his court never permitted between the officers and himself. They performed, under his eye, that which no others could do. The best document of his relation to his troops is the order of the day on the morning of the battle of Austerlitz, in which Napoleon promises the troops that he will keep his person out of reach of fire. This declaration, which is the reverse of that ordinarily made by generals and sovereigns on the eve of a battle, sufficiently explains the devotion of the army to their leader.

But though there is in particulars this identity between Napoleon and the mass of the people, his real strength lay in their conviction that he was their representative in his genius and aims, not only when he courted, but when he controlled, and even when he decimated them by his conscriptions. He knew, as well as any Jacobin in France, how to philosophize on liberty and equality; and when allusion was made to the precious blood of centuries, which was spilled by the killing of the Duc d'Enghien, he suggested, "Neither is my blood ditch-water." The people felt that no longer the throne was occupied and the land sucked of its nourishment, by a small class of legitimates, secluded from all community with the children of the soil, and holding the ideas and superstitions of a long-forgotten state of society. Instead of that vampyre, a man of themselves held, in the Tuileries, knowledge and ideas like their own, opening of course to them and their children all places of power and trust. The day of sleepy, selfish policy, ever narrowing the means and opportunities of young men, was ended, and a day of expansion and demand was come. A market for all the powers and productions of man was opened; brilliant prizes glittered in the eyes of youth and talent. The old, iron-bound, feudal France was changed into a young Ohio or New York; and those who smarted under the immediate rigors of the new monarch, pardoned them as the necessary severities of the military system which had driven out the oppressor. And even when the majority of the people had begun to ask whether they had really gained any thing under the exhausting levies of men and money of the new master, the whole talent of the country, in every rank and kindred, took his part and defended him as its natural patron. In 1814, when advised to rely on the higher classes, Napoleon said to those around him, "Gentlemen, in the situation in which I stand, my only nobility is the rabble of the Faubourgs."

Napoleon met this natural expectation. The necessity of his position required a hospitality to every sort of talent, and its appointment to trusts; and his feeling went along with this policy. Like every superior person, he undoubtedly felt a desire for men and compeers, and a wish to measure his power with other masters, and an impatience of fools and underlings. In Italy, he sought for men and found none. "Good God!" he said, "how rare men are! There are eighteen millions in Italy, and I have with difficulty found two,—Dandolo and Melzi." In later years, with larger experience, his respect for mankind was not increased. In a moment of bitterness he said to one of his oldest friends, "Men deserve the contempt with which they inspire me. I have only to put some gold-lace on the coat of my virtuous republicans and they immediately become just what I wish them." This impatience at levity was, however, an oblique tribute of respect to those able persons who commanded his regard not only when he found them friends and coadjutors but also when they resisted his will. He could not confound Fox and Pitt, Carnot, Lafayette and Bernadotte, with the danglers of his court; and in spite of the detraction which his systematic egotism dictated toward the great captains who conquered with and for him, ample acknowledgments are made by him to Lannes, Duroc, Kleber, Dessaix, Massena, Murat, Ney and Augereau. If he felt himself their patron and the founder of their fortunes, as when he said "I made my generals out of mud,"—he could not hide his satisfaction in receiving from them a seconding and support commensurate with the grandeur of his enterprise. In the Russian campaign he was so much impressed by the courage and resources of Marshal Ney, that he said, "I have two hundred millions in my coffers, and I would give them all for Ney." The characters which he has drawn of several of his marshals are discriminating, and though they did not content the insatiable vanity of French officers, are no doubt substantially just. And in fact every species of merit was sought and advanced under his government. "I know," he said, "the depth and draught of water of every one of my generals." Natural power was sure to be well received at his court.

Seventeen men in his time were raised from common soldiers to the rank of king, marshal, duke, or general; and the crosses of his Legion of Honor were given to personal valor, and not to family connexion. "When soldiers have been baptized in the fire of a battlefield, they have all one rank in my eyes."

When a natural king becomes a titular king, every body is pleased and satisfied. The Revolution entitled the strong populace of the Faubourg St. Antoine, and every horse-boy and powder-monkey in the army, to look on Napoleon as flesh of his flesh and the creature of *his* party: but there is something in the success of grand talent which enlists an universal sympathy. For in the prevalence of sense and spirit over stupidity and malversation, all reasonable men have an interest; and as intellectual beings we feel the air purified by the electric shock, when material force is overthrown by intellectual energies. As soon as we are removed out of the reach of local and accidental partialities, Man feels that Napoleon fights for him; these are honest victories; this strong steam-engine does our work. Whatever appeals to the imagination, by transcending the ordinary limits of human ability, wonderfully encourages and liberates us. This capacious head, revolving and disposing sovereignly trains of affairs, and animating such multitudes of agents; this eye, which looked through Europe; this prompt invention; this inexhaustible resource:—what events! what romantic pictures! what strange situations!—when spying the Alps, by a sunset in the Sicilian sea; drawing up his army for battle in sight of the Pyramids, and saying to his troops, "From the tops of those pyramids, forty centuries look down on you;" fording the Red Sea; wading in the gulf of the Isthmus of Suez. On the shore of Ptolemais, gigantic projects agitated him. "Had Acre fallen, I should have changed the face of the world." His army, on the night of the battle of Austerlitz, which was the anniversary of his inauguration as Emperor, presented him with a bouquet of forty standards taken in the fight. Perhaps it is a little puerile, the pleasure he took in making these contrasts glaring; as when he pleased himself with making kings wait in his antechambers, at Tilsit, at Paris and at Erfurt.

We can not, in the universal imbecility, indecision and indolence of men, sufficiently congratulate ourselves on this strong and ready actor, who took occasion by the beard, and showed us how much may be accomplished by the mere force of such virtues as all men possess in less degrees; namely, by punctuality, by personal attention, by courage and thoroughness. "The Austrians," he said, "do not know the value of time." I should cite him, in his earlier years, as a model of prudence. His power does not consist in any wild or extravagant force; in any enthusiasm like Mahomet's, or singular power of persuasion; but in the exercise of common-sense on each emergency, instead of abiding by rules and customs. The lesson he teaches is that which vigor always teaches;—that there is always room for it. To what heaps of cowardly doubts is not that man's life an answer. When he appeared it was the belief of all military men that there could be nothing new in war; as it is the belief of men to-day that nothing new can be undertaken in politics, or in church, or in letters, or in trade, or in farming, or in our social manners and customs; and as it is at all times the belief of society that the world is used up. But Bonaparte knew better than society; and moreover knew that he knew better. I think all men know better than they do; know that the institutions we so volubly commend are go-carts and baubles; but they dare not trust their presentiments. Bonaparte relied on his own sense, and did not care a bean for other people's. The world treated his novelties just as it treats everybody's novelties,—made infinite objection, mustered all the impediments; but he snapped his finger at their objections. "What creates great difficulty," he remarks, "in the profession of the land-commander, is the necessity of feeding so many men and animals. If he allows himself to be guided by the commissaries he will never stir, and all his expeditions will fail." An example of his common-sense is what he says of the passage of the Alps in winter, which all writers, one repeating after the other, had described as impracticable. "The winter," says Napoleon, "is not the most unfavorable season for the passage of lofty mountains. The snow is then firm, the weather settled, and there is nothing to fear from avalanches, the real and only danger to be apprehended in the Alps. On these high mountains there are often very fine days in December, of a dry cold, with extreme calmness in the air." Read his account, too, of the way in which battles are gained. "In all battles a moment occurs when the bravest troops, after having made the greatest efforts, feel inclined to run. That terror proceeds from a want of confidence in their own courage, and it only requires a slight opportunity, a pretence, to restore confidence to them. The art is, to give rise to the opportunity and to invent the pretence. At Arcola I won the battle with twenty-five horsemen. I seized that moment of lassitude, gave every man a trumpet, and gained the day with this handful. You see that two armies are two bodies which meet and endeavor to frighten each other; a moment of panic occurs, and that moment must be turned to advantage. When a man has been present in many actions, he distinguishes that moment without difficulty: it is as easy as casting up an addition."

This deputy of the nineteenth century added to his gifts a capacity for speculation on general topics. He delighted in running through the range of practical, of literary and of abstract questions. His opinion is always original and to the purpose. On the voyage to Egypt he liked, after dinner, to fix on three or four persons to support a proposition, and as many to oppose it. He gave a subject, and the discussions turned on questions of religion, the different kinds of government, and the art of war. One day he asked whether the planets were inhabited? On another, what was the age of the world? Then he proposed to consider the probability of the destruction of the globe, either by water or by fire: at another time, the truth or fallacy of presentiments, and the interpretation of dreams. He was very fond of talking of religion. In 1806 he conversed with Fournier, bishop of Montpellier, on matters of theology. There were two points on which they could not agree, viz. that of hell and that of salvation out of the pale of the church. The Emperor told Josephine that he disputed like a devil on these two points, on which the bishop was inexorable. To the philosophers he readily yielded all that was proved against religion as the work of men and time, but he would not hear of materialism. One fine night, on deck, amid a clatter of materialism, Bonaparte pointed to the stars, and said, "You may talk as long as you please, gentlemen, but who made all that?" He delighted in the conversation of men of science, particularly of Monge and Berthollet; but the men of letters he slighted; they were "manufacturers of phrases." Of medicine too he was fond of talking, and with those of its practitioners whom he most esteemed,—with Corvisart at Paris, and with Antonomarchi at St. Helena. "Believe me," he said to the last, "we had better leave off all these remedies: life is a fortress which neither you nor I know any thing about. Why throw obstacles in the way of its defence? Its own means are superior to all the apparatus of your laboratories. Corvisart candidly agreed with me that all your filthy mixtures are good for nothing. Medicine is a collection of uncertain prescriptions, the results of which, taken collectively, are more fatal than useful to mankind. Water, air and cleanliness are the chief articles in my pharmacopœia."

His memoirs, dictated to Count Montholon and General Gourgaud at St. Helena, have great value, after all the deduction that it seems is to be made from them on account of his known disingenuousness. He has the good-nature of strength and conscious superiority. I admire his simple, clear narrative of his battles;—good as Cæsar's; his good-natured and sufficiently respectful account of Marshal Wurmser and his other antagonists; and his own equality as a writer to his varying subject. The most agreeable portion is the Campaign in Egypt.

He had hours of thought and wisdom. In intervals of leisure, either in the camp or the palace, Napoleon appears as a man of genius directing on abstract questions the native appetite for truth and the impatience of words he was wont to show in war. He could enjoy every play of invention, a romance, a *bon mot*, as well as a stratagem in a campaign. He delighted to fascinate Josephine and her ladies, in a dim-lighted apartment, by the terrors of a fiction to which his voice and dramatic power lent every addition.

I call Napoleon the agent or attorney of the middle class of modern society; of the throng who fill the markets, shops, counting-houses, manufactories, ships, of the modern world, aiming to be rich. He was the agitator, the destroyer of prescription, the internal improver, the liberal, the radical, the inventor of means, the opener of doors and markets, the subverter of monopoly and abuse. Of course the rich and aristocratic did not like him. England, the centre of capital, and Rome and Austria, centres of tradition and genealogy, opposed him. The consternation of the dull and conservative classes, the terror of the foolish old men and old women of the Roman conclave, who in their despair took hold of any thing, and would cling to red-hot iron,—the vain attempts of statists to amuse and deceive him, of the emperor of Austria to bribe him; and the instinct of the young, ardent and active men every where, which pointed him out as the giant of the middle class, make his history bright and commanding. He had the virtues of the masses of his constituents: he had also their vices. I am sorry that the brilliant picture has its reverse. But that is the fatal quality which we discover in our pursuit of wealth, that it is treacherous, and is bought by the breaking or weakening of the sentiments; and it is inevitable that we should find the same fact in the history of this champion, who proposed to himself simply a brilliant career, without any stipulation or scruple concerning the means.

Bonaparte was singularly destitute of generous sentiments. The highest-placed individual in the most cultivated age and population of the world,—he has not the merit of common truth and honesty. He is unjust to his generals; egotistic and monopolizing; meanly stealing the credit of their great actions from Kellermann, from Bernadotte; intriguing to involve his faithful Junot in hopeless bankruptcy, in order to drive him to a distance from Paris, because the familiarity of his manners offends the new pride of his throne. He is a boundless liar. The official paper, his "Moniteur," and all his bulletins, are proverbs for saying what he wished to be believed; and worse,—he sat, in his premature old age, in his lonely island, coldly falsifying facts and dates and characters, and giving to history a theatrical *éclat*. Like all Frenchmen he has a passion for stage effect. Every action that breathes of generosity is poisoned by this calculation. His star, his love of glory, his doctrine of the immortality of the soul, are all French. "I must dazzle and astonish. If I were to give the liberty of the press, my power could not last three days." To make a great noise is his favorite design. "A great reputation is a great noise: the more there is made, the farther off it is heard. Laws, institutions, monuments, nations, all fall; but the noise continues, and resounds in after ages." His doctrine of immortality is simply fame. His theory of influence is not flattering. "There are two levers for moving men,—interest and fear. Love is a silly infatuation, depend upon it. Friendship is but a name. I love nobody. I do not even love my brothers: perhaps Joseph a little, from habit, and because he is my elder; and Duroc, I love him too; but why?—because his character pleases me: he is stern and resolute, and I believe the fellow never shed a tear. For my part I know very well that I have no true friends. As long as I continue to be what I am, I may have as many pretended friends as I please. Leave sensibility to women; but men should be firm in heart and purpose, or they should have nothing to do with war and government." He was thoroughly unscrupulous. He would steal, slander, assassinate, drown and poison, as his interest dictated. He had no generosity, but mere vulgar hatred; he was intensely selfish; he was perfidious; he cheated at cards; he was a prodigious gossip, and opened letters, and delighted in his infamous police, and rubbed his hands with joy when he had intercepted some morsel of intelligence concerning the men and women about him, boasting that "he knew every thing;" and interfered with the cutting the dresses of the women; and listened after the hurrahs and the compliments of the street, incognito. His manners were coarse. He treated women with low familiarity. He had the habit of pulling their ears and pinching their cheeks when he was in good humor, and of pulling the ears and whiskers of men, and of striking and horse-play with them, to his last days. It does not appear that he listened at key-holes, or at least that he was caught at it. In short, when you have penetrated through all the circles of power and splendor, you were not dealing with a gentleman, at last; but with an impostor and a rogue; and he fully deserves the epithet of *Jupiter Scapin*, or a sort of Scamp Jupiter.

In describing the two parties into which modern society divides itself,—the democrat and the conservative,—I said, Bonaparte represents the democrat, or the party of men of business, against the stationary or conservative party. I omitted then to say, what is material to the statement, namely that these two parties differ only as young and old. The democrat is a young conservative; the conservative is an old democrat. The aristocrat is the democrat ripe and gone to seed;—because both parties stand on the one ground of the supreme value of property, which one endeavors to get, and the other to keep. Bonaparte may be said to represent the whole history of this party, its youth and its age; yes, and with poetic justice its fate, in his own. The counter-revolution, the counter-party, still waits for its organ and representative, in a lover and a man of truly public and universal aims.

Here was an experiment, under the most favorable conditions, of the powers of intellect without conscience. Never was such a leader so endowed and so weaponed; never leader found such aids and followers. And what was the result of this vast talent and power, of these immense armies, burned cities, squandered treasures, immolated millions of men, of this demoralized Europe? It came to no result. All passed away like the smoke of his artillery, and left no trace. He left France smaller, poorer, feebler, than he found it; and the whole contest for freedom was to be begun again. The attempt was in principle suicidal. France served him with life and limb and estate, as long as it could identify its interests with him; but when men saw that after victory was another war; after the destruction of armies, new conscriptions; and they who had toiled so desperately were never nearer to the reward,—they could not spend what they had earned, nor repose on their down-beds, nor strut in their châteaux,—they deserted him. Men found that his absorbing egotism was deadly to all other men. It resembled the torpedo, which inflicts a succession of shocks on any one who takes hold of it, producing spasms which contract the muscles of the hand, so that the man can not open his fingers; and the animal inflicts new and more violent shocks, until he paralyzes and kills his victim. So this exorbitant egotist narrowed, impoverished and absorbed the power and existence of those who served him; and the universal cry of France and of Europe in 1814 was, "Enough of him;" "*Assez de Bonaparte.*"

It was not Bonaparte's fault. He did all that in him lay to live and thrive without moral principle. It was the nature of things, the eternal law of man and of the world which baulked and ruined him; and the result, in a million experiments, will be the same. Every experiment, by multitudes or by individuals, that has a sensual and selfish aim, will fail. The pacific Fourier will be as inefficient as the pernicious Napoleon. As long as our civilization is essentially one of property, of fences, of exclusiveness, it will be mocked by delusions. Our riches will leave us sick; there will be bitterness in our laughter, and our wine will burn our mouth. Only that good profits which we can taste with all doors open, and which serves all men.

1845 1850

THE CHARDON STREET CONVENTION

In the month of November, 1840, a Convention of Friends of Universal Reform assembled in the Chardon Street Chapel in Boston, in obedience to a call in the newspapers, signed by a few individuals, inviting all persons to a public discussion of the institutions of the Sabbath, the Church and the Ministry. The Convention organized itself by the choice of Edmund Quincy as Moderator, spent three days in the consideration of the Sabbath, and adjourned to a day in March of the following year, for the discussion of the second topic. In March, accordingly, a three-days' session was holden in the same place, on the subject of the Church, and a third meeting fixed for the following November, which was accordingly holden; and the Convention debated, for three days again, the remaining subject of the Priesthood. This Convention never printed any report of its deliberations, nor pretended to arrive at any result by the expression of its sense in formal resolutions;—the professed objects of those persons who felt the greatest interest in its meetings being simply the elucidation of truth through free discussion. The daily newspapers reported, at the time, brief sketches of the course of proceedings, and the remarks of the principal speakers. These meetings attracted a great deal of public attention, and were spoken of in different circles in every note of hope, of sympathy, of joy, of alarm, of abhorrence and of merriment. The composition of the assembly was rich and various. The singularity and latitude of the summons drew together, from all parts of New England and also from the Middle States, men of every shade of opinion from the straitest orthodoxy to the wildest heresy, and many persons whose church was a church of one member only. A great variety of dialect and of costume was noticed; a great deal of confusion, eccentricity and freak appeared, as well as of zeal and enthusiasm. If the assembly was disorderly, it was picturesque. Madmen, madwomen, men with beards, Dunkers, Muggletonians, Come-outers, Groaners, Agrarians, Seventh-day Baptists,

Quakers, Abolitionists, Calvinists, Unitarians and Philosophers,—all came successively to the top, and seized their moment, if not their hour, wherein to chide, or pray, or preach, or protest. The faces were a study. The most daring innovators and the champions-until-death of the old cause sat side by side. The still-living merit of the oldest New England families, glowing yet after several generations, encountered the founders of families, fresh merit, emerging, and expanding the brows to a new breadth, and lighting a clownish face with sacred fire. The assembly was characterized by the predominance of a certain plain, sylvan strength and earnestness, whilst many of the most intellectual and cultivated persons attended its councils. Dr. Channing, Edward Taylor, Bronson Alcott, Mr. Garrison, Mr. May, Theodore Parker, H. C. Wright, Dr. Osgood, William Adams, Edward Palmer, Jones Very, Maria W. Chapman and many other persons of a mystical or sectarian or philanthropic renown, were present, and some of them participant. And there was no want of female speakers; Mrs. Little and Mrs. Lucy Sessions took a pleasing and memorable part in the debate, and that flea of Conventions, Mrs. Abigail Folsom, was but too ready with her interminable scroll. If there was not parliamentary order, there was life, and the assurance of that constitutional love for religion and religious liberty which, in all periods, characterizes the inhabitants of this part of America.

There was a great deal of wearisome speaking in each of those three-days' sessions, but relieved by signal passages of pure eloquence, by much vigor of thought, and especially by the exhibition of character, and by the victories of character. These men and women were in search of something better and more satisfying than a vote or a definition, and they found what they sought, or the pledge of it, in the attitude taken by individuals of their number of resistance to the insane routine of parliamentary usage; in the lofty reliance on principles, and the prophetic dignity and transfiguration which accompanies, even amidst opposition and ridicule, a man whose mind is made up to obey the great inward Commander, and who does not anticipate his own action, but awaits confidently the new emergency for the new counsel. By no means the least value of this Convention, in our eye, was the scope it gave to the genius of Mr. Alcott, and not its least instructive lesson was the gradual but sure ascendency of his spirit, in spite of the incredulity and derision with which he is at first received, and in spite, we might add, of his own failures. Moreover, although no decision was had, and no action taken on all the great points mooted in the discussion, yet the Convention brought together many remarkable persons, face to face, and gave occasion to memorable interviews and conversations, in the hall, in the lobbies or around the doors.

1842

BROOK FARM

The West Roxbury Association was formed in 1841, by a society of members, men and women, who bought a farm in West Roxbury, of about two hundred acres, and took possession of the place in April. Mr. George Ripley was the President, and I think Mr. Charles Dana (afterwards well known as one of the editors of the New York Tribune) was the Secretary. Many members took shares by paying money, others held shares by their labor. An old house on the place was enlarged, and three new houses built. William Allen was at first and for some time the head farmer, and the work was distributed in orderly committees to the men and women. There were many employments more or less lucrative found for, or brought hither by these members,—shoemakers, joiners, sempstresses. They had good scholars among them, and so received pupils for their education. The parents of the children in some instances wished to live there, and were received as boarders. Many persons, attracted by the beauty of the place and the culture and ambition of the community, joined them as boarders, and lived there for years. I think the numbers of this mixed community soon reached eighty or ninety souls.

It was a noble and generous movement in the projectors, to try an experiment of better living. They had the feeling that our ways of living were too conventional and expensive, not allowing each to do what he had a talent for, and not permitting men to combine cultivation of mind and heart with a reasonable amount of daily labor. At the same time, it was an attempt to lift others with themselves, and to share the advantages they should attain, with others now deprived of them.

There was no doubt great variety of character and purpose in the members of the community. It consisted in the main of young people,—few of middle age, and none old. Those who inspired and organized it were of course persons impatient of the routine, the uniformity, perhaps they would say the squalid contentment of society around them, which was so timid and skeptical of any progress. One would say then that impulse was the rule in the society, without centripetal balance; perhaps it would not be severe to say, intellectual sans-culottism, an impatience of the formal, routinary character of our educational, religious, social and economical life in Massachusetts. Yet there was immense hope in these young people. There was nobleness; there were self-sacrificing victims who compensated for the levity and rashness of their companions. The young people lived a great deal in a short time, and came forth some of them perhaps with shattered constitutions. And a few grave sanitary influences of character were happily there, which, I was assured, were always felt.

George W. Curtis of New York, and his brother, of English Oxford, were members of the family from the first. Theodore Parker, the near neighbor of the farm and the most intimate friend of Mr. Ripley, was a frequent visitor. Mr. Ichabod Morton of Plymouth, a plain man formerly engaged through many years in the fisheries with success, eccentric,—with a persevering interest in education, and of a very democratic religion, came and built a house on the farm, and he, or members of his family, continued there to the end. Margaret Fuller, with her joyful conversation and large sympathy, was often a guest, and always in correspondence with her friends. Many ladies, whom to name were to praise, gave character and varied attraction to the place.

In and around Brook Farm, whether as members, boarders or visitors, were many remarkable persons, for character, intellect or accomplishments. I recall one youth of the subtlest mind, I believe I must say the subtlest observer and diviner of character I ever met, living, reading, writing, talking there, perhaps as long as the colony held together; his mind fed and overfed by whatever is exalted in genius, whether in Poetry or Art, in Drama or Music, or in social accomplishment and elegancy; a man of no employment or practical aims, a student and philosopher, who found his daily enjoyment not with the elders or his exact contemporaries so much as with the fine boys who were skating and playing ball or bird-hunting; forming the closest friendships with such, and finding his delight in the petulant heroism of boys; yet was he the chosen counsellor to whom the guardians would repair on any hitch or difficulty that occurred, and draw from him a wise counsel. A fine, subtle, inward genius, puny in body and habit as a girl, yet with an *aplomb* like a general, never disconcerted. He lived and thought, in 1842, such worlds of life; all hinging on the thought of Being or Reality as opposed to consciousness; hating intellect with the ferocity of a Swedenborg. He was the Abbé or spiritual father, from his religious bias. His reading lay in Æschylus, Plato, Dante, Calderon, Shakspeare, and in modern novels and romances of merit. There too was Hawthorne, with his cold yet gentle genius, if he failed to do justice to this temporary home. There was the accomplished Doctor of Music, who has presided over its literature ever since in our metropolis. Rev. William Henry Channing, now of London, was from the first a student of Socialism in France and England, and in perfect sympathy with this experiment. An English baronet, Sir John Caldwell, was a frequent visitor, and more or less directly interested in the leaders and the success.

Hawthorne drew some sketches, not happily, as I think; I should rather say, quite unworthy of his genius. No friend who knew Margaret Fuller could recognize her rich and brilliant genius under the dismal mask which the public fancied was meant for her in that disagreeable story.

The Founders of Brook Farm should have this praise, that they made what all people try to make, an agreeable place to live in. All comers, even the most fastidious, found it the pleasantest of residences. It is certain that freedom from household routine, variety of character and talent, variety of work, variety of means of thought and instruction, art, music, poetry, reading, masquerade, did not permit sluggishness or despondency; broke up routine. There is agreement in the testimony that it was, to most of the associates, education; to many, the most important period of their life, the birth of valued friendships, their first acquaintance with the riches of conversation, their training in behavior. The art of letter-writing, it is said, was immensely cultivated. Letters were always flying not only from house to house, but from room to room. It was a perpetual picnic, a French Revolution in small, an Age of Reason in a patty-pan.

In the American social communities, the gossip found such vent and sway as to become despotic. The institutions were whispering-galleries, in which the adored Saxon privacy was lost. Married women I believe uniformly decided against the community. It was to them like the brassy and lacquered life in hotels. The common school was well enough, but to the common nursery they had grave objections. Eggs might be hatched in ovens, but the hen on her own account much preferred the old way. A hen without her chickens was but half a hen.

It was a curious experience of the patrons and leaders of this noted community, in which the agreement with many parties was that they should give so many hours of instruction in mathematics, in music, in moral and intellectual philosophy, and so forth,—that in every instance the newcomers showed themselves keenly alive to the advantages of the society, and were sure to avail themselves of every means of instruction; their knowledge was increased, their manners refined,—but they became in that proportion averse to labor, and were charged by the heads of the departments with a certain indolence and selfishness.

In practice it is always found that virtue is occasional, spotty, and not linear or cubic. Good people are as bad as rogues if steady performance is claimed; the conscience of the conscientious runs in veins, and the most punctilious in some particulars are latitudinarian in others. It was very gently said that people on whom beforehand all persons would put the utmost reliance were not responsible. They saw the necessity that the work must be done, and did it not, and it of course fell to be done by the few religious workers. No doubt there was in many a certain strength drawn from the fury of dissent. Thus Mr. Ripley told Theodore Parker, "There is your accomplished friend ——: he would hoe corn all Sunday if I would let him, but all Massachusetts could not make him do it on Monday."

Of course every visitor found that there was a comic side to this Paradise of shepherds and shepherdesses. There was a stove in every chamber, and every one might burn as much wood as he or she would saw. The ladies took cold on washing-day; so it was ordained that the gentlemen-shepherds should wring and hang out clothes; which they punctually did. And it would sometimes occur that when they danced in the evening, clothespins dropped plentifully from their pockets. The country members naturally were surprised to observe that one man ploughed all day and one looked out of the window all day, and perhaps drew his picture, and both received at night the same wages. One would meet also some modest pride in their advanced condition, signified by a frequent phrase, "Before we came out of civilization."

The question which occurs to you had occurred much earlier to Fourier: "How in this charming Elysium is the dirty work to be done?" And long ago Fourier had exclaimed, "Ah! I have it," and jumped with joy. "Don't you see," he cried, "that nothing so delights the young Caucasian child as dirt? See the mud-pies that all children will make if you will let them. See how much more joy they find in pouring their pudding on the table-cloth than into their beautiful mouths. The children from six to eight, organized into companies with flags and uniforms, shall do this last function of civilization."

In Brook Farm was this peculiarity, that there was no head. In every family is the father; in every factory, a foreman; in a shop, a master; in a boat, the skipper; but in this Farm, no authority; each was master or mistress of his or her actions; happy, hapless anarchists. They expressed, after much perilous experience, the conviction that plain dealing was the best defence of manners and moral between the sexes. People cannot live together in any but necessary ways. The only candidates who will present themselves will be those who have tried the experiment of independence and ambition, and have failed; and none others will barter for the most comfortable equality the chance of superiority. Then all communities have quarrelled. Few people can live together on their merits. There must be kindred, or mutual economy, or a common interest in their business, or other external tie.

The society at Brook Farm existed, I think, about six or seven years, and then broke up, the Farm was sold, and I believe all the partners came out with pecuniary loss. Some of them had spent on it the accumulations of years. I suppose they all, at the moment, regarded it as a failure. I do not think they can so regard it now, but probably as an important chapter in their experience which has been of lifelong value. What knowledge of themselves and of each other, what various practical wisdom, what personal power, what studies of character, what accumulated culture many of the members owed to it! What mutual measure they took of each other! It was a close union, like that in a ship's cabin, of clergymen, young collegians, merchants, mechanics, farmers' sons and daughters, with men and women of rare opportunities and delicate culture, yet assembled there by a sentiment which all shared, some of them hotly shared, of the honesty of a life of labor and of the beauty of a life of humanity. The yeoman saw refined manners in persons who were his friends; and the lady or the romantic scholar saw the continuous strength and faculty in people who would have disgusted them but that these powers were now spent in the direction of their own theory of life.

I recall these few selected facts, none of them of much independent interest, but symptomatic of the times and country. I please myself with the thought that our American mind is not now eccentric or rude in its strength, but is beginning to show a quiet power, drawn from wide and abundant sources, proper to a Continent and to an educated people. If I have owed much to the special influences I have indicated, I am not less aware of that excellent and increasing circle of masters in arts and in song and in science, who cheer the intellect of our cities and this country to-day,—whose genius is not a lucky accident, but normal, and with broad foundation of culture, and so inspires the hope of steady strength advancing on itself, and a day without night.

c.1867 1883

From ENGLISH TRAITS

Coleridge, Carlyle, Wordsworth

From London, on the 5th August, I went to Highgate, and wrote a note to Mr. Coleridge, requesting leave to pay my respects to him. It was near noon. Mr. Coleridge sent a verbal message that he was in bed, but if I would call after one o'clock he would see me. I returned at one, and he appeared, a short, thick old man, with bright blue eyes and fine clear complexion, leaning on his cane. He took snuff freely, which presently soiled his cravat and neat black suit. He asked whether I knew Allston, and spoke warmly of his merits and doings when he knew him in Rome; what a master of the Titianesque he was, etc., etc. He spoke of Dr. Channing. It was an unspeakable misfortune that he should have turned out a Unitarian after all. On this, he burst into a declamation on the folly and ignorance of Unitarianism,—its high unreasonableness; and taking up Bishop Waterland's book, which lay on the table, he read with vehemence two or three pages written by himself in the fly-leaves,—passages, too, which, I believe, are printed in the Aids to Reflection. When he stopped to take breath, I interposed that "whilst I highly valued all his explanations, I was bound to tell him that I was born and bred a Unitarian." "Yes," he said, "I supposed so;" and continued as before. It was a wonder that after so many ages of unquestioning acquiescence in the doctrine of St. Paul,—the doctrine of the Trinity, which was also according to Philo Judæus the doctrine of the Jews before Christ,—this handful of Preistleians should take on themselves to deny it, etc., etc. He was very sorry that Dr. Channing, a man to whom he looked up,—no, to say that he looked *up* to him would be to speak falsely, but a man whom he looked *at* with so much interest,—should embrace such views. When he saw Dr. Channing he had hinted to him that he was afraid he loved Christianity for what was lovely and excellent,—he loved the good in it, and not the true;—"And I tell you, sir, that I have known ten persons who loved the good, for one person who loved the true; but it is a far greater virtue to love the true for itself alone, than to love the good for itself alone." He (Coleridge) knew all about Unitarianism perfectly well, because he had once been a Unitarian and knew what quackery it was. He had been called "the rising star of Unitarianism." He went on defining, or rather refining: "The Trinitarian doctrine was realism; the idea of God was not essential, but super-essential;" talked of *trinism* and *tetrakism* and much more, of which I only caught this, "that the will was that by which a person is a person; because, if one should push me in the street, and so I should force the man next me into the kennel, I should at once exclaim, I did not do it, sir, meaning it was not my will." And this also, that "if you should insist on your faith here in England, and I on mine, mine would be the hotter side of the fagot."

I took advantage of a pause to say that he had many readers of all religious opinions in America, and I proceeded to inquire if the "extract" from the Independent's pamphlet, in the third volume of the Friend, were a veritable quotation. He replied that it was really taken from a pamphlet in his possession entitled "A Protest of one of the Independents," or something to that effect. I told him how excellent I thought it and how much I wished to see the entire work. "Yes," he said, "the man was a chaos of truths, but lacked the knowledge that God was a God of order. Yet the passage would no doubt strike you more in the quotation than in the original, for I have filtered it."

When I rose to go, he said, "I do not know whether you care about poetry, but I will repeat some verses I lately made on my baptismal anniversary," and he recited with strong emphasis, standing, ten or twelve lines beginning,—

"Born unto God in Christ——"

He inquired where I had been travelling; and on learning that I had been in Malta and Sicily, he compared one island with the other, repeating what he had said to the Bishop of London when he returned from that country, that Sicily was an excellent school of political economy; for, in any town there, it only needed to ask what the government enacted, and reverse that, to know what ought to be done; it was the most felicitously opposite legislation to anything good and wise. There were only three things which the government had brought into that garden of delights, namely, itch, pox and famine. Whereas in Malta, the force of law and mind was seen, in making that barren rock of semi-Saracen inhabitants the seat of population and plenty. Going out, he showed me in the next apartment a picture of Allston's and told me that Montague, a picture-dealer, once came to see him, and glancing towards this, said, "Well, you have got a picture!" thinking it the work of an old master; afterwards, Montague, still talking with his back to the canvas, put up his hand and touched it and exclaimed, "By Heaven! this picture is not ten years old:"—so delicate and skilful was that man's touch.

I was in his company for about an hour, but find it impossible to recall the largest part of his discourse, which was often like so many printed paragraphs in his book,—perhaps the same,—so readily did he fall into certain commonplaces. As I might have foreseen, the visit was rather a spectacle than a conversation, of no use beyond the satisfaction of my curiosity. He was old and preoccupied, and could not bend to a new companion and think with him.

From Edinburgh I went to the Highlands. On my return I came from Glasgow to Dumfries, and being intent on delivering a letter which I had brought from Rome, inquired for Craigenputtock. It was a farm in Nithsdale, in the parish of Dunscore, sixteen miles distant. No public coach passed near it, so I took a private carriage from the inn. I found the house amid desolate heathery hills, where the lonely scholar nourished his mighty heart. Carlyle was a man from his youth, an author who did not need to hide from his readers, and as absolute a man of the world, unknown and exiled on that hill-farm, as if holding on his own terms what is best in London. He was tall and gaunt, with a cliff-like brow, self-possessed and holding his extraordinary powers of conversation in easy command; clinging to his northern accent with evident relish; full of lively anecdote and with a streaming humor which floated every thing he looked upon. His talk playfully exalting the familiar objects, put the companion at once into an acquaintance with his Lars and Lemurs, and it was very pleasant to learn what was predestined to be a pretty mythology. Few were the objects and lonely the man; "not a person to speak to within sixteen miles except the minister of Dunscore;" so that books inevitably made his topics.

He had names of his own for all the matters familiar to his discourse. Blackwood's was the "sand magazine;" Fraser's nearer approach to possibility of life was the "mud magazine;" a piece of road near by, that marked some failed enterprise, was the "grave of the last sixpence." When too much praise of any genius annoyed him he professed hugely to admire the talent shown by his pig. He had spent much time and contrivance in confining the poor beast to one enclosure in his pen, but pig, by great strokes of judgment, had found out how to let a board down, and had foiled him. For all that he still thought man the most plastic little fellow in the planet, and he liked Nero's death, "*Qualis artifex pereo!*" better than most history. He worships a man that will manifest any truth to him. At one time he had inquired and read a good deal about America. Landor's principle was mere rebellion; and *that* he feared was the American principle. The best thing he knew of that country was that in it a man can have meat for his labor. He had read in Stewart's book that when he inquired in a New York hotel for the Boots, he had been shown across the street and had found Mungo in his own house dining on roast turkey.

We talked of books. Plato he does not read, and he disparaged Socrates; and, when pressed, persisted in making Mirabeau a hero. Gibbon he called the "splendid bridge from the old world to the new." His own reading had been multifarious. Tristram Shandy was one of his first books after Robinson Crusoe, and Robertson's America an early favorite. Rousseau's Confessions had discovered to him that he was not a dunce; and it was now ten years since he had learned German, by the advice of a man who told him he would find in that language what he wanted.

He took despairing or satirical views of literature at this moment; recounted the incredible sums paid in one year by the great booksellers for puffing. Hence it comes that no newspaper is trusted now, no books are bought, and the booksellers are on the eve of bankruptcy.

He still returned to English pauperism, the crowded country, the selfish abdication by public men of all that public persons should perform. Government should direct poor men what to do. Poor Irish folk come wandering over these moors. My dame makes it a rule to give to every son of Adam bread to eat, and supplies his wants to the next house. But here are thousands of acres which might give them all meat, and nobody to bid these poor Irish go to the moor and till it. They burned the stacks and so found a way to force the rich people to attend to them.

We went out to walk over long hills, and looked at Criffel, then without his cap, and down into Wordsworth's country. There we sat down and talked of the immortality of the soul. It was not Carlyle's fault that we talked on that topic, for he had the natural disinclination of every nimble spirit to bruise itself against walls, and did not like to place himself where no step can be taken. But he was honest and true, and cognizant of the subtile links that bind ages together, and saw how every event affects all the future. "Christ died on the tree; that built Dunscore kirk yonder; that brought you and me together. Time has only a relative existence."

He was already turning his eyes towards London with a scholar's appreciation. London is the heart of the world, he said, wonderful only from the mass of human beings. He liked the huge machine. Each keeps its own round. The baker's boy brings muffins to the window at a fixed hour every day, and that is all the Londoner knows or wishes to know on the subject. But it turned out good men. He named certain individuals, especially one man of letters, his friend, the best mind he knew, whom London had well served.

On the 28th August I went to Rydal Mount, to pay my respects to Mr. Wordsworth. His daughters called in their father, a plain, elderly, white-haired man, not prepossessing, and disfigured by green goggles. He sat down, and talked with great simplicity. He had just returned from a journey. His health was good, but he had broken a tooth by a fall, when walking with two lawyers, and had said that he was glad it did not happen forty years ago; whereupon they had praised his philosophy.

He had much to say of America, the more that it gave occasion for his favorite topic,—that society is being enlightened by a superficial tuition, out of all proportion to its being restrained by moral culture. Schools do no good. Tuition is not education. He thinks more of the education of circumstances than of tuition. 'T is not question whether there are offences of which the law takes cognizance, but whether there are offences of which the law does not take cognizance. Sin is what he fears,—and how society is to escape without gravest mischiefs from this source. He has even said, what seemed a paradox, that they needed a civil war in America, to teach the necessity of knitting the social ties stronger. "There may be," he said, "in America some vulgarity in manner, but that's not important. That comes of the pioneer state of things. But I fear they are too much given to the making of money; and secondly, to politics; that they make political distinction the end and not the means. And I fear they lack a class of men of leisure,—in short, of gentlemen,—to give a tone of honor to the community. I am told that things are boasted of in the second class of society there, which, in England,—God knows, are done in England every day, but would never be spoken of. In America I wish to know not how many churches or schools, but what newspapers? My friend Colonel Hamilton, at the foot of the hill, who was a year in America, assures me that the newspapers are atrocious, and accuse members of Congress of stealing spoons!" He was against taking off the tax on newspapers in England,—which the reformers represent as a tax upon knowledge,—for this reason, that they would be inundated with base prints. He said he talked on political aspects, for he wished to impress on me and all good Americans to cultivate the moral, the conservative, etc., etc., and never to call into action the physical strength of the people, as had just now been done in England in the Reform Bill,—a thing prophesied by Delolme. He alluded once or twice to his conversation with Dr. Channing, who had recently visited him (laying his hand on a particular chair in which the Doctor had sat).

The conversation turned on books. Lucretius he esteems a far higher poet than Virgil; not in his system, which is nothing, but in his power of illustration. Faith is necessary to explain anything and to reconcile the foreknowledge of God with human evil. Of Cousin (whose lectures we had all been reading in Boston), he knew only the name.

I inquired if he had read Carlyle's critical articles and translations. He said he thought him sometimes insane. He proceeded to abuse Goethe's Wilhelm Meister heartily. It was full of all manner of fornication. It was like the crossing of flies in the air. He had never gone farther than the first part: so disgusted was he that he threw the book across the room. I deprecated this wrath, and said what I could for the better parts of the book, and he courteously promised to look at it again. Carlyle he said wrote most obscurely. He was clever and deep, but he defied the sympathies of every body. Even Mr. Coleridge wrote more clearly, though he had always wished Coleridge would write more to be understood. He led me out into his garden, and showed me the gravel walk in which thousands of his lines were composed. His eyes are much inflamed. This is no loss except for reading, because he never writes prose, and of poetry he carries even hundreds of lines in his head before writing them. He had just returned from a visit to Staffa, and within three days had made three sonnets on Fingal's Cave, and was composing a fourth when he was called in to see me. He said, "If you are interested in my verses perhaps you will like to hear these lines." I gladly assented, and he recollected himself for a few moments and then stood forth and repeated, one after the other, the three entire sonnets with great animation. I fancied the second and third more beautiful than his poems are wont to be. The third is addressed to the flowers, which, he said, especially the ox-eye daisy, are very abundant on the top of the rock. The second alludes to the name of the cave, which is "Cave of Music;" the first to the circumstance of its being visited by the promiscuous company of the steamboat.

This recitation was so unlooked for and surprising,—he, the old Wordsworth, standing apart, and reciting to me in a garden-walk, like a school-boy declaiming,—that I at first was near to laugh; but recollecting myself, that I had come thus far to see a poet and he was chanting poems to me, I saw that he was right and I was wrong, and gladly gave myself up to hear. I told him how much the few printed extracts had quickened the desire to possess his unpublished poems. He replied he never was in haste to publish; partly because he corrected a good deal, and every alteration is ungraciously received after printing; but what he had written would be printed, whether he lived or died. I said Tintern Abbey appeared to be the favorite poem with the public, but more contemplative readers preferred the first books of the Excursion, and the Sonnets. He said, "Yes, they are better." He preferred such of his poems as touched the affections, to any others; for whatever is didactic—what theories of society, and so on—might perish quickly; but whatever combined a truth with an affection was κτῆμα ἐς ἀεί, good to-day and good forever. He cited the sonnet, On the feelings of a high-minded Spaniard, which he preferred to any other (I so understood him), and the Two Voices; and quoted, with evident pleasure, the verses addressed To the Skylark. In this connection he said of the Newtonian theory that it might yet be superseded and forgotten; and Dalton's atomic theory.

When I prepared to depart he said he wished to show me what a common person in England could do, and he led me into the enclosure of his clerk, a young man to whom he had given this slip of ground, which was laid out, or its natural capabilities shown, with much taste. He then said he would show me a better way towards the inn; and he walked a good part of a mile, talking and ever and anon stopping short to impress the word or the verse, and finally parted from me with great kindness and returned across the fields.

Wordsworth honored himself by his simple adherence to truth, and was very willing not to shine; but he surprised by the hard limits of his thought. To judge from a single conversation, he made the impression of a narrow and very English mind; of one who paid for his rare elevation by general tameness and conformity. Off his own beat, his opinions were of no value. It is not very rare to find persons loving sympathy and ease, who expiate their departure from the common in one direction, by their conformity in every other.

1856

JOHN BROWN

BOSTON SPEECH

Mr. Chairman, and Fellow Citizens: I share the sympathy and sorrow which have brought us together. Gentlemen who have preceded me have well said that no wall of separation could here exist. This commanding event which has brought us together, eclipses all others which have occurred for a long time in our history, and I am very glad to see that this sudden interest in the hero of Harper's Ferry has provoked an extreme curiosity in all parts of the Republic, in regard to the details of his history. Every anecdote is eagerly sought, and I do not wonder that gentlemen find traits of relation readily between him and themselves. One finds a relation in the church, another in the profession, another in the place of his birth. He was happily a representative of the American Republic. Captain John Brown is a farmer, the fifth in descent from Peter Brown, who came to Plymouth in the Mayflower, in 1620. All the six have been farmers. His grandfather, of Simsbury, in Connecticut, was a captain in the Revolution. His father, largely interested as a raiser of stock, became a contractor to supply the army with beef, in the war of 1812, and our Captain John Brown, then a boy, with his father was present and witnessed the surrender of General Hull. He cherishes a great respect for his father, as a man of strong character, and his respect is probably just. For himself, he is so transparent that all men see him through. He is a man to make friends wherever on earth courage and integrity are esteemed, the rarest of heroes, a pure idealist, with no by-ends of his own. Many of you have seen him, and every one who has heard him speak has been impressed alike by his simple, artless goodness, joined with his sublime courage. He joins that perfect Puritan faith which brought his fifth ancestor to Plymouth Rock with his grandfather's ardor in the Revolution. He believes in two articles,—two instruments, shall I say?—the Golden Rule and the Declaration of Independence; and he used this expression in conversation here concerning them, "Better that a whole generation of men, women and children should pass away by a violent death than that one word of either should be violated in this country." There is a Unionist,—there is a strict constructionist for you. He believes in the Union of the States, and he conceives that the only obstruction to the Union is Slavery, and for that reason, as a patriot, he works for its abolition. The governor of Virginia has pronounced his eulogy in a manner that discredits the moderation of our timid parties. His own speeches to the court have interested the nation in him. What magnanimity, and what innocent pleading, as of childhood! You remember his words: "If I had interfered in behalf of the rich, the powerful, the intelligent, the so-called great, or any of their friends, parents, wives or children, it would all have been right. But I believe that to have interfered as I have done, for the despised poor, was not wrong, but right."

It is easy to see what a favorite he will be with history, which plays such pranks with temporary reputations. Nothing can resist the sympathy which all elevated minds must feel with Brown, and through them the whole civilized world; and if he must suffer, he must drag official gentlemen into an immortality most undesirable, of which they have already some disagreeable forebodings. Indeed, it is the *reductio ad absurdum* of Slavery, when the governor of Virginia is forced to hang a man whom he declares to be a man of the most integrity, truthfulness and courage he has ever met. Is that the kind of man the gallows is built for? It were bold to affirm that there is within that broad commonwealth, at this moment, another citizen as worthy to live, and as deserving of all public and private honor, as this poor prisoner.

But we are here to think of relief for the family of John Brown. To my eyes, that family looks very large and very needy of relief. It comprises his brave fellow sufferers in the Charlestown Jail; the fugitives still hunted in the mountains of Virginia and Pennsylvania; the sympathizers with him in all the states; and, I may say, almost every man who loves the Golden Rule and the Declaration of Independence, like him, and who sees what a tiger's thirst threatens him in the malignity of public sentiment in the slave states. It seems to me that a common feeling joins the people of Massachusetts with him.

I said John Brown was an idealist. He believed in his ideas to that extent that he existed to put them all into action; he said, "he did not believe in moral suasion, he believed in putting the thing through." He saw how deceptive the forms are. We fancy, in Massachusetts, that we are free; yet it seems the government is quite unreliable. Great wealth, great population, men of talent in the executive, on the bench,—all the forms right,—and yet, life and freedom are not safe. Why? Because the judges rely on the forms, and do not, like John Brown, use their eyes to see the fact behind the forms. They assume that the United States can protect its witness or its prisoner. And in Massachusetts that is true, but the moment he is carried out of the bounds of Massachusetts, the United States, it is notorious, afford no protection at all; the government, the judges, are an envenomed party, and give such protection as they give in Utah to honest citizens, or in Kansas; such protection as they gave to their own Commodore Paulding, when he was simple enough to mistake the formal instructions of his government for their real meaning. The state judges fear collision between their two allegiances; but there are worse evils than collision; namely, the doing substantial injustice. A good man will see that the use of a judge is to secure good government, and where the citizen's weal is imperilled by abuse of the federal power, to use that arm which can secure it, viz., the local government. Had that been done on certain calamitous occasions, we should not have seen the honor of Massachusetts trailed in the dust, stained to all ages, once and again, by the ill-timed formalism of a venerable bench. If judges cannot find law enough to maintain the sovereignty of the state, and to protect the life and freedom of every inhabitant not a criminal, it is idle to compliment them as learned and venerable. What avails their learning or veneration? At a pinch, they are no more use than idiots. After the mischance they wring their hands, but they had better never have been born. A Vermont judge, Hutchinson, who has the Declaration of Independence in his heart; a Wisconsin judge, who knows that laws are for the protection of citizens against kidnappers, is worth a court-house full of lawyers so idolatrous of forms as to let go the substance. Is any man in Massachusetts so simple as to believe that when a United States Court in Virginia, now, in its present reign of terror, sends to Connecticut, or New York, or Massachusetts, for a witness, it wants him for a witness? No; it wants him for a party; it wants him for meat to slaughter and eat. And your *habeas corpus* is, in any way in which it has been, or, I fear, is likely to be used, a nuisance, and not a protection; for it takes away his right reliance on himself, and the natural assistance of his friends and fellow citizens, by offering him a form which is a piece of paper.

But I am detaining the meeting on matters which others understand better. I hope, then, that, in administering relief to John Brown's family, we shall remember all those whom his fate concerns, all who are in sympathy with him, and not forget to aid him in the best way, by securing freedom and independence in Massachusetts.

1859

THOREAU

A queen rejoices in her peers,
And wary Nature knows her own,
By court and city, dale and down,
And like a lover volunteers,
And to her son will treasures more,
And more to purpose, freely pour
In one wood walk, than learned men
Will find with glass in ten times ten.

It seemed as if the breezes brought him,
It seemed as if the sparrows taught him,
As if by secret sign he knew
Where in far fields the orchis grew.

Henry David Thoreau was the last male descendant of a French ancestor who came to this country from the Isle of Guernsey. His character exhibited occasional traits drawn from this blood, in singular combination with a very strong Saxon genius.

He was born in Concord, Massachusetts, on the 12th of July, 1817. He was graduated at Harvard College in 1837, but without any literary distinction. An iconoclast in literature, he seldom thanked colleges for their service to him, holding them in small esteem, whilst yet his debt to them was important. After leaving the University, he joined his brother in teaching a private school, which he soon renounced. His father was a manufacturer of lead-pencils, and Henry applied himself for a time to this craft, believing he could make a better pencil than was then in use. After completing his experiments, he exhibited his work to chemists and artists in Boston, and having obtained their certificates to its excellence and to its equality with the best London manufacture, he returned home contented. His friends congratulated him that he had now opened his way to fortune. But he replied that he should never make another pencil. "Why should I? I would not do again what I have done once." He resumed his endless walks and miscellaneous studies, making every day some new acquaintance with Nature, though as yet never speaking of zoölogy or botany, since, though very studious of natural facts, he was incurious of technical and textual science.

At this time, a strong, healthy youth, fresh from college, whilst all his companions were choosing their profession, or eager to begin some lucrative employment, it was inevitable that his thoughts should be exercised on the same question, and it required rare decision to refuse all the accustomed paths and keep his solitary freedom at the cost of disappointing the natural expectations of his family and friends: all the more difficult that he had a perfect probity, was exact in securing his own independence, and in holding every man to the like duty. But Thoreau never faltered. He was a born protestant. He declined to give up his large ambition of knowledge and action for any narrow craft or profession, aiming at a much more comprehensive calling, the art of living well. If he slighted and defied the opinions of others, it was only that he was more intent to reconcile his practice with his own belief. Never idle or self-indulgent, he preferred, when he wanted money, earning it by some piece of manual labor agreeable to him, as building a boat or a fence, planting, grafting, surveying or other short work, to any long engagements. With his hardy habits and few wants, his skill in wood-craft, and his powerful arithmetic, he was very competent to live in any part of the world. It would cost him less time to supply his wants than another. He was therefore secure of his leisure.

A natural skill for mensuration, growing out of his mathematical knowledge and his habit of ascertaining the measures and distances of objects which interested him, the size of trees, the depth and extent of ponds and rivers, the height of mountains and the air-line distance of his favorite summits,—this, and his intimate knowledge of the territory about Concord, made him drift into the profession of land-surveyor. It had the advantage for him that it led him continually into new and secluded grounds, and helped his studies of Nature. His accuracy and skill in this work were readily appreciated, and he found all the employment he wanted.

He could easily solve the problems of the surveyor, but he was daily beset with graver questions, which he manfully confronted. He interrogated every custom, and wished to settle all his practice on an ideal foundation. He was a protestant *à outrance*, and few lives contain so many renunciations. He was bred to no profession; he never married; he lived alone; he never went to church; he never voted; he refused to pay a tax to the State; he ate no flesh, he drank no wine, he never knew the use of tobacco; and, though a naturalist, he used neither trap nor gun. He chose, wisely no doubt for himself, to be the bachelor of thought and Nature. He had no talent for wealth, and knew how to be poor without the least hint of squalor or inelegance. Perhaps he fell into his way of living without forecasting it much, but approved it with later wisdom. "I am often reminded," he wrote in his journal, "that if I had bestowed on me the wealth of Crœsus, my aims must be still the same, and my means essentially the same." He had no temptations to fight against,—no appetites, no passions, no taste for elegant trifles. A fine house, dress, the manners and talk of highly cultivated people were all thrown away on him. He much preferred a good Indian, and considered these refinements as impediments to conversation, wishing to meet his companion on the simplest terms. He declined invitations to dinner-parties, because there each was in every one's way, and he could not meet the individuals to any purpose. "They make their pride," he said, "in making their dinner cost much; I make my pride in making my dinner cost little." When asked at table what dish he preferred, he answered, "The nearest." He did not like the taste of wine, and never had a vice in his life. He said,—"I have a faint recollection of pleasure derived from smoking dried lily-stems, before I was a man. I had commonly a supply of these. I have never smoked anything more noxious."

He chose to be rich by making his wants few, and supplying them himself. In his travels, he used the railroad only to get over so much country as was unimportant to the present purpose, walking hundreds of miles, avoiding taverns, buying a lodging in farmers' and fishermen's houses, as cheaper, and more agreeable to him, and because there he could better find the men and the information he wanted.

There was somewhat military in his nature, not to be subdued, always manly and able, but rarely tender, as if he did not feel himself except in opposition. He wanted a fallacy to expose, a blunder to pillory, I may say required a little sense of victory, a roll of the drum, to call his powers into full exercise. It cost him nothing to say No; indeed he found it much easier than to say Yes. It seemed as if his first instinct on hearing a proposition was to controvert it, so impatient was he of the limitations of our daily thought. This habit, of course, is a little chilling to the social affections; and though the companion would in the end acquit him of any malice or untruth, yet it mars conversation. Hence, no equal companion stood in affectionate relations with one so pure and guileless. "I love Henry," said one of his friends, "but I cannot like him; and as for taking his arm, I should as soon think of taking the arm of an elm-tree."

Yet, hermit and stoic as he was, he was really fond of sympathy, and threw himself heartily and childlike into the company of young people whom he loved, and whom he delighted to entertain, as he only could, with the varied and endless anecdotes of his experiences by field and river: and he was always ready to lead a huckleberry-party or a search for chestnuts or grapes. Talking, one day, of a public discourse, Henry remarked that whatever succeeded with the audience was bad. I said, "Who would not like to write something which all can read, like Robinson Crusoe? and who does not see with regret that his page is not solid with a right materialistic treatment, which delights everybody?" Henry objected, of course, and vaunted the better lectures which reached only a few persons. But, at supper, a young girl, understanding that he was to lecture at the Lyceum, sharply asked him, "Whether his lecture would be a nice, interesting story, such as she wished to hear, or whether it was one of those old philosophical things that she did not care about." Henry turned to her, and bethought himself, and, I saw, was trying to believe that he had matter that might fit her and her brother, who were to sit up and go to the lecture, if it was a good one for them.

He was a speaker and actor of the truth, born such, and was ever running into dramatic situations from this cause. In any circumstance it interested all bystanders to know what part Henry would take, and what he would say; and he did not disappoint expectation, but used an original judgment on each emergency. In 1845 he built himself a small framed house on the shores of Walden Pond, and lived there two years alone, a life of labor and study. This action was quite native and fit for him. No one who knew him would tax him with affectation. He was more unlike his neighbors in his thought than in his action. As soon as he had exhausted the advantages of that solitude, he abandoned it. In 1847, not approving some uses to which the public expenditure was applied, he refused to pay his town tax, and was put in jail. A friend paid the tax for him, and he was released. The like annoyance was threatened the next year. But as his friends paid the tax, notwithstanding his protest, I believe he ceased to resist. No opposition or ridicule had any weight with him. He coldly and fully stated his opinion without affecting to believe that it was the opinion of the company. It was of no consequence if every one present held the opposite opinion. On one occasion he went to the University Library to procure some books. The librarian refused to lend them. Mr. Thoreau repaired to the President, who stated to him the rules and usages, which permitted the loan of books to resident graduates, to clergymen who were alumni, and to some others resident within a circle of ten miles' radius from the College. Mr. Thoreau explained to the President that the railroad had destroyed the old scale of distances,—that the library was useless, yes, and President and College useless, on the terms of his rules,—that the one benefit he owed to the College was its library,—that, at this moment, not only his want of books was imperative, but he wanted a large number of books, and assured him that he, Thoreau and not the librarian, was the proper custodian of these. In short, the President found the petitioner so formidable, and the rules getting to look so ridiculous, that he ended by giving him a privilege which in his hands proved unlimited thereafter.

No truer American existed than Thoreau. His preference of his country and condition was genuine, and his aversation from English and European manners and tastes almost reached contempt. He listened impatiently to news or *bonmots* gleaned from London circles; and though he tried to be civil, these anecdotes fatigued him. The men were all imitating each other, and on a small mould. Why can they not live as far apart as possible, and each be a man by himself? What he sought was the most energetic nature; and he wished to go to Oregon, not to London. "In every part of Great Britain," he wrote in his diary, "are discovered traces of the Romans, their funereal urns, their camps, their roads, their dwellings. But New England, at least, is not based on any Roman ruins. We have not to lay the foundations of our houses on the ashes of a former civilization."

But idealist as he was, standing for abolition of slavery, abolition of tariffs, almost for abolition of government, it is needless to say he found himself not only unrepresented in actual politics, but almost equally opposed to every class of reformers. Yet he paid the tribute of his uniform respect to the Anti-Slavery party. One man, whose personal acquaintance he had formed, he honored with exceptional regard. Before the first friendly word had been spoken for Captain John Brown, he sent notices to most houses in Concord that he would speak in a public hall on the condition and character of John Brown, on Sunday evening, and invited all people to come. The Republican Committee, the Abolitionist Committee, sent him word that it was premature and not advisable. He replied,—"I did not send to you for advice, but to announce that I am to speak." The hall was filled at an early hour by people of all parties, and his earnest eulogy of the hero was heard by all respectfully, by many with a sympathy that surprised themselves.

It was said of Plotinus that he was ashamed of his body, and 't is very likely he had good reason for it,—that his body was a bad servant, and he had not skill in dealing with the material world, as happens often to men of abstract intellect. But Mr. Thoreau was equipped with a most adapted and serviceable body. He was of short stature, firmly built, of light complexion, with strong, serious blue eyes, and a grave aspect,—his face covered in the late years with a becoming beard. His senses were acute, his frame well-knit and hardy, his hands strong and skilful in the use of tools. And there was a wonderful fitness of body and mind. He could pace sixteen rods more accurately than another man could measure them with rod and chain. He could find his path in the woods at night, he said, better by his feet than his eyes. He could estimate the measure of a tree very well by his eye; he could estimate the weight of a calf or a pig, like a dealer. From a box containing a bushel or more of loose pencils, he could take up with his hands fast enough just a dozen pencils at every grasp. He was a good swimmer, runner, skater, boatman, and would probably outwalk most countrymen in a day's journey. And the relation of body to mind was still finer than we have indicated. He said he wanted every stride his legs made. The length of his walk uniformly made the length of his writing. If shut up in the house he did not write at all.

He had a strong common sense, like that which Rose Flammock, the weaver's daughter in Scott's romance, commends in her father, as resembling a yardstick, which, whilst it measures dowlas and diaper, can equally well measure tapestry and cloth of gold. He had always a new resource. When I was planting forest trees, and had procured half a peck of acorns, he said that only a small portion of them would be sound, and proceeded to examine them and select the sound ones. But finding this took time, he said, "I think if you put them all into water the good ones will sink;" which experiment we tried with success. He could plan a garden or a house or a barn; would have been competent to lead a "Pacific Exploring Expedition;" could give judicious counsel in the gravest private or public affairs.

He lived for the day, not cumbered and mortified by his

memory. If he brought you yesterday a new proposition, he would bring you to-day another not less revolutionary. A very industrious man, and setting, like all highly organized men, a high value on his time, he seemed the only man of leisure in town, always ready for any excursion that promised well, or for conversation prolonged into late hours. His trenchant sense was never stopped by his rules of daily prudence, but was always up to the new occasion. He liked and used the simplest food, yet, when some one urged a vegetable diet, Thoreau thought all diets a very small matter, saying that "the man who shoots the buffalo lives better than the man who boards at the Graham House." He said,—"You can sleep near the railroad, and never be disturbed: Nature knows very well what sounds are worth attending to, and has made up her mind not to hear the railroad-whistle. But things respect the devout mind, and a mental ecstasy was never interrupted." He noted what repeatedly befell him, that, after receiving from a distance a rare plant, he would presently find the same in his own haunts. And those pieces of luck which happen only to good players happened to him. One day, walking with a stranger, who inquired where Indian arrow-heads could be found, he replied, "Everywhere," and stooping forward, picked one on the instant from the ground. At Mount Washington, in Tuckerman's Ravine, Thoreau had a bad fall, and sprained his foot. As he was in the act of getting up from his fall, he saw for the first time the leaves of the *Arnica mollis*.

His robust common sense, armed with stout hands, keen perceptions and strong will, cannot yet account for the superiority which shone in his simple and hidden life. I must add the cardinal fact, that there was an excellent wisdom in him, proper to a rare class of men which showed him the material world as a means and symbol. This discovery, which sometimes yields to poets a certain casual and interrupted light, serving for the ornament of their writing, was in him an unsleeping insight; and whatever faults or obstructions of temperament might cloud it, he was not disobedient to the heavenly vision. In his youth, he said, one day, "The other world is all my art; my pencils will draw no other; my jack-knife will cut nothing else; I do not use it as a means." This was the muse and genius that ruled his opinions, conversation, studies, work and course of life. This made him a searching judge of men. At first glance he measured his companion, and, though insensible to some fine traits of culture, could very well report his weight and calibre. And this made the impression of genius which his conversation sometimes gave.

He understood the matter in hand at a glance, and saw the limitations and poverty of those he talked with, so that nothing seemed concealed from such terrible eyes. I have repeatedly known young men of sensibility converted in a moment to the belief that this was the man they were in search of, the man of men, who could tell them all they should do. His own dealing with them was never affectionate, but superior, didactic, scorning their petty ways,—very slowly conceding, or not conceding at all, the promise of his society at their houses, or even at his own. "Would he not walk with them?" "He did not know. There was nothing so important to him as his walk; he had no walks to throw away on company." Visits were offered him from respectful parties, but he declined them. Admiring friends offered to carry him at their own cost to the Yellowstone River, —to the West Indies,—to South America. But though nothing could be more grave or considered than his refusals, they remind one, in quite new relations, of that fop Brummel's reply to the gentleman who offered him his carriage in a shower, "But where will *you* ride, then?"—and what accusing silences, and what searching and irresistible speeches, battering down all defenses, his companions can remember!

Mr. Thoreau dedicated his genius with such entire love to the fields, hills and waters of his native town, that he made them known and interesting to all reading Americans, and to people over the sea. The river on whose banks he was born and died he knew from its springs to its confluence with the Merrimack. He had made summer and winter observations on it for many years, and at every hour of the day and night. The result of the recent survey of the Water Commissioners appointed by the State of Massachusetts he had reached by his private experiments, several years earlier. Every fact which occurs in the bed, on the banks or in the air over it; the fishes, and their spawning and nests, their manners, their food; the shad-flies which fill the air on a certain evening once a year, and which are snapped at by the fishes so ravenously that many of these die of repletion; the conical heaps of small stones on the river-shallows, the huge nests of small fishes, one of which will sometimes overfill a cart; the birds which frequent the stream, heron, duck, sheldrake, loon, osprey; the snake, muskrat, otter, woodchuck and fox, on the banks; the turtle, frog, hyla and cricket, which make the banks vocal,—were all known to him, and, as it were, townsmen and fellow creatures; so that he felt an absurdity or violence in any narrative of one of these by itself apart, and still more of its dimensions on an inch-rule, or in the exhibition of its skeleton, or the specimen of a squirrel or a bird in brandy. He liked to speak of the manners of the river, as itself a lawful creature, yet with exactness, and always to an observed fact. As he knew the river, so the ponds in this region.

One of the weapons he used, more important to him than microscope or alcohol-receiver to other investigators, was a whim which grew on him by indulgence, yet appeared in gravest statement, namely, of extolling his own town and neighborhood as the most favored centre for natural observation. He remarked that the Flora of Massachusetts embraced almost all the important plants of America,—most of the oaks, most of the willows, the best pines, the ash, the maple, the beech, the nuts. He returned Kane's Arctic Voyage to a friend of whom he had borrowed it, with the remark, that "Most of the phenomena noted might be observed in Concord." He seemed a little envious of the Pole, for the coincident sunrise and sunset, or five minutes' day after six months: a splendid fact, which Annursnuc had never afforded him. He found red snow in one of his walks, and told me that he expected to find yet the *Victoria regia* in Concord. He was the attorney of the indigenous plants, and owned to a preference of the weeds to the imported plants, as of the Indian to the civilized man, and noticed, with pleasure, that the willow bean-poles of his neighbor had grown more than his beans. "See these weeds," he said, "which have been hoed at by a million farmers all spring and summer, and yet have prevailed, and just now come out triumphant over all lanes, pastures, fields and gardens, such is their vigor. We have insulted them with low names, too,—as Pigweed, Wormwood, Chickweed, Shad-blossom." He says, "They have brave names, too,—Ambrosia, Stellaria, Amelanchier, Amaranth, etc."

I think his fancy for referring everything to the meridian of Concord did not grow out of any ignorance or depreciation of other longitudes or latitudes, but was rather a playful expression of his conviction of the indifferency of all places, and that the best place for each is where he stands. He expressed it once in this wise: "I think nothing is to be hoped from you, if this bit of mould under your feet is not sweeter to you to eat than any other in this world, or in any world."

The other weapon with which he conquered all obstacles in science was patience. He knew how to sit immovable, a part of the rock he rested on, until the bird, the reptile, the fish, which had retired from him, should come back and resume its habits, nay, moved by curiosity, should come to him and watch him.

It was a pleasure and a privilege to walk with him. He knew the country like a fox or a bird, and passed through it as freely by paths of his own. He knew every track in the snow or on the ground, and what creature had taken this path before him. One must submit abjectly to such a guide, and the reward was great. Under his arm he carried an old music-book to press plants; in his pocket, his diary and pencil, a spy-glass for birds, microscope, jack-knife and twine. He wore a straw hat, stout shoes, strong gray trousers, to brave scrub-oaks and smilax, and to climb a tree for a hawk's or a squirrel's nest. He waded into the pool for the waterplants, and his strong legs were no insignificant part of his armor. On the day I speak of he looked for the Menyanthes, detected it across the wide pool, and, on examination of the florets, decided that it had been in flower five days. He drew out of his breast-pocket his diary, and read the names of all the plants that should bloom on this day, whereof he kept account as a banker when his notes fall due. The Cypripedium not due till to-morrow. He thought that, if waked up from a trance, in this swamp, he could tell by the plants what time of the year it was within two days. The red-start was flying about, and presently the fine grosbeaks, whose brilliant scarlet "makes the rash gazer wipe his eye," and whose fine clear note Thoreau compared to that of a tanager which has got rid of its hoarseness. Presently he heard a note which he called that of the night-warbler, a bird he had never identified, had been in search of twelve years, which always, when he saw it, was in the act of diving down into a tree or bush, and which it was vain to seek; the only bird which sings indifferently by night and by day. I told him he must beware of finding and booking it, lest life should have nothing more to show him. He said, "What you seek in vain for, half your life, one day you come full upon, all the family at dinner. You seek it like a dream, and as soon as you find it you become its prey."

His interest in the flower or the bird lay very deep in his mind, was connected with Nature,—and the meaning of Nature was never attempted to be defined by him. He would not offer a memoir of his observations to the Natural History Society. "Why should I? To detach the description from its connections in my mind would make it no longer true or valuable to me: and they do not wish what belongs to it." His power of observation seemed to indicate additional senses. He saw as with microscope, heard as with ear-trumpet, and his memory was a photographic register of all he saw and heard. And yet none knew better than he that it is not the fact that imports, but the impression or effect of the fact on your mind. Every fact lay in glory in his mind, a type of the order and beauty of the whole.

His determination on Natural History was organic. He confessed that he sometimes felt like a hound or a panther, and, if born among Indians, would have been a fell hunter. But, restrained by his Massachusetts culture, he played out the game in this mild form of botany and ichthyology. His intimacy with animals suggested what Thomas Fuller records of Butler the apiologist, that "either he had told the bees things or the bees had told him." Snakes coiled round his legs; the fishes swam into his hand, and he took them out of the water; he pulled the woodchuck out of its hole by the tail, and took the foxes under his protection from the hunters. Our naturalist had perfect magnanimity; he had no secrets: he would carry you to the heron's haunt, or even to his most prized botanical swamp,—possibly knowing that you could never find it again, yet willing to take his risks.

No college ever offered him a diploma, or a professor's chair; no academy made him its corresponding secretary, its discoverer or even its member. Perhaps these learned bodies feared the satire of his presence. Yet so much knowledge of Nature's secret and genius few others possessed; none in a more large and religious synthesis. For not a particle of respect had he to the opinions of any man or body of men, but homage solely to the truth itself; and as he discovered everywhere among doctors some leaning of courtesy, it discredited them. He grew to be revered and admired by his townsmen, who had at first known him only as an oddity. The farmers who employed him as a surveyor soon discovered his rare accuracy and skill, his knowledge of their lands, of trees, of birds, of Indian remains and the like, which enabled him to tell every farmer more than he knew before of his own farm; so that he began to feel a little as if Mr. Thoreau had better rights in his land than he. They felt, too, the superiority of character which addressed all men with a native authority.

Indian relics abound in Concord,—arrow-heads, stone chisels, pestles and fragments of pottery; and on the river-bank, large heaps of clam-shells and ashes mark spots which the savages frequented. These, and every circumstance touching the Indian, were important in his eyes. His visits to Maine were chiefly for love of the Indian. He had the satisfaction of seeing the manufacture of the bark canoe, as well as of trying his hand in its management on the rapids. He was inquisitive about the making of the stone arrow-head, and in his last days charged a youth setting out for the Rocky Mountains to find an Indian who could tell him that: "It was well worth a visit to California to learn it." Occasionally, a small party of Penobscot Indians would visit Concord, and pitch their tents for a few weeks in summer on the river-bank. He failed not to make acquaintance with the best of them; though he well knew that asking questions of Indians is like catechizing beavers and rabbits. In his last visit to Maine he had great satisfaction from Joseph Polis, an intelligent Indian of Oldtown, who was his guide for some weeks.

He was equally interested in every natural fact. The depth of his perception found likeness of law throughout Nature, and I know not any genius who so swiftly inferred universal law from the single fact. He was no pedant of a department. His eyes was open to beauty, and his ear to music. He found these, not in rare conditions, but wheresoever he went. He thought the best of music was in single strains; and he found poetic suggestion in the humming of the telegraph-wire.

His poetry might be bad or good; he no doubt wanted a lyric facility and technical skill, but he had the source of poetry in his spiritual perception. He was a good reader and critic, and his judgment on poetry was to the ground of it. He could not be deceived as to the presence or absence of the poetic element in any composition, and his thirst for this made him negligent and perhaps scornful of superficial graces. He would pass by many delicate rhythms; but he would have detected every live stanza or line in a volume and knew very well where to find an equal poetic charm in prose. He was so enamoured of the spiritual beauty that he held all actual written poems in very light esteem in the comparison. He admired Æschylus and Pindar; but when some one was commending them, he said that Æschylus and the Greeks, in describing Apollo and Orpheus, had given no song, or no good one. "They ought not to have moved trees, but to have chanted to the gods such a hymn as would have sung all their old ideas out of their heads, and new ones in." His own verses are often rude and defective. The gold does not yet run pure, is drossy and crude. The thyme and marjoram are not yet honey. But if he want lyric fineness and technical merits, if he have not the poetic temperament, he never lacks the causal thought, showing that his genius was better than his talent. He knew the worth of the Imagination for the uplifting and consolation of human life, and liked to throw every thought into a symbol. The fact you tell is of no value, but only the impression. For this reason his presence was poetic, always piqued the curiosity to know more deeply the secrets of his mind. He had many reserves, an unwillingness to exhibit to profane eyes what was still sacred in his own, and knew well how to throw a poetic veil over his experience. All readers of Walden will remember his mythical record of his disappointments:—

"I long ago lost a hound, a bay horse and a turtle-dove, and am still on their trail. Many are the travellers I have spoken concerning them, describing their tracks, and what calls they answered to. I have met one or two who have heard the hound, and the tramp of the horse, and even seen the dove disappear behind a cloud; and they seemed as anxious to recover them as if they had lost them themselves."

His riddles were worth the reading, and I confide that if at any time I do not understand the expression, it is yet just. Such was the wealth of his truth that it was not worth his while to use words in vain. His poem entitled "Sympathy" reveals the tenderness under that triple steel of stoicism, and the intellectual subtility it could animate. His classic poem on "Smoke" suggests Simonides, but is better than any poem of Simonides. His biography is in his verses. His habitual thought makes all his poetry a hymn to the Cause of causes, the Spirit which vivifies and controls his own:—

"I hearing get, who had but ears,
And sight, who had but eyes before;
I moments live, who lived but years,
And truth discern, who knew but learning's lore."

And still more in these religious lines:—

"Now chiefly is my natal hour,
And only now my prime of life;

I will not doubt the love untold,
Which not my worth nor want have bought,
Which wooed me young, and wooes me old,
And to this evening hath me brought."

Whilst he used in his writings a certain petulance of remark in reference to churches or churchmen, he was a person of a rare, tender and absolute religion, a person incapable of any profanation, by act or by thought. Of course, the same isolation which belonged to his original thinking and living detached him from the social religious forms. This is neither to be censured nor regretted. Aristotle long ago explained it, when he said, "One who surpasses his fellow citizens in virtue is no longer a part of the city. Their law is not for him, since he is a law to himself."

Thoreau was sincerity itself, and might fortify the convictions of prophets in the ethical laws by his holy living. It was an affirmative experience which refused to be set aside. A truth-speaker he, capable of the most deep and strict conversation; a physician to the wounds of any soul; a friend, knowing not only the secret of friendship, but almost worshipped by those few persons who resorted to him as their confessor and prophet, and knew the deep value of his mind and great heart. He thought that without religion or devotion of some kind nothing great was ever accomplished: and he thought that the bigoted sectarian had better bear this in mind.

His virtues, of course, sometimes ran into extremes. It was easy to trace to the inexorable demand on all for exact truth that austerity which made this willing hermit more solitary even than he wished. Himself of a perfect probity, he required not less of others. He had a disgust at crime, and no worldly success would cover it. He detected paltering as readily in dignified and prosperous persons as in beggars, and with equal scorn. Such dangerous frankness was in his dealing that his admirers called him "that terrible Thoreau," as if he spoke when silent, and was still present when he had departed. I think the severity of his ideal interfered to deprive him of a healthy sufficiency of human society.

The habit of a realist to find things the reverse of their appearance inclined him to put every statement in a paradox. A certain habit of antagonism defaced his earlier writings,—a trick of rhetoric not quite outgrown in his later, of substituting for the obvious word and thought its diametrical opposite. He praised wild mountains and winter forests for their domestic air, in snow and ice he would find sultriness, and commended the wilderness for resembling Rome and Paris. "It was so dry, that you might call it wet."

The tendency to magnify the moment, to read all the laws of Nature in the one object or one combination under your eye, is of course comic to those who do not share the philosopher's perception of identity. To him there was no such thing as size. The pond was a small ocean; the Atlantic, a large Walden Pond. He referred every minute fact to cosmical laws. Though he meant to be just, he seemed haunted by a certain chronic assumption that the science of the day pretended completeness, and he had just found out that the *savans* had neglected to discriminate a particular botanical variety, had failed to describe the seeds or count the sepals. "That is to say," we replied, "the blockheads were not born in Concord; but who said they were? It was their unspeakable misfortune to be born in London, or Paris, or Rome; but, poor fellows, they did what they could, considering that they never saw Bateman's Pond, or Nine-Acre Corner, or Becky Stow's Swamp; besides, what were you sent into the world for, but to add this observation?"

Had his genius been only contemplative, he had been fitted to his life, but with his energy and practical ability he seemed born for great enterprise and for command; and I so much regret the loss of his rare powers of action, that I cannot help counting it a fault in him that he had no ambition. Wanting this, instead of engineering for all America, he was the captain of a huckleberry-party. Pounding beans is good to the end of pounding empires one of these days; but if, at the end of years, it is still only beans!

But these foibles, real or apparent, were fast vanishing in the incessant growth of a spirit so robust and wise, and which effaced its defeats with new triumphs. His study of Nature was a perpetual ornament to him, and inspired his friends with curiosity to see the world through his eyes, and to hear his adventures. They possessed every kind of interest.

He had many elegancies of his own, whilst he scoffed at conventional elegance. Thus, he could not bear to hear the sound of his own steps, the grit of gravel; and therefore never willingly walked in the road, but in the grass, on mountains and in woods. His senses were acute, and he remarked that by night every dwelling-house gives out bad air, like a slaughter-house. He liked the pure fragrance of melilot. He honored certain plants with special regard, and, over all, the pond-lily,—then, the gentian, and the *Mikania scandens*, and "life-everlasting," and a bass-tree which he visited every year when it bloomed, in the middle of July. He thought the scent a more oracular inquisition than the sight,—more oracular and trustworthy. The scent, of course, reveals what is concealed from the other senses. By it he detected earthiness. He delighted in echoes, and said they were almost the only kind of kindred voices that he heard. He loved Nature so well, was so happy in her solitude, that he became very jealous of cities and the sad work which their refinements and artifices made with man and his dwelling. The axe was always destroying his forest. "Thank God," he said, "they cannot cut down the clouds!" "All kinds of figures are drawn on the blue ground with this fibrous white paint."

I subjoin a few sentences taken from his unpublished manuscripts, not only as records of his thought and feeling, but for their power of description and literary excellence:—

"Some circumstantial evidence is very strong, as when you find a trout in the milk."

"The chub is a soft fish, and tastes like boiled brown paper salted."

"The youth gets together his materials to build a bridge to the moon, or, perchance, a palace or temple on the earth, and, at length the middle-aged man concludes to build a wood-shed with them."

"The locust z-ing."

"Devil's-needles zigzagging along the Nut-Meadow brook."

"Sugar is not so sweet to the palate as sound to the healthy ear."

"I put on some hemlock-boughs, and the rich salt crackling of their leaves was like mustard to the ear, the crackling of uncountable regiments. Dead trees love the fire."

"The bluebird carries the sky on his back."

"The tanager flies through the green foliage as if it would ignite the leaves."

"If I wish for a horse-hair for my compass-sight I must go to the stable; but the hair-bird, with her sharp eyes, goes to the road."

"Immortal water, alive even to the superficies."

"Fire is the most tolerable third party."

"Nature made ferns for pure leaves, to show what she could do in that line."

"No tree has so fair a bole and so handsome an instep as the beech."

"How did these beautiful rainbow-tints get into the shell of the fresh-water clam, buried in the mud at the bottom of our dark river?"

"Hard are the times when the infant's shoes are second-foot."

"We are strictly confined to our men to whom we give liberty."

"Nothing is so much to be feared as fear. Atheism may comparatively be popular with God himself."

"Of what significance the things you can forget? A little thought is sexton to all the world."

"How can we expect a harvest of thought who have not had a seed-time of character?"

"Only he can be trusted with gifts who can present a face of bronze to expectations."

"I ask to be melted. You can only ask of the metals that they be tender to the fire that melts them. To nought else can they be tender."

There is a flower known to botanists, one of the same genus with our summer plant called "Life-Everlasting," a *Gnaphalium* like that, which grows on the most inaccessible cliffs of the Tyrolese mountains, where the chamois dare hardly venture, and which the hunter, tempted by its beauty, and by his love (for it is immensely valued by the Swiss maidens), climbs the cliffs to gather, and is sometimes found dead at the foot, with the flower in his hand. It is called by botanists the *Gnaphalium leontopodium*, but by the Swiss *Edelweisse*, which signifies *Noble Purity*. Thoreau seemed to me living in the hope to gather this plant, which belonged to him of right. The scale on which his studies proceeded was so large as to require longevity, and we were the less prepared for his sudden disappearance. The country knows not yet, or in the least part, how great a son it has lost. It seems an injury that he should leave in the midst his broken task which none else can finish, a kind of indignity to so noble a soul that he should depart out of Nature before yet he has been really shown to his peers for what he is. But he, at least, is content. His soul was made for the noblest society; he had in a short life exhausted the capabilities of this world; wherever there is knowledge, wherever there is virtue, wherever there is beauty, he will find a home.

1862

FATE

Delicate omens traced in air,
To the lone bard true witness bare;
Birds with auguries on their wings
Chanted undeceiving things,
Him to beckon, him to warn;
Well might then the poet scorn
To learn of scribe or courier
Hints writ in vaster character;
And on his mind, at dawn of day,
Soft shadows of the evening lay.
For the prevision is allied
Unto the thing so signified;
Or say, the foresight that awaits
Is the same Genius that creates.

It chanced during one winter a few years ago, that our cities were bent on discussing the theory of the Age. By an odd coincidence, four or five noted men were each reading a discourse to the citizens of Boston or New York, on the Spirit of the Times. It so happened that the subject had the same prominence in some remarkable pamphlets and journals issued in London in the same season. To me, however, the question of the times resolved itself into a practical question of the conduct of life. How shall I live? We are incompetent to solve the times. Our geometry cannot span the huge orbits of the prevailing ideas, behold their return and reconcile their opposition. We can only obey our own polarity. 'T is fine for us to speculate and elect our course, if we must accept an irresistible dictation.

In our first steps to gain our wishes we come upon immovable limitations. We are fired with the hope to reform men. After many experiments we find that we must begin earlier,—at school. But the boys and girls are not docile; we can make nothing of them. We decide that they are not of good stock. We must begin our reform earlier still,—at generation: that is to say, there is Fate, or laws of the world.

But if there be irresistible dictation, this dictation understands itself. If we must accept Fate, we are not less compelled to affirm liberty, the significance of the individual, the grandeur of duty, the power of character. This is true, and that other is true. But our geometry cannot span these extreme points and reconcile them. What to do? By obeying each thought frankly, by harping, or, if you will, pounding on each string, we learn at last its power. By the same obedience to other thoughts we learn theirs, and then comes some reasonable hope of harmonizing them. We are sure that, though we know not how, necessity does comport with liberty, the individual with the world, my polarity with the spirit of the times. The riddle of the age has for each a private solution. If one would study his own time, it must be by this method of taking up in turn each of the leading topics which belong to our scheme of human life, and by firmly stating all that is agreeable to experience on one, and doing the same justice to the opposing facts in the others, the true limitations will appear. Any excess of emphasis on one part would be corrected, and a just balance would be made.

But let us honestly state the facts. Our America has a bad name for superficialness. Great men, great nations, have not been boasters and buffoons, but perceivers of the terror of life, and have manned themselves to face it. The Spartan, embodying his religion in his country, dies before its majesty without a question. The Turk, who believes his doom is written on the iron leaf in the moment when he entered the world, rushes on the enemy's sabre with undivided will. The Turk, the Arab, the Persian, accepts the foreordained fate:—

> "On two days, it steads not to run from thy grave,
> The appointed, and the unappointed day;
> On the first, neither balm nor physican can save,
> Nor thee, on the second, the Universe slay."

The Hindoo under the wheel is as firm. Our Calvinists in the last generation had something of the same dignity. They felt that the weight of the Universe held them down to their place. What could *they* do? Wise men feel that there is something which cannot be talked or voted away,—a strap or belt which girds the world:—

> "The Destinee, ministre general,
> That executeth in the world over al,
> The purveiance that God hath seen beforne,
> So strong it is, that though the world had sworne
> The contrary of a thing by yea or nay,
> Yet sometime it shall fallen on a day
> That falleth not oft in a thousand yeer;
> For certainly, our appetités here,
> Be it of warre, or pees, or hate, or love,
> All this is ruled by the sight above."
>
> CHAUCER: *The Knighte's Tale.*

The Greek Tragedy expressed the same sense. "Whatever is fated that will take place. The great immense mind of Jove is not to be transgressed."

Savages cling to a local god of one tribe or town. The broad ethics of Jesus were quickly narrowed to village theologies, which preach an election or favoritism. And now and then an amiable parson, like Jung Stilling or Robert Huntington, believes in a pistareen-Providence, which, whenever the good man wants a dinner, makes that somebody shall knock at his door and leave a half-dollar. But Nature is no sentimentalist,—does not cosset or pamper us. We must see that the world is rough and surly, and will not mind drowning a man or a woman, but swallows your ship like a grain of dust. The cold, inconsiderate of persons, tingles your blood, benumbs your feet, freezes a man like an apple. The diseases, the elements, fortune, gravity, lightning, respect no persons. The way of Providence is a little rude. The habit of snake and spider, the snap of the tiger and other leapers and bloody jumpers, the crackle of the bones of his prey in the coil of the anaconda,—these are in the system, and our habits are like theirs. You have just dined, and however scrupulously the slaughter-house is concealed in the graceful distance of miles, there is complicity, expensive races,—race living at the expense of race. The planet is liable to shocks from comets, perturbations from planets, rendings from earthquake and volcano, alterations of climate, precessions of equinoxes. Rivers dry up by opening of the forest. The sea changes its bed. Towns and counties fall into it. At Lisbon an earthquake killed men like flies. At Naples three years ago ten thousand persons were crushed in a few minutes. The scurvy at sea, the sword of the climate in the west of Africa, at Cayenne, at Panama, at New Orleans, cut off men like a massacre. Our western prairie shakes with fever and ague. The cholera, the small-pox, have proved as mortal to some tribes as a frost to the crickets, which, having filled the summer with noise, are silenced by a fall of the temperature of one night. Without uncovering what does not concern us, or counting how many species of parasites hang on a bombyx, or groping after intestinal parasites or infusory biters, or the obscurities of alternate generation,—the forms of the shark, the *labrus*, the jaw of the sea-wolf paved with crushing teeth, the weapons of the grampus, and other warriors hidden in the sea, are hints of ferocity in the interiors of nature. Let us not deny it up and down. Providence has a wild, rough, incalculable road to its end, and it is of no use to try to whitewash its huge, mixed instrumentalities, or to dress up that terrific benefactor in a clean shirt and white neckcloth of a student in divinity.

Will you say, the disasters which threaten mankind are exceptional, and one need not lay his account for cataclysms every day? Aye, but what happens once may happen again, and so long as these strokes are not to be parried by us they must be feared.

But these shocks and ruins are less destructive to us than the stealthy power of other laws which act on us daily. An expense of ends to means is fate;—organization tyrannizing over character. The menagerie, or forms and powers of the spine, is a book of fate; the bill of the bird, the skull of the snake, determines tyranically its limits. So is the scale of races, of temperaments; so is sex; so is climate; so is the reaction of talents imprisoning the vital power in certain directions. Every spirit makes its house; but afterwards the house confines the spirit.

The gross lines are legible to the dull; the cabman is phrenologist so far, he looks in your face to see if his shilling is sure. A dome of brow denotes one thing, a pot-belly another; a squint, a pug-nose, mats of hair, the pigment of the epidermis, betray character. People seem sheathed in their tough organization. Ask Spurzheim, ask the doctors, ask Quetelet if temperaments decide nothing?—or if there be anything they do not decide? Read the description in medical books of the four temperaments and you will think you are reading your own thoughts which you had not yet told. Find the part which black eyes and which blue eyes play severally in the company. How shall a man escape from his ancestors, or draw off from his veins the black drop which he drew from his father's or his mother's life? It often appears in a family as if all the qualities of the progenitors were potted in several jars,—some ruling quality in each son or daughter of the house; and sometimes the unmixed temperament, the rank unmitigated elixir, the family vice is drawn off in a separate individual and the others are proportionally relieved. We sometimes see a change of expression in our companion and say his father or his mother comes to the windows of his eyes, and sometimes a remote relative. In different hours a man represents each of several of his ancestors, as if there were seven or eight of us rolled up in each man's skin,—seven or eight ancestors at least; and they constitute the variety of notes for that new piece of music which his life is. At the corner of the street you read the possibility of each passenger in the facial angle, in the complexion, in the depth of his eye. His parentage determines it. Men are what their mothers made them. You may as well ask a loom which weaves huckabuck why it does not make cashmere, as expect poetry from this engineer, or a chemical discovery from that jobber. Ask the digger in the ditch to explain Newton's laws; the fine organs of his brain have been pinched by overwork and squalid poverty from father to son for a hundred years. When each comes forth from his mother's womb, the gate of gifts closes behind him. Let him value his hands and feet, he has but one pair. So he has but one future, and that is already predetermined in his lobes and described in that little fatty face, pig-eye, and squat form. All the privilege and all the legislation of the world cannot meddle or help to make a poet or a prince of him.

Jesus said, "When he looketh on her, he hath committed adultery." But he is an adulterer before he has yet looked on the woman, by the superfluity of animal and the defect of thought in his constitution. Who meets him, or who meets her, in the street, sees that they are ripe to be each other's victim.

In certain men digestion and sex absorb the vital force, and the stronger these are, the individual is so much weaker. The more of these drones perish, the better for the hive. If, later, they give birth to some superior individual, with force enough to add to this animal a new aim and a complete apparatus to work it out, all the ancestors are gladly forgotten. Most men and most women are merely one couple more. Now and then one has a new cell or camarilla opened in his brain,—an architectural, a musical, or a philological knack; some stray taste or talent for flowers, or chemistry, or pigments, or story-telling; a good hand for drawing, a good foot for dancing, an athletic frame for wide journeying, etc.—which skill nowise alters rank in the scale of nature, but serves to pass the time; the life of sensation going on as before. At last these hints and tendencies are fixed in one or in a succession. Each absorbs so much food and force as to become itself a new center. The new talent draws off so rapidly the vital force that not enough remains for the animal functions, hardly enough for health; so that in the second generation, if the like genius appear, the health is visibly deteriorated and the generative force impaired.

People are born with the moral or with the material bias;—uterine brothers with this diverging destination; and I suppose, with high magnifiers, Mr. Frauenhofer or Dr. Carpenter might come to distinguish in the embryo, at the fourth day,—this is a Whig, and that a Freesoiler.

It was a poetic attempt to lift this mountain of Fate, to reconcile this despotism of race with liberty, which led the Hindoos to say, "Fate is nothing but the deeds committed in a prior state of existence." I find the coincidence of the extremes of Eastern and Western speculation in the daring statement of Schelling, "There is in every man a certain feeling that he has been what he is from all eternity, and by no means became such in time." To say it less sublimely,—in the history of the individual is always an account of his condition, and he knows himself to be a party to his present estate.

A good deal of our politics is physiological. Now and then a man of wealth in the heyday of youth adopts the tenet of broadest freedom. In England there is always some man of wealth and large connection, planting himself, during all his years of health, on the side of progress, who, as soon as he begins to die, checks his forward play, calls in his troops and becomes conservative. All conservatives are such from personal defects. They have been effeminated by position or nature, born halt and blind, through luxury of their parents, and can only, like invalids, act on the defensive. But strong natures, backwoodsmen, New Hampshire giants, Napoleons, Burkes, Broughams, Websters, Kossuths, are inevitable patriots, until their life ebbs and their defects and gout, palsy and money, warp them.

The strongest idea incarnates itself in majorities and nations, in the healthiest and strongest. Probably the election goes by avoirdupois weight, and if you could weigh bodily the tonnage of any hundred of the Whig and the Democratic party in a town on the Dearborn balance, as they passed the hay-scales, you could predict with certainty which party would carry it. On the whole it would be rather the speediest way of deciding the vote, to put the selectmen or the mayor and aldermen at the hay-scales.

In science we have to consider two things: power and circumstance. All we know of the egg, from each successive discovery, is, *another vesicle;* and if, after five hundred years you get a better observer or a better glass, he finds, within the last observed, another. In vegetable and animal tissue it is just alike, and all that the primary power or spasm operates is still vesicles, vesicles. Yes,—but the tyrannical Circumstance! A vesicle in new circumstances, a vesicle lodged in darkness,

Oken thought, became animal; in light, a plant. Lodged in the parent animal, it suffers changes which end in unsheathing miraculous capability in the unaltered vesicle, and it unlocks itself to fish, bird, or quadruped, head and foot, eye and claw. The Circumstance is Nature. Nature is what you may do. There is much you may not. We have two things,—the circumstance, and the life. Once we thought positive power was all. Now we learn that negative power, or circumstance, is half. Nature is the tyrannous circumstance, the thick skull, the sheathed snake, the ponderous, rock-like jaw; necessitated activity; violent direction; the conditions of a tool, like the locomotive, strong enough on its track, but which can do nothing but mischief off of it; or skates, which are wings on the ice but fetters on the ground.

The book of Nature is the book of Fate. She turns the gigantic pages,—leaf after leaf,—never re-turning one. One leaf she lays down, a floor of granite; then a thousand ages, and a bed of slate; a thousand ages, and a measure of coal; a thousand ages, and a layer of marl and mud: vegetable forms appear; her first misshapen animals, zoöphyte, trilobium, fish; then, saurians,—rude forms, in which she has only blocked her future statue, concealing under these unwieldy monsters the fine type of her coming king. The face of the planet cools and dries, the races meliorate, and man is born. But when a race has lived its term, it comes no more again.

The population of the world is a conditional population; not the best, but the best that could live now; and the scale of tribes, and the steadiness with which victory adheres to one tribe and defeat to another, is as uniform as the superposition of strata. We know in history what weight belongs to race. We see the English, French, and Germans planting themselves on every shore and market of America and Australia, and monopolizing the commerce of these countries. We like the nervous and victorious habit of our own branch of the family. We follow the step of the Jew, of the Indian, of the Negro. We see how much will has been expended to extinguish the Jew, in vain. Look at the unpalatable conclusions of Knox, in his

Fragment of Races;—a rash and unsatisfactory writer, but charged with pungent and unforgettable truths. "Nature respects race, and not hybrids." "Every race has its own *habitat*." "Detach a colony from the race, and it deteriorates to the crab." See the shades of the picture. The German and Irish millions, like the Negro, have a great deal of guano in their destiny. They are ferried over the Atlantic and carted over America, to ditch and to drudge, to make corn cheap and then to lie down prematurely to make a spot of green grass on the prairie.

One more fagot of these adamantine bandages is the new science of Statistics. It is a rule that the most casual and extraordinary events, if the basis of population is broad enough, become matter of fixed calculation. It would not be safe to say when a captain like Bonaparte, a singer like Jenny Lind, or a navigator like Bowditch would be born in Boston; but, on a population of twenty or two hundred millions, something like accuracy may be had.

'Tis frivolous to fix pedantically the date of particular inventions. They have all been invented over and over fifty times. Man is the arch machine of which all these shifts drawn from himself are toy models. He helps himself on each emergency by copying or duplicating his own structure, just so far as the need is. 'Tis hard to find the right Homer, Zoroaster, or Menu; harder still to find the Tubal Cain, or Vulcan, or Cadmus, or Copernicus, or Fust, or Fulton; the indisputable inventor. There are scores and centuries of them. "The air is full of men." This kind of talent so abounds, this constructive tool-making efficiency, as if it adhered to the chemic atoms; as if the air he breathes were made of Vaucansons, Franklins, and Watts.

Doubtless in every million there will be an astronomer, a mathematician, a comic poet, a mystic. No one can read the history of astronomy without perceiving that Copernicus, Newton, Laplace, are not new men, or a new kind of men, but that Thales, Anaximenes, Hipparchus, Empedocles, Aristarchus, Pythagoras, Œnipodes, had anticipated them; each had the same tense geometrical brain, apt for the same vigorous computation and logic; a mind parallel to the movement of the world. The Roman mile probably rested on a measure of a degree of the meridian. Mahometan and Chinese know what we know of leap-year, of the Gregorian calendar, and of the precession of the equinoxes. As in every barrel of cowries brought to New Bedford there shall be one *orangia*, so there will, in a dozen millions of Malays and Mahometans, be one or two astronomical skulls. In a large city, the most casual things, and things whose beauty lies in their casualty, are produced as punctually and to order as the baker's muffin for breakfast. Punch makes exactly one capital joke a week; and the journals contrive to furnish one good piece of news every day.

And not less work the laws of repression, the penalities of violated functions. Famine, typhus, frost, war, suicide and effete races must be reckoned calculable parts of the system of the world.

These are pebbles from the mountain, hints of the terms by which our life is walled up, and which show a kind of mechanical exactness, as of a loom or mill in what we call casual or fortuitous events.

The force with which we resist these torrents of tendency looks so ridiculously inadequate that it amounts to little more than a criticism or protest made by a minority of one, under compulsion of millions. I seemed in the height of a tempest to see men overboard struggling in the waves, and driven about here and there. They glanced intelligently at each other, but 'twas little they could do for one another; 'twas much if each could keep afloat alone. Well, they had a right to their eyebeams, and all the rest was Fate.

We cannot trifle with this reality, this cropping-out in our planted gardens of the core of the world. No picture of life can have any veracity that does not admit the odious facts. A man's power is hooped in by a necessity which, by many experiments, he touches on every side until he learns its arc.

The element running through entire nature, which we popularly call Fate, is known to us as limitation. Whatever limits us we call Fate. If we are brute and barbarous, the fate takes a brute and dreadful shape. As we refine, our checks become finer. If we rise to spiritual culture, the antagonism takes a spiritual form. In the Hindoo fables, Vishnu follows Maya through all her ascending changes, from insect and crawfish up to elephant; whatever form she took, he took the male form of that kind, until she became at last woman and goddess, and he a man and a god. The limitations refine as the soul purifies, but the ring of necessity is always perched at the top.

When the gods in the Norse heaven were unable to bind the Fenris Wolf with steel or with weight of mountains,—the one he snapped and the other he spurned with his heel,—they put round his foot a limp band softer than silk or cobweb, and this held him; the more he spurned it the stiffer it drew. So soft and so stanch is the ring of Fate. Neither brandy, nor nectar, nor sulphuric ether, nor hell-fire, nor ichor, nor poetry, nor genius, can get rid of this limp band. For if we give it the high sense in which the poets use it, even thought itself is not above Fate; that too must act according to eternal laws, and all that is wilful and fantastic in it is in opposition to its fundamental essence.

And last of all, high over thought, in the world of morals, Fate appears as vindicator, levelling the high, lifting the low, requiring justice in man, and always striking soon or late when justice is not done. What is useful will last, what is hurtful will sink. "The doer must suffer," said the Greeks; "you would soothe a Deity not to be soothed." "God himself cannot procure good for the wicked," said the Welsh triad. "God may consent, but only for a time," said the bard of Spain. The limitation is impassable by any insight of man. In its last and loftiest ascensions, insight itself and the freedom of the will is one of its obedient members. But we must not run into generalizations too large, but show the natural bounds or essential distinctions, and seek to do justice to the other elements as well.

Thus we trace Fate in matter, mind, and morals; in race, in retardations of strata, and in thought and character as well. It is everywhere bound or limitation. But Fate has its lord; limitation its limits,—is different seen from above and from below, from within and from without. For though Fate is immense, so is Power, which is the other fact in the dual world, immense. If Fate follows and limits Power, Power attends and antagonizes Fate. We must respect Fate as natural history, but there is more than natural history. For who and what is this criticism that pries into the matter? Man is not order of nature, sack and sack, belly and members, link in a chain, nor any ignominious baggage; but a stupendous antagonism, a dragging together of the poles of the Universe. He betrays his relation to what is below him,—thick-skulled, small-brained, fishy, quadrumanous, quadruped ill-disguised, hardly escaped into biped,—and has paid for the new powers by loss of some of the old ones. But the lightning which explodes and fashions planets, maker of planets and suns, is in him. On one side elemental order, sandstone and granite, rock-ledges, peat-bog, forest, sea and shore; and on the other part thought, the spirit which composes and decomposes nature,—here they are, side by side, god and devil, mind and matter, king and conspirator, belt and spasm, riding peacefully together in the eye and brain of every man.

Nor can he blink the freewill. To hazard the contradiction,—freedom is necessary. If you please to plant yourself on the side of Fate, and say, Fate is all; then we say, a part of Fate is the freedom of man. Forever wells up the impulse of choosing and acting in the soul. Intellect annuls Fate. So far as a man thinks, he is free. And though nothing is more disgusting than the crowing about liberty by slaves, as most men are, and the flippant mistaking for freedom of some paper preamble like a Declaration of Independence or the statute right to vote, by those who have never dared to think or to act,—yet it is wholesome to man to look not at Fate, but the other way: the practical view is the other. His sound relation to these facts is to use and command, not to cringe to them. "Look not on Nature, for her name is fatal," said the oracle. The too much contemplation of these limits induces meanness. They who talk much of destiny, their birth-star, etc., are in a lower dangerous plane, and invite the evils they fear.

I cited the instinctive and heroic races as proud believers in Destiny. They conspire with it; a loving resignation is with the event. But the dogma makes a different impression when it is held by the weak and lazy. 'T is weak and vicious people who cast the blame on Fate. The right use of Fate is to bring up our conduct to the loftiness of nature. Rude and invincible except by themselves are the elements. So let man be. Let him empty his breast of his windy conceits, and show his lordship by manners and deeds on the scale of nature. Let him hold his purpose as with the tug of gravitation. No power, no persuasion, no bribe shall make him give up his point. A man ought to compare advantageously with a river, an oak, or a mountain. He shall have not less the flow, the expansion, and the resistance of these.

'T is the best use of Fate to teach a fatal courage. Go face the fire at sea, or the cholera in your friend's house, or the burglar in your own, or what danger lies in the way of duty,—knowing you are guarded by the cherubim of Destiny. If you believe in Fate to your harm, believe it at least for your good.

For if Fate is so prevailing, man also is part of it, and can confront fate with fate. If the Universe have these savage accidents, our atoms are as savage in resistance. We should be crushed by the atmosphere, but for the reaction of the air within the body. A tube made of a film of glass can resist the shock of the ocean if filled with the same water. If there be omnipotence in the stroke, there is omnipotence of recoil.

1. But Fate against Fate is only parrying and defence: there are also the noble creative forces. The revelation of Thought takes man out of servitude into freedom. We rightly say of ourselves, we were born and afterward we were born again, and many times. We have successive experiences so important that the new forgets the old, and hence the mythology of the seven or the nine heavens. The day of days, the great day of the feast of life, is that in which the inward eye opens to the Unity in things, to the omnipresence of law:—sees that what is must be and ought to be, or is the best. This beatitude dips from on high down on us and we see. It is not in us so much as

we are in it. If the air come to our lungs, we breathe and live; if not, we die. If the light come to our eyes, we see; else not. And if truth come to our mind we suddenly expand to its dimensions, as if we grew to worlds. We are as lawgivers; we speak for Nature; we prophesy and divine.

This insight throws us on the party and interest of the Universe, against all and sundry; against ourselves as much as others. A man speaking from insight affirms of himself what is true of the mind: seeing its immortality, he says, I am immortal; seeing its invincibility, he says, I am strong. It is not in us, but we are in it. It is of the maker, not of what is made. All things are touched and changed by it. This uses and is not used. It distances those who share it from those who share it not. Those who share it not are flocks and herds. It dates from itself; not from former men or better men, gospel, or constitution or college, or custom. Where it shines, Nature is no longer intrusive, but all things make a musical or pictorial impression. The world of men show like a comedy without laughter: populations, interests, government, history; 't is all toy figures in a toy house. It does not overvalue particular truths. We hear eagerly every thought and word quoted from an intellectual man. But in his presence our own mind is roused to activity, and we forget very fast what he says, much more interested in the new play of our own thought than in any thought of his. 'T is the majesty into which we have suddenly mounted, the impersonality, the scorn of egotisms, the sphere of laws, that engage us. Once we were stepping a little this way and a little that way; now we are as men in a balloon, and do not think so much of the point we have left, or the point we would make, as of the liberty and glory of the way.

Just as much intellect as you add, so much organic power. He who sees through the design, presides over it, and must will that which must be. We sit and rule, and, though we sleep, our dream will come to pass. Our thought, though it were only an hour old, affirms an oldest necessity, not to be separated from thought, and not to be separated from will. They must always have coexisted. It apprises us of its sovereignty and godhead, which refuse to be severed from it. It is not mine or thine, but the will of all mind. It is poured into the souls of all men, as the soul itself which constitutes them men. I know not whether there be, as is alleged, in the upper region of our atmosphere, a permanent westerly current which carries with it all atoms which rise to that height, but I see that when souls reach a certain clearness of perception they accept a knowledge and motive above selfishness. A breath of will blows eternally through the universe of souls in the direction of the Right and Necessary. It is the air which all intellects inhale and exhale, and it is the wind which blows the worlds into order and orbit.

Thought dissolves the material universe by carrying the mind up into a sphere where all is plastic. Of two men, each obeying his own thought, he whose thought is deepest will be the strongest character. Always one man more than another represents the will of Divine Providence to the period.

2. If thought makes free, so does the moral sentiment. The mixtures of spiritual chemistry refuse to be analyzed. Yet we can see that with the perception of truth is joined the desire that it shall prevail; that affection is essential to will. Moreover, when a strong will appears, it usually results from a certain unity of organization, as if the whole energy of body and mind flowed in one direction. All great force is real and elemental. There is no manufacturing a strong will. There must be a pound to balance a pound. Where power is shown in will, it must rest on the universal force. Alaric and Bonaparte must believe they rest on a truth, or their will can be bought or bent. There is a bribe possible for any finite will. But the pure sympathy with universal ends is an infinite force, and cannot be bribed or bent. Whoever has had experience of the moral sentiment cannot choose but believe in unlimited power. Each pulse from that heart is an oath from the Most High. I know not what the word *sublime* means, if it be not the intimations, in this infant, of a terrific force. A text of heroism, a name and anecdote of courage, are not arguments but sallies of freedom. One of these is the verse of the Persian Hafiz, "'T is written on the gate of Heaven, 'Woe unto him who suffers himself to be betrayed by

Fate!'" Does the reading of history make us fatalists? What courage does not the opposite opinion show! A little whim of will to be free gallantly contending against the universe of chemistry.

But insight is not will, nor is affection will. Perception is cold, and goodness dies in wishes. As Voltaire said, 't is the misfortune of worthy people that they are cowards; "un des plus grands malheurs, des honnêtes gens c'est qu'ils sont des lâches." There must be a fusion of these two to generate the energy of will. There can be no driving force except through the conversion of the man into his will, making him the will, and the will him. And one may say boldly that no man has a right perception of any truth who has not been reacted on by it so as to be ready to be its martyr.

The one serious and formidable thing in nature is a will. Society is servile from want of will, and therefore the world wants saviours and religions. One way is right to go; the hero sees it, and moves on that aim, and has the world under him for root and support. He is to others as the world. His approbation is honor; his dissent, infamy. The glance of his eye has the force of sunbeams. A personal influence towers up in memory only worthy, and we gladly forget numbers, money, climate, gravitation, and the rest of Fate.

We can afford to allow the limitation, if we know it is the meter of the growing man. We stand against Fate, as children stand up against the wall in their father's house and notch their height from year to year. But when the boy grows to man, and is master of the house, he pulls down that wall and builds a new and bigger. 'T is only a question of time. Every brave youth is in training to ride and rule this dragon. His science is to make weapons and wings of these passions and retarding forces. Now whether, seeing these two things, fate and power, we are permitted to believe in unity? The bulk of mankind believe in two gods. They are under one dominion here in the house, as friend and parent, in social circles, in letters, in art, in love, in religion; but in mechanics, in dealing with steam and climate, in trade, in politics, they think they come under another; and that it would be a practical blunder to transfer the method and way of working of one sphere into the other. What good, honest, generous men at home, will be wolves and foxes on 'Change! What pious men in the parlor will vote for what reprobates at the polls! To a certain point, they believe themselves the care of a Providence. But in a steamboat, in an epidemic, in war, they believe a malignant energy rules.

But relation and connection are not somewhere and sometimes, but everywhere and always. The divine order does not stop where their sight stops. The friendly power works on the same rules in the next farm and the next planet. But where they have not experience they run against it and hurt themselves. Fate then is a name for facts not yet passed under the fire of thought; for causes which are unpenetrated.

But every jet of chaos which threatens to exterminate us is convertible by intellect into wholesome force. Fate is unpenetrated causes. The water drowns ship and sailor like a grain of dust. But learn to swim, trim your bark, and the wave which drowned it will be cloven by it and carry it like its own foam, a plume and a power. The cold is inconsiderate of persons, tingles your blood, freezes a man like a dew-drop. But learn to skate, and the ice will give you a graceful, sweet, and poetic motion. The cold will brace your limbs and brain to genius, and make you foremost men of time. Cold and sea will train an imperial Saxon race, which nature cannot bear to lose, and after cooping it up for a thousand years in yonder England, gives a hundred Englands, a hundred Mexicos. All the bloods it shall absorb and domineer: and more than Mexicos, the secrets of water and steam, the spasms of electricity, the ductility of metals, the chariot of the air, the ruddered balloon are awaiting you.

The annual slaughter from typhus far exceeds that of war; but right drainage destroys typhus. The plague in the sea-service from scurvy is healed by lemon juice and other diets portable or procurable; the depopulation by cholera and small-pox is ended by drainage and vaccination; and every other pest is not less in the chain of cause and effect, and may be fought off. And whilst art draws out the venom, it commonly extorts some benefit from the vanquished enemy. The mischievous torrent is taught to drudge for man; the wild beasts he makes useful for food, or dress, or labor; the chemic explosions are controlled like his watch. These are now the steeds on which he rides. Man moves in all modes, by legs of horses, by wings of wind, by steam, by gas of balloon, by electricity, and stands on tiptoe threatening to hunt the eagle in his own element. There's nothing he will not make his carrier.

Steam was till the other day the devil which we dreaded. Every pot made by any human potter or brazier had a hole in its cover, to let off the enemy, lest he should lift pot and roof and carry the house away. But the Marquis of Worcester, Watt, and Fulton bethought themselves that where was power was not devil, but was God; that it must be availed of, and not by any means let off and wasted. Could he lift pots and roofs and houses so handily? He was the workman they were in search of. He could be used to lift away, chain and compel other devils far more reluctant and dangerous, namely, cubic miles of earth, mountains, weight or resistance of water, machinery, and the labors of all men in the world; and time he shall lengthen, and shorten space.

It has not fared much otherwise with higher kinds of steam. The opinion of the million was the terror of the world, and it was attempted either to dissipate it, by amusing nations, or to pile it over with strata of society,—a layer of soldiers, over that a layer of lords, and a king on the top; with clamps and hoops of castles, garrisons, and police. But sometimes the religious principle would get in and burst the hoops and rive every mountain laid on top of it. The Fultons and Watts of politics, believing in unity, saw that it was a power, and by satisfying it (as justice satisfies everybody), through a different disposition of society,—grouping it on a level instead of piling it into a mountain,—they have contrived to make of this terror the most harmless and energetic form of a State.

Very odious, I confess, are the lessons of Fate. Who likes to have a dapper phrenologist pronouncing on his fortunes? Who likes to believe that he has, hidden in his skull, spine, and pelvis, all the vices of a Saxon or Celtic race, which will be sure to pull him down,—with what grandeur of hope and resolve he is fired,—into a selfish, huckstering, servile, dodging animal? A learned physician tells us the fact is invariable with the Neapolitan, that when mature he assumes the forms of the unmistakable scoundrel. That is a little overstated,—but may pass.

But these are magazines and arsenals. A man must thank his defects, and stand in some terror of his talents. A transcendent talent draws so largely on his forces as to lame him; a defect pays him revenues on the other side. The sufferance which is the badge of the Jew, has made him, in these days, the ruler of the rulers of the earth. If Fate is ore and quarry, if evil is good in the making, if limitation is power that shall be, if calamities, oppositions, and weights are wings and means,—we are reconciled.

Fate involves the melioration. No statement of the Universe can have any soundness which does not admit its ascending effort. The direction of the whole and of the parts is toward benefit, and in proportion to the health. Behind every individual closes organization; before him opens liberty,—the Better, the Best. The first and worse races are dead. The second and imperfect races are dying out, or remain for the maturing of higher. In the latest race, in man, every generosity, every new perception, the love and praise he extorts from his fellows, are certificates of advance out of fate into freedom. Liberation of the will from the sheaths and clogs of organization which he has outgrown, is the end and aim of this world. Every calamity is a spur and valuable hint; and where his endeavors do not yet fully avail, they tell as tendency. The whole circle of animal life —tooth against tooth, devouring war, war for food, a yelp of pain and a grunt of triumph, until at last the whole menagerie, the whole chemical mass is mellowed and refined for higher use —pleases at a sufficient perspective.

But to see how fate slides into freedom and freedom into fate, observe how far the roots of every creature run, or find if you can a point where there is no thread of connection. Our life is consentaneous and far-related. This knot of nature is so well tied that nobody was ever cunning enough to find the two ends. Nature is intricate, overlapped, interweaved and endless. Christopher Wren said of the beautiful King's College chapel, that "if anybody would tell him where to lay the first stone, he would build such another." But where shall we find the first atom in this house of man, which is all consent, inosculation and balance of parts?

The web of relation is shown in *habitat*, shown in hibernation. When hibernation was observed, it was found that whilst some animals became torpid in winter, others were torpid in summer: hibernation then was a false name. The *long sleep* is not an effect of cold, but is regulated by the supply of food proper to the animal. It becomes torpid when the fruit or prey it lives on is not in season, and regains its activity when its food is ready.

Eyes are found in light; ears in auricular air; feet on land; fins in water; wings in air; and each creature where it was meant to be, with a mutual fitness. Every zone has its own *Fauna*. There is adjustment between the animal and its food, its parasite, its enemy. Balances are kept. It is not allowed to diminish in numbers, nor to exceed. The like adjustments exist for man. His food is cooked when he arrives; his coal in the pit; the house ventilated; the mud of the deluge dried; his companions arrived at the same hour, and awaiting him with love, concert, laughter and tears. These are coarse adjustments, but the invisible are not less. There are more belongings to every creature than his air and his food. His instincts must be met, and he has predisposing power that bends and fits what is near him to his use. He is not possible until the invisible things are right for him, as well as the visible. Of what changes then in sky and earth, and in finer skies and earths, does the appearance of some Dante or Columbus apprise us!

How is this effected? Nature is no spendthrift, but takes the shortest way to her ends. As the general says to his soldiers, "If you want a fort, build a fort," so nature makes every creature do its own work and get its living,—is it planet, animal or tree. The planet makes itself. The animal cell makes itself;—then, what it wants. Every creature, wren or dragon, shall make its own lair. As soon as there is life, there is self-direction and absorbing and using of material. Life is freedom,—life in the direct ratio of its amount. You may be sure the new-born man is not inert. Life works both voluntarily and supernaturally in its neighborhood. Do you suppose he can be estimated by his weight in pounds, or that he is contained in his skin,—this reaching, radiating, jaculating fellow? The smallest candle fills a mile with its rays, and the papillæ of a man run out to every star.

When there is something to be done, the world knows how to get it done. The vegetable eye makes leaf, pericarp, root, bark, or thorn, as the need is; the first cell converts itself into stomach, mouth, nose, or nail, according to the want; the world throws its life into a hero or a shepherd, and puts him where he is wanted. Dante and Columbus were Italians, in their time; they would be Russians or Americans to-day. Things ripen, new men come. The adaptation is not capricious. The ulterior aim, the purpose beyond itself, the correlation by which planets subside and crystallize, then animate beasts and men,—will not stop but will work into finer particulars, and from finer to finest.

The secret of the world is the tie between person and event. Person makes event, and event person. The "times," "the age," what is that but a few profound persons and a few active persons who epitomize the times?—Goethe, Hegel, Metternich, Adams, Calhoun, Guizot, Peel, Cobden, Kossuth, Rothschild, Astor, Brunel, and the rest. The same fitness must be presumed between a man and the time and event, as between the sexes, or between a race of animals and the food it eats, or the inferior races it uses. He thinks his fate alien, because the copula is hidden. But the soul contains the event that shall befall it; for the event is only the actualization of its thoughts, and what we pray to ourselves for is always granted. The event is the print of your form. It fits you like your skin. What each does is proper to him. Events are the children of his body and mind. We learn that the soul of Fate is the soul of us, as Hafiz sings,—

> "Alas! till now I had not known,
> My guide and fortune's guide are one."

All the toys that infatuate men and which they play for,—houses, land, money, luxury, power, fame, are the selfsame thing, with a new gauze or two of illusion overlaid. And of all the drums and rattles by which men are made willing to have their heads broke, and are led out solemnly every morning to parade,—the most admirable is this by which we are brought to believe that events are arbitrary and independent of actions. At the conjuror's, we detect the hair by which he moves his puppet, but we have not eyes sharp enough to descry the thread that ties cause and effect.

Nature magically suits the man to his fortunes, by making these the fruit of his character. Ducks take to the water, eagles to the sky, waders to the sea margin, hunters to the forest, clerks to counting-rooms, soldiers to the frontier. Thus events grow on the same stem with persons; are sub-persons. The pleasure of life is according to the man that lives it, and not according to the work or the place. Life is an ecstasy. We know what madness belongs to love,—what power to paint a vile object in hues of heaven. As insane persons are indifferent to their dress, diet, and other accommodations, and as we do in dreams, with equanimity, the most absurd acts, so a drop more of wine in our cup of life will reconcile us to strange company and work. Each creature puts forth from itself its own condition and sphere, as the slug sweats out its slimy house on the pear-leaf, and the woolly aphides on the apple perspire their own bed, and the fish its shell. In youth we clothe ourselves with rainbows and go as brave as the zodiac. In age we put out another sort of perspiration,—gout, fever, rheumatism, caprice, doubt, fretting and avarice.

A man's fortunes are the fruit of his character. A man's friends are his magnetisms. We go to Herodotus and Plutarch for examples of Fate; but we are examples. "*Quisque suos pati-*

mur manes." The tendency of every man to enact all that is in his constitution is expressed in the old belief that the efforts which we make to escape from our destiny only serve to lead us into it: and I have noticed a man likes better to be complimented on his position, as the proof of the last or total excellence, than on his merits.

A man will see his character emitted in the events that seem to meet, but which exude from and accompany him. Events expand with the character. As once he found himself among toys, so now he plays a part in colossal systems, and his growth is declared in his ambition, his companions and his performance. He looks like a piece of luck, but is a piece of causation; the mosaic, angulated and ground to fit into the gap he fills. Hence in each town there is some man who is, in his brain and performance, an explanation of the tillage, production, factories, banks, churches, ways of living and society of that town. If you do not chance to meet him, all that you see will leave you a little puzzled; if you see him it will become plain. We know in Massachusetts who built New Bedford, who built Lynn, Lowell, Lawrence, Clinton, Fitchburg, Holyoke, Portland, and many another noisy mart. Each of these men, if they were transparent, would seem to you not so much men as walking cities, and wherever you put them they would build one.

History is the action and reaction of these two,—Nature and Thought; two boys pushing each other on the curbstone of the pavement. Everything is pusher or pushed; and matter and mind are in perpetual tilt and balance, so. Whilst the man is weak, the earth takes up him. He plants his brain and affections. By and by he will take up the earth, and have his gardens and vineyards in the beautiful order and productiveness of his thought. Every solid in the universe is ready to become fluid on the approach of the mind, and the power to flux it is the measure of the mind. If the wall remain adamant, it accuses the want of thought. To a subtle force it will stream into new forms, expressive of the character of the mind. What is the city in which we sit here, but an aggregate of incongruous materials which have obeyed the will of some man? The granite was reluctant, but his hands were stronger, and it came. Iron was deep in the ground and well combined with stone, but could not hide from his fires. Wood, lime, stuffs, fruits, gums, were dispersed over the earth and sea, in vain. Here they are, within reach of every man's day-labor,—what he wants of them. The whole world is the flux of matter over the wires of thought to the poles or points where it would build. The races of men rise out of the ground preoccupied with a thought which rules them, and divided into parties ready armed and angry to fight for this metaphysical abstraction. The quality of the thought differences the Egyptian and the Roman, the Austrian and the American. The men who come on the stage at one period are all found to be related to each other. Certain ideas are in the air. We are all impressionable, for we are made of them; all impressionable, but some more than others, and these first express them. This explains the curious contemporaneousness of inventions and discoveries. The truth is in the air, and the most impressionable brain will announce it first, but all will announce it a few minutes later. So women, as most susceptible, are the best index of the coming hour. So the great man, that is, the man most imbued with the spirit of the time, is the impressionable man;—of a fibre irritable and delicate, like iodine to light. He feels the infinitesimal attractions. His mind is righter than others because he yields to a current so feeble as can be felt only by a needle delicately poised.

The correlation is shown in defects. Möller, in his Essay on Architecture, taught that the building which was fitted accurately to answer its end would turn out to be beautiful though beauty had not been intended. I find the like unity in human structures rather virulent and pervasive; that a crudity in the blood will appear in the argument; a hump in the shoulder will appear in the speech and handiwork. If his mind could be seen, the hump would be seen. If a man has a see-saw in his voice, it will run into his sentences, into his poem, into the structure of his fable, into his speculation, into his charity. And as every man is hunted by his own dæmon, vexed by his own disease, this checks all his activity.

So each man, like each plant, has his parasites. A strong, astringent, bilious nature has more truculent enemies than the slugs and moths that fret my leaves. Such an one has curculios, borers, knifeworms; a swindler ate him first, then a client, then a quack, then smooth, plausible gentlemen, bitter and selfish as Moloch.

This correlation really existing can be divined. If the threads are there, thought can follow and show them. Especially when a soul is quick and docile, as Chaucer sings:—

> "Or if the soule of proper kind
> Be so parfite as men find,
> That it wot what is to come,
> And that he warneth all and some
> Of everiche of hir aventures,
> By avisions or figures;
> But that our flesh hath no might
> To understand it aright
> For it is warned too derkely."

Some people are made up of rhyme, coincidence, omen, periodicity, and presage: they meet the person they seek; what their companion prepares to say to them, they first say to him; and a hundred signs apprise them of what is about to befall.

Wonderful intricacy in the web, wonderful constancy in the design this vagabond life admits. We wonder how the fly finds its mate, and yet year after year, we find two men, two women, without legal or carnal tie, spend a great part of their best time within a few feet of each other. And the moral is that what we seek we shall find; what we flee from flees from us; as Goethe said, "what we wish for in youth, comes in heaps on us in old age," too often cursed with the granting of our prayer: and hence the high caution, that since we are sure of having what we wish, we beware to ask only for high things.

One key, one solution to the mysteries of human condition, one solution to the old knots of fate, freedom, and foreknowledge, exists; the propounding, namely, of the double consciousness. A man must ride alternately on the horses of his private and his public nature, as the equestrians in the circus throw themselves nimbly from horse to horse, or plant one foot on the back of one and the other foot on the back of the other. So when a man is the victim of his fate, has sciatica in his loins and cramp in his mind; a club-foot and a club in his wit; a sour face and a selfish temper; a strut in his gait and a conceit in his affection; or is ground to powder by the vice of his race;—he is to rally on his relation to the Universe, which his ruin benefits. Leaving the dæmon who suffers, he is to take sides with the Deity who secures universal benefit by his pain.

To offset the drag of temperament and race, which pulls down, learn this lesson, namely, that by the cunning co-presence of two elements, which is throughout nature, whatever lames or paralyzes you draws in with it the divinity, in some form, to repay. A good intention clothes itself with sudden power. When a god wishes to ride, any chip or pebble will bud and shoot out winged feet and serve him for a horse.

Let us build altars to the Blessed Unity which holds nature and souls in perfect solution, and compels every atom to serve an universal end. I do not wonder at a snow-flake, a shell, a summer landscape, or the glory of the stars; but at the necessity of beauty under which the universe lies; that all is and must be pictorial; that the rainbow and the curve of the horizon and the arch of the blue vault are only results from the organism of the eye. There is no need for foolish amateurs to fetch me to admire a garden of flowers, or a sun-gilt cloud, or a waterfall, when I cannot look without seeing splendor and grace. How idle to choose a random sparkle here or there, when the indwelling necessity plants the rose of beauty on the brow of chaos, and discloses the central intention of Nature to be harmony and joy.

Let us build altars to the Beautiful Necessity. If we thought men were free in the sense that in a single exception one fantastical will could prevail over the law of things, it were all one as if a child's hand could pull down the sun. If in the least particular one could derange the order of nature,—who would accept the gift of life?

Let us build altars to the Beautiful Necessity, which secures that all is made of one piece; that plaintiff and defendant, friend and enemy, animal and planet, food and eater are of one kind. In astronomy is vast space but no foreign system; in geology, vast time but the same laws as to-day. Why should we be afraid of Nature, which is no other than "philosophy and theology embodied"? Why should we fear to be crushed by savage elements, we who are made up of the same elements? Let us build to the Beautiful Necessity, which makes man brave in believing that he cannot shun a danger that is appointed, nor incur one that is not; to the Necessity which rudely or softly educates him to the perception that there are no contingencies; that Law rules throughout existence; a Law which is not intelligent but intelligence;—not personal nor impersonal—it disdains words and passes understanding; it dissolves persons; it vivifies nature; yet solicits the pure in heart to draw on all its omnipotence.

1851–3 1860

ILLUSIONS

Flow, flow the waves hated,
Accursed, adored,
The waves of mutation:
No anchorage is.
Sleep is not, death is not;
Who seem to die live.
House you were born in,
Friends of your spring-time,
Old man and young maid,
Day's toil and its guerdon,
They are all vanishing,
Fleeing to fables,
Cannot be moored.
See the stars through them,
Through treacherous marbles.
Know, the stars yonder,
The stars everlasting,
Are fugitive also,
And emulate, vaulted,
The lambent heat-lightning,
And fire-fly's flight.

When thou dost return
On the wave's circulation,
Beholding the shimmer,
The wild dissipation,
And, out of endeavor
To change and to flow,
The gas become solid,
And phantoms and nothings
Return to be things,
And endless imbroglio
Is law and the world,—
Then first shalt thou know,

That in the wild turmoil,
Horsed on the Proteus,
Thou ridest to power,
And to endurance.

Some years ago, in company with an agreeable party, I spent a long summer day in exploring the Mammoth Cave in Kentucky. We traversed, through spacious galleries affording a solid masonry foundation for the town and country overhead, the six or eight black miles from the mouth of the cavern to the innermost recess which tourists visit,—a niche or grotto made of one seamless stalactite, and called, I believe, Serena's Bower. I lost the light of one day. I saw high domes and bottomless pits; heard the voice of unseen waterfalls; paddled three quarters of a mile in the deep Echo River, whose waters are peopled with the blind fish; crossed the streams "Lethe" and "Styx;" plied with music and guns the echoes in these alarming galleries; saw every form of stalagmite and stalactite in the sculptured and fretted chambers;—icicle, orange-flower, acanthus, grapes and snowball. We shot Bengal lights into the vaults and groins of the sparry cathedrals and examined all the masterpieces which the four combined engineers, water, limestone, gravitation and time, could make in the dark.

The mysteries and scenery of the cave had the same dignity that belongs to all natural objects, and which shames the fine things to which we foppishly compare them. I remarked especially the mimetic habit with which nature, on new instruments, hums her old tunes, making night to mimic day, and chemistry to ape vegetation. But I then took notice and still chiefly remember that the best thing which the cave had to offer was an illusion. On arriving at what is called the "Star-Chamber," our lamps were taken from us by the guide and extinguished or put aside, and, on looking upwards, I saw or seemed to see the night heaven thick with stars glimmering more or less brightly over our heads, and even what seemed a comet flaming among them. All the party were touched with astonishment and pleasure. Our musical friends sung with much feeling a pretty song, "The stars are in the quiet sky," etc., and I sat down on the rocky floor to enjoy the serene picture. Some crystal specks in the black ceiling high overhead, reflecting the light of a half-hid lamp, yielded this magnificent effect.

I own I did not like the cave so well for eking out its sublimities with this theatrical trick. But I have had many experiences like it, before and since; and we must be content to be pleased without too curiously analyzing the occasions. Our conversation with nature is not just what it seems. The cloud-rack, the sunrise and sunset glories, rainbows and Northern Lights are not quite so spheral as our childhood thought them, and the part our organization plays in them is too large. The senses interfere everywhere and mix their own structure with all they report of. Once we fancied the earth a plane, and stationary. In admiring the sunset we do not yet deduct the rounding, coördinating, pictorial powers of the eye.

The same interference from our organization creates the most of our pleasure and pain. Our first mistake is the belief that the circumstance gives the joy which we give to the circumstance. Life is an ecstasy. Life is sweet as nitrous oxide; and the fisherman dripping all day over a cold pond, the switchman at the railway intersection, the farmer in the field, the negro in the rice-swamp, the fop in the street, the hunter in the woods, the barrister with the jury, the belle at the ball, all ascribe a certain pleasure to their employment, which they themselves give it. Health and appetite impart the sweetness to sugar, bread, and meat. We fancy that our civilization has got on far, but we still come back to our primers.

We live by our imaginations, by our admirations, by our sentiments. The child walks amid heaps of illusions, which he does not like to have disturbed. The boy, how sweet to him in his fancy! how dear the story of barons and battles! What a hero he is, whilst he feeds on his heroes! What a debt is his to imaginative books! He has no better friend or influence than Scott, Shakspeare, Plutarch and Homer. The man lives to other objects, but who dare affirm that they are more real?

Even the prose of the streets is full of refractions. In the life of the dreariest alderman, fancy enters into all details and colors them with rosy hue. He imitates the air and actions of people whom he admires, and is raised in his own eyes. He pays a debt quicker to a rich man than to a poor man. He wishes the bow and compliment of some leader in the state or in society; weighs what he says; perhaps he never comes nearer to him for that, but dies at last better contented for this amusement of his eyes and his fancy.

The world rolls, the din of life is never hushed. In London, in Paris, in Boston, in San Francisco, the carnival, the masquerade is at its height. Nobody drops his domino. The unities, the fictions of the piece it would be an impertinence to break. The chapter of fascinations is very long. Great is paint; nay, God is the painter; and we rightly accuse the critic who destroys too many illusions. Society does not love its unmaskers. It was wittily if somewhat bitterly said by D'Alembert, "*qu'un état de vapeur était un état très fâcheux, parcequ'il nous faisait voir les choses comme elles sont.*" I find men victims of illusion in all parts of life. Children, youths, adults and old men, all are led by one bawble or another. Yoganidra, the goddess of illusion, Proteus, or Momus, or Gylfi's Mocking,—for the Power has many names,—is stronger than the Titans, stronger than Apollo. Few have overheard the gods or surprised their secret. Life is a succession of lessons which must be lived to be understood. All is riddle, and the key to a riddle is another riddle. There are as many pillows of illusion as flakes in a snow-storm. We wake from one dream into another dream. The toys to be sure are various, and are graduated in refinement to the quality of the dupe. The intellectual man requires a fine bait; the sots are easily amused. But everybody is drugged with his own frenzy, and the pageant marches at all hours, with music and banner and badge.

Amid the joyous troop who give in to the charivari, comes now and then a sad-eyed boy whose eyes lack the requisite refractions to clothe the show in due glory, and who is afflicted with a tendency to trace home the glittering miscellany of fruits and flowers to one root. Science is a search after identity, and the scientific whim is lurking in all corners. At the State Fair a friend of mine complained that all the varieties of fancy pears in our orchards seem to have been selected by somebody who had a whim for a particular kind of pear, and only cultivated such as had that perfume; they were all alike. And I remember the quarrel of another youth with the confectioners, that when he racked his wit to choose the best comfits in the shops, in all the endless varieties of sweetmeat he could find only three flavors, or two. What then? Pears and cakes are good for something; and because you unluckily have an eye or nose too keen, why need you spoil the comfort which the rest of us find in them? I knew a humorist who in a good deal of rattle had a grain or two of sense. He shocked the company by maintaining that the attributes of God were two,—power and risibility, and that it was the duty of every pious man to keep up the comedy. And I have known gentlemen of great stake in the community, but whose sympathies were cold,—presidents of colleges and governors and senators,—who held themselves bound to sign every temperance pledge, and act with Bible societies and missions and peace-makers, and cry *Hist-a-boy!* to every good dog. We must not carry comity too far, but we all have kind impulses in this direction. When the boys come into my yard for leave to gather horse-chestnuts, I own I enter into nature's game, and affect to grant the permission reluctantly, fearing that any moment they will find out the imposture of that showy chaff. But this tenderness is quite unnecessary; the enchantments are laid on very thick. Their young life is thatched with them. Bare and grim to tears is the lot of the children in the hovel I saw yesterday; yet not the less they hung it round with frippery romance, like the children of the happiest fortune, and talked of "the dear cottage where so many joyful hours had flown." Well, this thatching of hovels is the custom of the country. Women, more than all, are the element and kingdom of illusion. Being fascinated, they fascinate. They see through Claude-Lorraines. And how dare any one, if he could, pluck away the *coulisses*, stage effects and ceremonies, by which they live? Too pathetic, too pitiable, is the region of affection, and its atmosphere always liable to *mirage*.

We are not very much to blame for our bad marriages. We live amid hallucinations; and this especial trap is laid to trip up our feet with, and all are tripped up first or last. But the mighty Mother who had been so sly with us, as if she felt that she owed us some indemnity, insinuates into the Pandora-box of marriage some deep and serious benefits and some great joys. We find a delight in the beauty and happiness of children that makes the heart too big for the body. In the worst-assorted connections there is ever some mixture of true marriage. Teague and his jade get some just relations of mutual respect, kindly observation, and fostering of each other; learn something, and would carry themselves wiselier if they were now to begin.

'T is fine for us to point at one or another fine madman, as if there were any exempts. The scholar in his library is none. I, who have all my life heard any number of orations and debates, read poems and miscellaneous books, conversed with many geniuses, am still the victim of any new page; and if Marmaduke, or Hugh, or Moosehead, or any other, invent a new style or mythology, I fancy that the world will be all brave and right if dressed in these colors, which I had not thought of. Then at once I will daub with this new paint; but it will not stick. 'T is like the cement which the peddler sells at the door; he makes broken crockery hold with it, but you can never buy of him a bit of the cement which will make it hold when he is gone.

Men who make themselves felt in the world avail themselves of a certain fate in their constitution which they know how to use. But they never deeply interest us unless they lift a corner of the curtain, or betray, never so slightly, their penetration of what is behind it. 'T is the charm of practical men that outside of their practicality are a certain poetry and play, as if they led the good horse Power by the bridle, and preferred to walk, though they can ride so fiercely. Bonaparte is intellectual, as well as Cæsar; and the best soldiers, sea-captains and railway men have a gentleness when off duty, a good-natured admission that there are illusions, and who shall say that he is not their sport? We stigmatize the cast-iron fellows who cannot so detach themselves, as "dragon-ridden," "thunder-stricken," and fools of fate, with whatever powers endowed.

Since our tuition is through emblems and indirections, it is well to know that there is method in it, a fixed scale and rank above rank in the phantasms. We begin low with coarse masks and rise to the most subtle and beautiful. The red men told Columbus "they had an herb which took away fatigue;" but he found the illusion of "arriving from the east at the Indies" more composing to his lofty spirit than any tobacco. Is not our faith in the impenetrability of matter more sedative than narcotics? You play with jackstraws, balls, bowls, horse and gun, estates and politics; but there are finer games before you. Is not time a pretty toy? Life will show you masks that are worth all your carnivals. Yonder mountain must migrate into your mind. The fine star-dust and nebulous blur in Orion, "the portentous year of Mizar and Alcor," must come down and be dealt with in your household thought. What if you shall come to discern that the play and playground of all this pompous history are radiations from yourself, and that the sun borrows his beams? What terrible questions we are learning to ask! The former men believed in magic, by which temples, cities, and men were swallowed up, and all trace of them gone. We are coming on the secret of a magic which sweeps out of men's minds all vestige of theism and beliefs which they and their fathers held and were framed upon.

There are deceptions of the senses, deceptions of the passions, and the structural, beneficent illusions of sentiment and of the intellect. There is the illusion of love, which attributes to the beloved person all which that person shares with his or her family, sex, age or condition, nay, with the human mind itself. 'T is these which the lover loves, and Anna Matilda gets the credit of them. As if one shut up always in a tower, with one window through which the face of heaven and earth could be seen, should fancy that all the marvels he beheld belonged to that window. There is the illusion of time, which is very deep; who has disposed of it?—or come to the conviction that what seems the *succession* of thought is only the distribution of wholes into causal series? The intellect sees that every atom carries the whole of nature; that the mind opens to omnipotence; that, in the endless striving and ascents, the metamorphosis is entire, so that the soul doth not know itself in its own act when that act is perfected. There is illusion that shall deceive even the elect. There is illusion that shall deceive even the performer of the miracle. Though he make his body, he denies that he makes it. Though the world exist from thought, thought is daunted in presence of the world. One after the other we accept the mental laws, still resisting those which follow, which however must be accepted. But all our concessions only compel us to new profusion. And what avails it that science has come to treat space and time as simply forms of thought, and the material world as hypothetical, and withal our pretension of *property* and even of self-hood are fading with the rest, if, at last, even our thoughts are not finalities, but the incessant flowing and ascension reach these also, and each thought which yesterday was a finality, to-day is yielding to a larger generalization?

With such volatile elements to work in, 't is no wonder if our estimates are loose and floating. We must work and affirm, but we have no guess of the value of what we say or do. The cloud is now as big as your hand, and now it covers a county. That story of Thor, who was set to drain the drinking-horn in Asgard and to wrestle with the old woman and to run with the runner Lok, and presently found that he had been drinking up the sea, and wrestling with Time, and racing with Thought, —describes us, who are contending, amid these seeming trifles, with the supreme energies of nature. We fancy we have fallen into bad company and squalid condition, low debts, shoe-bills, broken glass to pay for, pots to buy, butcher's meat, sugar, milk and coal. "Set me some great task, ye gods! and I will show my spirit." "Not so," says the good Heaven; "plod and plough, vamp your old coats and hats, weave a shoestring;

great affairs and the best wine by and by." Well, 't is all phantasm; and if we weave a yard of tape in all humility and as well as we can, long hereafter we shall see it was no cotton tape at all but some galaxy which we braided, and that the threads were Time and Nature.

We cannot write the order of the variable winds. How can we penetrate the law of our shifting moods and susceptibility? Yet they differ as all and nothing. Instead of the firmament of yesterday, which our eyes require, it is to-day an egg-shell which coops us in; we cannot even see what or where our stars of destiny are. From day to day the capital facts of human life are hidden from our eyes. Suddenly the mist rolls up and reveals them, and we think how much good time is gone that might have been saved had any hint of these things been shown. A sudden rise in the road shows us the system of mountains, and all the summits, which have been just as near us all the year, but quite out of mind. But these alternations are not without their order, and we are parties to our various fortune. If life seem a succession of dreams, yet poetic justice is done in dreams also. The visions of good men are good; it is the undisciplined will that is whipped with bad thoughts and bad fortunes. When we break the laws, we lose our hold on the central reality. Like sick men in hospitals, we change only from bed to bed, from one folly to another; and it cannot signify much what becomes of such castaways, wailing, stupid, comatose creatures, lifted from bed to bed, from the nothing of life to the nothing of death.

In this kingdom of illusions we grope eagerly for stays and foundations. There is none but a strict and faithful dealing at home and a severe barring out of all duplicity or illusion there. Whatever games are played with us, we must play no games with ourselves, but deal in our privacy with the last honesty and truth. I look upon the simple and childish virtues of veracity and honesty as the root of all that is sublime in character. Speak as you think, be what you are, pay your debts of all kinds. I prefer to be owned as sound and solvent, and my word as good as my bond, and to be what cannot be skipped, or dissipated, or undermined, to all the *éclat* in the universe. This reality is the foundation of friendship, religion, poetry, and art. At the top or at the bottom of all illusions, I set the cheat which still leads us to work and live for appearances; in spite of our conviction, in all sane hours, that it is what we really are that avails with friends, with strangers, and with fate or fortune.

One would think from the talk of men that riches and poverty were a great matter; and our civilization mainly respects it. But the Indians say that they do not think the white man, with his brow of care, always toiling, afraid of heat and cold, and keeping within doors, has any advantage of them. The permanent interest of every man is never to be in a false position, but to have the weight of nature to back him in all that he does. Riches and poverty are a thick or thin costume; and our life—the life of all of us—identical. For we transcend the circumstance continually and taste the real quality of existence; as in our employments, which only differ in the manifestations but express the same laws; or in our thoughts, which wear no silks and taste no ice-creams. We see God face to face every hour, and know the savor of nature.

The early Greek philosophers Heraclitus and Xenophanes measured their force on this problem of identity. Diogenes of Apollonia said that unless the atoms were made of one stuff, they could never blend and act with one another. But the Hindoos, in their sacred writings, express the liveliest feeling, both of the essential identity and of that illusion which they conceive variety to be. "The notions, '*I am*,' and '*This is mine*,' which influence mankind, are but delusions of the mother of the world. Dispel, O Lord of all creatures! the conceit of knowledge which proceeds from ignorance." And the beatitude of man they hold to lie in being freed from fascination.

The intellect is stimulated by the statement of truth in a trope, and the will by clothing the laws of life in illusions. But the unities of Truth and of Right are not broken by the disguise. There need never be any confusion in these. In a crowded life of many parts and performers, on a stage of nations, or in the obscurest hamlet in Maine or California, the same elements offer the same choices to each new comer, and, according to his election, he fixes his fortune in absolute Nature. It would be hard to put more mental and moral philosophy than the Persians have thrown into a sentence,—

"Fooled thou must be, though wisest of the wise:
Then be the fool of virtue, not of vice."

There is no chance and no anarchy in the universe. All is system and gradation. Every god is there sitting in his sphere. The young mortal enters the hall of the firmament; there is he alone with them alone, they pouring on him benedictions and gifts, and beckoning him up to their thrones. On the instant, and incessantly, fall snow-storms of illusions. He fancies himself in a vast crowd which sways this way and that and whose movement and doings he must obey: he fancies himself poor, orphaned, insignificant. The mad crowd drives hither and thither, now furiously commanding this thing to be done, now that. What is he that he should resist their will, and think or act for himself? Every moment new changes and new showers of deceptions to baffle and distract him. And when, by and by, for an instant, the air clears and the cloud lifts a little, there are the gods still sitting around him on their thrones, —they alone with him alone.

c. 1851 1860

CIVILIZATION

We flee away from cities, but we bring
The best of cities with us, these learned classifiers,
Men knowing what they seek, armed eyes of experts.
We praise the guide, we praise the forest life:
But will we sacrifice our dear-bought lore
Of books and arts and trained experiment,
Or count the Sioux a match for Agassiz?
O no, not we! . . .
. . . Witness the mute all hail
The joyful traveller gives, when on the verge
Of craggy Indian wilderness he hears
From a log cabin stream Beethoven's notes
On the piano, played with master's hand.
"Well done!" he cries; "the bear is kept at bay,
The lynx, the rattlesnake, the flood, the fire:
All the fierce enemies, ague, hunger, cold,
This thin spruce roof, this clayed log wall,
This wild plantation will suffice to chase.
Now speed the gay celerities of art,
What in the desert was impossible
Within four walls is possible again,—
Culture and libraries, mysteries of skill,
Traditioned fame of masters, eager strife
Of keen competing youths, joined or alone,
To outdo each other and extort applause.
Mind wakes a new-born giant from her sleep.
Twirl the old wheels! Time takes fresh start again,
On for a thousand years of genius more."

A certain degree of progress from the rudest state in which man is found,—a dweller in caves, or on trees, like an ape,—a cannibal, and eater of pounded snails, worms and offal,—a certain degree of progress from this extreme is called Civilization. It is a vague, complex name, of many degrees. Nobody has attempted a definition. Mr. Guizot, writing a book on the subject, does not. It implies the evolution of a highly organized man, brought to supreme delicacy of sentiment, as in practical power, religion, liberty, sense of honor, and taste. In the hesitation to define what it is, we usually suggest it by negations. A nation that has no clothing, no iron, no alphabet, no marriage, no arts of peace, no abstract thought, we call barbarous. And after many arts are invented or imported, as among the Turks and Moorish nations, it is often a little complaisant to call them civilized.

Each nation grows after its own genius, and has a civilization of its own. The Chinese and Japanese, though each complete in his way, is different from the man of Madrid or the man of New York. The term imports a mysterious progress. In the brutes is none; and in mankind to-day the savage tribes are gradually extinguished rather than civilized. The Indians of this country have not learned the white man's work; and in Africa the negro of to-day is the negro of Herodotus. In other races the growth is not arrested, but the like progress that is made by a boy "when he cuts his eye-teeth," as we say,—childish illusions passing daily away and he seeing things really and comprehensively,—is made by tribes. It is the learning the secret of cumulative power, of advancing on one's self. It implies a facility of association, power to compare, the ceasing from fixed ideas. The Indian is gloomy and distressed when urged to depart from his habits and traditions. He is overpowered by the gaze of the white, and his eye sinks. The occasion of one of these starts of growth is always some novelty that astounds the mind and provokes it to dare to change. Thus there is a Cadmus, a Pytheas, a Manco Capac at the beginning of each improvement,—some superior foreigner importing new and wonderful arts, and teaching them. Of course he must not know too much, but must have the sympathy, language and gods of those he would inform. But chiefly the seashore has been the point of departure, to knowledge as to commerce. The most advanced nations are always those who navigate the most. The power which the sea requires in the sailor makes a man of him very fast, and the change of shores and population clears his head of much nonsense of his wigwam.

Where shall we begin or end the list of those feats of liberty and wit, each of which feats made an epoch of history? Thus the effect of a framed or stone house is immense on the tranquillity, power, and refinement of the builder. A man in a cave or in a camp, a nomad, will die with no more estate than the wolf or the horse leaves. But so simple a labor as a house being achieved, his chief enemies are kept at bay. He is safe from the teeth of wild animals, from frost, sun-stroke, and weather; and fine faculties begin to yield their fine harvest. Invention and art are born, manners and social beauty and delight. 'T is wonderful how soon a piano gets into a log hut on the frontier. You would think they found it under a pine stump. With it comes a Latin grammar,—and one of those tow-head boys has written a hymn on Sunday. Now let colleges, now let senates take heed! for here is one who opening these fine tastes on the basis of the pioneer's iron constitution, will gather all their laurels in his strong hands.

When the Indian trail gets widened, graded and bridged to a good road, there is a benefactor, there is a missionary, a pacificator, a wealth-bringer, a maker of markets, a vent for industry. Another step in civility is the change from war, hunting, and pasturage, to agriculture. Our Scandinavian forefathers have left us a significant legend to convey their sense of the importance of this step. "There was once a giantess who had a daughter, and the child saw a husbandman ploughing in the field. Then she ran and picked him up with her finger and thumb, and put him and his plough and his oxen into her apron, and carried them to her mother, and said, 'Mother, what sort of a beetle is this that I found wriggling in the sand?' But the mother said, 'Put it away, my child; we must begone out of this land, for these people will dwell in it.' " Another success is the post-office, with its educating energy augmented by cheapness and guarded by a certain religious sentiment in mankind; so that the power of a wafer or a drop of wax or gluten to guard a letter, as it flies over sea, over land and comes to its address as if a battalion of artillery brought it, I look upon as a fine meter of civilization.

The division of labor, the multiplication of the arts of peace, which is nothing but a large allowance to each man to choose his work according to his faculty,—to live by his better hand,—fills the State with useful and happy laborers; and they, creating demand by the very temptation of their productions, are rapidly and surely rewarded by good sale: and what a police and ten commandments their work thus becomes. So true is Dr. Johnson's remark that "men are seldom more innocently employed than when they are making money."

The skilful combinations of civil government, though they usually follow natural leadings, as the lines of race, language, religion, and territory, yet require wisdom and conduct in the rulers, and in their result delight the imagination. "We see insurmountable multitudes obeying, in opposition to their strongest passions, the restraints of a power which they scarcely perceive, and the crimes of a single individual marked and punished at the distance of half the earth."

Right position of woman in the State is another index. Poverty and industry with a healthy mind read very easily the laws of humanity, and love them: place the sexes in right relations of mutual respect, and a severe morality gives that essential charm to woman which educates all that is delicate, poetic, and self-sacrificing; breeds courtesy and learning, conversation and wit, in her rough mate; so that I have thought a sufficient measure of civilization is the influence of good women.

Another measure of culture is the diffusion of knowledge, overrunning all the old barriers of caste, and, by the cheap press, bringing the university to every poor man's door in the newsboy's basket. Scraps of science, of thought, of poetry are in the coarsest sheet, so that in every house we hesitate to burn a newspaper until we have looked it through.

The ship, in its latest complete equipment, is an abridgment and compend of a nation's arts: the ship steered by compass and chart, longitude reckoned by lunar observation and by chronometer, driven by steam; and in wildest sea-mountains, at vast distances from home,—

> "The pulses of her iron heart
> Go beating through the storm."

No use can lessen the wonder of this control by so weak a creature of forces so prodigious. I remember I watched, in crossing the sea, the beautiful skill whereby the engine in its constant working was made to produce two hundred gallons of fresh water out of salt water, every hour,—thereby supplying all the ship's want.

The skill that pervades complex details; the man that maintains himself; the chimney taught to burn its own smoke; the farm made to produce all that is consumed on it; the very prison compelled to maintain itself and yield a revenue, and, better still, made a reform school and a manufactory of honest men out of rogues, as the steamer made fresh water out of salt, —all these are examples of that tendency to combine antagonisms and utilize evil which is the index of high civilization.

Civilization is the result of highly complex organization. In the snake, all the organs are sheathed; no hands, no feet, no fins, no wings. In bird and beast the organs are released and begin to play. In man they are all unbound and full of joyful action. With this unswaddling he receives the absolute illumination we call Reason, and thereby true liberty.

Climate has much to do with this melioration. The highest civility has never loved the hot zones. Wherever snow falls there is usually civil freedom. Where the banana grows the animal system is indolent and pampered at the cost of higher qualities: the man is sensual and cruel. But this scale is not invariable. High degrees of moral sentiment control the unfavorable influences of climate; and some of our grandest examples of men and of races come from the equatorial regions,—as the genius of Egypt, of India and of Arabia.

These feats are measures or traits of civility; and temperate climate is an important influence, though not quite indispensable, for there have been learning, philosophy and art in

Iceland, and in the tropics. But one condition is essential to the social education of man, namely, morality. There can be no high civility without a deep morality, though it may not always call itself by that name, but sometimes the point of honor, as in the institution of chivalry; or patriotism, as in the Spartan and Roman republics; or the enthusiasm of some religious sect which imputes its virtue to its dogma; or the cabalism or *esprit de corps* of a masonic or other association of friends.

The evolution of a highly destined society must be moral; it must run in the grooves of the celestial wheels. It must be catholic in aims. What is *moral?* It is the respecting in action catholic or universal ends. Hear the definition which Kant gives of moral conduct: "Act always so that the immediate motive of thy will may become a universal rule for all intelligent beings."

Civilization depends on morality. Everything good in man leans on what is higher. This rule holds in small as in great. Thus all our strength and success in the work of our hands depend on our borrowing the aid of the elements. You have seen a carpenter on a ladder with a broad-axe chopping upward chips from a beam. How awkward! at what disadvantage he works! But see him on the ground, dressing his timber under him. Now, not his feeble muscles but the force of gravity brings down the axe; that is to say, the planet itself splits his stick. The farmer had much ill-temper, laziness and shirking to endure from his hand-sawyers, until one day he bethought him to put his saw-mill on the edge of a waterfall; and the river never tires of turning his wheel; the river is good-natured, and never hints an objection.

We had letters to send: couriers could not go fast enough nor far enough; broke their wagons, foundered their horses; bad roads in spring, snowdrifts in winter, heats in summer; could not get the horses out of a walk. But we found out that the air and earth were full of Electricity, and always going our way,—just the way we wanted to send. *Would he take a message?* Just as lief as not; had nothing else to do; would carry it in no time. Only one doubt occurred, one staggering objection,—he had no carpet-bag, no visible pockets, no hands, not so much as a mouth, to carry a letter. But after much thought and many experiments we managed to meet the conditions, and to fold up the letter in such invisible compact form as he could carry in those invisible pockets of his, never wrought by needle and thread,—and it went like a charm.

I admire still more than the saw-mill the skill which, on the seashore, makes the tides drive the wheels and grind corn, and which thus engages the assistance of the moon, like a hired hand, to grind, and wind, and pump, and saw, and split stone, and roll iron.

Now that is the wisdom of a man, in every instance of his labor, to hitch his wagon to a star, and see his chore done by the gods themselves. That is the way we are strong, by borrowing the might of the elements. The forces of steam, gravity, galvanism, light, magnets, wind, fire, serve us day by day and cost us nothing.

Our astronomy is full of examples of calling in the aid of these magnificent helpers. Thus, on a planet so small as ours, the want of an adequate base for astronomical measurements is early felt, as, for example, in detecting the parallax of a star. But the astronomer, having by an observation fixed the place of a star,—by so simple an expedient as waiting six months and then repeating his observation, contrived to put the diameter of the earth's orbit, say two hundred millions of miles, between his first observation and his second, and this line afforded him a respectable base for his triangle.

All our arts aim to win this vantage. We cannot bring the heavenly powers to us, but if we will only choose our jobs in directions in which they travel, they will undertake them with the greatest pleasure. It is a peremptory rule with them that *they never go out of their road.* We are dapper little busybodies and run this way and that way superserviceably; but they swerve never from their foreordained paths,—neither the sun, nor the moon, nor a bubble of air, nor a mote of dust.

And as our handiworks borrow the elements, so all our social and political action leans on principles. To accomplish anything excellent the will must work for catholic and universal ends. A puny creature, walled in on every side, as Daniel wrote,—

> "Unless above himself he can
> Erect himself, how poor a thing is man!"

but when his will leans on a principle, when he is the vehicle of ideas, he borrows their omnipotence. Gibraltar may be strong, but ideas are impregnable, and bestow on the hero their invincibility. "It was a great instruction," said a saint in Cromwell's war, "that the best courages are but beams of the Almighty." Hitch your wagon to a star. Let us not fag in paltry works which serve our pot and bag alone. Let us not lie and steal. No god will help. We shall find all their teams going the other way,—Charles's Wain, Great Bear, Orion, Leo, Hercules: every god will leave us. Work rather for those interests which the divinities honor and promote,—justice, love, freedom, knowledge, utility.

If we can thus ride in Olympian chariots by putting our works in the path of the celestial circuits, we can harness also evil agents, the powers of darkness, and force them to serve against their will the ends of wisdom and virtue. Thus a wise government puts fines and penalties on pleasant vices. What a benefit would the American government, not yet relieved of its extreme need, render to itself and to every city, village, and hamlet in the states, if it would tax whiskey and rum almost to the point of prohibition! Was it Bonaparte who said that he found vices very good patriots?—"he got five millions from the love of brandy, and he should be glad to know which of the virtues would pay him as much." Tobacco and opium have broad backs, and will cheerfully carry the load of armies, if you choose to make them pay high for such joy as they give and such harm as they do.

These are traits and measures and modes; and the true test of civilization is, not the census, nor the size of cities, nor the crops,—no, but the kind of man the country turns out. I see the vast advantages of this country, spanning the breadth of the temperate zone. I see the immense material prosperity,—towns on towns, states on states, and wealth piled in the massive architecture of cities: California quartz-mountains dumped down in New York to be repiled architecturally alongshore from Canada to Cuba, and thence westward to California again. But it is not New York streets, built by the confluence of workmen and wealth of all nations, though stretching out towards Philadelphia until they touch it, and northward until they touch New Haven, Hartford, Springfield, Worcester and Boston,—not these that make the real estimation. But when I look over this constellation of cities which animate and illustrate the land, and see how little the government has to do with their daily life, how self-helped and self-directed all families are,—knots of men in purely natural societies, societies of trade, of kindred blood, of habitual hospitality, house and house, man acting on man by weight of opinion, of longer or better-directed industry; the refining influence of women, the invitation which experience and permanent causes open to youth and labor:—when I see how much each virtuous and gifted person, whom all men consider, lives affectionately with scores of excellent people who are not known far from home, and perhaps with great reason reckons these people his superiors in virtue and in the symmetry and force of their qualities,—I see what cubic values America has, and in these a better certificate of civilization than great cities or enormous wealth.

In strictness, the vital refinements are the moral and intellectual steps. The appearance of the Hebrew Moses, of the Indian Buddh; in Greece, of the Seven Wise Masters, of the acute and upright Socrates, and of the stoic Zeno; in Judæa, the advent of Jesus, and, in modern Christendom, of the realists Huss, Savonarola, and Luther,—are casual facts which carry forward races to new convictions and elevate the rule of life. In the presence of these agencies it is frivolous to insist on the invention of printing or gunpowder, of steam-power or gas-light, percussion-caps and rubber-shoes, which are toys thrown off from that security, freedom, and exhilaration which a healthy morality creates in society. These arts add a comfort and smoothness to house and street life; but a purer morality, which kindles genius, civilizes civilization, casts backward all that we held sacred into the profane, as the flame of oil throws a shadow when shined upon by the flame of the Bude-light. Not the less the popular measures of progress will ever be the arts and the laws.

But if there be a country which cannot stand any one of these tests,—a country where knowledge cannot be diffused without perils of mob law and statute law; where speech is not free; where the post-office is violated, mail-bags opened and letters tampered with; where public debts and private debts outside of the State are repudiated; where liberty is attacked in the primary institution of social life; where the position of the white woman is injuriously affected by the outlawry of the black woman; where the arts, such as they have, are all imported, having no indigenous life; where the laborer is not secured in the earnings of his own hands; where suffrage is not free or equal;—that country is, in all these respects, not civil, but barbarous; and no advantages of soil, climate, or coast can resist these suicidal mischiefs.

Morality and all the incidents of morality are essential; as, justice to the citizen, and personal liberty. Montesquieu says: "Countries are well cultivated, not as they are fertile, but as they are free;" and the remark holds not less but more true of the culture of men than of the tillage of land. And the highest proof of civility is that the whole public action of the State is directed on securing the greatest good of the greatest number.

c. 1861 1870

EXTRACTS FROM THE JOURNALS

November 11, 1842.

Time is the little grey man who takes out of his breast-pocket first a pocketbook, then a Dollond telescope, then a Turkey carpet, then four saddled and bridled nags and a sumptuous canvas tent. We are accustomed to chemistry and it does not surprise us. But chemistry is but a name for changes and developments as wonderful as those of this Breast-Pocket.

I was a little chubby boy trundling a hoop in Chauncy Place, and spouting poetry from Scott and Campbell at the Latin School. But Time, the little grey man, has taken out of his vest-pocket a great, awkward house (in a corner of which I sit down and write of him), some acres of land, several full-grown and several very young persons, and seated them close beside me; then he has taken that chubbiness and that hoop quite away (to be sure he has left the declamation and the poetry), and here left a long, lean person threatening to be a little grey man, like himself.

May 24, 1864.

Yesterday, May 23, we buried Hawthorne in Sleepy Hollow, in a pomp of sunshine and verdure, and gentle winds. James Freeman Clarke read the service in the church and at the grave. Longfellow, Lowell, Holmes, Agassiz, Hoar, Dwight, Whipple, Norton, Alcott, Hillard, Fields, Judge Thomas, and I attended the hearse as pallbearers. Franklin Pierce was with the family. The church was copiously decorated with white flowers delicately arranged. The corpse was unwillingly shown,—only a few moments to this company of his friends. But it was noble and serene in its aspect,—nothing amiss,—a calm and powerful head. A large company filled the church and the grounds of the cemetery. All was so bright and quiet that pain or mourning was hardly suggested, and Holmes said to me that it looked like a happy meeting.

Clarke said in the church that Hawthorne had done more

justice than any other to the shades of life, shown a sympathy with the crime in our nation, and, like Jesus, was the friend of sinners.

I thought there was a tragic element in the event, that might be more fully rendered,—in the painful solitude of the man, which, I suppose, could not longer be endured, and he died of it.

June, 1864.

Within, I do not find wrinkles and used heart, but unspent youth.

EMERSON'S LAST LETTER TO CARLYLE

Baltimore, Md., 5 January, 1872.

My dear Carlyle,—I received from you through Mr. Chapman, just before Christmas, the last rich instalment of your Library Edition; viz. Vols. IV.–X. *Life of Friedrich;* Vols. I.–III. *Translations from German;* one volume *General Index;* eleven volumes in all,—and now my stately collection is perfect. Perfect too is your Victory. But I clatter my chains with joy, as I did forty years ago, at your earliest gifts. Happy man you should be, to whom the Heaven has allowed such masterly completion. You shall wear your crown at the Pan-Saxon Games with no equal or approaching competitor in sight,—well earned by genius and exhaustive labor, and with nations for your pupils and praisers. I count it my eminent happiness to have been so nearly your contemporary, and your friend,—permitted to detect by its rare light the new star almost before the Easterners had seen it, and to have found no disappointment, but joyful confirmation rather, in coming close to its orb. Rest, rest, now for a time, I pray you, and be thankful. Meantime, I know well all your perversities, and give them a wide berth. They seriously annoy a great many worthy readers, nations of readers sometimes,—but I heap them all as style, and read them as I read Rabelais's gigantic humors which astonish in order to force attention, and by and by are seen to be the rhetoric of a highly virtuous gentleman who *swears*. I have been quite too busy with fast succeeding *jobs* (I may well call them), in the last year, to have read much in these proud books; but I begin to see daylight coming through my fogs, and I have not lost in the least my appetite for reading,—resolve with my old Harvard professor, "to retire and read the Authors."

I am impatient to deserve your grand Volumes by reading in them with all the haughty airs that belong to seventy years which I shall count if I live till May, 1873. Meantime I see well that you have lost none of your power, and I wish that you would let in some good Eckermann to dine with you day by day, and be competent to report your opinions,—for you can speak as well as you can write, and what the world to come should know. . . .

Affectionately,

R. W. Emerson.

EMERSON'S POEMS

GOOD-BYE

Good-bye, proud world! I'm going home:
Thou art not my friend, and I'm not thine.
Long through thy weary crowds I roam;
A river-ark on the ocean brine,
Long I've been tossed like the driven foam;
But now, proud world! I'm going home.

Good-bye to Flattery's fawning face;
To Grandeur with his wise grimace;
To upstart Wealth's averted eye;
To supple Office, low and high;
To crowded halls, to court and street;
To frozen hearts and hasting feet;
To those who go, and those who come;
Good-bye, proud world! I'm going home.

I am going to my own hearth-stone,
Bosomed in yon green hills alone,—
A secret nook in a pleasant land,
Whose groves the frolic fairies planned;
Where arches green, the livelong day,
Echo the blackbird's roundelay,
And vulgar feet have never trod
A spot that is sacred to thought and God.

O, when I am safe in my sylvan home,
I tread on the pride of Greece and Rome;
And when I am stretched beneath the pines,
Where the evening star so holy shines,
I laugh at the lore and the pride of man,
At the sophist schools and the learned clan;
For what are they all, in their high conceit,
When man in the bush with God may meet?

1823 1839

EACH AND ALL

Little thinks, in the field, yon red-cloaked clown
Of thee from the hill-top looking down;
The heifer that lows in the upland farm,
Far-heard, lows not thine ear to charm;
The sexton, tolling his bell at noon,
Deems not that great Napoleon
Stops his horse, and lists with delight,
Whilst his files sweep round yon Alpine height;
Nor knowest thou what argument
Thy life to thy neighbor's creed has lent.
All are needed by each one;
Nothing is fair or good alone.
I thought the sparrow's note from heaven,
Singing at dawn on the alder bough;
I brought him home, in his nest, at even;
He sings the song, but it cheers not now,
For I did not bring home the river and sky;—
He sang to my ear,—they sang to my eye.
The delicate shells lay on the shore;
The bubbles of the latest wave
Fresh pearls to their enamel gave,
And the bellowing of the savage sea
Greeted their safe escape to me.
I wiped away the weeds and foam,
I fetched my sea-born treasures home;
But the poor, unsightly, noisome things
Had left their beauty on the shore
With the sun and the sand and the wild uproar.
The lover watched his graceful maid,
As 'mid the virgin train she strayed,
Nor knew her beauty's best attire
Was woven still by the snow-white choir.
At last she came to his hermitage,
Like the bird from the woodlands to the cage;—

The gay enchantment was undone,
A gentle wife, but fairy none.
Then I said, "I covet truth;
Beauty is unripe childhood's cheat;
I leave it behind with the games of youth:"—
As I spoke, beneath my feet
The ground-pine curled its pretty wreath,
Running over the club-moss burrs;
I inhaled the violet's breath;
Around me stood the oaks and firs;
Pine-cones and acorns lay on the ground;
Over me soared the eternal sky,
Full of light and of deity;
Again I saw, again I heard,
The rolling river, the morning bird;—
Beauty through my senses stole;
I yielded myself to the perfect whole.

1839

THE PROBLEM

I like a church; I like a cowl;
I love a prophet of the soul;
And on my heart monastic aisles
Fall like sweet strains, or pensive smiles;
Yet not for all his faith can see
Would I that cowlèd churchman be.

Why should the vest on him allure,
Which I could not on me endure?

Not from a vain or shallow thought
His awful Jove young Phidias brought;
Never from lips of cunning fell
The thrilling Delphic oracle;
Out from the heart of nature rolled
The burdens of the Bible old;

The litanies of nations came,
Like the volcano's tongue of flame,
Up from the burning core below,—
The canticles of love and woe:
The hand that rounded Peter's dome
And groined the aisles of Christian Rome
Wrought in a sad sincerity;
Himself from God he could not free;
He builded better than he knew;—
The conscious stone to beauty grew.

Know'st thou what wove yon woodbird's nest
Of leaves, and feathers from her breast?
Or how the fish outbuilt her shell,
Painting with morn each annual cell?
Or how the sacred pine-tree adds
To her old leaves new myriads?
Such and so grew these holy piles,
Whilst love and terror laid the tiles.
Earth proudly wears the Parthenon,
As the best gem upon her zone,
And Morning opes with haste her lids
To gaze upon the Pyramids;
O'er England's abbeys bends the sky,
As on its friends, with kindred eye;
For out of Thought's interior sphere
These wonders rose to upper air;
And Nature gladly gave them place,
Adopted them into her race,
And granted them an equal date
With Andes and with Ararat.

These temples grew as grows the grass;
Art might obey, but not surpass.
The passive Master lent his hand
To the vast soul that o'er him planned;
And the same power that reared the shrine

Bestrode the tribes that knelt within.
Ever the fiery Pentecost
Girds with one flame the countless host,
Trances the heart through chanting choirs,
And through the priest the mind inspires.
The word unto the prophet spoken
Was writ on tables yet unbroken;
The word by seers or sibyls told,
In groves of oak, or fanes of gold,
Still floats upon the morning wind,
Still whispers to the willing mind.
One accent of the Holy Ghost
The heedless world hath never lost.
I know what say the fathers wise,—
The Book itself before me lies,
Old *Chrysostom*, best Augustine,
And he who blent both in his line,
The younger *Golden Lips* or mines,
Taylor, the Shakspeare of divines.
His words are music in my ear,
I see his cowlèd portrait dear;
And yet, for all his faith could see,
I would not the good bishop be.

1839 1840

URIEL

It fell in the ancient periods
  Which the brooding soul surveys,
Or ever the wild Time coined itself
  Into calendar months and days.

This was the lapse of Uriel,
Which in Paradise befell.
Once, among the Pleiads walking,
Seyd overheard the young gods talking;
And the treason, too long pent,
To his ears was evident.

The young deities discussed
Laws of form, and metre just,
Orb, quintessence, and sunbeams,
What subsisteth, and what seems.
One, with low tones that decide,
And doubt and reverend use defied,
With a look that solved the sphere,
And stirred the devils everywhere,
Gave his sentiment divine
Against the being of a line.
"Line in nature is not found;
Unit and universe are round;
In vain produced, all rays return;
Evil will bless, and ice will burn."
As Uriel spoke with piercing eye,
A shudder ran around the sky;
The stern old war-gods shook their heads,
The seraphs frowned from myrtle-beds;
Seemed to the holy festival
The rash word boded ill to all;
The balance-beam of Fate was bent;
The bounds of good and ill were rent;
Strong Hades could not keep his own,
But all slid to confusion.

A sad self-knowledge, withering, fell
On the beauty of Uriel;
In heaven once eminent, the god
Withdrew, that hour, into his cloud;
Whether doomed to long gyration
In the sea of generation,
Or by knowledge grown too bright
To hit the nerve of feebler sight.
Straightway, a forgetting wind
Stole over the celestial kind,
And their lips the secret kept,
If in ashes the fire-seed slept.

But now and then, truth-speaking things
Shamed the angels' veiling wings;
And, shrilling from the solar course,
Or from fruit of chemic force,
Procession of a soul in matter,
Or the speeding change of water,
Or out of the good of evil born,
Came Uriel's voice of cherub scorn,
And a blush tinged the upper sky,
And the gods shook, they knew not why.

c. 1838 1847

THE SPHINX

The Sphinx is drowsy,
  Her wings are furled:
Her ear is heavy,
  She broods on the world.
"Who'll tell me my secret,
  The ages have kept?—
I awaited the seer
  While they slumbered and slept:—

"The fate of the man-child,
  The meaning of man;
Known fruit of the unknown;
  Dædalian plan;
Out of sleeping a waking,
  Out of waking a sleep;
Life death overtaking;
  Deep underneath deep?

"Erect as a sunbeam,
  Upspringeth the palm;
The elephant browses,
  Undaunted and calm;
In beautiful motion
  The thrush plies his wings;

Kind leaves of his covert,
  Your silence he sings.

"The waves, unashamèd,
  In difference sweet,
Play glad with the breezes,
  Old playfellows meet;
The journeying atoms,
  Primordial wholes,
Firmly draw, firmly drive,
  By their animate poles.

"Sea, earth, air, sound, silence,
  Plant, quadruped, bird,
By one music enchanted,
  One deity stirred,—
Each the other adorning,
  Accompany still;
Night veileth the morning,
  The vapor the hill.

"The babe by its mother
  Lies bathèd in joy;
Glide its hours uncounted,—
  The sun is its toy;
Shines the peace of all being,
  Without cloud, in its eyes;
And the sum of the world
  In soft miniature lies.

"But man crouches and blushes,
  Absconds and conceals;
He creepeth and peepeth,
  He palters and steals;
Infirm, melancholy,
  Jealous glancing around,
An oaf, an accomplice,
  He poisons the ground.

"Out spoke the great mother,
Beholding his fear;—
At the sound of her accents
Cold shuddered the sphere:—
'Who has drugged my boy's cup?
Who has mixed my boy's bread?
Who, with sadness and madness,
Has turned my child's head?'"

I heard a poet answer
Aloud and cheerfully,
"Say on, sweet Sphinx! thy dirges
Are pleasant songs to me.
Deep love lieth under
These pictures of time;
They fade in the light of
Their meaning sublime.

"The fiend that man harries
Is love of the Best;
Yawns the pit of the Dragon,
Lit by rays from the Blest.
The Lethe of Nature
Can't trance him again,
Whose soul sees the perfect,
Which his eyes seek in vain.

"To vision profounder,
Man's spirit must dive;
His aye-rolling orb
At no goal will arrive;
The heavens that now draw him
With sweetness untold,
Once found,—for new heavens
He spurneth the old.

"Pride ruined the angels,
Their shame them restores;

Lurks the joy that is sweetest
In stings of remorse.
Have I a lover
Who is noble and free?—
I would he were nobler
Than to love me.

"Eterne alternation
Now follows, now flies;
And under pain, pleasure,—
Under pleasure, pain lies.
Love works at the centre,
Heart-heaving alway;
Forth speed the strong pulses
To the borders of day.

"Dull Sphinx, Jove keep thy five wits;
Thy sight is growing blear;
Rue, myrrh and cummin for the Sphinx,
Her muddy eyes to clear!"
The old Sphinx bit her thick lip,—
Said, "Who taught thee me to name?
I am thy spirit, yoke-fellow;
Of thine eye I am eyebeam.

"Thou art the unanswered question;
Couldst see thy proper eye,
Always it asketh, asketh;
And each answer is a lie.
So take thy quest through nature,
It through thousand natures ply;
Ask on, thou clothed eternity;
Time is the false reply."

Uprose the merry Sphinx,
And crouched no more in stone;
She melted into purple cloud,
She silvered in the moon;

She spired into a yellow flame;
She flowered in blossoms red;
She flowed into a foaming wave:
She stood Monadnoc's head.

Through a thousand voices
Spoke the universal dame;
"Who telleth one of my meanings,
Is master of all I am."

1841

TO J. W.

Set not thy foot on graves;
Hear what wine and roses say;
The mountain chase, the summer waves,
The crowded town, thy feet may well delay.

Set not thy foot on graves;
Nor seek to unwind the shroud
Which charitable Time
And Nature have allowed
To wrap the errors of a sage sublime.

Set not thy foot on graves;
Care not to strip the dead
Of his sad ornament,
His myrrh, and wine, and rings,

His sheet of lead,
And trophies burièd:
Go, get them where he earned them when alive;
As resolutely dig or dive.

Life is too short to waste
In critic peep or cynic bark,

Quarrel or reprimand:
'T will soon be dark;
Up! mind thine own aim, and
God speed the mark!

1847

HAMATREYA

Bulkeley, Hunt, Willard, Hosmer, Meriam, Flint,
Possessed the land which rendered to their toil
Hay, corn, roots, hemp, flax, apples, wool and wood.
Each of these landlords walked amidst his farm,
Saying, " 'T is mine, my children's and my name's.
How sweet the west wind sounds in my own trees!
How graceful climb those shadows on my hill!
I fancy these pure waters and the flags
Know me, as does my dog: we sympathize;
And, I affirm, my actions smack of the soil."

Where are these men? Asleep beneath their grounds:
And strangers, fond as they, their furrows plough.
Earth laughs in flowers, to see her boastful boys
Earth-proud, proud of the earth which is not theirs;
Who steer the plough, but cannot steer their feet
Clear of the grave.
They added ridge to valley, brook to pond,
And sighed for all that bounded their domain;
"This suits me for a pasture; that's my park;
We must have clay, lime, gravel, granite-ledge,
And misty lowland, where to go for peat.
The land is well,—lies fairly to the south.
'T is good, when you have crossed the sea and back,
To find the sitfast acres where you left them."
Ah! the hot owner sees not Death, who adds
Him to his land, a lump of mould the more.
Hear what the Earth says:—

EARTH-SONG

"Mine and yours;
Mine, not yours.
Earth endures;
Stars abide—
Shine down in the old sea;
Old are the shores;
But where are old men?
I who have seen much,
Such have I never seen.

"The lawyer's deed
Ran sure,
In tail,
To them, and to their heirs
Who shall succeed,
Without fail,
Forevermore.

"Here is the land,
Shaggy with wood,
With its old valley,
Mound and flood.
But the heritors?—
Fled like the flood's foam.
The lawyer, and the laws,
And the kingdom,
Clean swept herefrom.

"They called me theirs,
Who so controlled me;
Yet every one
Wished to stay, and is gone,
How am I theirs,
If they cannot hold me,
But I hold them?"

When I heard the Earth-song,
I was no longer brave;
My avarice cooled
Like lust in the chill of the grave.

1847

THE RHODORA:

ON BEING ASKED, WHENCE IS THE FLOWER?

In May, when sea-winds pierced our solitudes,
I found the fresh Rhodora in the woods,
Spreading its leafless blooms in a damp nook,
To please the desert and the sluggish brook.
The purple petals, fallen in the pool,
Made the black water with their beauty gay;
Here might the red-bird come his plumes to cool,
And court the flower that cheapens his array.
Rhodora! if the sages ask thee why
This charm is wasted on the earth and sky,
Tell them, dear, that if eyes were made for seeing,
Then Beauty is its own excuse for being:
Why thou wert there, O rival of the rose!
I never thought to ask, I never knew:
But, in my simple ignorance, suppose
The self-same Power that brought me there brought you.

1834 1839

THE HUMBLE-BEE

Burly, dozing humble-bee,
Where thou art is clime for me.
Let them sail for Porto Rique,
Far-off heats through seas to seek;
I will follow thee alone,
Thou animated torrid-zone!
Zigzag steerer, desert cheerer,
Let me chase thy waving lines;

Keep me nearer, me thy hearer,
Singing over shrubs and vines.

Insect lover of the sun,
Joy of thy dominion!
Sailor of the atmosphere;
Swimmer through the waves of air;
Voyager of light and noon;
Epicurean of June;
Wait, I prithee, till I come
Within earshot of thy hum,—
All without is martyrdom.

When the south wind, in May days,
With a net of shining haze
Silvers the horizon wall,
And with softness touching all,
Tints the human countenance
With a color of romance,
And infusing subtle heats,
Turns the sod to violets,
Thou, in sunny solitudes,
Rover of the underwoods,
The green silence dost displace
With thy mellow, breezy bass.

Hot midsummer's petted crone,
Sweet to me thy drowsy tone
Tells of countless sunny hours,
Long days, and solid banks of flowers;
Of gulfs of sweetness without bound
In Indian wildernesses found;
Of Syrian peace, immortal leisure,
Firmest cheer, and bird-like pleasure.
Aught unsavory or unclean
Hath my insect never seen;
But violets and bilberry bells,
Maple-sap and daffodels,

Grass with green flag half-mast high,
Succory to match the sky,
Columbine with horn of honey,
Scented fern, and agrimony,
Clover, catchfly, adder's-tongue
And brier-roses, dwelt among;
All beside was unknown waste,
All was picture as he passed.

Wiser far than human seer,
Yellow-breeched philosopher!
Seeing only what is fair,
Sipping only what is sweet,
Thou dost mock at fate and care,
Leave the chaff, and take the wheat.
When the fierce northwestern blast
Cools sea and land so far and fast,
Thou already slumberest deep;
Woe and want thou canst outsleep;
Want and woe, which torture us,
Thy sleep makes ridiculous.

1839

THE SNOW-STORM

Announced by all the trumpets of the sky,
Arrives the snow, and, driving o'er the fields,
Seems nowhere to alight: the whited air
Hides hills and woods, the river, and the heaven,
And veils the farm-house at the garden's end.
The sled and traveller stopped, the courier's feet
Delayed, all friends shut out, the housemates sit
Around the radiant fireplace, enclosed
In a tumultuous privacy of storm.

Come see the north wind's masonry.
Out of an unseen quarry evermore

Furnished with tile, the fierce artificer
Curves his white bastions with projected roof
Round every windward stake, or tree, or door.
Speeding, the myriad-handed, his wild work
So fanciful, so savage, nought cares he
For number or proportion. Mockingly,
On coop or kennel he hangs Parian wreaths;
A swan-like form invests the hidden thorn;
Fills up the farmer's lane from wall to wall,
Maugre the farmer's sighs; and at the gate
A tapering turret overtops the work.
And when his hours are numbered, and the world
Is all his own, retiring, as he were not,
Leaves, when the sun appears, astonished Art
To mimic in slow structures, stone by stone,
Built in an age, the mad wind's nightwork,
The frolic architecture of the snow.

1841

WOODNOTES—I

I

When the pine tosses its cones
To the song of its waterfall tones,
Who speeds to the woodland walks?
To birds and trees who talks?
Cæsar of his leafy Rome,
There the poet is at home.
He goes to the river-side,—
Not hook nor line hath he;
He stands in the meadows wide,—
Nor gun nor scythe to see.
Sure some god his eye enchants:
What he knows nobody wants.
In the wood he travels glad,
Without better fortune had,
Melancholy without bad.

Knowledge this man prizes best
Seems fantastic to the rest:
Pondering shadows, colors, clouds,
Grass-buds and caterpillar-shrouds,
Boughs on which the wild bees settle,
Tints that spot the violet's petal,
Why Nature loves the number five,
And why the star-form she repeats:
Lover of all things alive,
Wonderer at all he meets,
Wonderer chiefly at himself,
Who can tell him what he is?
Or how meet in human elf
Coming and past eternities?

2

And such I knew, a forest seer,
A minstrel of the natural year,
Foreteller of the vernal ides,
Wise harbinger of spheres and tides,
A lover true, who knew by heart
Each joy the mountain dales impart;
It seemed that Nature could not raise
A plant in any secret place,
In quaking bog, on snowy hill,
Beneath the grass that shades the rill,
Under the snow, between the rocks,
In damp fields known to bird and fox,
But he would come in the very hour
It opened in its virgin bower,
As if a sunbeam showed the place,
And tell its long-descended race.
It seemed as if the breezes brought him,
It seemed as if the sparrows taught him;
As if by secret sight he knew
Where, in far fields, the orchis grew.

Many haps fall in the field
Seldom seen by wishful eyes
But all her shows did Nature yield,
To please and win this pilgrim wise.
He saw the partridge drum in the woods;
He heard the woodcock's evening hymn;
He found the tawny thrushes' broods;
And the shy hawk did wait for him;
What others did at distance hear,
And guessed within the thicket's gloom,
Was shown to this philosopher,
And at his bidding seemed to come.

3

In unploughed Maine he sought the lumberers' gang
Where from a hundred lakes young rivers sprang;
He trode the unplanted forest floor, whereon
The all-seeing sun for ages hath not shone;
Where feeds the moose, and walks the surly bear,
And up the tall mast runs the woodpecker.
He saw beneath dim aisles, in odorous beds,
The slight Linnæa hang its twin-born heads,
And blessed the monument of the man of flowers,
Which breathes his sweet fame through the northern bowers.
He heard, when in the grove, at intervals,
With sudden roar the aged pine-tree falls,—
One crash, the death-hymn of the perfect tree,
Declares the close of its green century.
Low lies the plant to whose creation went
Sweet influence from every element;
Whose living towers the years conspired to build,
Whose giddy top the morning loved to gild.
Through these green tents, by eldest Nature dressed,
He roamed, content alike with man and beast.
Where darkness found him he lay glad at night;
There the red morning touched him with its light.

Three moons his great heart him a hermit made,
So long he roved at will the boundless shade.
The timid it concerns to ask their way,
And fear what foe in caves and swamps can stray,
To make no step until the event is known,
And ills to come as evils past bemoan.
Not so the wise; no coward watch he keeps
To spy what danger on his pathway creeps;
Go where he will, the wise man is at home,
His hearth the earth,—his hall the azure dome;
Where his clear spirit leads him, there's his road
By God's own light illumined and foreshowed.

4

'T was one of the charmèd days
When the genius of God doth flow;
The wind may alter twenty ways,
A tempest cannot blow;
It may blow north, it still is warm;
Or south, it still is clear;
Or east, it smells like a clover-farm;
Or west, no thunder fear.
The musing peasant, lowly great,
Beside the forest water sate;
The rope-like pine-roots crosswise grown
Composed the network of his throne;
The wide lake, edged with sand and grass,
Was burnished to a floor of glass,
Painted with shadows green and proud
Of the tree and of the cloud.
He was the heart of all the scene;
On him the sun looked more serene;
To hill and cloud his face was known,—
It seemed the likeness of their own;
They knew by secret sympathy
The public child of earth and sky.

"You ask," he said, "what guide
Me through trackless thickets led,
Through thick-stemmed woodlands rough and wide.
I found the water's bed.
The watercourses were my guide;
I travelled grateful by their side,
Or through their channel dry;
They led me through the thicket damp,
Through brake and fern, the beavers' camp,
Through beds of granite cut my road,
And their resistless friendship showed:
The falling waters led me,
The foodful waters fed me,
And brought me to the lowest land,
Unerring to the ocean sand.
The moss upon the forest bark
Was pole-star when the night was dark;
The purple berries in the wood
Supplied me necessary food;
For Nature ever faithful is
To such as trust her faithfulness.
When the forest shall mislead me,
When the night and morning lie,
When sea and land refuse to feed me,
'T will be time enough to die;
Then will yet my mother yield
A pillow in her greenest field,
Nor the June flowers scorn to cover
The clay of their departed lover."

1840

FABLE

The mountain and the squirrel
Had a quarrel,
And the former called the latter "Little Prig;"
Bun replied,

"You are doubtless very big;
But all sorts of things and weather
Must be taken in together,
To make up a year
And a sphere.
And I think it no disgrace
To occupy my place.
If I'm not so large as you,
You are not so small as I,
And not half so spry.
I'll not deny you make
A very pretty squirrel track;
Talents differ; all is well and wisely put;
If I cannot carry forests on my back,
Neither can you crack a nut."

1845 1847

ODE

INSCRIBED TO W. H. CHANNING

Though loath to grieve
The evil time's sole patriot,
I cannot leave
My honied thought
For the priest's cant,
Or statesman's rant.

If I refuse
My study for their politique,
Which at the best is trick,
The angry Muse
Puts confusion in my brain.

But who is he that prates
Of the culture of mankind,
Of better arts and life?

Go, blindworm, go,
Behold the famous States
Harrying Mexico
With rifle and with knife!

Or who, with accent bolder,
Dare praise the freedom-loving mountaineer?
I found by thee, O rushing Contoocook!
And in thy valleys, Agiochook!
The jackals of the negro-holder.

The God who made New Hampshire
Taunted the lofty land
With little men;—
Small bat and wren
House in the oak:—
If earth-fire cleave
The upheaved land, and bury the folk,
The southern crocodile would grieve.
Virtue palters; Right is hence;
Freedom praised, but hid;
Funeral eloquence
Rattles the coffin-lid.

Canada 1940

What boots thy zeal,
O glowing friend,
That would indignant rend
The northland from the south?
Wherefore? to what good end?
Boston Bay and Bunker Hill
Would serve things still;—
Things are of the snake.

North & South both devoted to their property

The horseman serves the horse,
The neatherd serves the neat,
The merchant serves the purse,
The eater serves his meat;

'T is the day of the chattel,
Web to weave, and corn to grind;
Things are in the saddle,
And ride mankind.

There are two laws discrete,
Not reconciled,—
Law for man, and law for thing;
The last builds town and fleet,
But it runs wild,
And doth the man unking.

'T is fit the forest fall,
The steep be graded,
The mountain tunnelled,
The sand shaded,
The orchard planted,
The glebe tilled,
The prairie granted,
The steamer built.

Let man serve law for man;
Live for friendship, live for love,
For truth's and harmony's behoof;
The state may follow how it can,
As Olympus follows Jove.

Yet do not I implore
The wrinkled shopman to my sounding woods,
Nor bid the unwilling senator
Ask votes of thrushes in the solitudes.
Every one to his chosen work;—
Foolish hands may mix and mar;
Wise and sure the issues are.
Round they roll till dark is light,
Sex to sex, and even to odd;—
The over-god

Who marries Right to Might,
Who peoples, unpeoples,—
He who exterminates
Races by stronger races,
Black by white faces,—
Knows to bring honey
Out of the lion;
Grafts gentlest scion
On pirate and Turk.

The Cossack eats Poland,
Like stolen fruit;
Her last noble is ruined,
Her last poet mute:
Straight, into double band
The victors divide;
Half for freedom strike and stand;—
The astonished Muse finds thousands at her side.

1847

FORBEARANCE

Hast thou named all the birds without a gun?
Loved the wood-rose, and left it on its stalk?
At rich men's tables eaten bread and pulse?
Unarmed, faced danger with a heart of trust?
And loved so well a high behavior,
In man or maid, that thou from speech refrained,
Nobility more nobly to repay?
O, be my friend, and teach me to be thine!

1842

FORERUNNERS

Long I followed happy guides,
I could never reach their sides;

Their step is forth, and, ere the day
Breaks up their leaguer, and away.
Keen my sense, my heart was young,
Right good-will my sinews strung,
But no speed of mine avails
To hunt upon their shining trails.
On and away, their hasting feet
Make the morning proud and sweet;
Flowers they strew,—I catch the scent;
Or tone of silver instrument
Leaves on the wind melodious trace;
Yet I could never see their face.
On eastern hills I see their smokes,
Mixed with mist by distant lochs.
I met many travellers
Who the road had surely kept;
They saw not my fine revellers,—
These had crossed them while they slept.
Some had heard their fair report,
In the country or the court.
Fleetest couriers alive
Never yet could once arrive,
As they went or they returned,
At the house where these sojourned.
Sometimes their strong speed they slacken,
Though they are not overtaken;
In sleep their jubilant troop is near,—
I tuneful voices overhear;
It may be in wood or waste,—
At unawares 't is come and past.
Their near camp my spirit knows
By signs gracious as rainbows.
I thenceforward and long after
Listen for their harp-like laughter,
And carry in my heart, for days,
Peace that hallows rudest ways.

1846

ODE TO BEAUTY

Who gave thee, O Beauty,
The keys of this breast,—
Too credulous lover
Of blest and unblest?
Say, when in lapsed ages
Thee knew I of old?
Or what was the service
For which I was sold?
When first my eyes saw thee,
I found me thy thrall,
By magical drawings,
Sweet tyrant of all!
I drank at thy fountain
False waters of thirst;
Thou intimate stranger,
Thou latest and first!
Thy dangerous glances
Make women of men;
New-born, we are melting
Into nature again.

Lavish, lavish promiser,
Nigh persuading gods to err!
Guest of million painted forms,
Which in turn thy glory warms!
The frailest leaf, the mossy bark,
The acorn's cup, the raindrop's arc,
The swinging spider's silver line,
The ruby of the drop of wine,
The shining pebble of the pond,
Thou inscribest with a bond,
In thy momentary play,
Would bankrupt nature to repay.

Ah, what avails it
To hide or to shun
Whom the Infinite One
Hath granted his throne?
The heaven high over
Is the deep's lover;
The sun and sea,
Informed by thee,
Before me run
And draw me on,
Yet fly me still,
As Fate refuses
To me the heart Fate for me chooses.
Is it that my opulent soul
Was mingled from the generous whole;
Sea-valleys and the deep of skies
Furnished several supplies;
And the sands whereof I'm made
Draw me to them, self-betrayed?
I turn the proud portfolio
Which holds the grand designs
Of Salvator, of Guercino,
And Piranesi's lines.
I hear the lofty pæans
Of the masters of the shell,
Who heard the starry music
And recount the numbers well;
Olympian bards who sung
Divine Ideas below,
Which always find us young
And always keep us so.
Oft, in streets or humblest places,
I detect far-wandering graces,
Which, from Eden wide astray,
In lowly homes have lost their way.

Thee gliding through the sea of form,
Like the lightning through the storm,

Somewhat not to be possessed,
Somewhat not to be caressed,
No feet so fleet could ever find,
No perfect form could ever bind.
Thou eternal fugitive,
Hovering over all that live,
Quick and skilful to inspire
Sweet, extravagant desire,
Starry space and lily-bell
Filling with thy roseate smell,
Wilt not give the lips to taste
Of the nectar which thou hast.

All that's good and great with thee
Works in close conspiracy;
Thou hast bribed the dark and lonely
To report thy features only,
And the cold and purple morning
Itself with thoughts of thee adorning;
The leafy dell, the city mart,
Equal trophies of thine art;
E'en the flowing azure air
Thou hast touched for my despair;
And, if I languish into dreams,
Again I meet the ardent beams.
Queen of things! I dare not die
In Being's deeps past ear and eye;
Lest there I find the same deceiver
And be the sport of Fate forever.
Dread Power, but dear! if God thou be,
Unmake me quite, or give thyself to me!

1843

GIVE ALL TO LOVE

Give all to love;
Obey thy heart;
Friends, kindred, days,

Estate, good-fame,
Plans, credit and the Muse,—
Nothing refuse.

'T is a brave master;
Let it have scope:
Follow it utterly,
Hope beyond hope:
High and more high
It dives into noon,
With wing unspent,
Untold intent;
But it is a god,
Knows its own path
And the outlets of the sky.

It was never for the mean;
It requireth courage stout.
Souls above doubt,
Valor unbending,
It will reward,—
They shall return
More than they were,
And ever ascending.

Leave all for love;
Yet, hear me, yet,
One word more thy heart behoved,
One pulse more of firm endeavor,—
Keep thee to-day,
To-morrow, forever,
Free as an Arab
Of thy beloved.

Cling with life to the maid;
But when the surprise,
First vague shadow of surmise

Flits across her bosom young,
Of a joy apart from thee,
Free be she, fancy-free;
Nor thou detain her vesture's hem,
Nor the palest rose she flung
From her summer diadem.

Though thou loved her as thyself,
As a self of purer clay,
Though her parting dims the day,
Stealing grace from all alive;
Heartily know,
When half-gods go,
The gods arrive.

1847

INITIAL, DÆMONIC AND CELESTIAL LOVE

I. The Initial Love

Venus, when her son was lost,
Cried him up and down the coast,
In hamlets, palaces and parks,
And told the truant by his marks,—
Golden curls, and quiver and bow.
This befell how long ago!
Time and tide are strangely changed,
Men and manners much deranged:
None will now find Cupid latent
By this foolish antique patent.
He came late along the waste,
Shod like a traveller for haste;
With malice dared me to proclaim him.
That the maids and boys might name him.

Boy no more, he wears all coats,
Frocks and blouses, capes, capotes;

He bears no bow, or quiver, or wand,
Nor chaplet on his head or hand.
Leave his weeds and heed his eyes,—
All the rest he can disguise.
In the pit of his eye 's a spark
Would bring back day if it were dark;
And, if I tell you all my thought,
Though I comprehend it not,
In those unfathomable orbs
Every function he absorbs;
Doth eat, and drink, and fish, and shoot,
And write, and reason, and compute,
And ride, and run, and have, and hold,
And whine, and flatter, and regret,
And kiss, and couple, and beget,
By those roving eyeballs bold.

Undaunted are their courages,
Right Cossacks in their forages;
Fleeter they than any creature,—
They are his steeds, and not his feature;
Inquisitive, and fierce, and fasting,
Restless, predatory, hasting;
And they pounce on other eyes
As lions on their prey;
And round their circles is writ,
Plainer than the day,
Underneath, within, above,—
Love—love—love—love.
He lives in his eyes;
There doth digest, and work, and spin,
And buy, and sell, and lose, and win;
He rolls them with delighted motion,
Joy-tides swell their mimic ocean.
Yet holds he them with tautest rein,
That they may seize and entertain

The glance that to their glance opposes,
Like fiery honey sucked from roses.
He palmistry can understand,
Imbibing virtue by his hand
As if it were a living root;
The pulse of hands will make him mute;
With all his force he gathers balms
Into those wise, thrilling palms.

Cupid is a casuist,
A mystic and a cabalist,—
Can your lurking thought surprise,
And interpret your device.
He is versed in occult science,
In magic and in clairvoyance,
Oft he keeps his fine ear strained,
And Reason on her tiptoe pained
For aëry intelligence,
And for strange coincidence.
But it touches his quick heart
When Fate by omens takes his part,
And chance-dropped hints from Nature's sphere
Deeply soothe his anxious ear.

Heralds high before him run;
He has ushers many a one;
He spreads his welcome where he goes,
And touches all things with his rose.
All things wait for and divine him,—
How shall I dare to malign him,
Or accuse the god of sport?
I must end my true report,
Painting him from head to foot,
In as far as I took note,
Trusting well the matchless power
Of this young-eyed emperor

Will clear his fame from every cloud
With the bards and with the crowd.

He is wilful, mutable,
Shy, untamed, inscrutable,
Swifter-fashioned than the fairies,
Substance mixed of pure contraries;
His vice some elder virtue's token,
And his good is evil-spoken.
Failing sometimes of his own,
He is headstrong and alone;
He affects the wood and wild,
Like a flower-hunting child;
Buries himself in summer waves,
In trees, with beasts, in mines and caves,
Loves nature like a hornèd cow,
Bird, or deer, or caribou.

Shun him, nymphs, on the fleet horses!
He has a total world of wit;
O how wise are his discourses!
But he is the arch-hypocrite,
And, through all science and all art,
Seeks alone his counterpart.
He is a Pundit of the East,
He is an augur and a priest,
And his soul will melt in prayer,
But word and wisdom is a snare;
Corrupted by the present toy
He follows joy, and only joy.
There is no mask but he will wear;
He invented oaths to swear;
He paints, he carves, he chants, he prays,
And holds all stars in his embrace.
He takes a sovran privilege
Not allowed to any liege;
For Cupid goes behind all law,
And right into himself does draw;

For he is sovereignly allied,—
Heaven's oldest blood flows in his side,—
And interchangeably at one
With every king on every throne,
That no god dare say him nay,
Or see the fault, or seen betray:
He has the Muses by the heart,
And the stern Parcæ on his part.

His many signs cannot be told;
He has not one mode, but manifold,
Many fashions and addresses,
Piques, reproaches, hurts, caresses.
He will preach like a friar,
And jump like a Harlequin;
He will read like a crier,
And fight like a Paladin.
Boundless is his memory;
Plans immense his term prolong;
He is not of counted age,
Meaning always to be young.
And his wish is intimacy,
Intimater intimacy,
And a stricter privacy;
The impossible shall yet be done,
And, being two, shall still be one.
As the wave breaks to foam on shelves,
Then runs into a wave again,
So lovers melt their sundered selves,
Yet melted would be twain.

II. The Dæmonic Love

Man was made of social earth,
Child and brother from his birth,
Tethered by a liquid cord
Of blood through veins of kindred poured.

Next his heart the fireside band
Of mother, father, sister, stand;
Names from awful childhood heard
Throbs of a wild religion stirred;—
Virtue, to love, to hate them, vice;
Till dangerous Beauty came, at last,
Till Beauty came to snap all ties;
The maid, abolishing the past,
With lotus wine obliterates
Dear memory's stone-incarved traits,
And, by herself, supplants alone
Friends year by year more inly known.
When her calm eyes opened bright,
All else grew foreign in their light.
It was ever the self-same tale,
The first experience will not fail;
Only two in the garden walked,
And with snake and seraph talked.

Close, close to men,
Like undulating layer of air,
Right above their heads,
The potent plain of Dæmons spreads.
Stands to each human soul its own,
For watch and ward and furtherance,
In the snares of Nature's dance;
And the lustre and the grace
To fascinate each youthful heart,
Beaming from its counterpart,
Translucent through the mortal covers,
Is the Dæmon's form and face.
To and fro the Genius hies,—
A gleam which plays and hovers
Over the maiden's head,
And dips sometimes as low as to her eyes.
Unknown, albeit lying near,

To men, the path to the Dæmon sphere;
And they that swiftly come and go
Leave no track on the heavenly snow.
Sometimes the airy synod bends,
And the mighty choir descends,
And the brains of men thenceforth,
In crowded and in still resorts,
Teem with unwonted thoughts:
As, when a shower of meteors
Cross the orbit of the earth,
And, lit by fringent air,
Blaze near and far,
Mortals deem the planets bright
Have slipped their sacred bars,
And the lone seaman all the night
Sails, astonished, amid stars.

Beauty of a richer vein,
Graces of a subtler strain,
Unto men these moonmen lend,
And our shrinking sky extend.
So is man's narrow path
By strength and terror skirted;
Also (from the song the wrath
Of the Genii be averted!
The Muse the truth uncolored speaking)
The Dæmons are self-seeking:
Their fierce and limitary will
Draws men to their likeness still.
The erring painter made Love blind,—
Highest Love who shines on all;
Him, radiant, sharpest-sighted god,
None can bewilder;
Whose eyes pierce
The universe,
Path-finder, road-builder,

Mediator, royal giver;
Rightly seeing, rightly seen,
Of joyful and transparent mien.
'T is a sparkle passing
From each to each, from thee to me,
To and fro perpetually;
Sharing all, daring all,
Levelling, displacing
Each obstruction, it unites
Equals remote, and seeming opposites.
And ever and forever Love
Delights to build a road:
Unheeded Danger near him strides,
Love laughs, and on a lion rides.
But Cupid wears another face,
Born into Dæmons less divine:
His roses bleach apace,
His nectar smacks of wine.
The Dæmon ever builds a wall,
Himself encloses and includes,
Solitude in solitudes:
In like sort his love doth fall.
He doth elect
The beautiful and fortunate,
And the sons of intellect,
And the souls of ample fate,
Who the Future's gates unbar,—
Minions of the Morning Star.
In his prowess he exults,
And the multitude insults.
His impatient looks devour
Oft the humble and the poor;
And, seeing his eye glare,
They drop their few pale flowers,
Gathered with hope to please,
Along the mountain towers,—
Lose courage, and despair.

He will never be gainsaid,—
Pitiless, will not be stayed;
His hot tyranny
Burns up every other tie.
Therefore comes an hour from Jove
Which his ruthless will defies,
And the dogs of Fate unties.
Shiver the palaces of glass;
Shrivel the rainbow-colored walls,
Where in bright Art each god and sibyl dwelt
Secure as in the zodiac's belt;
And the galleries and halls,
Wherein every siren sung,
Like a meteor pass.
For this fortune wanted root
In the core of God's abysm,—
Was a weed of self and schism;
And ever the Dæmonic Love
Is the ancestor of wars
And the parent of remorse.

III. The Celestial Love

But God said,
"I will have a purer gift;
There is smoke in the flame;
New flowerets bring, new prayers uplift,
And love without a name.
Fond children, ye desire
To please each other well;
Another round, a higher,
Ye shall climb on the heavenly stair,
And selfish preference forbear;
And in right deserving,
And without a swerving
Each from your proper state,
Weave roses for your mate.

"Deep, deep are loving eyes,
Flowed with naphtha fiery sweet;
And the point is paradise,
Where their glances meet:
Their reach shall yet be more profound,
And a vision without bound:
The axis of those eyes sun-clear
Be the axis of the sphere:
So shall the lights ye pour amain
Go, without check or intervals,
Through from the empyrean walls
Unto the same again."

Higher far into the pure realm,
Over sun and star,
Over the flickering Dæmon film,
Thou must mount for love;
Into vision where all form
In one only form dissolves;
In a region where the wheel
On which all beings ride
Visibly revolves;
Where the starred, eternal worm
Girds the world with bound and term;
Where unlike things are like;
Where good and ill,
And joy and moan,
Melt into one.

There Past, Present, Future, shoot
Triple blossoms from one root;
Substances at base divided,
In their summits are united;
There the holy essence rolls,
One through separated souls;
And the sunny Æon sleeps
Folding Nature in its deeps,

And every fair and every good,
Known in part, or known impure,
To men below,
In their archetypes endure.
The race of gods,
Or those we erring own,
Are shadows flitting up and down
In the still abodes.
The circles of that sea are laws
Which publish and which hide the cause.

Pray for a beam
Out of that sphere,
Thee to guide and to redeem.
O, what a load
Of care and toil,
By lying use bestowed,
From his shoulders falls who sees
The true astronomy,
The period of peace.
Counsel which the ages kept
Shall the well-born soul accept.
As the overhanging trees
Fill the lake with images,—
As garment draws the garment's hem,
Men their fortunes bring with them.
By right or wrong,
Lands and goods go to the strong.
Property will brutely draw
Still to the proprietor;
Silver to silver creep and wind,
And kind to kind.

Nor less the eternal poles
Of tendency distribute souls.
There need no vows to bind
Whom not each other seek, but find.

They give and take no pledge or oath,—
Nature is the bond of both:
No prayer persuades, no flattery fawns,—
Their noble meanings are their pawns.
Plain and cold is their address,
Power have they for tenderness;
And, so thoroughly is known
Each other's counsel by his own,
They can parley without meeting;
Need is none of forms of greeting;
They can well communicate
In their innermost estate;
When each the other shall avoid,
Shall each by each be most enjoyed.

Not with scarfs or perfumed gloves
Do these celebrate their loves:
Not by jewels, feasts and savors,
Not by ribbons or by favors,
But by the sun-spark on the sea,
And the cloud-shadow on the lea,
The soothing lapse of morn to mirk,
And the cheerful round of work.
Their cords of love so public are,
They intertwine the farthest star:
The throbbing sea, the quaking earth,
Yield sympathy and signs of mirth;
Is none so high, so mean is none,
But feels and seals this union;
Even the fell Furies are appeased.
The good applaud, the lost are eased.

Love's hearts are faithful, but not fond,
Bound for the just, but not beyond;
Not glad, as the low-loving herd,
Of self in other still preferred,

But they have heartily designed
The benefit of broad mankind.
And they serve men austerely,
After their own genius, clearly,
Without a false humility;
For this is Love's nobility,—
Not to scatter bread and gold,
Goods and raiment bought and sold;
But to hold fast his simple sense,
And speak the speech of innocence,
And with hand and body and blood,
To make his bosom-counsel good.
He that feeds men serveth few;
He serves all who dares be true.

1847

THE APOLOGY

Think me not unkind and rude
  That I walk alone in grove and glen;
I go to the god of the wood
  To fetch his word to men.

Tax not my sloth that I
  Fold my arms beside the brook;
Each cloud that floated in the sky
  Writes a letter in my book.

Chide me not, laborious band,
  For the idle flowers I brought;
Every aster in my hand
  Goes home loaded with a thought.

There was never mystery
  But 't is figured in the flowers;
Was never secret history
  But birds tell it in the bowers.

One harvest from thy field
  Homeward brought the oxen strong;
A second crop thine acres yield
  Which I gather in a song.

1847

MERLIN

I

Thy trivial harp will never please
Or fill my craving ear;
Its chords should ring as blows the breeze,
Free, peremptory, clear.
No jingling serenader's art,
Nor tinkle of piano strings,
Can make the wild blood start
In its mystic springs.
The kingly bard
Must smite the chords rudely and hard,
As with hammer or with mace;
That they may render back
Artful thunder, which conveys
Secrets of the solar track,
Sparks of the supersolar blaze.
Merlin's blows are strokes of fate,
Chiming with the forest tone,
When boughs buffet boughs in the wood;
Chiming with the gasp and moan
Of the ice-imprisoned flood;
With the pulse of manly hearts;
With the voice of orators;
With the din of city arts;
With the cannonade of wars;
With the marches of the brave;
And prayers of might from martyrs' cave.

Great is the art,
Great be the manners, of the bard.
He shall not his brain encumber
With the coil of rhythm and number;
But, leaving rule and pale forethought,
He shall aye climb
For his rhyme.
"Pass in, pass in," the angels say,
"In to the upper doors,
Nor count compartments of the floors,
But mount to paradise
By the stairway of surprise."

Blameless master of the games,
King of sport that never shames,
He shall daily joy dispense
Hid in song's sweet influence.
Forms more cheerly live and go,
What time the subtle mind
Sings aloud the tune whereto
Their pulses beat,
And march their feet,
And their members are combined.

By Sybarites beguiled,
He shall no task decline;
Merlin's mighty line
Extremes of nature reconciled,—
Bereaved a tyrant of his will,
And made the lion mild.
Songs can the tempest still,
Scattered on the stormy air,
Mould the year to fair increase,
And bring in poetic peace.

He shall not seek to weave,
In weak, unhappy times,

Efficacious rhymes;
Wait his returning strength.
Bird that from the nadir's floor
To the zenith's top can soar,—
The soaring orbit of the muse exceeds that journey's
 length.
Nor profane affect to hit
Or compass that, by meddling wit,
Which only the propitious mind
Publishes when 't is inclined.
There are open hours
When the God's will sallies free,
And the dull idiot might see
The flowing fortunes of a thousand years;—
Sudden, at unawares,
Self-moved, fly-to the doors,
Nor sword of angels could reveal
What they conceal.

II

The rhyme of the poet
Modulates the king's affairs;
Balance-loving Nature
Made all things in pairs.
To every foot its antipode;
Each color with its counter glowed;
To every tone beat answering tones,
Higher or graver;
Flavor gladly blends with flavor;
Leaf answers leaf upon the bough;
And match the paired cotyledons.
Hands to hands, and feet to feet,
In one body grooms and brides;
Eldest rite, two married sides
In every mortal meet.
Light's far furnace shines,

Smelting balls and bars,
Forging double stars,
Glittering twins and trines.
The animals are sick with love,
Lovesick with rhyme;
Each with all propitious Time
Into chorus wove.

Like the dancers' ordered band,
Thoughts come also hand in hand;
In equal couples mated,
Or else alternated;
Adding by their mutual gage,
One to other, health and age.
Solitary fancies go
Short-lived wandering to and fro,
Most like to bachelors,
Or an ungiven maid,
Not ancestors,
With no posterity to make the lie afraid,
Or keep truth undecayed.
Perfect-paired as eagle's wings,
Justice is the rhyme of things;
Trade and counting use
The self-same tuneful muse;
And Nemesis,
Who with even matches odd,
Who athwart space redresses
The partial wrong,
Fills the just period,
And finishes the song.

Subtle rhymes, with ruin rife,
Murmur in the house of life,
Sung by the Sisters as they spin;
In perfect time and measure they
Build and unbuild our echoing clay.

As the two twilights of the day
Fold us music-drunken in.

1846 1847

BACCHUS

Bring me wine, but wine which never grew
In the belly of the grape,
Or grew on vine whose tap-roots, reaching through
Under the Andes to the Cape,
Suffer no savor of the earth to scape.

Let its grapes the morn salute
From a nocturnal root,
Which feels the acrid juice
Of Styx and Erebus;
And turns the woe of Night,
By its own craft, to a more rich delight.

We buy ashes for bread;
We buy diluted wine;
Give me of the true,—
Whose ample leaves and tendrils curled
Among the silver hills of heaven
Draw everlasting dew;
Wine of wine,
Blood of the world,
Form of forms, and mould of statures,
That I intoxicated,
And by the draught assimilated,
May float at pleasure through all natures;
The bird-language rightly spell,
And that which roses say so well.

Wine that is shed
Like the torrents of the sun
Up the horizon walls,

Or like the Atlantic streams, which run
When the South Sea calls.

Water and bread,
Food which needs no transmuting,
Rainbow-flowering, wisdom-fruiting,
Wine which is already man,
Food which teach and reason can.

Wine which Music is,—
Music and wine are one,—
That I, drinking this,
Shall hear far Chaos talk with me;
Kings unborn shall walk with me;
And the poor grass shall plot and plan
What it will do when it is man.
Quickened so, will I unlock
Every crypt of every rock.

I thank the joyful juice
For all I know;—
Winds of remembering
Of the ancient being blow,
And seeming-solid walls of use
Open and flow.

Pour, Bacchus! the remembering wine;
Retrieve the loss of me and mine!
Vine for vine be antidote,
And the grape requite the lote!
Haste to cure the old despair,—
Reason in Nature's lotus drenched,
The memory of ages quenched;
Give them again to shine;
Let wine repair what this undid;
And where the infection slid,

A dazzling memory revive;
Refresh the faded tints,
Recut the aged prints,
And write my old adventures with the pen
Which on the first day drew,
Upon the tablets blue,
The dancing Pleiads and eternal men.

1846 1847

THRENODY

The South-wind brings
Life, sunshine and desire,
And on every mount and meadow
Breathes aromatic fire;
But over the dead he has no power,
The lost, the lost, he cannot restore;
And, looking over the hills, I mourn
The darling who shall not return.

I see my empty house,
I see my trees repair their boughs;
And he, the wondrous child,
Whose silver warble wild
Outvalued every pulsing sound
Within the air's cerulean round,—
The hyacinthine boy, for whom
Morn well might break and April bloom,
The gracious boy, who did adorn
The world whereinto he was born,
And by his countenance repay
The favor of the loving Day,—
Has disappeared from the Day's eye;
Far and wide she cannot find him;
My hopes pursue, they cannot bind him.
Returned this day, the South-wind searches,
And finds young pines and budding birches;

But finds not the budding man;
Nature, who lost, cannot remake him;
Fate let him fall, Fate can't retake him;
Nature, Fate, men, him seek in vain.

And whither now, my truant wise and sweet,
O, whither tend thy feet?
I had the right, few days ago,
Thy steps to watch, thy place to know:
How have I forfeited the right?
Hast thou forgot me in a new delight?
I hearken for thy household cheer,
O eloquent child!
Whose voice, an equal messenger,
Conveyed thy meaning mild.
What though the pains and joys
Whereof it spoke were toys
Fitting his age and ken,
Yet fairest dames and bearded men,
Who heard the sweet request,
So gentle, wise and grave,
Bended with joy to his behest
And let the world's affairs go by,
A while to share his cordial game,
Or mend his wicker wagon-frame,
Still plotting how their hungry ear
That winsome voice again might hear;
For his lips could well pronounce
Words that were persuasions.

Gentlest guardians marked serene
His early hope, his liberal mien;
Took counsel from his guiding eyes
To make this wisdom earthly wise.
Ah, vainly do these eyes recall
The school-march, each day's festival,
When every morn my bosom glowed
To watch the convoy on the road;

The babe in willow wagon closed,
With rolling eyes and face composed;
With children forward and behind,
Like Cupids studiously inclined;
And he the chieftain paced beside,
The centre of the troop allied,
With sunny face of sweet repose,
To guard the babe from fancied foes.
The little captain innocent
Took the eye with him as he went;
Each village senior paused to scan
And speak the lovely caravan.
From the window I look out
To mark thy beautiful parade,
Stately marching in cap and coat
To some tune by fairies played;—
A music heard by thee alone
To works as noble led thee on.

Now Love and Pride, alas! in vain,
Up and down their glances strain.
The painted sled stands where it stood;
The kennel by the corded wood;
His gathered sticks to stanch the wall
Of the snow-tower, when snow should fall;
The ominous hole he dug in the sand,
And childhood's castles built or planned;
His daily haunts I well discern,—
The poultry-yard, the shed, the barn,—
And every inch of garden ground
Paced by the blessed feet around,
From the roadside to the brook
Whereinto he loved to look.
Step the meek fowls where erst they ranged;
The wintry garden lies unchanged;
The brook into the stream runs on;
But the deep-eyed boy is gone.

On that shaded day,
Dark with more clouds than tempests are,
When thou didst yield thy innocent breath
In birdlike heavings unto death,
Night came, and Nature had not thee;
I said, "We are mates in misery."
The morrow dawned with needless glow;
Each snowbird chirped, each fowl must crow;
Each tramper started; but the feet
Of the most beautiful and sweet
Of human youth had left the hill
And garden,—they were bound and still.
There's not a sparrow or a wren,
There's not a blade of autumn grain,
Which the four seasons do not tend
And tides of life and increase lend;
And every chick of every bird,
And weed and rock-moss is preferred.
O ostrich-like forgetfulness!
O loss of larger in the less!
Was there no star that could be sent,
No watcher in the firmament,
No angel from the countless host
That loiters round the crystal coast,
Could stoop to heal that only child,
Nature's sweet marvel undefiled,
And keep the blossom of the earth,
Which all her harvests were not worth?
Not mine,—I never called thee mine,
But Nature's heir,—if I repine,
And seeing rashly torn and moved
Not what I made, but what I loved,
Grow early old with grief that thou
Must to the wastes of Nature go,—
'T is because a general hope
Was quenched, and all must doubt and grope.
For flattering planets seemed to say

This child should ills of ages stay,
By wondrous tongue, and guided pen,
Bring the flown Muses back to men.
Perchance not he but Nature ailed,
The world and not the infant failed.
It was not ripe yet to sustain
A genius of so fine a strain,
Who gazed upon the sun and moon
As if he came unto his own,
And, pregnant with his grander thought,
Brought the old order into doubt.
His beauty once their beauty tried;
They could not feed him, and he died,
And wandered backward as in scorn,
To wait an æon to be born.
Ill day which made this beauty waste,
Plight broken, this high face defaced!
Some went and came about the dead;
And some in books of solace read;
Some to their friends the tidings say;
Some went to write, some went to pray;
One tarried here, there hurried one;
But their heart abode with none.
Covetous death bereaved us all,
To aggrandize one funeral.
The eager fate which carried thee
Took the largest part of me:
For this losing is true dying;
This is lordly man's down-lying,
This his slow but sure reclining,
Star by star his world resigning.

O child of paradise,
Boy who made dear his father's home,
In whose deep eyes
Men read the welfare of the times to come,

I am too much bereft.
The world dishonored thou hast left.
O truth's and nature's costly lie!
O trusted broken prophecy!
O richest fortune sourly crossed!
Born for the future, to the future lost!

The deep Heart answered, "Weepest thou?
Worthier cause for passion wild
If I had not taken the child.
And deemest thou as those who pore,
With aged eyes, short way before,—
Think'st Beauty vanished from the coast
Of matter, and thy darling lost?
Taught he not thee—the man of eld,
Whose eyes within his eyes beheld
Heaven's numerous hierarchy span
The mystic gulf from God to man?
To be alone wilt thou begin
When worlds of lovers hem thee in?
To-morrow, when the masks shall fall
That dizen Nature's carnival,
The pure shall see by their own will,
Which overflowing Love shall fill,
'T is not within the force of fate
The fate-conjoined to separate.
But thou, my votary, weepest thou?
I gave thee sight—where is it now?
I taught thy heart beyond the reach
Of ritual, bible, or of speech;
Wrote in thy mind's transparent table,
As far as the incommunicable;
Taught thee each private sign to raise
Lit by the supersolar blaze.
Past utterance, and past belief,
And past the blasphemy of grief

The mysteries of Nature's heart;
And though no Muse can these impart,
Throb thine with Nature's throbbing breast
And all is clear from east to west.

"I came to thee as to a friend;
Dearest, to thee I did not send
Tutors, but a joyful eye,
Innocence that matched the sky,
Lovely locks, a form of wonder,
Laughter rich as woodland thunder,
That thou might'st entertain apart
The richest flowering of all art:
And, as the great all-loving Day
Through smallest chambers takes its way,
That thou might'st break thy daily bread
With prophet, savior and head;
That thou might'st cherish for thine own
The riches of sweet Mary's Son,
Boy-Rabbi, Israel's paragon.
And thoughtest thou such guest
Would in thy hall take up his rest?
Would rushing life forget her laws,
Fate's glowing revolution pause?
High omens ask diviner guess;
Not to be conned to tediousness
And know my higher gifts unbind
The zone that girds the incarnate mind.
When the scanty shores are full
With Thought's perilous, whirling pool;
When frail Nature can no more,
Then the Spirit strikes the hour:
My servant Death, with solving rite,
Pours finite into infinite.
Wilt thou freeze love's tidal flow,
Whose streams through Nature circling go?

Nail the wild star to its track
On the half-climbed zodiac?
Light is light which radiates,
Blood is blood which circulates,
Life is life which generates,
And many-seeming life is one,—
Wilt thou transfix and make it none?
Its onward force too starkly pent
In figure, bone, and lineament?
Wilt thou, uncalled, interrogate,
Talker! the unreplying Fate?
Nor see the genius of the whole
Ascendant in the private soul,
Beckon it when to go and come,
Self-announced its hour of doom?
Fair the soul's recess and shrine,
Magic-built to last a season;
Masterpiece of love benign,
Fairer that expansive reason
Whose omen 't is, and sign.
Wilt thou not ope thy heart to know
What rainbows teach, and sunsets show?
Verdict which accumulates
From lengthening scroll of human fates,
Voice of earth to earth returned,
Prayers of saints that inly burned,—
Saying, *What is excellent,*
As God lives, is permanent;
Hearts are dust, hearts' loves remain;
Heart's love will meet thee again.
Revere the Maker; fetch thine eye
Up to his style, and manners of the sky.
Not of adamant and gold
Built he heaven stark and cold;
No, but a nest of bending reeds,
Flowering grass and scented weeds;

Or like a traveller's fleeing tent,
Or bow above the tempest bent;
Built of tears and sacred flames,
And virtue reaching to its aims;
Built of furtherance and pursuing,
Not of spent deeds, but of doing.
Silent rushes the swift Lord
Through ruined systems still restored,
Broadsowing, bleak and void to bless,
Plants with worlds the wilderness;
Waters with tears of ancient sorrow
Apples of Eden ripe to-morrow.
House and tenant go to ground,
Lost in God, in Godhead found."

c. 1842–4 1847

CONCORD HYMN

SUNG AT THE COMPLETION OF THE BATTLE MONUMENT, JULY 4, 1837

By the rude bridge that arched the flood,
  Their flag to April's breeze unfurled,
Here once the embattled farmers stood
  And fired the shot heard round the world.

The foe long since in silence slept;
  Alike the conqueror silent sleeps;
And Time the ruined bridge has swept
  Down the dark stream which seaward creeps.

On this green bank, by this soft stream,
  We set to-day a votive stone;
That memory may their deed redeem,
  When, like our sires, our sons are gone.

Spirit, that made those heroes dare
To die, and leave their children free,
Bid Time and Nature gently spare
The shaft we raise to them and thee.

1837

REJECTED POEMS

THOUGHT

I am not poor, but I am proud,
Of one inalienable right,
Above the envy of the crowd,—
Thought's holy light.

Better it is than gems or gold,
And oh! it cannot die,
But thought will glow when the sun grows cold,
And mix with Deity.

1823 1903

GRACE

How much, preventing God, how much I owe
To the defences thou hast round me set;
Example, custom, fear, occasion slow,—
These scorned bondmen were my parapet.
I dare not peep over this parapet
To gauge with glance the roaring gulf below,
The depths of sin to which I had descended,
Had not these me against myself defended.

1842

THE BOHEMIAN HYMN

In many forms we try
To utter God's infinity,
But the boundless hath no form,
And the Universal Friend
Doth as far transcend
An angel as a worm.

The great Idea baffles wit,
Language falters under it,
It leaves the learned in the lurch;
Nor art, nor power, nor toil can find
The measure of the eternal Mind,
Nor hymn, nor prayer, nor church.

c. 1840 1904

LATER POEMS

BRAHMA

If the red slayer think he slays,
  Or if the slain think he is slain,
They know not well the subtle ways
  I keep, and pass, and turn again.

Far or forgot to me is near;
  Shadow and sunlight are the same;
The vanished gods to me appear;
  And one to me are shame and fame.

They reckon ill who leave me out;
  When me they fly, I am the wings;
I am the doubter and the doubt,
  And I the hymn the Brahmin sings.

The strong gods pine for my abode,
  And pine in vain the sacred Seven;
But thou, meek lover of the good!
  Find me, and turn thy back on heaven.

1856 God is everywhere 1857

ODE

SUNG IN THE TOWN HALL, CONCORD
JULY 4, 1857

O tenderly the haughty day
  Fills his blue urn with fire;
One morn is in the mighty heaven,
  And one in our desire.

The cannon booms from town to town,
  Our pulses beat not less,
The joy-bells chime their tidings down,
  Which children's voices bless.

For He that flung the broad blue fold
  O'er-mantling land and sea,
One third part of the sky unrolled
  For the banner of the free.

The men are ripe of Saxon kind
  To build an equal state,—
To take the statute from the mind
  And make of duty fate.

United States! the ages plead,—
  Present and Past in under-song,—
Go put your creed into your deed,
  Nor speak with double tongue.

For sea and land don't understand,
  Nor skies without a frown

See rights for which the one hand fights
By the other cloven down.

Be just at home; then write your scroll
Of honor o'er the sea,
And bid the broad Atlantic roll,
A ferry of the free.

And henceforth there shall be no chain,
Save underneath the sea
The wires shall murmur through the main
Sweet songs of liberty.

The conscious stars accord above,
The waters wild below,
And under, through the cable wove,
Her fiery errands go.

For He that worketh high and wise,
Nor pauses in his plan,
Will take the sun out of the skies
Ere freedom out of man.

1857 1867

BOSTON HYMN

READ IN MUSIC HALL, JANUARY 1, 1863

The word of the Lord by night
To the watching Pilgrims came,
As they sat by the seaside,
And filled their hearts with flame.

God said, I am tired of kings,
I suffer them no more;
Up to my ear the morning brings
The outrage of the poor.

Think ye I made this ball
A field of havoc and war,
Where tyrants great and tyrants small
Might harry the weak and poor?

My angel,—his name is Freedom,—
Choose him to be your king;
He shall cut pathways east and west
And fend you with his wing.

Lo! I uncover the land
Which I hid of old time in the West,
As the sculptor uncovers the statue
When he has wrought his best;

I show Columbia, of the rocks
Which dip their foot in the seas
And soar to the air-borne flocks
Of clouds and the boreal fleece.

I will divide my goods;
Call in the wretch and slave:
None shall rule but the humble,
And none but Toil shall have.

I will have never a noble,
No lineage counted great;
Fishers and choppers and ploughmen
Shall constitute a state.

Go, cut down trees in the forest
And trim the straightest boughs;
Cut down trees in the forest
And build me a wooden house.

Call the people together,
The young men and the sires,

The digger in the harvest field,
Hireling and him that hires;

And here in a pine state-house
They shall choose men to rule
In every needful faculty,
In church and state and school.

Lo, now! if these poor men
Can govern the land and sea
And make just laws below the sun,
As planets faithful be.

And ye shall succor men;
'T is nobleness to serve;
Help them who cannot help again:
Beware from right to swerve.

I break your bonds and masterships,
And I unchain the slave:
Free be his heart and hand henceforth
As wind and wandering wave.

I cause from every creature
His proper good to flow:
As much as he is and doeth,
So much he shall bestow.

But, laying hands on another
To coin his labor and sweat,
He goes in pawn to his victim
For eternal years in debt.

To-day unbind the captive,
So only are ye unbound;
Lift up a people from the dust,
Trump of their rescue, sound!

Pay ransom to the owner
And fill the bag to the brim.
Who is the owner? The slave is owner,
And ever was. Pay him.

O North! give him beauty for rags,
And honor, O South! for his shame;
Nevada! coin thy golden crags
With Freedom's image and name.

Up! and the dusky race
That sat in darkness long,—
Be swift their feet as antelopes,
And as behemoth strong.

Come, East and West and North,
By races, as snow-flakes,
And carry my purpose forth,
Which neither halts nor shakes.

My will fulfilled shall be,
For, in daylight or in dark,
My thunderbolt has eyes to see
His way home to the mark.

1862 1863

DAYS

Daughters of Time, the hypocritic Days,
Muffled and dumb like barefoot dervishes,
And marching single in an endless file,
Bring diadems and fagots in their hands.
To each they offer gifts after his will,
Bread, kingdoms, stars, and sky that holds them all.
I, in my pleached garden, watched the pomp,
Forgot my morning wishes, hastily

Took a few herbs and apples, and the Day
Turned and departed silent. I, too late,
Under her solemn fillet saw the scorn.

c. 1852 1857

SEASHORE

I heard or seemed to hear the chiding Sea
Say, Pilgrim, why so late and slow to come?
Am I not always here, thy summer home?
Is not my voice thy music, morn and eve?
My breath thy healthful climate in the heats,
My touch thy antidote, my bay thy bath?
Was ever building like my terraces?
Was ever couch magnificent as mine?
Lie on the warm rock-ledges, and there learn
A little hut suffices like a town.
I make your sculptured architecture vain,
Vain beside mine. I drive my wedges home,
And carve the coastwise mountain into caves.
Lo! here is Rome and Nineveh and Thebes,
Karnak and Pyramid and Giant's Stairs
Half piled or prostrate; and my newest slab
Older than all thy race.

Behold the Sea,
The opaline, the plentiful and strong,
Yet beautiful as is the rose in June,
Fresh as the trickling rainbow of July;
Sea full of food, the nourisher of kinds,
Purger of earth, and medicine of men;
Creating a sweet climate by my breath,
Washing out harms and griefs from memory,
And, in my mathematic ebb and flow,
Giving a hint of that which changes not.
Rich are the sea-gods:—who gives gifts but they?
They grope the sea for pearls, but more than pearls:

They pluck Force thence, and give it to the wise.
For every wave is wealth to Dædalus,
Wealth to the cunning artist who can work
This matchless strength. Where shall he find, O waves!
A load your Atlas shoulders cannot lift?

I with my hammer pounding evermore
The rocky coast, smite Andes into dust,
Strewing my bed, and, in another age,
Rebuild a continent of better men.
Then I unbar the doors: my paths lead out
The exodus of nations: I disperse
Men to all shores that front the hoary main.

I too have arts and sorceries;
Illusion dwells forever with the wave.
I know what spells are laid. Leave me to deal
With credulous and imaginative man;
For, though he scoop my water in his palm,
A few rods off he deems it gems and clouds.
Planting strange fruits and sunshine on the shore,
I make some coast alluring, some lone isle,
To distant men, who must go there, or die.

c. 1857 1867

TWO RIVERS

Thy summer voice, Musketaquit,
Repeats the music of the rain;
But sweeter rivers pulsing flit
Through thee, as thou through Concord Plain.

Thou in thy narrow banks art pent:
The stream I love unbounded goes
Through flood and sea and firmament;
Through light, through life, it forward flows.

I see the inundation sweet,
I hear the spending of the stream
Through years, through men, through Nature fleet,
Through love and thought, through power and dream.

Musketaquit, a goblin strong,
Of shard and flint makes jewels gay;
They lose their grief who hear his song,
And where he winds is the day of day.

So forth and brighter fares my stream,—
Who drink it shall not thirst again;
No darkness stains its equal gleam,
And ages drop in it like rain.

1856 1858

WALDEINSAMKEIT

I do not count the hours I spend
In wandering by the sea;
The forest is my loyal friend,
Like God it useth me.

In plains that room for shadows make
Of skirting hills to lie,
Bound in by streams which give and take
Their colors from the sky;

Or on the mountain-crest sublime,
Or down the oaken glade,
O what have I to do with time?
For this the day was made.

Cities of mortals woe-begone
Fantastic care derides,
But in the serious landscape lone
Stern benefit abides.

Sheen will tarnish, honey cloy,
And merry is only a mask of sad,

But, sober on a fund of joy,
The woods at heart are glad.

There the great Planter plants
Of fruitful worlds the grain,
And with a million spells enchants
The souls that walk in pain.

Still on the seeds of all he made
The rose of beauty burns;
Through times that wear and forms that fade,
Immortal youth returns.

The black ducks mounting from the lake,
The pigeon in the pines,
The bittern's boom, a desert make
Which no false art refines.

Down in yon watery nook,
Where bearded mists divide,
The gray old gods whom Chaos knew,
The sires of Nature, hide.

Aloft, in secret veins of air,
Blows the sweet breath of song,
O, few to scale those uplands dare,
Though they to all belong!

See thou bring not to field or stone
The fancies found in books;
Leave authors' eyes, and fetch your own,
To brave the landscape's looks.

Oblivion here thy wisdom is,
Thy thrift, the sleep of cares;
For a proud idleness like this
Crowns all thy mean affairs.

1857 1858

TERMINUS

It is time to be old,
To take in sail:—
The god of bounds,
Who sets to seas a shore,
Came to me in his fatal rounds,
And said: "No more!
No farther shoot
Thy broad ambitious branches, and thy root.
Fancy departs: no more invent;
Contract thy firmament
To compass of a tent.
There's not enough for this and that,
Make thy option which of two;
Economize the failing river,
Not the less revere the Giver,
Leave the many and hold the few.
Timely wise accept the terms,
Soften the fall with wary foot;
A little while
Still plan and smile,
And,—fault of novel germs,—
Mature the unfallen fruit.
Curse, if thou wilt, thy sires,
Bad husbands of their fires,
Who, when they gave thee breath,
Failed to bequeath
The needful sinew stark as once,
The Baresark marrow to thy bones,
But left a legacy of ebbing veins,
Inconstant heat and nerveless reins,—
Amid the Muses, left thee deaf and dumb,
Amid the gladiators, halt and numb."

As the bird trims her to the gale,
I trim myself to the storm of time,

I man the rudder, reef the sail,
Obey the voice at eve obeyed at prime:
"Lowly faithful, banish fear,
Right onward drive unharmed;
The port, well worth the cruise, is near,
And every wave is charmed."

1866 1867

I man the rudder, reef the sail,
Obey the voice at eve obeyed at prime:
"Lowly faithful, banish fear,
Right onward drive unharmed;
The port, well worth the cruise, is near,
And every wave is charmed."

1867 1866

NOTES

These notes are intended to supplement the general remarks of the Introduction with more detailed comments on the text. They suggest comparisons and cross-references as frequently as possible. The complete notes of the Centenary Edition of Emerson's Works, prepared by Edward W. Emerson, should be consulted for further information and comment.

Early Journals and Letters

Emerson began keeping a regular journal in 1820, in his junior year at Harvard College. The custom of journal-writing was a common one in his time, and his journals may be compared with Thoreau's and Hawthorne's, especially as these three are conveniently selected in "The Heart of ——'s Journals" series, published by Houghton Mifflin Co. The present very brief selections can only suggest the quality of the complete Journals. They possess a combination of personal self-revelation with artistic creation. Most of Emerson's ideas found their first, informal expression in this medium. For a description of the method and purpose of his Journals, see an essay by Bliss Perry, "Emerson's Savings Bank," in *The Praise of Folly and Other Papers.*

Emerson was a voluminous letter-writer. His correspondence with Carlyle, occupying two good-sized volumes, is probably the most famous in nineteenth-century English literature. The first and the last of Emerson's letters are here reprinted. On his first visit to England, he had called on Carlyle at Craigenputtock, August 25, 1833. He described this visit in a later book, *English Traits* (see Selections, p. 283), and in his *Journals.* It was the start of a lifelong friendship, which was renewed constantly by correspondence, and twice again in person, on Emerson's later visits to England. Carlyle's letters to Emerson will be found quoted frequently in these Notes.

Emerson's letter to the Rev. Henry Ware, Jr., is one of his most extraordinary utterances. Ware had been his predecessor in the pastorate of the Second Church of Boston, and in 1838 was a professor at the Harvard Divinity School. Having heard Emerson's Divinity School Address, he wrote him a friendly letter of protest, arguing against certain passages. Emerson's reply (the only formal one he made to his critics) expresses with a sort of Socratic mock-humility his determination not to argue the matter. Actually, of course, he was not at all incapable of such argument, as his sermon on "The Lord's Supper" had clearly proved. (See Introduction, "Religion.")

Nature

Nature was Emerson's first book, published in September, 1836. It had been taking shape in his mind for over three years, as a *Journal* entry for September 6, 1833, shows. It was written soon after he moved to Concord, first in the Old Manse, and later in his own house. It was published anonymously, in an edition of 500 copies. From the first it was not popular, and was not reprinted until 1849, when it was included in the volume of *Nature, Addresses and Lectures*, which now constitutes the first volume of the Centenary Edition.

Although *Nature* has never been popular, it has always possessed a unique appeal to readers at all sympathetic with Emerson. Carlyle wrote with enthusiasm: "Your little azure-colored *Nature* gave me true satisfaction. I read it, and then lent it about to all my acquaintance that had a sense for such things; from whom a similar verdict always came back. You say it is the first chapter of something greater. I call it rather the Foundation and Ground-plan on which you may build whatsoever of great and true has been given you to build."

G. E. Woodberry writes that "it has the bloom of the mind upon it," and O. W. Firkins describes it as expressing "the elation of spiritual discovery." These phrases suggest its quality. It expresses an enthusiasm, born of joy in emancipation from the formal duties of the ministry, but tempered by sorrow at the death of his first wife, and of his brothers.

For the philosophical background and implications of *Nature*, see the Introduction, "Philosophy." It has often been said that *Nature* expresses all of Emerson's later ideas, at least in the germ.

"The American Scholar"

This address, delivered before the Phi Beta Kappa Society of Harvard University, and its guests, on August 31, 1837, proved as popular as *Nature* had proved limited in its appeal. A vivid account of the circumstances of the address is given by Bliss Perry in "Emerson's Most Famous Speech," in *The Praise of Folly and Other Papers*. Holmes described the speech as "our intellectual Declaration of Independence," and certainly it marked the beginning of "The Golden Day" of American Literature. Holmes and Lowell heard it with enthusiasm, Thoreau was a member of the graduating class and either heard or read it immediately, while Carlyle described his enthusiasm from the other side of the Atlantic. The words of these men are typical:

Lowell wrote: "The Puritan revolt had made us ecclesiastically, and the Revolution politically independent, but we were still socially and intellectually moored to English thought, till Emerson cut the cable and gave us a chance at the dangers and the glories of blue water. . . . His oration before the Phi Beta Kappa Society at Cambridge, some thirty years ago, was an event without any former parallel in our literary annals, a scene to be always treasured in the memory for its picturesqueness and its inspiration. What crowded and breathless aisles, what windows clustering with eager heads, what enthusiasm of approval, what grim silence of foregone dissent!"

Holmes wrote: "Nothing like it had been heard in the halls of Harvard since Samuel Adams supported the affirmative of the question, 'Whether it be lawful to resist the chief magistrate, if the commonwealth cannot otherwise be preserved.' It was easy to find fault with an expression here and there. The dignity, not to say the formality of an academic assembly, was startled by the realism that looked for the infinite in 'the meal in the firkin; the milk in the pan.' They could understand the deep thoughts suggested by 'the meanest flower that blows,' but these domestic illustrations had a kind of nursery homeliness about them which the grave professors and sedate clergymen were unused to expect on so stately an occasion. But the young men went out from it as if a prophet had been proclaiming to them, 'Thus saith the Lord.' No listener ever forgot that address, and among all the noble utterances of the speaker it may be questioned if one ever contained more truth in language more like that of immediate inspiration."

Carlyle repeated the praise: "My friend! you know not what you have done for me there. . . . Lo, out of the West comes a clear utterance, clearly recognizable as a man's voice, and I have a kinsman and brother; God be thanked for it. I could have wept to read that speech; the clear high melody of it went tingling through my heart. . . . Miss Martineau tells me, 'Some say it is inspired, some say it is mad.' Exactly so; no say could be suitabler. But for you, my dear friend, I say and pray heartily: May God grant you strength; for you have a fearful work to do! Fearful I call it; and yet it is great, and the greatest."

Five hundred copies of the oration were printed and sold in a month. Now, as its centenary approaches, its popularity increases. Next to "Self-Reliance," it has proved to be Emerson's most effective piece of writing. For a discussion of the theories of "The American Scholar" in relation to Emerson's own life, see the Introduction, "America."

"The Divinity School Address"

The ideas which most hearers accepted with enthusiasm in "The American Scholar," created a furore when applied to religion and given expression in "The Divinity School Address," on July 15, 1838, less than a year later. They aroused immediate controversy, which thrived in newspapers and pamphlets. The chief opponent of the address was Professor Andrews Norton of the Divinity School, while its chief defender was George Ripley—later the leader of the Brook Farm community. Emerson himself took little part in the controversy, but stated his position in a letter to Henry Ware, Jr., reprinted elsewhere in this volume. His Journals describe the effects of the speech:

"Yesterday at the Φ. B. K. anniversary. Steady, steady. I am convinced that if a man will be a true scholar, he shall have perfect freedom. The young people and the mature hint at odium, and the aversion of faces to be presently encountered in society. I say, No: I fear it not. . . . Society has no bribe for me, neither in politics, nor church, nor college, nor city. My resources are far from exhausted. If they will not hear me lecture, I shall have leisure for my book which wants me."

Actually, the officers of Harvard College were so disturbed by the radicalism of the Address that Emerson was not invited to lecture again for over a generation. But time softened the bitterness of the disputes, and on the centenary of his birth, in 1903, a memorial tablet was set up in the chapel of the Divinity School where he had spoken.

The issues are as vivid now as they were in 1838—the controversy being essentially that between the Modernists and the Fundamentalists. In this address, Emerson's modernism was aggressive, and his statements still repel the conservative. For a detailed analysis and criticism of the issues involved, see G. E. Woodberry, *Emerson*, 55 ff., and the Introduction, "Religion."

Essays, First Series

In March, 1841, Emerson published his first, and most famous, book of essays. From this volume "Self-Reliance," "Compensation," and "The Over-Soul" have been selected, but many other essays are almost as important; such as: "History," "Spiritual Laws," and "Friendship."

"Self-Reliance"

By universal consent, "Self-Reliance" is Emerson's greatest essay. Its title has come to stand for the whole of his philosophy, and whenever his writings are reprinted, it appears. In this essay, Emerson describes his radical philosophy in such universal terms that it does not seem as extreme as the Divinity School Address, yet so vividly that it arouses the most indifferent reader. It abounds in epigrams and quotable passages, yet possesses a greater organic unity than most of his essays. The chief danger in studying the essay is to take the sentences so much for granted as to forget their import.

Although "Self-Reliance" outlines a radical system of ethics, it qualifies this radicalism significantly. The last two sentences of the essay sum this up: "Nothing can bring you peace but yourself. Nothing can bring you peace but the triumph of principles." In others words, the "self" is closely related to the over-self, which is only another name for God, or the laws of the world. In the final analysis, self-reliance is described as much the same as God-reliance. The radicalism appears in allowing the individual the responsibility of choosing for himself which principles he believes right. It may be suggested that this responsibility is much the same as that required by the "High Religion" (as Walter Lippmann defines the term in *A Preface to Morals*) of all truly mature men, and that it is opposed only to the immature acceptance of external discipline required of children. Emerson wrote: "Society everywhere is in conspiracy against the *manhood* of every one of its members." This "manhood," or spiritual maturity, he preached with an enthusiasm suggesting that of all the prophets of the "high religion" of spiritual maturity.

"Compensation"

Emerson had been pondering the idea of compensation from his early college days, as his Journals indicate. The essay is one of his most original and contains some of his best epigrammatic and proverbial wisdom. It also illustrates his ability to fuse the scientific theory of his time with his own thoughts on morals and conduct. (See Introduction, "Religion.") The essay was never delivered as a lecture.

Philosophically the doctrine of compensation has one serious flaw, but within its limits it has proved remarkably suggestive. That "crime and punishment grow out of one stem" was a favorite theme of later nineteenth-century writers, and is illustrated by such novels as Hawthorne's *The Scarlet Letter* and Dostoievski's *Crime and Punishment*. But objection may be made that the law of compensation is not "perfect," as Emerson maintained. If the murderer is punished for his crime, whether captured or not, by a deterioration of his own character, no compensation seems to exist for his innocent victim, who has been murdered. The workings of the law of compensation are somewhat one-sided.

"The Over-Soul"

This essay is probably the most disputed of all Emerson's writing. From the beginning it has been derided by "tough-minded" people, but it has been enthusiastically praised by all readers who appreciate mysticism. It lacks the universal appeal of "Self-Reliance," but appeals even more strongly to a large group. Holmes deprecated it, and Carlyle wrote (in his Preface to the English edition of the *Essays*), "I do not advise the British public to trouble itself much with all that." Recently, critics like Ludwig Lewisohn have emphasized the necessity of discarding its mysticism in order to discover the true meaning of Emerson's message. But the religion of the Over-Soul was a part of Emerson's true message, and to many it seems an all-important part. It may be compared to "Brahma" in Emerson's poetry: few people pretend to understand it wholly, but it is artistically perfect, and produces a definite emotional effect even on readers who do not understand it.

"The Young American"

This essay was first delivered as a lecture before the Mercantile Library Association of Boston on February 7, 1844, and was first published in the last number of the *Dial*, April, 1844. It best illustrates the application of Emerson's ideas to the economic thought of his time and of our own. (See Introduction, "Individualism and Socialism.") It is divided into three distinct parts. If the first, dealing with "the values of land," sounds antiquated to us, the other two, dealing with "Commerce" and "Government," are as fresh today as they were ninety years ago.

Essays, Second Series

The second volume of essays was published in 1844, three years after the first. It lacks some of the freshness and vigor of the earlier writings, but possesses a firmer texture and a more mature wisdom. The sensational extremes of "Self-Reliance" and "The Over-Soul" are absent, but the very titles "Experience" and "Politics" suggest a more deeply considered and sober approach. Besides these two essays and "The Poet," "Manners" and "New England Reformers" are of major importance.

"Experience"

The second essay in the volume, "Experience," is one of the most extraordinary that Emerson ever wrote. It was never given as a lecture, and bears all the marks of having been written all at once, in a mood of reaction after the death of his son. It has repelled many readers by its false, and seemingly heartless remark, near the beginning, concerning this personal tragedy. But, although Emerson seems not to have realized it, this grief stirred him deeply, and caused him to write one of his most brilliant essays. It might almost be said that readers, in direct proportion to their own intellectual originality, have appreciated this essay. It is not one of the most popular, nor one of the most perfect, but it certainly is one of the most powerful that Emerson ever wrote. " 'Experience,' " writes O.W. Firkins, "seems one of the boldest essays in literature, though its boldness has an almost casual air, as if a man should blow up a minister by way of correction of the monotony of an evening walk."

Like all of Emerson's essays, this particularly has been accused of formlessness. Therefore it seems worth while to brief its argument: I. What is reality? "All things swim and glitter" (4 paragraphs). II. Passing moods seem to be "the lords of life" (3 paragraphs). III. "The party-colored wheel must revolve very fast to appear white" (3 paragraphs). IV. Therefore, accept life as it comes: "Its chief good is for well-mixed people" (3 paragraphs). V. Power, "the vital force supplied from the eternal," will assert itself, unconsciously (2 paragraphs). VI. "The universal impulse to believe" (2 paragraphs). VII. Accept the illusions, or moods, for what they are (5 paragraphs). VIII. The possibility of discovering truth by piecing together the "fragments" which partial experience offers (3 paragraphs, to end).

For a more complete discussion of this essay, see the Introduction, "Philosophy."

"Politics"

This is one of the most sane and balanced of the essays. Dealing with a subject distasteful to him, Emerson yet wrote a striking essay, which sounds almost as fresh today as when first published. It should be read in connection with "The Young American," which is more detailed and specific, and with "Civilization," a later essay, brilliant in spots, though less well balanced.

"The Poet"

This was the first essay of the Second Series, but is reprinted in this place because it serves as a good introduction to the later volume of *Representative Men.* For its relation to Emerson's and to Whitman's poetry, see the Introduction, "Poetry." Ludwig Lewisohn ranks it as Emerson's best essay, after "Self-Reliance." (See *Expression in America,* 127 ff.)

Representative Men

Representative Men was published in 1850, after having been delivered frequently in lecture form for five years previously. The volume challenges comparison with Carlyle's *Heroes and Hero-Worship*, published in 1840. The underlying conceptions of the two are quite different, however —Carlyle describing the hero as a sort of divinely gifted individual, independent of circumstance, while Emerson described him as representative of a certain type of human endeavor, deriving his strength from this "representative" quality.

"Plato" and "Napoleon"

Emerson regarded Plato as the greatest man (exclusive of Jesus, whom he avoided describing), because he was both philosopher and, to a high degree, poet. The essay on "Plato" is selected because it best illustrates Emerson's ideas and because it was his own favorite. Its subject matter is often abstract and difficult, and many readers (such as Carlyle) have preferred the more colorful essay on "Napoleon." The essays on "Montaigne" and "Shakspeare" are also excellent.

Occasional Essays

Under this heading have been grouped various essays dealing with concrete and specific subjects, but taken from different sources, and written for different occasions.

The first two illustrate Emerson's attitude toward the reform movements of his time. The essay on "New England Reformers" describes much the same subject matter, but in more impersonal and philosophic terms. Since Emerson was personally interested in these reformers, and observed them at first hand, his more informal essays on them seem more revealing.

"The Chardon Street Convention of Friends of Universal Reform" was one of the early meetings of miscellaneous reformers typical of the early Transcendental times. The general atmosphere of the period has been vividly described by Lowell in his essay on "Thoreau," in *My Study Windows.* Emerson's essay, written closer to the event than Lowell's, is imbued with the same detached humor, and with a rather more sympathetic understanding. It was first published in the *Dial* for July, 1842, and was reprinted in *Lectures and Biographical Sketches* (vol. X of the Centenary Edition).

The essay on "Brook Farm" is reprinted from an essay included in the same volume, entitled "Historic Notes of Life and Letters in New England." It was written about 1867, and not published until 1883, and therefore has the tone of retrospect. "The Brook Farm Institute of Agriculture and Education" was founded in 1841, and lasted until 1846. Because of its subject matter, this essay is reprinted in its present early position.

Emerson's "First Visit to England" is described in the first chapter of *English Traits,* published in 1856. This visit occurred in 1833, and a second visit in 1847. Emerson's account of his conversations with Coleridge, Carlyle, and Wordsworth is essentially personal, and is interesting for the light which it throws both on Emerson and on his subjects. The rest of *English Traits* is a combination of travel diary and analysis of English civilization, something on the order of Count Keyserling's books today.

Emerson's speech on John Brown at Boston, November 18, 1859, shows him in the rôle of public character, vividly concerned with the events of his time. Although he did not possess the crusading ardor of Thoreau, whose speeches on John Brown were more eloquent than his, he did understand and express the significance of the occasion clearly. The speech was an informal one, delivered without the polish of his formal orations, but it possesses a sincerity and conviction superior to them. The careless paragraphing and punctuation of the address makes it difficult reading, but the vigor of the language more than overcomes this weakness of composition.

Emerson's essay on "Thoreau," written shortly after his friend's death in 1862, is his best biographical and critical essay. Although he had known and admired Thoreau all his life, he kept a remarkably objective attitude toward him, and avoided an uncritical enthusiasm. If he seems to have done Thoreau less than perfect justice, it is because Thoreau's greatness was of a sort which only time and perspective can make completely manifest. The essay appeared in the *Atlantic Monthly* for August, 1862, and was reprinted in *Lectures and Biographical Sketches.*

The Conduct of Life

Published in 1860, fourteen years after his last volume of essays on general subjects, *The Conduct of Life* represents a new and different Emerson —and one too often neglected. The old revolutionary enthusiasm has disappeared, but in its place has come a breadth of perspective unequaled, perhaps, in American Literature. On the one hand, these essays, as their title implies, are less "transcendental" than the earlier ones, and more directly ethical; but on the other, they introduce new elements which give Emerson's thought "that suggestion of eternity which is the sign-royal of greatness." The bent towards Oriental ideas, which the "Plato" essay had foreshadowed, here finds its fullest expression, as the first and last essays on "Fate" and "Illusions" suggest by their titles. Between these two extremes the essays on "Power," "Worship," and "Beauty" are noteworthy.

Of *The Conduct of Life*, Carlyle wrote to Emerson: "You have grown older, more pungent, piercing:—I never read from you before such lightning-gleams of meaning as are to be found here. The finale of all, that ot 'Illusions' falling on us like snow-showers, but again of 'the gods sitting steadfast on their thrones' all the while,—what a *Fiat Lux* is there, into the deeps of a philosophy, which the vulgar has not, which hardly three men living have, yet dreamt of! Well done, I say; and so let that matter rest."

"Fate"

"Fate" and "Power" were published as twin essays, the one qualifying the other. But Emerson so inclined towards Power that he qualified his treatment of Fate in the first essay, making the second seem almost unnecessary. Less than halfway through "Fate," Emerson begins emphasizing Power: "But Fate has its lord; limitation its limits. . . . Fate is immense, so is Power. . . ."

"Illusions"

To many this has seemed Emerson's most beautiful essay. In it his prose, always eloquent, rises to the pitch of poetry, so that the final paragraph produces a unique impression of exaltation in the mind. Carlyle remarked upon it, and critics since then have constantly quoted the passage. (For a discussion of the sources from which Emerson elaborated it see F. I. Carpenter, *Emerson and Asia*, 63–65.) But in describing the artistry, it is too often forgotten that the essay means something,—something central to Emerson's philosophy. His later essay on "Works and Days" in *Society and Solitude* explains the idea of "Illusions" in more prosaic, and more easily comprehensible terms, and the student interested in Emerson's ideas will read that essay also.

"Civilization"

The volume of essays entitled *Society and Solitude* represents a distinct falling off of power, although the title essay, and "Civilization," "Works and Days," and "Books" are all interesting for different reasons. "Civilization" is rather an inferior essay as a whole, but it contains several unforgettable passages, especially the famous "Hitch your wagon to a star." This has been so often misinterpreted that it should be read carefully in its context. Then it will be seen to say not merely "Aim high," but also, "by so doing, see your 'chores done by the gods themselves.'"

Poems

For a discussion of Emerson's poetry as a whole, see the Introduction, "Poetry," and references in the Bibliography. Emerson's first volume of *Poems* was published in 1847.

"Good-bye" was written at the age of twenty. Being the expression of a mood, it has often been misunderstood. It should be read in connection with the essays "Self-Reliance" and "Society and Solitude."

"Each and All" is a poetic expression of the problem of "unity and variety," best described in the essay on "Plato."

"The Problem" suggests Emerson's philosophy of art, and should be read in connection with "The Poet."

"Uriel" is a sort of poetic fable describing the circumstances of the Divinity School Address, in 1838.

"The Sphinx" is, perhaps, Emerson's most typical poem, though certainly not his most popular. He placed it first in his first collection of poems, but later editors, yielding to public opinion, have given it a less prominent place.

"To J. W." was addressed to the Reverend John Weiss, who had criticized Goethe's morals too narrowly. Compare Emerson's own essay on "Goethe" in *Representative Men*.

"Hamatreya" was inspired by a passage from the *Vishnu Purana* (see *Emerson and Asia*, 122 ff.). It bears a close relation to passages from the essay on "Plato."

"The Humble-Bee" describes Emerson's "philosophy of laziness." See also the essay on "Spiritual Laws."

"The Snow-Storm" has always been popular. Whittier used a part of it as a motto for his "Snow-Bound."

"Woodnotes" probably is an indirect sketch of the character of Thoreau.

In the "Ode Inscribed to W. H. Channing," Emerson defends his early inaction over the questions of slavery and the Mexican War.

"Forerunners" was first published under the title of "Guides."

The "Ode to Beauty" was first published in the *Dial* for October, 1843. It may be compared with Emerson's essay on "Beauty" in *The Conduct of Life*.

"Give All to Love" is typical of Emerson's thought in its less popular aspects. It may be compared to his essay on "Love," and to his longer poem on "Initial, Dæmonic, and Celestial Love."

"Initial, Dæmonic, and Celestial Love" treats its theme more fully than the shorter poem "Give All to Love," and more effectively than the longer essay on "Love" in the *Essays, First Series*. The idea of the three planes of love is from Plato's *Banquet*.

"The Apology" is an early poem, comparable to "Good-bye."

"Merlin" was one of Emerson's names for the ideal poet, who shall possess perfectly the emancipating power of expression.

"Bacchus" is a poet's poem. To some readers it seems mere nonsense, but to sympathetic readers it is one of Emerson's greatest. It attempts to describe the dionysiac inspiration of the ideal poet.

"Threnody" mourns the death of Emerson's son, Waldo, at the age of five. It was written over two periods, and is dual in mood. The first part describes the mood of grief; the second, the recovery from grief. It is probably Emerson's most successful long poem.

Rejected Poems

These poems Emerson rejected from his final collections for different reasons.

"Thought" was a youthful composition, expressing an enthusiasm for the pure intellect which he later qualified. See his essay on "Experience."

"Grace" seems to contradict the philosophy of "Self-Reliance." See G. R. Elliott, "Some Remarks on Emerson's 'Grace' and 'Self-Reliance,'" in *New England Quarterly* II, 99–104 (January, 1929).

"The Bohemian Hymn" has always been a waif among Emerson's poems. No explanation of the title is known.

May Day and Other Pieces

This second volume of Emerson's poems was published in 1867.

In "Brahma," the "I" is the impersonal creative energy of the universe. The poem may be compared with Whitman's "Pensive on Her Dead Gazing." For a complete discussion of the poem, see *Emerson and Asia*, 110 ff.

The "Ode," sung at Concord in 1857, and the "Boston Hymn," read on January 1, 1863, reflect Emerson's increasing preoccupation with the question of slavery. At a meeting held to celebrate the Emancipation Proclamation, the "Boston Hymn" created such enthusiasm that its reading was interrupted for several minutes by the cheering.

"Days" is one of the most perfect and frequently-quoted of Emerson's poems.

"Two Rivers" may be read as a parable of Transcendentalism. The Notes of the Centenary Edition describe the circumstances of its composition.

"Terminus" reveals once again Emerson's self-knowledge. It was written at the age of 63, and marks the end of his active literary career.

INDEX OF TITLES OF ALL SELECTIONS AND OF FIRST LINES OF POEMS

Titles are in italics and first lines of poems are in roman type.